POWER, CORRUPTION and PIES

Twelve Years of the Best Football Writing from When Saturday Comes

MAINSTREAM PUBLISHING

EDINBURGH AND LONDON

First published in 1997 by Two Heads Publishing
This edition published in 1999 by
MAINSTREAM PUBLISHING COMPANY (EDINBURGH) LTD
7 Albany Street
Edinburgh EH1 3UG

ISBN 1 84018 199 0

Every effort has been made to credit the copyright holders
of photographs and articles in this book. The publisher
apologises for any inadvertant omissions

A CIP catalogue record for this book is available from the British
Library

Cover photographs: Colorsport, Allsport, Alistair Berg
Illustrations: Dave Robinson and Tim Bradford
Cover design: Doug Cheeseman
Thanks to: Richard Guy and Jamie Rainbow

Available from Sportspages bookshops in London and Manchester,
plus all good newsagents in the UK and Ireland
For subscription details write to:
When Saturday Comes, 17a Perseverance Works,
38 Kingsland Road, London E2 8DD
Printed by in Great Britain by Biddles Ltd

Contents

1996

1997

1998

Foreword

THE PROBLEM WITH IRELAND IS ITS DISTANCE FROM ENGLAND. IN THE LAST century, it contributed to Whitehall's reaction to the Great Famine, and the resultant starvation of millions. Add to that centuries of rebellion, slaughter, misunderstanding, war, intolerance and neglect. Today, it makes going to football very expensive and inconvenient.

I am very happily Irish. "Thank God we're surrounded by water," goes the old song, and so says all of me. Except on Saturday afternoons. (And Sundays. And some Mondays. And every other Wednesday. And Thursdays, while the Cup-Winners Cup was with us and Chelsea were in it.) On Saturday afternoons I go down to the sea and curse it, every millimetre of it, every radioactive drop. I'm not alone. The shore and docks of Dublin are lined with men and boys – and women too, remember – ten-deep, feet firmly on our beloved soil but souls hovering over Anfield, Old Trafford and Stamford Bridge. (On a clear day you can see the ball in the air over Goodison.)

We get over to the odd game. We have children, to give us a reasonable, reliable excuse to travel. We roar and whinge with the best of them. But we're visitors. We're outsiders. We have Sky Sports 1,2 and 3 but they make us feel even more alone. We can watch the goals from angles once the province of porn directors, we can phone in our vote for Man of the Match, we can see Andy Gray loading his VCR from a swivel chair moving at speed – but we're not there. We're far away. We're so far away, we need to see Andy Cole shaking his head in disbelief seven times – "Ah! I see it now! He missed."

The distancing effect of modern television presentation was brought home to me not long ago when I was watching Iceland v Ireland. The football was dreadful and the crowd was freezing; it was very, very quiet out there, so Mick McCarthy's voice, like something coming over the wall of a zoo, could be heard throughout the game, and I would swear on the head of my first-born man-child that I heard him shouting at Mark Kennedy, just as the latter received his first of two yellow cards for dissent, "I'll fuckin' do you!" And, for a few seconds, as I explained to the same man-child why Captain Fantastic had said such a thing – if, indeed, he had – I was in Reykjavik; the two of us were there, happily frozen, bang up against the pitch.

I remember Saturdays when I was a kid, towards the end of the season when the weather improved; I'd climb onto the kitchen roof with the Bush transistor and try to grab the waves coming over the Irish Sea from the BBC, the ones hardy enough to make it through the soup of high pressure. The misery of pacing that flat, tar-covered roof, the growing, mocking certainty that I was wasting my time, searching for commentary without falling off, have left me with a hatred of sunshine and calm. I was alone up there, the boy in the bubble, a wee bag of sweating alienation.

Years later, perhaps too late, I found *When Saturday Comes*. I read it and immediately felt that I belonged; I was part of a community. It was intelligent and funny, world-weary and enthusiastic. I passed it on to friends; it gathered beer and coffee stains, was handled fondly and as carefully as a *samizdat* publication in eastern Europe before the Wall came down. It entered our vocabulary and it freed us. It lifted the weekly curse of being born on an island on the wrong side of Wales.

On the subject of Wales, I want now to record my family's contribution to Welsh football. My grandfather's name was Tim Doyle. He died before I could know him but, by all accounts, he was a lovely, gentle man. In 1921 he was a tram driver and, in his spare time, he was a member of the IRA. He, with some other men and a box of matches, set fire to the Customs House in Dublin, thereby destroying most of the country's records and crippling the civil service. Seventy years later Vinnie Jones arrived in Ireland looking for proof that his granny was Irish. He didn't find it. Granda and his Vestas had got there before him. So Vinnie went back to England and discovered that he was Welsh.

Thank you, Granda. Thank you, *WSC*.

Roddy Doyle

Introduction

THE NEW FOOTBALL WRITING APPARENTLY STARTED SOME TIME IN THE mid-1990s. There was no such name for what *When Saturday Comes* was doing when it began, but we know you won't hold that against us.

The articles in this book have been selected from issues of *WSC* between No 12 (January 1988) and No 138 (August 1998). No contributions have been included from the first 11 issues, as these were reproduced in full as *The First Eleven* in 1992 and reprinted in 1998. We have attempted to select articles simply on the basis of quality, without going out of our way to achieve a rigid balance across time and subject matter.

The date of each article is the date which appeared on the cover of that issue. Some anomalies may appear in the text as the magazine has usually been published in the second week of the month preceding the cover date (and if you can follow that, you might be able to explain the Champions League qualification process to us).

The editorial in No 12 which starts the book was written by Mike Ticher (when he was much younger and angrier). All the others are by Andy Lyons except where stated, with additional input from John Duncan (1988-90),Philip Cornwall (1990-97) and Mike Ticher (1998). Where articles appeared as part of a series in the magazine, such as The Positive Touch or More Than A Match, this has been indicated next to the date.

We have attempted to eliminate some of the many style inconsistencies which crop up over ten years of a magazine's life, but inevitably many others remain (don't write in). A handful of pieces have been cut slightly, but apart from such minor tinkering and small factual corrections, everything appears as it was originally published, including the suggestion that *South Pacific* was written in the 1930s.

Thanks to everyone who has been involved with *WSC* over the years, especially those who still haven't been paid. Some contributors to *Power, Corruption and Pies* have gone on to greater things since they first wrote for *WSC*, but most remain in the anonymity they craved. A couple of them may not even exist.

Power, Corruption and Pies
Compiled and edited by Doug Cheeseman, Andy Lyons and Mike Ticher

1988

Plenty of Courage, No Convictions

A proposed sponsorship of the FA Cup was given short shrift in
When Saturday Comes ten years ago. Little did we know what
indignities were to follow.

WSC No 12, January 1988 – Editorial

WELL, THAT'S IT THEN. MIGHT AS WELL PACK UP AND GO HOME. THAT MUST
have been the reaction of many football fans to the news that the FA are
prepared to allow the FA Cup to be sponsored by Courage, or anyone else
who comes along with a few million quid and no scruples. Whatever else
happens in football, ever again, this is the moment when it finally
surrendered any remaining integrity, dignity or sensitivity. So what is
there left to do, apart from writing rude letters to Mr Millichip?

The first and most important thing is that this should make everyone
finally accept that the FA have relinquished all credibility as competent
or acceptable administrators and are simply not fit to run football at any
level. There's no point talking of reforming or having a dialogue with a
body that does things like this.

They've got to go. The only question is, how? The immediate reaction
might be that a few Molotov cocktails lobbed into Lancaster Gate might
do the trick, but no doubt some will see practical objections to this

strategy. The only answer is for the fans to channel their disgust and despondency into organised and vehement protest. The Football Supporters Association is there, waiting to do the job, if only its membership was more numerous and more radical.

However, if we are honest, we have to admit that neither the FSA nor anyone else is going to achieve the revolution which is necessary in the immediate future. Any amount of bitter adjectives will not shift the Millichips and Crokers overnight. And that means that we have to live with the current status quo for the time being: there really is only despair to look forward to. ○

Pass the Duchy

Luxembourg are pretty useless and they always have been.
Andy Lyons celebrated an enviable record of under-achievement.

WSC No 14, April 1988

JUST WHY ARE LUXEMBOURG SO UNUTTERABLY CRAP AT FOOTBALL? IT IS HIGH time that we gave due consideration to a question posed on millions of trembling lips, from Lisbon to Istanbul. The country's diminutive size is obviously a handicap. As a land mass, Luxembourg might best be described as 'pert'. It can only accommodate a few dozen people at any one time, half of whom are permanently engaged in issuing stamps. Thus, home advantage counts for little, when corners have to be taken from well inside Belgium, though it is possible that visitors might be unsettled by the difficulties experienced in finding a parking space for the team coach.

Luxembourg has also been lumbered with a national language which looks like a fusion of the most boring bits of French, German and Dutch. This could be important because any player possessed of what might appear to an outsider to be a thoroughly out-of-control name would surely be spurred on to sterling deeds on the pitch as a form of self-assertion. A glance at any Luxembourg team line-up, however, would reveal a woeful lack of genuinely silly names – a few worthy of a smirk perhaps, but no real thigh slappers. Nonetheless, the fact that the team fielded for the most recent thrill-packed heavyweight bout against Cyprus contained a centre-forward called Grimberger hints at promise for the future.

The crux of the problem is that the playing conditions in the country are unlikely to present problems for visiting teams. This is clearly not the case with the other European minnows, Malta and, of course, Cyprus, whose respective climates present a stiff challenge to opponents, not least because of the heat's cumulative effect on the pitch (hard and sandy) and the groundsman (asleep under a tree). Thus, any attempt to run with the ball or string a few passes together founders upon the discovery of small boulders left undisturbed since the Ice Age, plus unexploded mines, archeological excavations and the occasional itinerant goat-herd ambling across the penalty area with his charges, and making little discernible effort to prevent them from nibbling away at the six-yard box.

Perhaps Luxembourg could learn something from the South American predilection for hurling thousands of pieces of paper into the air as the teams emerge from the tunnel. Why not instead bombard visitors with EEC memoranda? No-one would be so cockily certain of gaining an away victory if they continually had to fend off a barrage of weighty documents outlining the economic grievances of Portuguese fish-gutters, or the latest batch of divorce statistics from Baden-Württemberg.

The history of performances by teams representing the Grand Duchy in international matches and European club competitions amounts to a catalogue of unremitting failure. They seem to enjoy it all nevertheless, and like Mother Teresa and her British counterpart Peter Reid, have clearly devoted themselves to brightening the lives of others. Why else would they have embarked on a defeat-packed tour of Israel, Turkey and – let's mention them once more – Cyprus in 1985, if not from a laudable desire to present the locals with a rare opportunity to kick some Northern European ass for an hour and a half (a bit like the Crusades in reverse)?

Luxembourg have entered every World Cup tournament since 1934, and played in all the Olympic qualifying rounds from 1920 onwards. They always turn up when required, boots in one hand, flasks and sandwiches in the other, never crying off en masse because of 'headcolds' or a collective dental appointment.

One of their early matches might even have had major repercussions in international affairs. A 5-4 home victory over France in 1914 demonstrated that the latter's defences could be breached with consummate ease, which must have dealt quite a blow to their morale on the eve of World War I. Our team were to wait 30 years for their next victory, a draw against Egypt in 1928 being the only (relatively) bright spot in an era jammed solid with spanking defeats. All hell broke loose in 1946 however, with Belgium and Norway seen off to the tune of 4-1 and 2-1 in successive matches. This remains the only winning sequence yet put together by Luxembourg.

Cynics might point out that a few British soldiers, among them Stanley Matthews, Raich Carter and Tommy Lawton, then serving in the army on the Rhine, disappeared around this time, returning to barracks after a few weeks with a lorry-load of cheese and a signed thank-you letter from the Grand Duke... but that's just idle conjecture.

Triumphs now rained in thick and fast. The 1948 Olympics witnessed a merciless 6-0 pummelling of doughty Afghanistan, with the British amateur team also being given a bit of a seeing-to (5-3) just four years later. The two greatest moments in the history of the Luxembourg national team, however, occurred in the early sixties. In 1961, Portugal were defeated 4-2 in a World Cup qualifier, with the debutant Eusebio being comprehensively outshone by a 21-year-old locksmith called Ady Schmidt, who scored a hat-trick. Almost before you could say 'mini-renaissance', they stormed through to the second round of the 1962-64 European Nations Cup after a thoroughly deserved first round bye, and then sent Holland tumbling out of the tournament before losing to Denmark in a quarter-final replay.

For this cornucopia of achievements, the entire national squad were elected as 'Sportsmen of the Year'. The only individual footballers to have won this coveted trophy were Standard Liège centre-back Louis Pilot in the 1960s, and French-based striker Roby Langers last year. (Langers just pipped one Fonsi Grethen, who apparently enjoys the dubious honour of being the world's number one billiards player.) It would seem, then, that the local populace is too embarrassed to register a proper appreciation of their footballers' contribution to the European game.

It is true that in all matches played since 1911 they have yet to take their tally of wins into double figures, but obviously cold statistics do not reveal the complete picture. Perhaps the government will eventually strike commemorative medals to mark the achievements of the last two Luxembourg teams to have obtained a point in competitive matches (v Sweden in 1979 and Scotland in 1987). Two players, Reiter and Weis, played in both games. In Britain, knighthoods have been gained for less.

In between these matches, the side went through a bit of a bad patch, the lowest point being a 0-2 reversal against the USA in Dudelange, not, perhaps, the most uplifting of home venues. The same might also apply to Ettelbruck, where three years ago a teeming throng of 500 enthusiasts were left screaming deliriously for more after their favourites had battled through a 0-0 humdinger with Iceland. Needless to say, the attendance for the latter encounter is reckoned to be amongst the lowest ever for an international fixture between two European countries.

It would offend against common decency to reveal the sum total of goals conceded by teams from Luxembourg in European club tournaments. Suffice to say that if that exact number of people gathered together in the same place and stamped their feet in unison, there would be an earthquake. Only a keen disciple of the Marquis de Sade would want to probe much further, but the general gist is four victories, including a walkover, out of 83 ties played. Jeunesse D'Esch top the rankings with two wins, and are also the most successful club in domestic competitions, marginally ahead of the magnificent Red Boys Differdange, who would take on all-comers in a contest to find the best club name in the world.

Two lesser outfits, Jeunesse Hautcharage and US Rumelange jointly hold the record for the biggest aggregate defeat in Europe, 21-0, which was set up by the former against Chelsea in 1971, and cheekily equalled by their compatriots a year later. What could Hautcharage's coach possibly have said to his players at half-time in the second leg, when they were already fourteen goals down in the tie? A bit of understated irony, perhaps – "We'll have to emerge from our cautious defensive shell now," or even an attempt to divert their attention from the matter in hand: "Well, what does everyone want for Christmas then? – apart from a few rudimentary ball skills, ha ha ha, oh come on lads, just my little joke..."

Luxembourg's hard-won status as the losers of European football could yet face a concerted challenge from two directions. Five years ago, Liechtenstein entered the international arena with a 1-0 home win over Malaysia, in a match arranged to help prepare the latter for a prestigious tournament in Kuala Lumpur (and what a boost it must have been). This was followed by a win against China, which may have set back the game's development there by a couple of centuries. More recently, however, they did the decent thing and succumbed to a 19-0 aggregate defeat against Switzerland in an Olympic qualifier. One imagines that they would be more than capable of maintaining that level of performance if involved in regular competition.

Meanwhile, San Marino, a small roped-off area in the middle of Italy, have apparently decided to enter a team in the next European under-21 championships, where they will face Italy and the ever-obliging Swiss. They have one well-known player, Massimo Bonini of Juventus (who has steadfastly refused to take out Italian nationality, his mind obviously set on leading his countrymen to a succession of moral victories), but where will the other ten come from? Are there any mineshafts to whistle down in San Marino? At least they have picked up a bit of international experience recently, having participated in one of the most bizarre footballing encounters of modern times during last year's Mediterranean Games in Syria, when they took on the Lebanon in a first round tie.

However, both Liechtenstein and San Marino would have to go some before they begin to match the admirable level of consistency achieved by Luxembourg. The national eleven really hit their stride after the First World War and are currently in possession of a long-term lease on the small, but homely, basement of European football. Here's to the next 75 years. ○

Limited Shelf Life

Annelise Jespersen chronicled yet another sad and shabby chapter in the catalogue of ground desecrations.

WSC No 16, June 1988

I WOULDN'T SAY THAT TOTTENHAM HOTSPUR LIE TO THEIR FANS, BUT WHEN I wrote to chairman Irving Scholar asking what the club intended doing with the Shelf terracing in the East Stand, I received a reassuring letter from secretary Peter Barnes saying that no definite agreement had been reached. "When the club has made a decision, rest assured we will inform our supporters accordingly, as we value your support." That was in March. Three months earlier, Haringey council had received a planning application from Tottenham for permission to build 36 luxury boxes along the Shelf, losing 11,700 standing places.

I wouldn't say Tottenham were confident that their application would be quietly passed by the council, but they didn't bother to send anyone to the planning meeting on April 11th to speak for them. Twenty Spurs fans who found out about the meeting at the last minute raised enough objections to defer a decision until the next meeting on May 3rd.

And I certainly wouldn't say that Tottenham are devious, but as a concession to consultation they called a meeting with the council and supporters – at very short notice, with no publicity and for 9 o'clock on a Wednesday morning (April 20th). It was made clear at that meeting that the club plans to go ahead with its 'refurbishment' of the East Stand, whatever the feelings of the fans, and that the council is virtually powerless to do anything about it, because there are no planning grounds on which to turn down the application.

However, a Left On The Shelf? campaign is trying to make it as difficult – and embarrassing – as possible for the plans to continue. A public meeting, which Irving Scholar says he wants to attend, was scheduled to take place at the Supporters Club on April 28th, and it was hoped that hundreds (thousands?) of fans would go to the planning committee meeting on May 3rd.

Some form of protest was also planned for the final home game against Luton the following evening. Mobilising support has been more difficult than it might have been, because the Luton match was the only home game left after the club's intentions had become known, but fans were leafletted at Charlton and Liverpool, and there has been considerable press interest.

Local papers have given the campaign publicity, an *Evening Standard* article resulted in protest phone calls to the club and the newspaper, and a few sympathetic nationals have also publicised the meetings and (we hope) caused Mr Scholar to blush over his cereal.

The main objection of Left On The Shelf? is, of course, that supporters have not been consulted about the drastic changes that are planned, and there has been no debate in which fans could challenge some of the more ludicrous reasons put forward for the refurbishment (as the club insists on calling it). For example, Tottenham cite the necessity of meeting the standards of the Safety of Sports Grounds Act as "a major purpose of the refurbishment", claiming that the current dangers include the storage of groundsman's equipment (a fire hazard) under the stand and "inadequate means of escape and of segregation of different sections of the crowd".

I would welcome any measures to improve safety, especially as it is difficult to evacuate the Shelf quickly in an emergency, but these could be met by building more stairways, improving the lighting on the existing ones, and by removing the perimeter fence in front of the lower tier of terracing. I know of no part of the Sports Grounds Act which suggests making grounds safer by building luxury boxes. And as for the storage of groundsman's equipment – it's equivalent to moving house because the ashtrays are overflowing.

Mr Scholar says that the only way the safety measures can be paid for is by having executive boxes, or else by charging £15 a game to stand on the Shelf. No figure has been provided for the cost of the 'safety improvements', but I find this explanation unbelievable from a company which has recently sold its training ground for more than £4 million (and has not bought a new one), has its own successful sports and leisurewear business (Hummel UK), has recently bought three adjoining shops in North London for £1.2 million, has bought two clothing factories in Leicester, has its own publishing division and a travel agency, has recently obtained the exclusive rights for marketing and selling England souvenirs, and made a £4.3 million profit last year. (It has also sold Clive Allen for £1 million, but I am hopeful that that money will be spent on buying three new goalkeepers).

Another reason for the "refurbishment" according to Mr Scholar, is the attitude of the police. In a letter to one fan, he said that the club had "consistent criticism and complaints" from the police about trouble in the Shelf and the number of arrests that occur there, and he told another supporter that the boys in blue "virtually rule football in London" and that a lot of the impetus for the changes is coming from them.

In discussions with the London branch of the Football Supporters Association, an officer from the Met's public order department has said that the Shelf is one of safest areas of any London ground, because no away fans ever get into it. He also told me that while the police might suggest extra fencing, moving fans etc, they aren't really in a position to ask for boxes to be built. Admittedly, there is a section of the Shelf from which missiles can be thrown at away supporters, but this could be overcome by building a higher segregating fence, or by making a larger 'no-go' area between the fans. Or even by building the boxes in the corner section separating home and away supporters...

The planning application also includes the possibility of a creche and baby changing area, "to encourage families" and to benefit women with children. Again, I would welcome these, but how many families are going to be hiring the boxes? And who says families don't already come to football? They might not fit into the standard mortgage advert of jolly, smiling, middle-class couple and two jolly, smiling children (one of each), but in the area where I stand, regular attenders include a mother and daughter, a mother and son, several married couples, a father and two sons, and an assortment of young kiddies. One I know of stands on the Shelf with 12 members of his family. So just what kind of families is the club trying to encourage?

Supposing for a moment that there are thousands of 'families' and 'women with children' out there, just waiting for a creche, where will they go when the capacity has been reduced by 9,640? It seems that the new plans leave very little space for anyone who isn't a season-ticket holder. The remaining section of terracing will hold 8,000, and two-thirds of it will be reserved for season-tickets, leaving several thousand regulars who currently stand on the lower tier, and at either end of the Shelf, to fight it out for the remaining section. Casual fans and floaters won't even get a look-in. (The only other terrace for home fans, at the Paxton Road end, is members-only.)

Mr Scholar says that there are plans to make the Paxton Road end all standing, but he told one supporter this would be done next summer, and another that it would be carried out within five years. What are we supposed to think? He also suggested that a lot of people stand on the Shelf because the perimeter fence blocks the view from the lower tier, rather than because the Shelf offers one of the best terrace views in the country. We suggested that the fence be taken down for the Luton game, to see how many people still stand on the Shelf, but naturally he refused.

Yet another worrying (and cynical) aspect of the club's plans is that at the beginning of the season they were offering two-year season-tickets at a special price, which many Shelf fans bought. There was, of course, no indication that people who bought these might have to stand somewhere completely different next season, although it is highly unlikely that the plans were suddenly thought up this season.

People bought the season-tickets on the understanding that they would be standing in the same place next season, so it seems as if the club could be in breach of contract. Mr Scholar says these people will be given a seat or a refund if they don't want to stand on the lower terrace, but nothing has been put in writing, and in any case, a seat on the Paxton (the likeliest place) is hardly a fair exchange for a spot on the Shelf. And if some fans take up the offer of a seat they could be split up from their families or friends, hardly the sort of thing we want to see happen at a club trying to foster a family-all-friends-together image.

By the time you read this, either the Shelf will be about to be reduced to rubble, or else the council planning committee will have deferred the decision yet again until a fuller meeting between council, club and fans can take place. I fear that it won't be the latter. In the end, the most distressing aspect is not the lack of consultation, or even the actual loss of the terrace places, but that Irving Scholar does not recognise where the soul of the club is, does not realise how dead the ground will be with 36 luxury boxes on one side facing 72 on the other, does not remember, in Patrick Barclay's words, how the club's image was formed with the assistance not only of a great team, but a great place.

Spurs and their fans, it seems, are becoming a tiny part of Tottenham Hotspur plc, a company which depends on the fans' loyalty to the team (I know of no supporters who have any feelings of warmth for the actual club), a company which knows that, no matter how much we protest, if we lose the Shelf we will still renew our season-tickets. After Keith Burkinshaw had been forced out as manager, he commented that "there used to be a football club over there". That was a very long time ago, Keith. ○

The Risk Business

Three years after Bradford and Heysel, fans were still regarded as a security risk. Mike Ticher wondered about their own safety.

WSC No 17, July 1988

THE BRADFORD FIRE, JUST OVER THREE YEARS AGO, EXPOSED IN THE MOST vivid manner possible the complacent attitudes in football towards safety. Since then, strict new regulations have had a big impact on both clubs' finances and the general experience of going to a football ground. It is widely assumed that lessons have been learnt and procedures tightened, and that consequently watching football is now a much safer pastime than it was before 1985.

It's an assumption which shouldn't be allowed to go unchallenged. The introduction of membership schemes, together with imbecile ticket arrangements and 'over-zealous' policing have led on occasions to situations where fans have been put at considerable personal risk.

It's easy to be alarmist about safety standards, and to see dangers where perhaps none really exist. However, this critical attitude is surely infinitely preferable to the 'it-couldn't-happen-here' syndrome, which was clearly so prevalent before Bradford. Are things really different now? Or have we lapsed back into complacency? Simon Inglis, author of *The Football Grounds of Great Britain*: "The clubs have responded extremely well in general. They really had no choice when the new rules came in, and I think they've realised that there's nothing they can do except go along with them. There is a whole new attitude towards grounds in general – that they can't afford to be complacent. No authority wants to be like West Yorkshire." Inglis is currently researching grounds outside Britain, and is confident that many in Europe would not meet British safety standards.

Such standards are determined by the Safety of Sports Grounds Act, 1975, which was heavily amended after Bradford, and guidelines for clubs and local authorities are set out in the *Guide to Safety at Sports Grounds*, known as the Green Guide. This is a voluntary code, with no legal force, but it forms the basis for most thinking about sports grounds' safety.

The quotes in italics below are from the Green Guide. We talked to stewards at a number of grounds (more or less randomly selected) to try to find out how closely the guidelines are followed.

"Effective training and supervision should be provided by management so that all stewards, whether regular or casual, know not only what their duties are, but how to carry them out and why. This is especially important in emergencies when it is essential that stewards and their supervisors are fully aware of and practised in the part they are to play in the plans drawn up with the emergency services."

The amount of training undergone by the stewards we interviewed varied enormously. At Arsenal, for example, we were told that they'd "seen the Bradford video so many times I've lost count", and at Grimsby (where they dealt effectively with a fire this season during a Littlewoods Cup tie against Halifax) they have "lots of meetings about fire regulations" and are well clued-up on what to do in an emergency. At QPR, too, they meet "three or four times a season" for briefings with fire chiefs.

By contrast, other clubs seem content to give the stewards brief instruction at the start of the season at a meeting with police and fire officers, and then more or less leave them to it. Aston Villa are one of these, and one of their stewards told us: "At the meeting, a lot was said about remote-controlled door-locks, fire alarms, extinguishers etc. Unfortunately, no-one bothered to tell us where these things are." Stewards at Luton described their meeting as a "pep talk from the police". Oxford United's stewards assured us that most of the training was "on the job".

By far the most worrying responses came from Wembley. Stewards for matches at Wembley are recruited by two security firms, unconnected to Wembley Stadium Ltd, and to describe the training of their stewards as 'minimal' is perhaps being a bit kind. There is no instruction about fire drills, evacuation procedure or where to find first aid, apart from three sheets of paper handed out at the beginning of the day. We were assured that "most people wouldn't know where the toilets are".

The majority of Wembley stewards don't get paid, and so their primary motivation for becoming one is to get in free to see the game. As a result, many leave their allotted posts almost immediately after the start of the game, and checks on whether they are in position are said to be almost non-existent. Our contact was stewarding the rugby league cup final when a spectator in an adjacent bay collapsed. There were no stewards working in that bay, and he had to run halfway round the ground to find a first aid post, having had no instruction as to where they were located. Similarly, he had no idea where he was supposed to go in the event of a fire, or which way he should send people.

"Exercises should be carried out so as to ensure that emergency procedures operate smoothly, and a record kept of the duration of the exercise, details of the instruction given and by whom."

In general clubs seemed pretty hot on emergency drills – from their own information most held full-scale evacuation practices in conjunction with the fire services at least twice a season. This includes Aston Villa, who, as we've seen, did not favourably impress their own steward as far as training was concerned. Villa's stadium manager also came up with the rather surprising statement that the Bradford fire was a "one-off", and the circumstances did not apply anywhere else, least of all Villa Park. Once again, Wembley appeared hopelessly inadequate. Since stewards are hired virtually on the day, mainly through knowing someone else who is already a steward, there is no feasible way of carrying out full-scale practices with all the stewards. Indeed, Wembley have no idea how many stewards will be in operation on a particular day, since they rely on regulars to turn up. Thus at that same rugby league game, out of a notional full complement of 200, there were only 90 stewards present. Each bay is supposed to be covered by 10 stewards, but in some cases this was down to as few as four, and that's even before they disappear to watch the game from a better vantage point.

After Heysel, the Recreation Committee of the now-defunct Greater London Council published a report looking into many aspects of football ground safety. On stewarding, they had this to say: "Stewards are often only employed on a haphazard basis... they often are ill-trained in the nature of the responsibilities that go with the job." In many cases this still seems to be true. None of the stewards we talked to was paid more than £10 per game (roughly £2 an hour) for doing a job with a huge amount of responsibility and, supposedly, thorough training.

The general attitude towards stewarding was that it was something to be done more or less out of love for the club (literally in one case, Arsenal), although at Forest it was claimed that some of the stewards were in fact County fans "doing it for the money" (£9.50 per game). At the same club, our steward said that many OAPs did it for the same reason, and even his wife turned up if they were short.

Without intending to be dismissive to the people who do the job, such ad hoc recruitment arrangements scarcely inspire confidence.

"Every steward should be fully appraised in writing of his duties and responsibilities and should carry on him a general check list of them... Stewards should attend pre-match briefings (with police)."

Degrees of liaison with the police varied wildly. Some were restricted to the initial pre-season chat. Very few seemed to have meetings before every game, – although in one case (Arsenal), the 'squad leaders' did do so, and then briefed their squad of stewards in turn. At a couple of clubs (Grimsby and Oxford) there was contact on match-days via walkie-talkies, but this seemed to be the exception.

Interestingly, every single steward asked, interpreted a question about contact with the police as a cue to talk about potential violence. None seemed particularly aware that there might be a joint role in more mundane (but equally important) crowd control. Responses to questions on crowd control techniques ranged from "what's that?" to "it's common sense, isn't it?". Supporters who have been unnecessarily herded into inadequate areas of the ground, or who have seen crowd pressures build up intolerably, might question such assumptions.

Our steward at QPR confirmed that they are "not very educated on the layout of the ground", a view echoed, as we've already seen, at Villa Park. And it's from Villa, a regular FA Cup semi-final venue and allegedly one of the easiest grounds to evacuate, that we get the last word on stewarding: "If the worst did happen, myself and two others, both as 'well trained' as I am, would be responsible for getting hundreds of away supporters out of the stands, over fences and everything else designed for your comfort and safety, and into a 'safe' area. My feelings, and that of most stewards, is that if a fire occurs, then it's a case of getting yourself out first, then worrying about other people. If you think that irresponsible and selfish, then can I ask what you would have done if you'd been a Bradford steward?"

If that depresses or frightens you, let's go back to the Green Guide for some comic relief:

"Public address equipment should be installed so that broadcast messages can be heard under reasonable conditions (including emergencies) by all persons of normal hearing."

And if you think that's a joke, this one'll really crack you up:

"Where a pitch perimeter barrier fence is installed to keep spectators off the pitch, care is needed to ensure that it does not impair the visibility of the playing area from the terraces... Failure to provide spectators with an unobstructed view invites them to stretch and strain, and so generates dangerous pressures within the crowd."

Side issues, perhaps, but fences and "everything else designed for your safety and comfort" are no laughing matter. No-one will need reminding that one of the main causes of the high death toll at Bradford was the fact that the exit gates at the back of the stand were locked and unattended during the game. Or that the conditions of the Safety of Sports Grounds Act would have obliged them to erect a fence in front of the Main Stand the following year.

"Provision of such gates or access points (in perimeter fences) is particularly important to allow full access to the playing area where it is likely to be used as a place of safety in an emergency. Such gates or access points should be properly stewarded."

One of the clubs we looked at in our brief survey was Oxford United. As anyone who has stood in the Cuckoo Lane End, or indeed the home end, will know, the fences are so high that views of the near end of the pitch are strictly limited. Certainly they would present an insurmountable barrier to anyone trying to escape on to the pitch in an emergency. This obviously means that it is essential for evacuation to take place quickly and efficiently through the gates at the front of the terracing. These gates are supposed to be manned by stewards, one to every two gates, who are in radio contact with the police, and the overall co-ordinator of crowd control at the Manor. On the day we were there, there was no permanent presence of stewards immediately in front of any of the four gates, although there were two or three stewards in neighbouring areas of the ground who might have been able to reach them all fairly quickly in an emergency (given that the problem was confined to one area). According to the official we spoke to at Oxford, Mr McGeough, ("Don't quote me or I'll deny this conversation ever took place"), stewards at this end are placed so as not to obstruct the view of spectators! Quite honestly, it would be impossible to obstruct it any more than it is already.

Perhaps more worrying is the fact that, on the day we were there at least, it would have been obstructed by the advertising hoardings which, in places, form a continuous line along the edge of the pitch. These hoardings are not fixed in position and are constructed of light materials, and Mr McGeough was adamant that they could be swiftly knocked aside and out of the way in the event of an emergency. It was at this point in the conversation that Mr McGeough became uncontrollably abusive and so we were unable to find out whether a full-scale practice had been carried out to test his assertion. However, in a letter, he asserted that "fire drills are periodically staged without everyone turned on to the pitch which is not necessary. We have conducted two fire drills this season so far and have received one unannounced matchday inspection by a fire service official."

The unbelievably aggressive attitude of the club should not necessarily be taken to mean that they have anything to hide as far as safety in their ground goes. It may very well be possible that they could evacuate the Cuckoo Lane End in the two minutes recommended by the Green Guide. In normal circumstances, timing people leaving a big game, the whole ground was empty in considerably less than the eight minutes recommended for this operation. However, this assumes that the gates at the rear of the terracing are fully in operation. These are kept locked during the game, but manned by police and stewards with two-way radios. Assuming that information received about any crisis was accurate, and action to open these gates was prompt, supporters didn't panic etc, there might be no reason to have to get people on to the pitch.

However, no-one can predict with any certainty the nature of an emergency at a football ground. As the people of Bradford know only too well, a catastrophe can happen at the most unexpected places and times. There can be no justification for making any assumptions about safety that have not been thoroughly tested, or for complacency, or for refusing to answer reasonable questions about a subject which should be a deadly serious one for football fans. Do the gates open properly at the Cuckoo Lane End? Would the hoardings be an obstruction to people trying to get out? To a layman's eye it certainly looks like a dangerous situation.

"All exit gates, unless secured in an open position, should be manned at all

times while the ground is used by the public and be capable of being opened immediately from inside by anyone in an emergency."

Evidence of similar situations was to be found at several other grounds, with gates in high fencing either unstewarded or non-existent. The events at the Chelsea v Middlesbrough game showed one thing for sure – that there was no steward on the gate in the fencing in front of the Shed. On this occasion it was unlocked, but in another time and at another place it might just as easily have been locked. This also applies to exit gates at the rear of stands and terraces. Once again at Chelsea, I have often seen the gates leading to the street padlocked during the game, with no-one in attendance.

It's impossible to draw any hard and fast conclusions from a 'survey' which is inevitably sketchy and incomplete. However, since we've started looking at this issue, matchdays haven't quite been the same. When you start looking for possible lapses, they appear by the dozen. The question is, how many of these are due to a layman's misunderstanding of how clubs would respond to a crisis, and to what extent they are in control, and how many are genuine and potentially fatal hazards? The chances are that we'll find out the hard way. O

Snob Values

David Wangerin saw Wimbledon win the 1988 Cup final.
Or at least he thought he did.

WSC No 18, August 1988

THE LAST TIME I ATTENDED, OR INDEED WITNESSED, A FOOTBALL MATCH, THE team scoring the most goals was officially declared the winner of the contest. It was easy to check on the progress of a match by tallying the goals scored by each side and assessing the likelihood of either team's scoring before the final whistle.

Since the rise of Wimbledon Football Club, however, a number of 'purists' or 'experts' (their term, not mine) want to change this means of determining a winner. Let not the number of goals decide the outcome, they seem to be saying; instead, let us have 'style points' like there are in figure-skating. After all, Wimbledon play such crude, elementary, no-talent football, why should they 'win' merely because they happen to score more goals than their opposition?

With the FA Cup final over, and Wimbledon deserved winners of it, are Liverpool to be felt sorry for because the 'style points' system was not officially in use? We were treated in the pre-match build-up to BBC TV's resident 'expert', Jimmy Hill, who told the world that this particular Liverpool side were the best since the Creation, not only in England, but the world. We were also treated to drivel such as this in the newspapers: "Not only should Liverpool, the favourites and the champions, win the FA Cup this afternoon.They must... All those who believe in 'the beautiful game' will not deny them yet another trophy." (Stuart Jones, *The Times*)

No-one got sent off. No-one got his legs amputated. It was far from the best final played, but one could say that about almost any other. Liverpool have been known to bore the pants off people in their day.

Yet, at the conclusion of the match, there was Jimmy Hill, vainly trying to stick to his guns, lamenting that Liverpool "had played one match too many" and were suffering in the heat. I doubt if any such comments were made for Luton Town, who played many more matches than Liverpool this season, and still managed to beat Arsenal just when it looked least likely. So we are left to ponder Mr Hill's comment that the greatest team ever produced could not manage 90 minutes of football played in 80 degree weather.

In fairness, Liverpool do have a fantastic team, but with £10.5 million to spend on players, why shouldn't they? Would Kenny Dalglish be manager of the year at Wimbledon, where gates of 6,000 for First Division football aren't unheard of, and whose best FA Cup crowd of the season was almost 2,000 less than Liverpool's worst?

The really good result for the game was Wimbledon's triumph. In a year when Liverpool matches were shown on television more often than not (three live matches in February alone), when the paucity of First Division talent showed from virtually the first week of the season, the team from the wrong side of the tracks showed us that you have to put the ball in the back of the net, regardless of who or what you are, or are supposed to be. And, somewhere among the drivel of the snobs, Simon Barnes of *The Times* reminded us: "I am not condoning the dirty play that Wimbledon have such a name for: but why are their long ball tactics considered immoral and a disgrace to the game? If you get beaten in a running race, it is no good complaining that the other person didn't run gracefully enough." ○

Ain't No Cure for Somerton Blues

As Lincoln returned to the League and Newport departed, John Davies reflected on the joy and despair of automatic promotion and relegation to the Conference.

WSC No 19, September 1988

AT LUNCH TIME ON THE DAY THAT NEWPORT SLID OUT OF THE LEAGUE, THERE were queues outside every pub and every chip shop in town. Rotund Welshmen poured off trains, clattering empty Fosters cans underfoot and jabbering in excitable high pitched tones about the historic occasion that they were about to witness. The only problem was that this scene was happening in Cardiff. The crowds were there for the Welsh Rugby Union Cup final (Llanelli-Neath) and Newport County were the last thing on anyone's mind.

That's the way of things in south Wales. If Newport had been bidding for promotion that day (as Cardiff had been a week previously), the reaction from the populace would have been identical. Rugby fans like to think of themselves as fair-minded. They're not inclined to kick a local football team when it's down. But for Newport their reaction was worse than that – they just ignored them. On the saddest day of their (pretty miserable) Football League life.

After Cardiff, Newport was quiet. To get to the orange shambles of Somerton Park you jump over the railings outside the station, and follow the one-way system the wrong way until you're on the West Ham bridge (it's not really called the West Ham bridge but it's painted claret and blue and the connection seems appropriate). Then follows a 55-minute hike from the town's old industrial heartland out through suburbia and beyond. Newport County could not have got farther from the town centre if they had tried.

In 1987-88, their 60th and last season in the League, about 1,500 regulars managed to drag themselves along to home games at Somerton Park. On the day that Newport dived, 2,560 passed through the turnstiles. The attendance was swelled by the curious and the madly romantic, including a bloke who had travelled from Aberdeen just to see the game, which he did from the enlightened perspective that 24 hours of solid drinking inevitably bring.

What was curious about this occasion was that it almost entirely lacked emotion. We were expecting long faces. We didn't see them. We were expecting long emotional speeches through the tannoy. We got a pleasant, almost jolly sort of welcome. We were expecting tears and cheers as the teams came out. Instead polite handclaps rebounded off the deserted grandstand back to us, as the players battled through an offensive wall of cameramen onto the (surprisingly healthy looking) pitch. It dawned on us that the die-hards' placid acceptance of this most disastrous demotion was due to the fact that they had seen it coming virtually all season.

Newport's demise has been well documented: a combination of lacklustre performances, uninspired management and abysmal administration dropped them into the Fourth Division after seven seasons in the Third – missing promotion to the Second by one place in 1982-83. This combination reached its nadir some time in the middle of the season. Chairman Brian Stent pulled out, taking his financial base with him, and manager Brian Eastick was dropped, along with half of the first team, in an essential cost-cutting programme.

Newport ended their League careers as a team which consisted mainly of YTS lads battling bravely against dismal but experienced Fourth Division opponents, and losing. Their last ten games yielded nine defeats, with a memorable run of three consecutive four-nils, a 6-0 and 6-1 contributing to a tally of For 5, Against 33. Only the shock 2-0 win over mighty Darlington gave any cheer to Somerton's suffering few. It was undignified and certainly hard on the youngsters, but certainly no less than Newport deserved.

Automatic relegation from the League is hard but fair – Newport have had it coming since they had to apply for re-election in 1923. That was the first of ten appeals to maintain their League status, a statistic that they share with Rochdale. In 1931 they were actually rejected and spent a season out in the cold, before returning in place of Thames, and their contribution to the history of the game since then has hardly been spectacular.

They ended their one full season in the Second Division (1946-47) in 22nd place, with 23 points gained and 133 goals conceded, mirroring last season's record (25 and 105). In 1980 their best-ever team of modern years (Tynan, Aldridge, Gary Plumley et al) won them their only Welsh Cup. Cloud Nine was scaled the following season with the celebrated run to the European Cup Winners' Cup quarter-finals, where the East

Germans of Carl Zeiss Jena brought them back to earth with a whimper. From then on it was steady decline, ending on a sunny May day that turned to rain, in a 0-1 defeat at the hands of (oh, the irony) Rochdale.

At the end of the game there was no show of mass hysteria. Da Boyz invaded the pitch, firstly in an attempt to wrench the jerseys off the retreating Newport apprentices, secondly to tear up to the Rochdale end for a bout of taunting. Polite handclaps echoed around the ground again, but passing Inter City trains drowned them out, and the crowd – regulars and voyeurs alike – shuffled off coyly into a rain shower. A League club had died and no-one seemed to care.

Newport's future is uncertain. On one level they seem to be looking forward realistically to their future in the Conference. The souvenir programme (good at £1) bore that out, carrying one feature entitled 'Looking Forward in Amber – Into The Conference' and another on the non-League pyramid system. A veteran supporter of 26 years backed that up too, breaking off from lamenting the club's lost financial opportunity in John Aldridge (failing to insist on a 10 per cent clause in their deal with Oxford which would have earned them £80,000 from his move to Liverpool) to meditate on the pros and cons of next season's opposition.

On another level, however, the non-League future for which Newport seem to be preparing themselves is less like the silicon-slick operations of teams like Barnet, and more akin to the grubby waste ground of sub-Southern League land. Our veteran supporter spoke with an almost parental admiration about some of Newport's remaining good players (Glynne Millett, Darren Peacock, and buccaneering winger Robbie Taylor) and the same players smiled and waved their boots at him as they left the ground. It is unfortunate that pally communal gestures, which so often characterise clubs on football's underside, gestures which often reflect what is good about the game, often belong to clubs without ambition, content to play out season after season with mundane teams, grotesque grounds and tiny attendances.

In a sense Newport have always been such a club. It remains to be seen whether their enormous will to survive can be translated into a more positive will to succeed in the future. Lincoln City – or Thames? For Newport County, decision time has arrived. Oh, and incidentally Llanelli beat Neath 28-13. ○

A Game of Two Channels

The advent of satellite TV finally put a gun to ITV's head.
WSC was first in the queue to pull the trigger.

WSC No 19, September 1988 – Editorial

UNTIL THIS YEAR THE BBC AND ITV CO-OPERATED IN A CARTEL WHICH JOINTLY negotiated terms for the transmission of League and Cup football. In the absence of competition they were able to keep their costs down to an artificially low level. The last TV agreement, which expired at the end of 1987-88 has been worth £6.2 million over a two year period, yet in the final year of the contract some of the matches broadcast on ITV were believed to have generated in excess of £1 million each in advertising revenue.

In recent seasons both have adhered to the argument that programmes of recorded highlights were no longer sufficiently popular to be worth retaining as part of their regular sports service. This position has been maintained in the face of statistical evidence to the contrary. As a fairly recent example, on January 31st, 1987 three FA Cup fourth round highlights matches broadcast on BBC1 drew an audience of 6.2 million. ITV's live game the following day attracted only 5.2 million. However, in the last three years both channels' output has centred around live broadcasts.

At the beginning of June the League AGM voted in favour of opening negotiations with the satellite company British Satellite Broadcasting, which hoped to begin transmission of English League football from the beginning of the 1989-90 season. BSB also proposed the formation in association with the League and FA of a profit-sharing company which would transmit over 20 hours of sports coverage, including live and recorded football, spread evenly throughout the week.

Profits would accrue from advertising, sponsorship and worldwide video sales. The deal was not intended to be exclusive, the League's negotiators having declared their willingness to enter into separate agreements with either or both of the two main channels. ITV refused to countenance the idea of buying programmes from BSB, and set about constructing the schismatic offer shortly to be put before a handful of First Division clubs. The BBC publicly echoed their rival's stance, but shortly afterwards concluded an agreement with the satellite company.

As anyone who has wearily endeavoured to follow the process of events would confirm, the ensuing flurry of activity resembled the conclusion of a rather messy divorce; with secret meetings in airport hotels, speedily arranged midnight rendezvous, emotional accusations and emphatic denials.

After six fraught weeks had elapsed, two bids emerged which, at the time of writing, were the definitive offers made by both parties, and, as such, likely to be placed before the EGM of the League on August 8th, when a decision is expected.

There are varied reports of the new figure proposed by the BBC/BSB partnership, but it is believed to be in the region of £45 million for the first four years of a ten-year agreement, with the First Division clubs set to receive 90 per cent of the cash. They would each be paid a straight fee estimated at £100,000 per annum plus £125,000 for each home game covered, with the away team receiving 25 per cent of this. From the beginning of 1988-89 the BBC would broadcast seven Sunday live matches and 16 highlights programmes during the course of the season. The following year BSB would begin transmitting live games on weekday evenings.

The revised ITV package is claimed to be at least £1 million in excess of the BBC/BSB proposal, the inference being that they are prepared to improve upon any bid made by their competitors. In a departure from their previous position, which centred around the sole rights to televise the home games of ten selected teams, with no payments to other League members, there would be some money, possibly 10 per cent, set aside for clubs outside the First Division.

Three years' experience of achingly predictable match scheduling suggests both channels believe that the most successful First Division teams invariably provide entertaining games which will ensure large TV audiences. Success and popularity are mistakenly equated with quality. The interests of those 50 per cent of fans who regularly attend matches outside the top flight have been consistently and criminally under-represented.

There is little reason to suppose that ITV, in particular, would seek to change this basic policy if their package was accepted on August 8th. The largest clubs would still be guaranteed a regular flow of TV appearances, enabling them to attract larger sponsorship and merchandising deals. We would still be just a step away from a Super (sic) League, albeit in the slightly modified form of a Premier Division within the League structure.

Those likely to be involved in such a scheme, possibly still dazed by the effects of hammering out a deal with the "ebullient and dynamic" (*Daily Mirror*) Greg Dyke, have already begun to murmur about the need to effect some kind of 'streamlining' wheeze in the near future. Philip Carter, for one, is swiftly emerging as an inordinately keen follower of the Scottish game, taking every opportunity to point out that gates have shown a steady increase in recent seasons. This side-steps the screamingly obvious fact that there is no equitable basis for comparison between English football and its Scottish counterpart. Given its population, there will only ever be scope for, at most, a dozen or so professional teams in Scotland. This is surely not the case in England.

Nonetheless, let us assume that a Premier League, comprising 12 clubs, is proposed in a couple of years' time. Though craving a monopoly on success, the self-appointed 'Big Five' would still require a few obliging playmates to fulfil the role of prospective cannon fodder. Lured by dreams of a perpetually replenished stock of TV cash tumbling into their outstretched hands, a group of First Division clubs declare themselves in favour...

A fair degree of open-ended competition is clearly vital to the continued popularity of football. Time and again we have seen examples of teams reinvigorated by the impetus gained from a successful season in a lower division (eg Aston Villa, Sunderland, Middlesbrough, Wolves last season). This would be largely denied by the restrictive requirements of the Premier Division.

With perhaps one team relegated per season, and that possibly dependent upon the financial standing of the projected replacement, the competitive element would be reduced to the bare minimum, with only the championship at stake. Encounters between the biggest clubs would, in any case, be irreparably damaged through repetition. A vast number of the season's games would come to seem entirely meaningless. In fairly quick time, those supporters who chose to follow their clubs in the restructured competition would feel their interest wane, as would the television audience.

In such a situation, ITV, dependent on ratings to maintain advertising revenue, might begin to doubt the advisability of renewing the contract. Perhaps they would endeavour to persuade their pliable footballing dependants to institute a few rule changes which would make the game a little more... interesting. Football might soon come to bear as little relation to real sport as, say, professional wrestling.

Obviously, ITV will always be required to tailor its output in order to satisfy commercial interests. However, as a public service, the BBC has responsibilities which are not incumbent upon its rival. It might be argued that it has a duty to provide adequate coverage of a sport which, last season, was watched by more than 18 million people. The BBC/BSB package offers a return, at last, to regular highlights programmes covering a broad spectrum of League football. The BBC's football broadcasts in any case habitually attract larger audiences than ITV, even when the latter has sole rights to theoretically more attractive matches. For example, ITV's exclusive coverage of this year's Littlewoods Cup final attracted 4.6 million viewers, whilst the less glamorous Oxford v Luton semi-final on the BBC drew 6.6 million.

In the long term, their joint package in association with BSB appears to be offering the better of the two deals. The experiences of European countries, where satellite coverage has become an integral part of sports broadcasting, suggests that a greater choice presented to the viewer, accompanied by new techniques in marketing and presentation, tends to increase interest. Through foreign sales, BSB could generate a substantial payout for our domestic football bodies as well as boosting the international profile of the English game. Football would be linked to expanding developments in communications technology. The game's authorities would be in a position to maintain a far greater degree of control than previously over the way in which the product is presented.

ITV's approach, with exclusivity as the cornerstone, is based on the mistaken belief that it makes commercial sense to restrict the scope of the product on offer to ensure an acceptable level of quality and consumer interest. The alternative option offers the prospect of football no longer being perceived purely as a commodity to be shaped to television's will, and of the profits generated being used constructively for the long-term benefits of the sport.

Over the years, our football authorities have developed a tenacious consistency in their approach to problems that have confronted them. They can almost always be relied upon to choose the wrong option. Keep your fingers crossed. ○

Peruvian Rhapsody

Our man in Lima, Phil Ball, documented some odd goings-on in Peruvian football and lost his watch in the process.

WSC No 21, November 1988

ASK ANY BRITISH PERSON UNDER THE AGE OF 25 WHAT THEY KNOW ABOUT Peru, and they'll tell you Paddington. Ask any British person over that age what they know about Peru and they'll say Cubillas. The test rarely fails, though the more knowledgeable elders may throw in a Chumpitaz for good measure. Lovely name that. No wonder so many people remember it.

Travel 8,000 miles to the arid west coast of South America and ask a three-year-old Peruvian child the whereabouts of a country called Scotland and the question will be met by a shrug of the shoulders. However, should one subsequently venture to ask the same child the name of Scotland's goalie in the 1978 World Cup, the reply will be as immediate as it will be confident: "Alan Rough." Since I had the privilege to work in this beautiful yet benighted country for four years, I can vouch for the truth of the above. It would, however, be less than informative to add that the answer to the question was often decorated with the observation "*Era un huevon*," which means roughly, "He was a pillock."

Alan Rough is inextricably written into Peruvian culture because he has come to represent the symbol of First World fallibility, the last line of defence against New World trickery. It says a lot for the way in which South Americans, and Peruvians in particular, regard our soccer. They would never claim superiority, for that is too permanent, too uninteresting. Rather it boils down to the concept of the *pendejada*, or 'buggering folks about', that dominates South American soccer and which the Brits, so convinced that they still represent the Corinthian values, find so hard to understand and come to terms with.

This gulf in thinking was best exemplified by the Hand of God. The Peruvians I spoke to were delighted by Maradona's goal and couldn't understand the fuss. Neither could they understand why one of the four defenders later left in Maradona's wake didn't just take his legs. *Huevones* (pillocks). If you don't cheat you're dumb. Indeed one might conclude that England were beaten not by superior technique but

35

because they were pillocks. Why on earth didn't Lineker punch Barnes' second cross into the onion bag instead of waiting to be pushed by Brown, the Argentinian defender? The Peruvian commentator implied as much during the post-match analysis, shaking his head with a rather respectful but at the same time condescending wisdom.

If you go to Peru expecting the richness of club soccer that exists in Brazil or Argentina you'll be disappointed. The capital city, Lima, contains seven million of the country's 17 million people. Such centralization is rarely conducive to a competitive league structure. League games are poorly attended, and the only factionalism which really exists is the traditional rivalry between the two top clubs, Alianza and Universitario. They meet twice a year in what is termed *El Clásico*, and the Estadio Nacional fills up to its 60,000 capacity. This fixture divides the city but in a rather muted way. Fathers pass on their allegiances to sons and the press fuels the occasion, but the fixture contains none of that territorial and regionalistic passion that we have in Britain.

Only Hungeritos, a diminutive team from the Amazonian region of Iquitos, have recently managed to create something of a new phenomenon in Peruvian football, namely the regional identification. Promoted from their amateur status by dint of winning the Peruvian equivalent of the FA Vase, the country has watched in fascination as this energetic bunch of Brian Flynns has attempted to participate in the national league. Their basic problem has been the lack of funds required to finance each game, for Iquitos is stranded in a jungle wilderness 1,000 miles from Lima. Flying a team is expensive, even if they do all get on board for half price, but their antics have spawned a thousand wisecracks and an affectionate interest.

Plane journeys are not such a funny subject in Peru at the moment, however. The aforementioned Alianza, returning from a jungle fixture last year, drowned to a man when the pilot misjudged the approach to a fog-shrouded Lima airport. Clinging onto driftwood in the cold Pacific, the pilot survived, but in one fell swoop had managed to decimate the entire first team squad of the country's premier side. The incident provoked little media interest in Britain, yet imagine the kerfuffle if such a tragedy were to happen to a major European side.

So what's all this stuff about football being a religion out there? Well, it is, but strictly at the national level. When the national side plays, it is not an occasion, rather an orgy. You must arrive at least three hours before the 4 pm kick-off to witness the kinetic build-up. Everyone must be

whipped up into a patriotic frenzy, especially during World Cup qualifiers. Do not take your watch, for there is a 100 per cent chance you will
not return home with it. The stadium has no clock, for that too was
stolen, and the referee simply waits for the sun to dip below the western
stand before blowing the final whistle. I witnessed a turgid 0-0 draw with
Colombia in 1985 and lost a good Timex.

The pre-match events were bizarre. Buxom wenches tripped onto the
pitch in high-heels and skimpy bathing costumes and stood waving in
the centre of the cauldron whilst the crowd chanted, "*Que buen culo*"
(what a good arse). The team physiotherapist squatted on his knees for a
full hour urging the baying macho hordes to sing patriotic songs.

One of these was the catchy: "*Arriba, abajo, arriba Peru, carajo!*" (Up,
down, up Peru, fucking hell!). Not quite *Abide With Me*! Parachutists,
attempting to hit the centre circle, whizzed by the stadium and landed in
remote backyards. When one managed to hit the pitch, the crowd rose
and screamed "*Peru campeon!*" (Peru champions!) as though this feat had
somehow guaranteed them a place in the final in Mexico.

When Argentina arrived to play, the fever pitch was bubonic.
Maradona unwisely informed a journalist at the airport that no one could
mark him out of the game. He had not reckoned on Rena, Peru's equivalent of a mass-murderer on amphetamines. The only time Diego was
able to demonstrate his skills was in the pre-match warm-up where he
flicked up a can of coke and, to the whistles of the crowd, kept it up with
feet and knees for a good five minutes. Peru won 1-0, almost destroying
Argentina's chances of qualifying, and Maradona was subjected to what
can only be described as homosexual assault. The referee did nothing,
for this was all part for the scheme of things. The Argentinians could
wait for their revenge.

Rena, like Rough, is now a cult figure. Parents tell their children that if
they misbehave, Rena will come and get them. Though we are told *ad
nauseam* in Britain that the South Americans admire only skill, the truth is
that they admire any player who conforms to the tradition of the *pendejada*.
Hence a good foul is equal in status to a good nutmeg. Interestingly, the
only English player the Peruvians admired during the '86 World Cup was
Chris Waddle. Lineker's lack of technique was obvious to them, Hoddle
was too laid back – but Waddle did a few nutmegs, took players on for no
apparent reason, showed a few tantrums. They would never chuck Mars
Bars at him, for he played like the average Peruvian plays on the beach, in
the street, in the mountains, in the kitchen.

Another little-known fact in Britain is that South Americans grow up not playing football but *fulbito*. This is crucial to understanding the nature of their game. The whole continent is littered with stone or concrete pitches, probably 25 yards by 12. It is a sophisticated form of six-a-side which naturally develops every player's close control, dummying skills and an aversion to the long ball.

In remote Andean villages there may be no school, but there will be a *fulbito* pitch. When Brian Glanville eulogised the recent Colombian performances at Wembley and took unusual time out to spit venom at British coaching techniques, he was overlooking the fundamental fact that we put primary school children onto huge muddy pitches in the depths of winter and expect them to develop an awareness of possession, control and space.

South Americans cannot help but do this. In Peru every male biped plays in a *fulbito* league, which also contributes to poor League attendances. Every team must have the same six players. These are *Gordo, Flaco, Chino, Feo, Cholo, Animal*, which mean respectively Fatty, Skinny, Chinky, Ugly, Darky, Animal. No other names are ever heard. Since male bipeds include lawyers and politicians the nicknames serve to democratise the game. There is a *fulbito* pitch inside the grounds of the Presidential Palace and Alan Garcia, the present 6" 5' incumbent, is a *gordo*.

If the prevailing characteristics of a nation's culture can be judged by its attitude to football, then Peru is a piquant, chaotic yet endearing country with piquant, endearing and chaotic football. The national side stands no chance of qualifying for Italy, largely due to the Alianza tragedy. Still, *Arriba, abajo, arriba Peru, carajo*, as they say in Lima. ○

Inside image: ID CARD / NAME: M. THATCHER / ADDRESS: 10 DOWNING ST LONDON SW1 / PROFESSION: POLITICAL HOOLIGAN / TEAM SUPPORTED: THE TRUE BLUES / SIGNATURE: MThatcher

Alas Smith and Bloor

Peter Bloor celebrated a Stoke City pair notable for their loyalty as well as their talent.

WSC No 23, January 1989 – The Positive Touch

IN THE FIRST PLACE, SIMPLY HAVING THE SAME SURNAME AS ALAN BLOOR WAS sufficient reason for me to adopt him as a favourite. His footballing abilities didn't come into it, for it was his mere presence in the Stoke City team of the late 1960s that enabled me to tell what the sociologists now call my primary school peer group, that I was related to A Footballer. My story had as much truth in it as an Eric Gates penalty appeal, but happily, Alan Bloor was to prove there were better reasons to take to him than a shared difficulty in getting people to correctly spell our surname.

In 1969, Bill Shankly declared that "Alan Bloor is good enough to represent England in the World Cup...", while a newspaper report from the previous year told of how "Bloor charged round the midfield, launched several threatening solos against the quaking defence and unleashed a shot of Cape Kennedy power..."

Forget Martin Peters being ten years ahead of his time, here was the original Ronald Koeman thundering out of the Potteries mist, years before anybody realised that Leeds United weren't the only link between the words 'football' and 'clog'. It is quite probable that Shankly, rarely a man to shrink from hyperbole, was guilty of some exaggeration in his claim, but this did not concern the Stoke fans, who appreciated the contribution 'Bluto' made, particularly during the club's most successful period, in the first half of the 1970s.

It is sometimes felt that the teams Tony Waddington assembled were a midlands version of West Ham, with players such as Dobing, Hudson and Greenhoff confirming, and even creating, that impression. What does tend to be overlooked is the fact that behind these players was a defence which made sure nobody kicked sand in Stoke City's face, even when the likes of Hudson and Greenhoff were performing the football equivalent of sharing a beach towel with the opposition's girlfriends.

At the heart was Alan Bloor, usually alongside Denis Smith, who had originally come into the team because of an injury to his future partner, but who was to become one of the all-time Victoria Ground favourites, as much because he so obviously cared as for any great football ability.

Here was a player who was also a fan, who played for the reserves on his wedding day and who was to sustain numerous fractures and gashes in the cause of Stoke City, but nonetheless played whenever possible because he loved the club. For instance, at the end of the 1978-79 season, and with promotion to the First Division apparently slipping away, he turned out at Wrexham with a burst blood-vessel, a gashed shin and a back strain, displaying an attitude carried to the very end of his Stoke career in 1982.

Having played until the end of November 1981, only to be made available on free transfer, Smith did not reappear in the first team until April, by which time the half-witted management of Ritchie Barker had put the club in dire danger of relegation. In a rare moment of clear thinking, Barker brought Denis back with seven games left, not because he was necessarily any better than those who had been playing but because he personified the attitude and spirit needed at that moment.

The first and final games of the five he played sum up his career at Stoke. In the first, against Wolves (making their then seasonal trip between the top two divisions), Stoke battled back from conceding the traditional Kenny Hibbitt goal to win 2-1. Denis had a quiet game, finishing it needing just three stitches in a cut eye. In the last match, with Stoke only needing a draw against West Brom to send Leeds down, but winning 3-0 with ten minutes to go, he put in a tackle that sent the ball bulleting for a corner.

Acknowledging the resulting cheer with a wave as he hit the ground,

Denis had shown us that with just minutes of his 13-year Stoke career left, he was still determined that nothing was going to get past him. This fact was appreciated by the fans, who chanted his name unceasingly until the final whistle and stayed, demanding a lap of honour so that we could thank the man who represented us on the field.

In contrast, Alan Bloor's departure was much more muted, in keeping with the character of the man himself. After 12 seasons of regular service he was released by Alan Durban in summer 1978 and decided not to stay in football, a plan he put into action by first joining Port Vale and then by entering the furniture business. Altogether less demonstrative than Smith, but no less committed, he was the Charles Bronson of the Potteries, rarely if ever being seen to smile. Even on the photograph of the 1972 League Cup winning team, his efforts to win a part in a *Death Wish* film are in marked contrast to the smirks, grins and outright beams of his colleagues.

No matter, the opposites of Smith and Bloor made for a formidable partnership, which was instrumental in making Stoke one of the best teams in the country for a time. Together they put in many afternoons of stern red and white striped defending, none more glorious than in the League Cup final of 1972, when their success in subduing Osgood and Garland contributed in no small measure to their team's victory.

Both were local men, both cared for the local club, the only one they ever wanted to play for. It showed, and the fans reacted accordingly. The super leaguers and the 'If it moves sign it'/'If it pays, move' (Adrian Heath, Paul Stewart) fraternity won't understand that, which is their loss (in all ways bar financial, unfortunately). So it is Stoke City's loss that the present management seemingly does not appreciate the club's tradition of having local players in the team. Parochial it may be, but it establishes a sense of identity, even community, otherwise lost when committed young locals like Graham Shaw and Chris Hemming are shabbily treated in favour of couldn't care less signings like Simon Stainrod. That, though, is another story, albeit one which will hopefully be re-written come the glorious day of Denis Smith's return as manager.

For now, it is the attitude of him and Alan Bloor which remind us of an ideal, which may now be unattainable in an age of new values, of whizz-kid chairmen and executive boxes, of share flotations and shady TV deals. Our thanks are due to both Smith and Bloor for showing us how it can be, and what we have lost. ○

Scouts Honour

Eric Foster's experiences as a football scout included this alarming encounter at Luton.

WSC No 26, April 1989

DURING MY FIRST 15 YEARS AS A SCOUT, I WATCHED THE GAME FROM THE terraces. Although I had a representative's card which guaranteed me a stand seat at least, and often a place in the director's box, I much preferred to stand out in the open.

There was one ground that I actually disliked and that was Kenilworth Road. Even in the Sixties there was an atmosphere of subdued violence there, a certain brutish nastiness I didn't encounter elsewhere.

One balmy September evening in 1968, I was there to watch a certain Stuart Boam of Mansfield Town. Luton were top of the Third Division, having achieved promotion the season before, while Mansfield, two places below, had just suffered a 3-0 defeat at the hands of Barrow. The referee was Mr Malcolm Sinclair of Guildford, which was usually good enough to guarantee a home win. In all, I had seen 17 games refereed by this gentleman, all of them home wins. Just coincidence of course!

There was a dramatic start to the game. In the first minute, a half-hit shot was fumbled by the Mansfield goalkeeper, Dave Hollins, who dived on the ball, clutching it to his chest before anyone could reach it. Luton's Bruce Rioch ignored the fact that the ball was safely in the keeper's possession and hit it with all the might of his renowned left foot. Instant pandemonium: fists flew, bodies crumpled, but eventually order was restored and Rioch got his marching orders.

I was standing on the terraces at the opposite end to this mayhem. No sooner had the game re-started than there was a disturbance behind me. Turning round, I gazed in awe at the arrival of a tall, blond, bronzed Tarzan, shirt open to his navel, gold medallion around his neck.

Accompanying him was an equally striking female in vermilion blouse and slacks. This Adonis was obviously no stranger to that part of the ground. As he and his companion made their way down the terrace steps, it transpired that he was known as 'King'.

He had arrived late, obviously missing the frantic opening minutes. In reply to his "What do you think of it so far?" (shades of Mr Eric

Morecambe) he was informed that 'Brucey' had been sent off. His face darkened and there immediately followed a catalogue of foul language which contained several expletives I'd never heard before, all directed at the referee, who was obviously a ****** in the pay of Mansfield.

He spent the rest of the first half moving around the terraces behind the goal, orchestrating the violence that was to be unleashed after the interval. I quickly lost interest in the game and became absorbed by the antics of the crowd. The football had, in fact, degenerated, as many such games do. Frequent fouls, Luton players seeking to get Mansfield players dismissed, an irresolute referee and a crowd baying for blood.

As the opposition goalkeeper took up his position for the second half, he was at once the target for showers of coins, apple cores, the odd pebble and, of course, a barrage of the choicest language. 'King' had organised well. By now, the referee had become an almost willing accomplice. A sending off to level numbers, a highly dubious home penalty and it was not a game to judge any player's ability. The ball was passed as if it were a live grenade.

I rarely left a match before full-time, but was thoroughly sickened by what had been witnessed. As I reached my car, parked a good mile from the ground, I heard the roar which signalled that Luton had won and Mr Sinclair had achieved his 18th success.

It was April 1969 when I received the dread summons – a report, please, on Luton v Brighton. This time I vowed not to watch from the terraces but from the safety of the directors' box. Arriving early, and making my way to the stand, I saw, coming toward me, the Adonis observed on my previous visit, the 'King' himself. Only this time, no shirt open to the waist, no gold medallion on his chest. This time, he was resplendent in his police uniform. ○

But First the Bad News

John Duncan monitored the coverage of the Hillsborough disaster.

WSC No 28, June 1989

IN MEDIA TERMS, TRAGEDY IS THE BEST KIND OF BAD NEWS. BUT FOR THE PRESS and television, Hillsborough was in a class of its own. It was surely the first time that disaster has occurred when newspapers and TV have all their facilities present and manned.

The papers have an established routine in these circumstances. Get pictures, get survivors, play guess the cause and pull out a few quotes from dignitaries. However, a football tragedy is rather different, with, uniquely, the victims being perceived as part of the problem. No-one blames airline passengers for plane crashes.

The imagery and phraseology of a disaster give one a disturbing feeling that an attempt was being made to glamourise the whole thing. In the tabloids, each story has its distinctive slogan and graphic, like cheap film adverts. It was **Gates of Hell** for the *Sun* and **Cage of Death** for *Today*. The *Star* picked **Cup of Tears** as the motif for its coverage, and there were references everywhere throughout the week to the **Tunnel of Death**. These all sound like cheap paperback titles because that is the tone that they are seeking.

Disaster as entertainment (which is all the tabloids claim to be) has to be packaged in a way that sanitises the horror by dramatising it. We are bombarded with such an enormous amount of information, with pictures and stories both heroic and tragic, that it is very difficult to take in.The way in which the story is told places it alongside soaps and mini series with a dramatic, barely believable plot and rapidly developing story line. Media treatment degrades the human tragedy by telling the story on an epic scale and by using real disaster as just another tool in the ratings wars.

The first problem for the press was to distinguish between the good guys and the bad guys. The media are accustomed to blaming supporters so most were unable to resist at least a sideswipe straight away. By Tuesday, a few were really having a go. The *People* went for the headline **Bodies Spiked As Crazed Mob Flee**. The story beneath was a simple tale of how people tried to get out and couldn't. Who exactly the crazed mob were wasn't made clear.

So, most papers were perfectly willing to swallow stories of misdemeanour by supporters. The blame was put on "hundreds of non ticket holders... crushing hundreds under foot" (*Sunday Mirror*). In the *Sunday Times* "ticketless Liverpool fans poured into the Hillsborough Stadium through an open gate". The *Sunday Telegraph* found Dennis Howell willing to assert that there were "obviously large crowds milling about outside the gates without tickets".

The evidence for all this appears to have been fans let into the ground who still had their full tickets. While one may assume that some got in this way it's all a bit flimsy as hard evidence on which to apportion such a significant degree of blame. But, as with everything that involved in the treatment of fans, prejudice (not necessary malicious) reshapes the truth.

The problem that pressmen everywhere had to wrestle with was that TV pictures spoiled any attempt to blacken the fans. After clumsily failing to smear supporters who got on the pitch, the *Sun* were forced into what, for them, amounts to a grovelling apology under the headline **Fan's Film Clears Fans**. Their only attempt to retire gracefully was a letter from a reader which read rather similarly to a *Sun* editorial. The reader, Mrs Clementson of Portsmouth is either not on the phone (there are no Clementsons in Portsmouth) or she doesn't exist. Make your own mind up.

Peter McKay in the London *Evening Standard* had decided to have a go as early as Monday. "The police often make wrong decisions. Soccer management is frequently greedy and uncaring. But fans are the biggest danger to other fans and we had better not lose sight of that." And why does he believe fans have to share the blame? "They accept a crowd penning system that would be controversial if used for cattle because it is the price they pay for behaving badly."

So, we should be more active in resisting such things that are wrong? Don't be silly. McKay wouldn't want us to resist the sort of common sense solution that he and so many of his colleagues have come up with. "Perhaps the best solution of all would be to cancel the 1990 home soccer season. The time could be used to upgrade dodgy grounds and establish just which entrance scheme for fans will work. Soccer managements would howl..." But should they be ignored, or arrested for impertinence like so many fans who have complained about anything at a football match.

A big disaster gives every two-bit columnist (and two-bit is a generous description of Peter McKay) a chance to fill their columns with attempts at either sympathetic words of comfort and concern or bigotry.The first place to look for the latter is always arch hypocrite Auberon Waugh in the *Sunday Telegraph*. But his column of April 23rd started promisingly. "This new breed of Chief Constable finds it more congenial to terrorize law abiding citizens than to tackle the malice and perversity of the criminal element."

Surely this wasn't dear old Auberon talking? Yes it was. Only he was talking about the actions of the police at Henley and Ascot who were apparently taking the shameful and oppressive step of stopping cars to check for drunkeness. When it came to Hillsborough things were different, and the well-informed Waugh identified the problem instantly. "Of all the Liverpool supporters who had been in early to give them time to settle down, 3,000 were still rioting outside the gate, many of them without tickets, a few minutes before kick off, having for the most part spent the time drinking." It is, naturally, quite absurd for anyone to assume that Henley or Ascot goers might be drunk, but obvious when you are talking about football fans.

Alongside Waugh in the *Sunday Telegraph*, Frank Johnson tells it how it is. "Going to football is now the recreation of what Marx called the lumpen proletariat and what the rest of us are content to call yobs." Johnson moans about how crowds used to be much bigger but people were mainly good humoured. The difference is more one of age than facts. People like Johnson regard crushing and crowd problems of the past with nostalgia. Like rationing, or the Blitz, life was hard but fair. What was once 'just part of growing up in those days' is now regarded with terror by the Frank Johnsons of the world. In the same breath as remembering huge crowds and people peeing in your pocket, they decry the mob instinct and public urination.

They say you can tell a lot about a paper by the letters it receives. In the *Sun*, most backed the paper's stance. Mrs E of Farnham blamed Liverpool fans, "If they arrived in good time and in good order tragedy could have been averted." And Mrs E Spencer of Chesterfield says, "When we encountered the totally out of control crowd we went home. When will people take responsibility for their own behaviour." Mrs Spencer obviously arrived as late as the irresponsible fans she mentions – doubtless she will be handing herself into the local police station. If not she had better hope that Mrs E of Farnham doesn't catch up with her.

Today managed to find one reader who knew exactly what caused it all. "I wonder if the powers that be realise it is the players who trigger off the mass hysteria of crowds? Watching sports programmes one sees players having scored leap on one another's backs and then dash to their supporters to receive their acclaim. This does not occur at hockey or rugby matches where fans are not caged like animals. Control the players and the crowds will settle down." There's always one, isn't there?

The coverage in the quality press was largely excellent. The tone of most of the writing was depressed rather than aggressive, and in much of the best pieces you could sense the frustration of the writers who had seen it before but thought that things had changed for the better. Among the non football writers who chipped in, most notable was Jeremy Seabrook, who wrote an excellent piece in the *Guardian*.

Then, suprisingly there was the *Daily Express* whose assessment of the police stories of looting and robbery was remarkably sensible. "No-one can justify loutish behaviour by Liverpool fans. And there was some of that. But on balance it seems that the police have more questions to answer than fans." When the *Daily Express* says things like that, then there must be something fishy going on.

Anthony Burgess in the *Daily Telegraph* satisfied himself with talking guff. "Support for the local or national team can be invested with a frenzy that cuts at the roots of what we call civilised behaviour. And the support itself is more abstract or nominal than genuinely civic or patriotic." He can barely disguise his disdain for football supporters, "Crowds as Elias Canetti has pointed out are primitive beasts very low on the evolutionary scale."

He doesn't really like football either. "For many thousands of Britons there is nothing more important on a Saturday afternoon than watching 22 men kicking a piece of leather about. There is something wrong with our culture if we have come to this."

Burgess perhaps typified much of the media coverage of Hillsborough, too vast to cover here. He knew nothing and cared less. Everyone thinks that disaster gives them a right to pontificate or sympathise in the guise of 'Making Sure It Never Happens Again.'

However, all they succeed in doing is vulgarising the tragedy that they decry. Worse still, they set the agenda for what happens beyond the disaster itself, leaving others to sort out the mess of crackpot ideas they leave behind. Perversely, their attempts to shout that it must never happen again help to ensure that it probably will, by confusing issues and turning inquiries into debates. Their attentions hinder the process of learning and twist tragedy into a self perpetuating media circus, not far from soap opera. ○

Heaven Knowles

What would you do if a football idol knocked on your door and asked you about God? Julian Richards offered some tips from his personal experience.

WSC No29, July 1989

BY 1965, THE MYOPIC BOARD OF DIRECTORS AT WOLVERHAMPTON WANDERERS had condemned themselves to second-class soccer for the first time in two generations. The glorious old-golden days and nights, the Brylcreem and baggy pants had passed me by in my cradle. Molineux had become a decaying Victorian palace theatre – the cast something of a music hall joke.

Never mind: big, blond Ron Flowers was still there directing defensive traffic like some great white lighthouse; there was little Joe Wilson, the archetypal bullet-headed, barrel-chested, bow-legged, beer-bellied right back; young Graham Hawkins skulking dangerously amongst the Central League stiffs, vengefully plotting his minor role in the future sinking of the once-titanic club. And then there was 'Knocker' Knowles.

As a schoolboy, one of my proudest boasts was that I actually 'knew' Peter Knowles. In fact, it was my Dad who happened to get nearer to the great man than many opposing defenders ever did. One Saturday morning in 1965, Knocker was ejected from Dad's clothing store for distracting the attention of the lovely Cathy in Lingerie. Later that same day I was amongst the privileged who witnessed the 20-year-old score his second successive hat-trick.

As a talented young footballer, Knowles seemed to thrive on controversy and infamy. He was variously described as arrogant, precocious, imprudent, irresponsible. Fortunately, he was all of those things – and much more besides. I remember how Knocker enlivened one of those dour, dreary encounters with Bolton Wanderers: parking his backside on the ball on the centre spot, taunting bovine opposition defenders to come and get it, then, after a ticking off from the ref, hoofing the leather over the old Molineux Street stand and on to New Invention. I recall some of his many goals: typically, dummying a clumsy half-wit wing half on the edge of the penalty area and then, with either of those telescopic legs, catapulting ball from boot to roof of net. PK taking the piss again. A thoroughbred among workhorses.

George Best's romps at Old Trafford (and in bedrooms and bars between Barnet and Benidorm) were widely reckoned to have been responsible for the rapid transformation of manager Wilf McGuinness's coiffure from black to grey to white to non-existent in not much more than half a season. Similarly, in order to avoid premature aging, Ronnie Allen was prompted by Peter Knowles' antics to relieve West Brom of the dubious services of another inside left. David Burnside was not only balding and aging but also bore an uncanny resemblance to Coco the Clown. Allen used Burnside as a stick with which to beat the juggling, wriggling Knowles. If Knocker's jiggery-pokery on a Saturday was considered to be bad form, you could bet your shirt that 'Sideburn' would turn out the following Wednesday wearing the No 10 jersey.

To be fair, it was rumoured that the latter had once been a reasonably useful and popular inside forward. During his brief twilight sojourn at Molineux, however, he demonstrated two particularly alarming characteristics; a tendency to deliver long sweeping backpasses to a tremulous Fred Davies in goal and an ability to trip over his own boot-laces and fall flat on his face.

For a young green lad, those Second Division Molineux years of 1965-67 provided a thorough grounding in the good, bad and downright ugly of professional football. Were it not for Peter Knowles, the Coventrys and the Carlisles would have clouded our Saturday skies. Had it not been for the mercenary stoppers with names like Nutton, Woodhead and Savage, I may never have appreciated the subtleties of unarmed combat. Without the hapless Sideburn, the gentle art of character assassination might have remained elusive.

On those bitter, damp, cheerless January evenings, my heart ached for the likes of David Burnside: at those moments when the restless hubbub of a football ground is severed by a lone, acid-sharp voice of abuse reverberating through stand and terraces; when professional confidence and pride may be ruptured by the precision timing of a scalpel tongue.

One day, early in 1969, Peter Knowles publicly declared his allegiance to the Jehovah's Witness movement, having apparently been converted on the doorstep. He also announced his intention to quit football.

One can only speculate as to his true motivation. Knowles himself expressed a profound disillusion with the increased competitiveness and commercialism within the game. However, it has been suggested that Knocker lacked the appetite for a hard tackle and that, in fact, he simply used religion as an excuse for 'bottling out'. And yet, he had already proved his worth at England youth and under-23 level and seemed destined to gain far more than his brother Cyril's four full caps. Indeed, Knowles' talent and good looks might have made him one of the most successful and highly paid players of his era.

Ronnie Allen's successor, Bill McGarry, hardly a world-renowned leader of men, could not be expected to influence Peter's decision. In fact, he succeeded only in retaining the registration of Wolves' most valuable asset, in the vain hope that he would one day return (and also, no doubt, to deflect approaches from other clubs).

So, Jehovah summoned Peter Knowles after an emotional farewell Molineux match against Nottingham Forest. At just 24 years of age, Knocker renounced all unnecessary material possessions, hung up his boots and resigned himself to the Lord.

In recent years, I have occasionally seen the prodigal son return to the scene of his former glory, to bear testimony and give thanks to Old Wolves, such as the sublimely elegant John Richards. I have witnessed the cherubic figure protrude from the players' tunnel to render a businesslike yet ghostly second-half performance beneath the unforgiving Molineux floodlights; still, even now, transiently reminiscent of those old past masters – the Whites, the Baxters – who continue to haunt the No 10 jersey.

But I am finally left with the image of Peter Knowles standing divinely on our doorstep, some ten years after illuminating my grey, Wolverhampton Saturday afternoons. And I am left standing, with my own words echoing in my ears: "Er... I'm sorry, not today, thank you... I don't believe in it..." O

Reading the Reviews

Rob McIlveen paid tribute to a legendary publication familiar to anyone who began watching football in the late Sixties or early Seventies.

WSC No 29, July 1989

PICTURE IF YOU WILL THE FOLLOWING SCENE. IT'S A SUNDAY. YOU'RE GOD AND it's been bloody hard work all round creating this and that. You've written your letter to the Rush family pointing out that somebody had to get the last nose out of the box and bollocked Tottenham for appointing some geezer called Venables when you clearly said "somebody venerable." There isn't much that you, the creator, haven't seen. But wait, nestling in the mahogany-effect magazine rack you picked up when creating the first MFI sale, is something that's even older than you!

I talk, of course of the *Football League Review*, the one-time official journal of, believe it or not, the Football League. For many clubs, especially in the lower divisions, the advent of this 'add-on' journal saved them from acute embarrassment. Grimsby Town, for example, used to print 1,500 or so sheets of A4 sized paper, fold them in half and then staple each around a copy of the Review. The finished product was, of course, 'the programme' and the club charged nine old pence for what was, in effect, one sheet of paper plus something that was probably distributed free to them.

Those were, as they say, the days. The cover was always worth a laugh, one I will always treasure being that which shows Hartlepool United ball boys posing as though for a team picture circa 1968. According to the 'cover story' which the Review always printed pages away from the cover, the lads were "dedicated Hartlepool United fans" who, after their Saturday duties, returned on Sunday mornings "to sweep the terraces". The manager, a certain Gus McLean is quoted as saying "just show them that the club is interested in them and they'll be fans for life".

The 'fans' were aged ten or so when the picture was taken, so they'll be around 30 today. I often look at their scowling faces and wonder how many of them are inside for mass murder, rape and other equally unsavoury behaviour. We can be sure of one thing – none of them gives a bugger now about either Hartlepool United or Gus McLean.

The inside front cover often featured 'Soccer Strips', which required the reader to guess the identity of the club whose kit was featured. This always struck me as a pointless exercise as many of the pictures had obviously been air-brushed, presumably because the player involved was either wearing the away strip or playing for another club. How else can you explain why Ralph Coates' Tottenham socks managed to stay up when they appeared to be a good deal wider than his legs. And what was a Spurs player doing on the pitch during a Burnley v Everton game anyway?

The inside cover was just as bad. For unexplained reasons, they demanded that we 'Collect Club Badges' and printed pictures of metal lapel badges (which could be purchased by the likes of you and me) and the official blazer variety (which invariably could not). It goes without saying that not once did I see my own team, Grimsby, featured. Sure, I could tell you how much a packet of No 10 or Park Plain Drive cost (3/6 and 4/5 respectively) but couldn't even begin to describe either of Grimsby's badges.

I often wondered if different versions of the *Review* were distributed to various grounds in such a way that the home supporter would never see a reference to his own team. Those of you who tried in vain to secure a picture of Peter Storey in the *Soccer Stars* collection will appreciate my conspiracy theory (though in Storey's case it's probably fair to assume that Plod snapped up all the pictures for their 'Wanted' posters).

Equally baffling was a feature entitled 'Top Ten Review'. This was a postal poll of votes for "the most attractive footballing hunk of manhood you know". Overall, Eoin Hand won more often than anyone else (even George Best) but, week by week, there were some surprises. I remember seeing Trevor Hockey feature at No 1 once, as well as Wyn Davies and Ian Callaghan.

What intrigued me though was why anyone could be bothered to collect and register votes. Apparently, the *Review* used to get over 1,000 letters per week on this subject. God knows how such a poll would be received nowadays and how many people would behave like 'Honest Shirley of Newcastle' and admit that several signatures were not genuine.

These people were keen. As Peter Savage wrote (yes, a male collecting votes for a footballer!) "the girls have been neglecting their duties for a few weeks so I got together with a few boy pals to collect votes for Coventry's Neil Martin". Hmmm. The fans who collected the most votes for a player received a free Mettoy ball. One suspects that Peter was hoping for a couple as his reward, both Neil Martin brand.

People like Peter would undoubtedly have been avid readers of features such as 'Man Behind The Ball' and 'Man And Manager', a look at any footballer or manager who had a hobby that their kind are not supposed to have. My favourite was Mike Rogan, who, when not keeping goal for Workington (surely a full-time occupation) alternated between disc jockey at his local youth club and model train enthusiast.

Then there was one-time Middlesbrough manager Stan Anderson with his stamp collection and Colin Appleton telling us that "whenever I'm tired or strained, I go under the stairs and fetch it out". "It" was a carpenter's kit. As Appleton explained: "Messing about with wood is a real freedom to me". Poor old Colin got more freedom than he bargained for since Barrow, whom he was managing at the time, were kicked out of the League shortly after.

The most obvious way for fans to make a contribution to the review was through 'Post Bag', allegedly 'The Best Forum In Football'. Forum, however, was hardly the word. Any letter which even hinted at criticism was given short shrift and, of course, the feature attracted some real plonkers. Take Peter Hartland and Graham Weston who wrote to say they had walked ten miles around Geneva to find an English newspaper with the football results in. "We're Wolves fans," they concluded, as if this was justification for their behaviour.

Readers also filled out the pages of the *Review,* through 'Make Friends With Other Fans', which seems now to have been a forerunner of a kinky contact mag. Thus, Miss C Driscoll of Parsons Green, London begged the magazine to help her find a Saints supporter who she met at a Southampton v QPR game. Innocent enough so far, but wait, the man in question "unfortunately cut his head so I used my scarf to mop up the blood". What Miss Driscoll could have wanted him for is something only present day bloodied Saints fans could tell us.

Other correspondents were more concerned with the exchange of pennants, badges, programmes and the like. More often than not they were Polish, Czech or Hungarian, like Pavel Randa of Lodenice, who pleaded for the *Review* to "press in their beautiful journal" his letter. He even requested that they show a picture of him in national costume. The cruel bastards duly did. I would have sent him my club's badge, if only I'd known what it looked like and where I could get it from...

Even in the less economically constrained late Sixties, sponsorship abounded. 'John White', who claimed to produce "shoes that lead the League" with names like The Cad and The Rogue, operated a crowd behaviour award scheme, with £100 given monthly to the fans judged the most sporting' in each division. Potentially laudable, if not for two things. First, their claim that "the rowdies and rioters are getting far more publicity than they are worth" was given further support, rather than anything else, by their scheme. Second, it gave rise to a 'we know more songs than you and want you to publish them' mentality. Thus the *Review* was obliged to print the words to "I'm a knock-kneed chicken, I'm a bow-legged hen" and "Hey up, hey up, we are the Busby boys" etc in its supposedly serious pages.

It comes as little surprise to learn that the John White Supporters' Cup was the only trophy Workington Town ever won in the Football League and look what it did for them. Exactly what they did with their £100 is anybody's guess. Mine is that they used it to get pissed out of their heads and smash up an away ground or two.

In a similar, worthy, vein, Ford Motors claimed that their sponsorship would help stamp out "this sort of malarkey," the latter being defined in a series of a dozen pictures showing various types of foul being committed. Of course, prior to the ad appearing, few players even knew about the sort of illegal behaviour which subsequently became common-place. Pontins also got in on the act, awarding a free holiday for two at any of their camps, for the 'fan of the week'. Now, wasn't that an incentive to see all 92 clubs clock up 3,643 miles, and watch the reserves every Thursday night?

The rest of the magazine carried the views of several notables including Harry Brown (and his astonishingly boring editorial), Bryon Butler (and his equally tedious 'Press Box' section) and Bob Baldwin (and his numbingly-tiresome 'Meet the People' column) as well as some geezer called Walter Pilkington. For some reason, he was given a whole page, devoted to facts and figures. Did you know, for example, that four of the 14 ever-presents in the First Division in 1947-48 were goalkeepers? More pertinently, did you care?

Sadly, the *Review* faded away in the 1970s. A pity really, for in spite of the foregoing, I and a lot of others, did enjoy it. Rather like those people who can tell you exactly what they were doing when the news came through that Kennedy had been assassinated, I remember vividly the day that my programme lost 24 of its 28 pages. As a Grimsby supporter, I had plenty of opportunity to read the *Review* between 3 pm and 4.45 pm. Imagine my horror when I discovered I would be forced to watch a whole 90 minutes from then on.

I still treasure my copies of the *Review* and know that one look at Gordon Nisbet's 1973 hairstyle will always cheer me up, as will my colour picture of a thin Francis Lee. The *Review* is dead. Long live the *Review*! ○

Tough and Super-Tough

The first instalment of the true story of British football,
as told to Harry Pearson.

WSC No 30, August 1989

"THE BALL WAS HEAVIER IN THEM DAYS," MY GRANDFATHER WOULD SAY waggling his false front tooth up and down reflectively, "It was like a bloody cannonball," he'd say, and laugh.

"It soaked up water like a camel's hump and the mud stuck to it an' all. On a wet day that ball weighed more than the King of Persia's Christmas pudding. I've seen Jack Carr at Ayresome Park get under a kick from the opposition goalkeeper and the ball would drive him into the ground like a steamhammer driving in a rivet. He'd be sunk in the ground up to his neck. They had a gang of navvies on hand just to dig him out. They weren't allowed on until half or full-time, mind. Sometimes he'd spend 85 minutes of the game like that; on the edge of the penalty area with only his head visible above the mud. And he still made a contribution.

"And that pitch was muddy. There was none of this drainage or underground heating or astrakhan surfaces or all that jesse-ing about. That pitch was like the Somme. And if we were playing Sunderland so was the game.

"Aye it was like the Somme on the third day that pitch. Boro brought down this new winger from Scotland. Ten minutes into the game he fell into a crater over by the left touchline. They never recovered the body. But nobody kicked up a stink. Players were tough in those days. Death was a way of life to them.

"The goalkeepers were the toughest of the lot. They didn't get protection from the refs like they do now. I remember Dixie Dean shoulder-charging Tim Williamson so hard he sent him straight back through the net and up through the roof of the stand. He landed, third bounce, on a tramp steamer that was sailing down the Tees. When he woke up, he was in Trinidad. And the ref just waved play on.

"They were stronger, too. They had to be to run about in those boots. They weren't like these modern things, they're just sand shoes. In those days the players made their own. Billy Pease had a pair he'd knocked up out of old off-cuts of steel plate stitched together with half-inch cable. They were so heavy it took four normal men to carry them and they say that on a wet day when his right boot filled up with water it weighed the same as a class-three destroyer. His left boot was sunk by a U-boat during the Dunkirk evacuation.

"And there was none of this moaning about the minimum wage. Andrew Wilson would have played for the Boro for no more than couple of smacks on the back of the head with a five pound lump hammer. And when times were hard, he'd have settled for one.

"Times were tough, then. But there was none of this hooliganism. My cousin Dave once laid out Leslie Compton, mind. But that was under extreme provocation. There wasn't a jury in the land that would have convicted him. Except for the one that did." O

Regional Differences

At a time when League re-organisation was being mooted once again, Roger Titford looked back at a previous restructuring and suggested that a terrible error had been made.

WSC No 31, September 1989

SO IT'S GOODBYE DARLINGTON, HELLO MAIDSTONE. WHILST IT'S ALWAYS SAD to see a club forcibly removed from a position they've held for 60 years, it does represent a further step towards rectifying one of the worst mistakes the Football League ever made – the formation of Division Three North in 1921.

The decision to introduce the division was highly debatable at the time and time would appear to have proven the doubters right. The cost to the League as a whole has not only been the stagnation of the lower divisions but also the appalling Woodbine imagery of poverty clubs as the butt of music-hall jokes. "I asked what time's the kick-off-and they said what time can you get here" or "the chairman found half a dozen courting couples in the stand one night and said it was the biggest crowd we'd had all season", etc etc *ad nauseam*.

Division Three North evolved as a regional response to the Southern League's First Division becoming the Third Division of the Football League in 1920. The old Southern League was a strong competition from which several important League sides had already emerged, Tottenham and Fulham for instance. In the ten seasons prior to 1920 no less than 36 Southern League sides had reached the last 16 of the FA Cup (and three went on to the semi finals). Only two northern non-Leaguers reached this stage in the same period.

The inclusion of 22 southern clubs redressed the original imbalance in the Football League which, when founded in 1888, had comprised only northern and midland clubs. Half the members of this original Third Division have gone on to play in the First Division. By comparison, the story of Division Three North is woeful. There was no obvious source of new clubs in the north. The best were already in the League and rugby league was strong in Yorkshire, Lancashire and Cumbria.

The League Management Committee was split over the issue and, unusually, did not make a recommendation to the full members' meeting in March 1921. Some applications were turned away (including such future soccer hotbeds as Castleford, Wakefield, Lancaster and West Stanley), the rest were strictly vetted. Despite this, they could still not give enthusiastic backing to the aspirations of the remaining 14 'suitable' candidates. Only financial guarantees, the generally optimistic mood of the game and the country's post-war prosperity turned the day their way.

Though it has never been publicly stated, it seems the League came to regret the decision. They have always adopted a *laissez-faire* attitude towards failing clubs, most notably Accrington Stanley in 1962. Moreover, there was no meaningful expansion after 1921, merely the addition of six places in the next 67 years.

At the time, gate receipts for Division 3N were about half those of its southern equivalent. This kind of economic disparity showed up in the longer term, never more so than after the formation of a national Third Division at the end of 1957-58. The bottom halves of the two regional sections became Fourth Division. Within three seasons, the effect of promotion and relegation between the two was that Third Division in effect became Division 3S re-christened.

Last season, 17 of the 24 sides in the Fourth Division would have been in the old Division 3N. More telling still is that former members of that section accounted for 92 of the 111 applications for re-election between 1959 and 1986.

It's hard to comment on the playing style and standard of the old Division 3N, there not being a lot of examples on the shelves of my local video store. The only memory of that era which seems to have survived in wider public consciousness is Michael Parkinson's recollections of the division's most famous son, Skinner Normanton. The general sense was of a hard game played by hard men in hard times and relished as such is suggested by this extract from Ward & Allister's *Barnsley – A Study in Football 1953-1959*:

"Thomas was on one leg when Johnson collided with him. Shotton and Ward suddenly saw Thomas flying across the track towards their trainer's box. They jumped to cushion the impact, but Thomas connected with the solid concrete structure. Spectators on the terrace craned forward. Shotton started to separate the red cinder from splashes of blood." The beautiful game it wasn't.

Born in a year of optimism, Division 3N's beginnings were damaged by the economic stump of 1922 and the clubs' poor preparations. From the start, spectator facilities at several grounds were awful and Darlington, Lincoln, Stalybridge, Halifax and Rochdale were known to be struggling. In the inaugural season, the latter two applied for re-election, and they still cling on to League status despite being locked in the bottom half of the Fourth Division for the past decade with only two promotions between them in 60 seasons.

Half of the 16 teams who came into the League in 1921 have since departed. Some of the others have had respectable lower division careers, though none has yet reached the First Division. Between them, Hartlepool, Halifax, Rochdale, Crewe (newly blessed) and Darlington (no more) have been re-elected 56 times and gained only nine promotions! They average a manager every two years, hold a disproportionately large share of the worst playing records and 'own' some of the most startlingly decrepit facilities (Darlington and, to a small extent, Crewe, should be excepted from the last charge).

Together they, and much of the rest of the old Third Division North have given football its seedy, breadline image without ever bringing much glory to their towns or, indeed, crowds from them.

The good news is that the solution to the mistake of 1921 exists and is at work – the new system of automatic relegation from the League. Playing standards and attendances in the Fourth Division do seem to be improving, clubs like Crewe are rising to the challenge and the Conference is proving to be an effective feeder league. When clubs switch back and forth regularly between the two divisions, say in five years' time, we'll know the deadwood's been cleared out of the coal cellar and the time will be right to welcome back, if they make it on merit, Darlington, Barrow, Bradford Park Avenue... O

Local Lad Makes Good

The second part of the absolutely true (honest) story of British football, as told to Harry Pearson.

WSC No 31, September 1989

"Groin strain!" My grandfather would snort as he closed one eye ruminatively and stared into the distance with the other as if gazing through an invisible telescope. "They didn't get groin strain in those days," he'd say, and chuckle.

"George Camsell was as tough as a tortoise sandwich. He followed a scientific fitness programme. Every day he climbed a sixty foot ladder, 100 times, with a 50lb pound bucket of rivets in either hand. It wasn't called callisthenics. It wasn't called weight training. It was called a day's work and he was glad to get it. And he never had a groin strain in his life.

"Mind, after his first 45 minutes against Sunderland, he never had a groin either. Aye, it was a man's game in those days. There were no tactics. Most of those lads couldn't have even spelt 4-3-3 never mind played in it. The nearest Jock Marshall ever got to a coach was when he caught the train to Ormesby. But his tackles were as hard as Jack Dempsey's left hook. When they landed they made a bang like a tugboat's boiler exploding through over-stoking. And he didn't wear shin pads. He just filled his socks with quick-dry concrete.

"Jock Marshall's shoulder charge was so powerful that during the week he worked for a demolition firm as a wrecking ball. But compared to 'Pudden' Carr, he was a right Shirley Temple. They didn't need tactics because they were that skilful. Billy Birrel was so clever that he once sold the opposition full back a dummy and knocked in a hat-trick while the lad was still searching for him in the South Stand.

"And he was quick too. The only thing I've ever seen run faster than Billy Birrel was when our Alf played a steam hose over a dray horse's arse. You should've seen it shift! It went off down Parliament Road like a TT racer. And with 48 kegs of Cameron's bouncing about on the wagon an' all. The beer went west, but nobody moaned – there was plenty of ale to go round in those days. Jim Baxter hadn't come to the north east yet.

"And the players were respected. When Andrew 'Wingy' Wilson walked down the street, he didn't get mobbed. People treated him as a gentleman. They called him Mr 'Wingy' Wilson. He got his nickname because he had lost an arm in the Great War. The fans at Ayresome Park always had a sense of humour.

"It was before the maximum wage was abolished. Poverty gave those players a sense of purpose. They were as poor as we were and lived in the same areas. We lived in the same street as Jiddler Murray and if he didn't get carried off unconscious at least three times during the game, our Joe would go round to his house on Sunday morning and land him a fourpenny one. There was a strong link between the players and the community in those days.

"And Jiddler didn't mind. He understood. It cost a shilling to get into Ayresome Park. You could get a new suit, two tickets for the opera house and a pie and peas supper for that. As our Joe said, 'We've paid good money and we've a right to complain'. Not that we ever did pay, mind. When we got back to the turnstiles Joe would grab the gateman by the ears and me and Alf and Davey would crawl in underneath. But Jiddler Murray didn't know that." ○

A Race Apart

Dave Hill described the difficulties he encountered in writing his acclaimed book about John Barnes, Out Of His Skin.

WSC No 32, October 1989

AS I WRITE, THE SPORTS DEPARTMENTS OF LIVERPOOL'S TWO LOCAL RADIO stations are deciding whether to speak to me or not. The problem is, I have written this book about John Barnes and his success in becoming the first black player to make it big on Merseyside. It is a football saga about much more than a few balls in the back of the net. By telling the story of Barnes, it tries to shed some critical light on the values of the two big clubs and how they reflect both the racism of the city of Liverpool and the bigotry which flourishes throughout English football. This, it appears, has thrown our men at the microphones into a defensive panic.

The book was written without Barnes' co-operation. Therefore, in a fearless display of editorial independence, the local commercial radio station, Radio City, told my publisher's press officer they could not ask me along to discuss it unless 'Barnesie' said it was all right. I await a decision with interest. In the meantime, the whole business strikes me as a perfect example of the way the football industry bureaucrats, managers and media alike prefer to deal with all the crises that afflict it, that is, by scratching their heads in confusion, then running a mile.

There is a conspiracy of silence surrounding racism in football and all kinds of people, willingly and otherwise, are implicated in it. This ranges from the failure of TV commentators to acknowledge the existence of terrace abuse to the disinterest of reporters in breaking stories about what have effectively been colour bars at certain clubs. One soccer hack confidently assured me that the board of one well-known Northern club once ordered the manager not to sign a particular black defender because "that sort of player would not be suitable here".

Largely this is a product of the mind-numbing insularity of the football world. People working in it appear to be oblivious to wider social changes even when they impinge most dramatically on the world of sport. Half a century after Jesse Owens, a quarter of a century after Martin Luther King, and 21 years after two American sprinters gave the Black Power salute from the Olympic medal rostrum, some of these dickheads don't even know what a black person is.

The other day, a news reporter from the BBC related to me a conversation he had with a Well-Known Television Football Commentator. The topic was Ruud Gullit and the abuse to which he has been routinely subjected by England supporters. The Well-Known Television Football Commentator's view was that "there's a bit too much fuss about this racism business. After all, you can't call Ruud Gullit black, can you?" Of course not. How silly. And Bob Marley – wasn't he lead singer with the Hitler Youth?

This kind of mind-blowing vacuity is present at all levels of the game, sometimes just the benign expression of received 'wisdoms', but nicely spiced here and there with a dose of authentic, out and out xenophobia. Anyone who has read Hunter Davies' book, *The Glory Game*, will be familiar with the tin-hatted chauvinism of the then team coach Eddie Baily ("These darkies should go back to the jungle where they belong" and so on).

Less malevolent, but almost as tiresome to those branded with them, are bizarre myths about the supposed physical and temperamental failings of blacks. 'No bottle' is a particular favourite, lack of concentration another. "You don't want too many of them in your defence", one backroom bod told me, "they cave in under pressure". Then there is the curious conviction that blacks are susceptible to the cold and won't go out when it rains. Incredibly, Baily Of The Spurs was not the last of the breed.

Vile words like 'coon' and 'nigger' have yet to acquire the forbidden status they rightly enjoy in other areas of British life. Get Tommy Smith, the former 'Iron Man Of Anfield', talking on the subject of black people. He uses these pernicious terms like other folk say 'knife' and 'fork'.

But the saddest participants of all in this pact of indifference are the black players themselves. This is not, by and large, a willing complicity. It is not because they do not care when managers and team mates expect them to respond with a cheery grin to gags about suntans, or when a crowd assails them with monkey chants and flying bananas. Rather, it is because they have the most to lose by speaking out.

Danny Thomas, the former Coventry and Spurs full back, recalls having to handle such puerile nonsense in his early days with the midlands club. "I used to get some of that", he remembers, "but I noticed that if I was standing with big Garry Thompson it didn't happen nearly so much." Garth Crooks, speaking recently on Channel Four's *After Dark*, can now admit to being deeply hurt by Stoke team-mates mocking him for using an afro comb on his hair.

The inability of many white players to respect these sensitivities is well illustrated by an anecdote related by Bruce Grobbelaar in his 1986 autobiography, concerning himself, Howard Gayle, the black Scouser who played five times for Liverpool in the early Eighties and Daley Thompson, who dropped in on a training session. Gayle supposedly challenged Thompson to a race with 'Brucie' as the starter;

"It was all very serious until I said: 'Ready, steady, pick up your lips, GO!' Howard was not at all amused and found nothing to smile about," writes a puzzled Bruce. Gayle is a son of Liverpool 8 whose black citizens' lives were described in the recent Gifford Report as "uniquely horrific". Grobbelaar is a former conscript in Ian Smith's Rhodesian army. And he expected Howard Gayle to laugh. At the same time, anyone making artic-ulate noises to a journalist is likely to get it in the neck. Sometimes it's much easier not to rock the boat, not to be seen to be making a fuss. After all, someone might say, as Grobbelaar did of the assertive Howard Gayle, that you've "got a chip on your shoulder".

Brendan Batson of the PFA was, with Cyrille Regis and Laurie Cunningham, a member of the most visibly 'black' team in England during the late Seventies, Ron Atkinson's West Brom. Only in retirement does he feel able to explain how the issue of racism impinged, subtly but routinely, on relations with his peers and superiors, and admit how hurtful the attentions of the terrace tormentors were. To have gone public at the time, he says, would only have encouraged them and isolated him still more.

This obligation to stay silent is reinforced by the whole ethos of the game. To insist that your blackness deserves simple respect is often to break rank with 'the lads' in the dressing room. "After all, what's so special about you, Kunta Kinte, ha ha? Can't you take a joke?" What all this adds up to is that dear old sporting phobia, Fear of Politics, or, put another way: "Let's not dwell on the negative aspects, Brian. Let's concentrate on the good things in the game."

"If only Real Life would leave us alone," squeal the football mullahs. "All we want to do is get on with our little game." Meanwhile, any progress that has been made in challenging football's racist ideology is due almost entirely to the courage, resilience and sheer bloodied determination of the black players themselves.

In playing terms, their triumphs are easy to see. For a start, they are out on the field, participating at the highest levels of the national game. They continue to make inroads into parts of the sport from which they have been effectively excluded before. Clearly, it is a healthy sign that English League players voted in Garth Crooks, to chair the PFA, their own representative body. Finally, too, a black man has been appointed to a responsible backroom position – at Coventry, Cyrille Regis has been made team coach.

The first black manager, though well overdue, is surely just a matter of time. Further, as a younger generation of managers comes through (Dalglish is a key example) a gradual acceptance that a black man can fill roles demanding tenacity and responsibility is also being reflected in playing terms.

In England, the most celebrated black players have functioned on the wing, or in defence, usually at full-back. This is almost entirely the result of self-fulfilling prophecy born of the old prejudices as expressed by one Liverpool FC back-room staffer: "They're fast, aren't they?" Look at Arsenal's championship-winning squad. Paul Davies, David Rocastle and Michael Thomas, all differently gifted, but all integral to the Gunners' midfield. Even the long-suffering utility scapegoat Gus Caesar can hardly be dismissed as soft.

But let's not join the mute chorus of complacency. The fact that blacks are, in objective statistical terms, actually over-represented on the pitch when compared to the general population, emphasises that sport is one of the few careers where, turning elements of prejudice to their advantage, they have a chance to excel. Meanwhile, the situation is reversed at the turnstiles. Some clubs, of course, are more conscientious than others. But up and down the country the glaring indifference of the football industry to terrace racism can only be a disincentive to black people to turn up.

Imagine how you, white reader, would feel if you were black and were obliged to hear your fellow supporters greet the opposition's black striker with the mantra: "Kill, kill, kill the nigger." Better by far to stay at home.

The theory survives, even among fair minded white football supporters, that drawing attention to the problem of racism makes it worse. It is an understandable viewpoint, for it is true that the prime terrace perpetrators are far from averse to a spot of publicity. But, in the long term, nothing encourages ignorance and prejudice like neglect. The efforts of Leeds' Supporters Against Racism and Fascism prove that a consensus can be mobilised against organised turds like the NF. Would that the most powerful interest groups in the game had the same vision and determination.

Racism is a subject in itself, but it is also the most overt manifestation of a wider malaise. What fuels hooliganism if not an irrational disdain for the citizens of another district or town? What drives the 'Bulldog Army' to terrorise the citizens of other nations, but naked national chauvinism? To cure the disease, people in power must find the courage to diagnose it. Meanwhile, as the empire crashes around their ears, most prefer to stick their heads in the sand. ○

Dawn of the Tripehounds

The concluding chapter of the true story of British football as told to Harry Pearson.

WSC No 32, October 1989

"THE NORTH HAD ALL THE BEST SIDES IN THOSE DAYS," MY GRANDFATHER would say, and he'd look over the pink pages of the *Sports Gazette* and wink, "because floodlights hadn't been invented," he'd say and laugh.

"It was darker then an' all. There was smoke from the chimneys and the flarestacks, steam from the cooling towers and fumes from the chemical plants. The sky was as black as jet. By three o'clock of a winter's afternoon, you couldn't have seen Moby Dick if he was sitting in your lap, never mind a football. That gave the northern lads an advantage because they were used to it. Most of Boro's players worked down the ironstone mines. They knew how to get about in the dark. Owen Williams would scamper down the wing clutching onto a pit pony's tail. He'd cut the ball across and George Camsell would scurry into the penalty area on all fours, a Davey lamp between his teeth, and nod it into the net.

"What a forward line that was! Every one of them was an international. Even Owen Williams' pit pony had two caps for Wales. Aye, that was the best set of forwards I ever saw. Not that I ever did see them, mind. It was too bloody dark. You had to use your imagination. Boro fans were used to that. When you listened to the wireless you had to imagine the action. And in the north east during the depression you had to imagine the wireless an' all.

"Every Saturday, 40,000 supporters would pack into Ayresome just to see the lights on the pit helmets bobbing about in the smog. Those lamps were the targets for the players' passes, which were deadly accurate. There was many a Boro fan went to light up a cigarette and got his teeth knocked out by a Bobby Baxter 40 yarder. Nowadays they just boot the ball into orbit and if it lands on the pitch they call it a pass. But in those days the passes were pin-point. If they weren't you lost the ball in the blackness. And that was serious, because the ball cost more than the entire Boro team.

"I remember one time the coach, Charlie Cole, come up with a crafty solution. He bought a bloodhound from the Durham Prison Authority and played it at wing-half. Before the game he smothered the ball in gravy so's the dog could track it. Fifteen minutes into the game the ball vanished. The bloodhound dashed off. Seconds later he was back, dribbling it down the wing. He flicked it into the middle. Billy Birrel laid it out to 'Wingy' Wilson and he smashed it into the goal. It's the only time in Football League history anyone's ever netted a steak and kidney pudding.

"They transferred the dog to Sunderland after that. He wasn't the most skilful player that ever turned out for the Rokermen. But he was the brainiest.

"When I say 40,000 turned every Saturday, I mean every Saturday. It didn't matter if Boro were playing at home or not. The fans were loyal. There weren't any part-timers in those days. And, except for a few military policemen on the lookout for deserters, there were no bobbies in the ground. They weren't needed to control that crowd. Everybody controlled one another. If there was roughneck or a baloney-merchant stood near us, our Joe would snatch the bloke's cap off and drop it over the back of the stand – it was about thirty foot down. 'Any more out of you', he'd say 'and you're following it.' People listened to reason in those days.

"Aye there's three things that ruined north east football: the invention of floodlights, the passing of the Clean Air Act and the tripehounds. But I'll tell you about those when you're older."

And, basically like, that's it. ◯

1990

Facing Mecca

John Duncan traced the convoluted ownership of Wembley
Stadium and ended up wondering what it had to do with football.

WSC No 40, June 1990

WEMBLEY MAY JUST BE A FAMOUS OLD FOOTBALL STADIUM TO YOU AND ME BUT
in fact it is a great deal more than that. As a company its history is a fascinating study in the cloudy relationship between football and business.
From the twin towers stretches a business conglomerate that is now big
in greyhounds, and whose activities have included discotheques,
ticketing equipment, betting interests and even an outside catering
company called Yankee Doodle Dandy.

There are several key personalities involved in Wembley plc of 1990.
One is Jarvis Astaire, most famous for his activities in the boxing world,
where he had a long time partnership with Mickey Duff. Chairman of the
company is Brian Wolfson. Wolfson gave up his law studies at Liverpool
University to try and save the family engineering company. From the
ashes of that company came a small property firm. He built a quarry,
added haulage and building businesses, and even found himself renting
artificial flowers sprayed with essences of summer, spring, autumn or
winter. He was headhunted by Granada's Sidney Bernstein and became

managing director of Granada's TV rental arm. In 1986 he was appointed chairman of the British Institute of Management.

Business life at Wembley has always been interesting. The stadium was built in 300 working days in 1922-23 as the centrepiece of the 1924 British Empire Exhibition. It has been a private company ever since. From 1960 Wembley had been owned by British Electric Traction, a sprawling industrial concern, but by the mid-Eighties they were restructuring their business and declared they were looking for partners in Wembley. In July 1984 51 per cent of Wembley was bought by Arena Consortium which was chaired by Labour MP John Silkin. The money to finance the deal was raised through Standard Chartered, one of South Africa's big two banks, which has regular dealings with the Pretoria government.

In June 1985 Silkin was issued with a writ for fraudulent conspiracy over the sale of shares in another company, London Leisure and Arts Centre, a transaction which had given control of Wembley to the discredited businessman Abdul Shamji, who was later at the centre of the Johnson Matthey scandal. Because of opposition from other shareholders and directors he was never able to take complete control at Wembley. Shamji was recently jailed for perjury after lying in court about his personal wealth.

In July 1985 Peter de Savary announced he was interested in buying out Shamji for £5 million. But in October 1985 Brian Wolfson's engineering company AngloNordic announced plans to buy out LLAC for about £6 million, and promised a £500 million redevelopment of the complex.

It is Wolfson who has been behind the more recent aggressive marketing of Wembley. A Liverpool fan, he claims jokingly that he bought Wembley because he could never get Cup final tickets.

Wembley as a company has sought to acquire and expand. It now owns Pacer, a ticketing company in the US specialising in cinema systems. In May 1989 Wembley bought Meridian Holdings, a company which specialises in refitting sports arenas and leisure centres. In June 1989 it purchased Juliana Holdings, another property and leisure company which owned discotheques and catering companies. Wembley sold off part of the company for £10 million, but still owns several discotheques around the world.

Not all shareholders are happy at Wembley's performance. One of them, Ronnie Duis, feels that the company is too quick to spend money acquiring new companies and servicing debts rather than giving a good return to its shareholders. He has seen the value of the shares slip from 130p when he bought them to 87p as we went to press.

The FA appears to have an odd relationship with Wembley. Wembley receive 25 per cent of gate receipts for the FA Cup final and international matches. Wembley makes the money from the programme sales, catering, parking and advertising. They have a 21-year agreement which commenced in 1982 to use the ground for all internationals and the FA Cup final. In notes to the financial statements of 1986 it states that "under the terms of an agreement with the FA which commenced on June 25th 1982 repairs to the stadium costing £4,000,000 will be carried out. £3,500,000 will be incurred during the first five years of which £2,500,000 will be met by the Football Association." Though details of the contract are not available these notes seem to imply that Wembley gets to have a tenant who pays for repairs as well! Lucky them.

The main improvements to the stadium seem to be the building of executive boxes and the installation of seating. Seated or not many still complain about having to wade through other people's piss to get to the toilet, and at the price of food and programmes and the problems of entry. When huge-sounding sums are declared to have been spent the numbers have to be put into context. £188,000 sounds like a lot of money, but that is only what it costs to paint the outside of the stadium. It cost £96,000 to put up road signs directing traffic to the ground.

Plans for the future of Wembley Stadium include a museum of sport. David Griffiths, Wembley's general manager, described it as "a purpose-built Disneyland sport experience where customers start their ride between the twin towers and enjoy an interactive computerised experience".

But even as Wembley Stadium itself becomes less central to the group that bears its name, football becomes less significant as an activity in the stadium itself. Football now accounts for only about 15 per cent of the people who come through the gates. Wembley calculate that they make £1.5 million from football, but that the stadium costs £500,000 a month to run. The problem for Wembley plc is that the association with football is the key element in the legendary status of the stadium. However it is rumoured that Wembley wouldn't really be that bothered to lose the FA contract. They are thought to believe that two of the London clubs would die to play their home fixtures there.

Wembley plc has transformed itself from a quaint, old-fashioned, slightly run down company into a thrusting, acquisitive and profitable concern. The route it has taken makes an intriguing tale. Meanwhile the stadium that gives the company its name plays host to greyhounds and rock has-beens, football pushed aside as a visible but peripheral activity. Wembley. Venue of legends, or just a big hospitality tent? ○

The Final Straw

Harry Pearson was determined to see his team, Middlesbrough, in their first Wembley appearance, even if it was only the Zenith Data Systems Cup final.

WSC No 40, June 1990

MIDDLESBOREANS ARE PRONE TO SCHIZOPHRENIA. SANDWICHED BETWEEN THE voluble expansiveness of the Geordies and the dour tight-fistedness of the Tykes they are torn between two extremes: do they race to the bar and get the first round in, or hide in a corner and pretend they've lost their wallet? Somewhere along the line an uneasy compromise has been reached.

My father and I were talking after Middlesbrough's victory over Aston Villa had earned them a place in their first ever Wembley final. "Old........." Dad said, naming a famous Teesside garage owner, "always promised that if the Boro ever got to Wembley he'd buy all his staff grandstand tickets and put them up at the Savoy for the weekend."

"Why'd he do that?" I asked. "I don't know," my father replied, "but I bet he's bloody glad he's dead."

Aware of his fondness for the grand gesture, I should have been a little more cautious when replying to a relative stranger who called me up and said, "I've got a mate who can get tickets. D'you want some?"

Experience should have made me wary. Whenever there is a cup-tie there is always a 'mate'. The mate's uncle was at school with the manager or his sister-in-law works in the cobblers where the star striker gets his winkle-pickers re-sharpened. The mate is like the local carpet warehouse – he's convenient and cheap, but he doesn't deliver. As the days pass by in a whirl of anxious telephone calls, the mate's tenuous connections with the world of professional football are severed one by one. His uncle dies and his sister-in-law runs away with a Betterware salesman.

Gripped by despair you go to the pub and sit at the bar trying to unravel one of life's knottiest conundrums: when you were a regular and couldn't get tickets you assumed that the part-timers had snaffled them all. ("Where were they at Carlisle away in February '67?", you raged, forgetting in your anger that on the freezing Wednesday night in question you were not at Brunton Park yourself, but were cosily tucked up in bed, reading *Billy's Boots* by torchlight.) Yet now you are a part-timer the tickets remain equally elusive. Just who actually gets them is a question that will probably remain unanswered even when future, hyperintelligent beings, their ganglia flashing and pinging like pin-ball machines, have discovered how it was that Ray Wilkins got 84 caps for England.

Hours later, your perceptions heightened by a mind-expanding cocktail of black-and-tan and pickled eggs, you are granted a blinding insight: nobody gets tickets! The only people present are the players and club officials. The crowd scenes are all done with mirrors and a hidden film projector. It's just like *Scooby Doo*. "And I'd have gotten away with it too," snarls Graham Kelly, as the Sheriff and his deputies prepare to haul him downtown, "if it hadn't been for this meddlesome kid!"

And all the people who claim they've been to a Cup final? They're obviously suffering from the same kind of mass delusion that makes 15,000 Londoners believe they left the Blind Beggar pub just seconds before Ronnie Kray walked in and started blasting away with a Luger.

Two days later you're at a party. "I wish you'd said sooner. Gary down the print shop can get tickets for anything. He could've got you a ticket for the Last Supper could Gal. Cor blimey. Not 'arf. I'm seeing him tomorrow. I'll give you a bell Monday."

Monday dawns cold and bleak. "You know that Gary I was telling you about? You won't believe what's happened to him..."

"Don't tell me, let me guess. He's been eaten by a ten foot high pink penguin from the planet Pluto."

"Oh, you seen the *Sunday Sport*."

Three weeks to go. As the precious seconds tick away a cabal of desperate men hatch a dramatic plot. In the gloom beneath the North Stand, muffled voices can be heard. Every now and then a phrase permeates up through the darkness: "Supporters club... kidnap... false beard... disguised in the purple, silken robes of the Papal Nuncio..." The plan is so convoluted and improbable it makes *Mission: Impossible* seem like a trip to the off-licence for a four-pack of Strongarm.

Even the steel nerved (and haired) Jim Phelps would have baulked at this one: "Three tickets for the Cup final? Are you crazy? I quit! And I'm taking the man with a thousand faces, the blonde who creates a diversion, and the guy-whose-neck's-so-thick-it's-wider-than-his-head with me." Faced with a twin-pronged assault from idiocy and incompetence the plot collapses quicker than the Fisher Athletic defence.

Thus it was I found myself, just 16 days before my team's first ever Wembley appearance, without a ticket. It was at this point that my girlfriend made her suggestion. "Why don't you phone up the stadium," she said, "and book them with your credit card?" I looked at her and shook my head sadly. The poor, innocent child. What did she know of British football's history and rituals, of its favouritism and corruption, its nepotism and its I-know-a-blokiness? Then suddenly it hit me. I leapt from my chair and slapped my fist into the palm of my hand. "It's a wild and madcap scheme, Ginger," I cried, "but it might just work!" It didn't.○

Political Football

Rick Everitt described why Charlton fans formed a political party to argue the case for their club's return home to Greenwich from their exile at Selhurst Park.

WSC No 41, July 1990

YOU SHOULD HAVE SEEN THE LOOK ON THE ASSISTANT'S FACE IN THE CLUB shop when we asked him for 60 rosettes. He couldn't have been more surprised if the replica kit had come in before Christmas.

Not that he was the only one taken aback by the emergence of the Valley Party. It was more in desperation than anything else that we first threatened to take on Labour-controlled Greenwich Council in all 36 wards at the local elections. No-one, least of all ourselves, believed that we could emerge as a credible political force.

'Charlton Apathetic' was the club's unspoken nickname for a generation. But when, on January 31st, Greenwich finally threw out the club's ambitious plans for an all-seater stadium, they treated the supporters with such apparent contempt that dozens of angry fans demanded a call to arms.

Early Valley Party meetings soon expanded to such an extent that we were forced to seek a bigger hall. Richard Hunt, a director of an advertising agency and lifelong Charlton fan, pitched in with an almost free publicity campaign that eventually took in four different designs of poster on 25 giant hoardings across the borough. Even Channel 4 boss Michael Grade wrote a piece pledging support in the *Guardian.*

We had no coherent ideology, little political experience and no manifesto save for one single pledge – to get Charlton home. Slowly, the other parties realised that this was rather more than just a publicity stunt. In the safe Labour wards around the ground, canvassers were working overtime to persuade people not to vote Valley. Labour loudspeaker vans toured the borough announcing how much the council wanted the club back. An illegal leaflet even appeared, urging people not to vote for us.

But it was far too late. What the politicians had failed to understand is that the roots of football loyalty go just as deep as those of political parties. While probably as little as 30 per cent of Charlton's modern support comes from the borough of Greenwich, the older generation who made up the vast Valley crowds of the Forties and Fifties are still there. We also had by far the biggest army of volunteers of any party, more than 250 of them completing the last of three 85,000-plus leaflet drops to every home on the eve of poll.

Our only major hiccup came the previous Saturday, when Charlton's vice-chairman, Mike Norris, made the extraordinary announcement that hopes of a return to The Valley were fading. It was an own goal of Scottish proportions, lending weight to the council's whispering campaign that the directors were not quite what they seemed. Party workers were furious. Otherwise, the club, and particularly chairman Roger Alwen, had been 100 per cent behind us.

Even so, we awoke on election morning without the slightest idea of just how many we were going to get. The best estimate was about 8,000, more than enough to make our point.

Polling day remains a blur. Tannoy cars, mobile phones, a rented open-top double-decker bus, lifts, leaflets and last-minute pleas. Across the borough, Labour were worried; in Sherard, formerly their safest ward, they were frantic. An hour before the polls closed, I spent a farcical ten minutes trailing a Labour loudspeaker van around the estate contradicting their demand for people to come out and support council leader Quentin Marsh with our own appeal to vote for the Valley Party's Kevin Fox. Even a Labour teller in one of the ward's polling stations confided she had voted Valley.

By 10 pm, when the declarations started, we were ready for anything.

The first results were poor, 5.4 and 4 per cent. We consoled ourselves that at least they weren't derisory. Then came a message from Les Turner, the candidate in Hornfair Ward, Charlton. He was ahead in the boxes counted so far. We dreamed impossible dreams.

Les didn't win, but the Valley Party collected an astonishing 14 per cent of the vote there. Tangible backing from the very streets around the ground that the council said were up in arms against us. Those first two results, in the only Liberal seats, proved to be the worst of the evening. In Middle Park, Eltham, Paul Ellis and Chris Wilkins took 24 per cent. And in Sherard, Kevin Fox, though he eventually trailed Marsh by 350, polled a majestic 992.

Now we were ecstatic, but the best was yet to come. Shortly after three o'clock came the news that Simon Oelman, chair of the planning committee that had thrown out the club's plans, had been defeated by the SDP. Oelman's personal vote had collapsed. As a trophy, his head meant more to us than the FA Cup itself.

Just for good measure, the deposed councillor, leaving the count in tears, tried to assault a Valley Party photographer and was arrested by the police. Our man declined to press charges, but the atmosphere inside the town hall deteriorated sharply, with some Labour activists evidently keen to level the score.

Valley Party workers were variously accused of being extreme right-wingers, Tories and raving fascists, a charge which some of us were able to refute by displaying our Labour Party membership cards.

By dawn we had 14,838 votes and 10.9 per cent of those cast, a haul beyond our wildest dreams and the council's worst nightmare. In the solidly working-class parliamentary constituency of Woolwich we beat the Tories, while across the borough our candidates out-scored the Liberal Democrats by two to one. True, we had no seats, but if our opponents saw that as a defeat then it was measure of how credible we had become to them.

Surprisingly, the new planning chair now says that Greenwich have never been opposed to Charlton returning to The Valley at all.

The likelihood seems to be that in order to save the council's face, the club will offer to turn the pitch around, thus moving the troublesome commercial facilities further into the ground. Personally, I don't much like the idea, but then, as one candidate put it to me recently: "They can turn the pitch upside down as long as they play at The Valley." O

Taylor the Expected

News of Graham Taylor's appointment as England manager was received with cautious optimism. If only we'd known.

WSC No 41, July 1990 – Editorial

THE MOST SURPRISING ASPECT OF BOBBY ROBSON'S MOVE TO PSV EINDHOVEN IS the fact that, with all that money from the Philips corporation at their disposal, PSV should choose Wobbly Bobby to be their next coach. After all, he can hardly be said to have coped well with the day-to-day pressures imposed on an international football manager throughout his eight-year tenure in charge of England. During what will now come to be known as the 'Robson era', England's only performance of note in an international tournament came in the 1986 World Cup and that, as we know, was more by accident than design. Like Don Revie before him, Robson has stumbled through the job without ever really evolving a consistent strategy.

And now, it seems another adequately successful man will take Robson's place. Like Robson, Graham Taylor has never won the League title, but he has achieved good results with, by and large, moderate players. At times he has struggled – notably during Villa's first season back in the First Division. However, he took Villa from relegation candidates to second-best-in-the-League status in one season. This has been achieved without reliance on outstanding international stars, but with a good sense of team spirit binding together a team of veterans at the back (Mountfield, McGrath, Spink), and youth up front (Platt, Daley). If he could instil the same kind of team commitment in the national side, then England too might even become the second best.

But does Taylor have the temperament for the job? Undoubtedly he has better relations with the press and fans than Robson – at Watford he was largely responsible for the sense of community involvement which propelled the whole town into the limelight, not just those directly involved with the club. He generally answers questions from the press with disarming honesty – which will ensure he never goes into party politics. Some of those answers, however, have betrayed weaknesses which raise question marks about Taylor's suitability. His description of the Ian Ormondroyd purchase ("I just panicked") does not inspire confidence. Villa appeared to go into freefall towards the end of the 1988-89 season, and in the two championship campaigns of '88 and '90, Taylor was unable to sustain his team's challenge to the end.

Nonetheless, appointing a man who specialises in gallant near-misses to the post will at least mean England have a manager who matches the potential of the team as it currently stands. Another eight mediocre years would at least lower supporters' expectations to a more realistic level.

Is it logical to suppose that the best equipped individual for the job is necessarily one who has had experience of managing a First Division club? After all, Michel Platini hasn't got a coaching badge and had no experience whatsoever of club management prior to taking charge of the French team. Yet he seems to have inspired a revival in their fortunes and some argue that he might have taken them to Italy had he been appointed a few months earlier. It is fair to assume that Platini picked up considerable knowledge of the international game from having played at the top level for a decade. The same applies to Franz Beckenbauer. On the continent, many players are absorbed into the national coaching infrastructure upon their retirement and are given an opportunity to impart knowledge collected over the duration of a career.

In contrast, all we seem to possess is a mish-mash of half-baked ideas (of which the School of Excellence is the best example) patched together by the old-boy network. There are plenty of former England international players whose accumulated experience has never been put to practical use. Instead, the football authorities here seem intent on grasping the easiest available option, ie the appointment of a workmanlike manager such as Graham Taylor. Taylor's promotion to the job would indicate that the football establishment absolutely refuses to accept that there is anything wrong with the English game.

Robson made an unimpressive start back in 1982, and didn't appear to learn much in the years that followed. If England under Taylor failed to qualify for the next European Championship finals, the new boss would stay on – because an early dismissal would be tantamount to recognising that his employers had failed too. And we can't have that can we? ○

An Uneasy Alliance

Jonathan Bousfield watched a Yugoslav league match whose violence hinted at the political chaos to come.

WSC No 41, July 1990

AS YUGOSLAVIA'S CONSTITUENT NATIONALITIES DRIFT TOWARDS DIVORCE, THE country's football league has become the latest federal structure to show signs of imminent collapse. On the night of May 13th TV viewers across Europe had their increasingly regular diet of pan-European hooligan exotica augmented by disturbingly violent images from Zagreb, where police fought a desperate battle to keep apart supporters of the local team Dynamo, and the visiting fans of Red Star Belgrade.

This end of season clash between the major clubs of Yugoslavia's biggest and most volatile republics, Croatia and Serbia, put the finishing touches to a season of unprecedented ugliness. The sheer level of violence experienced over the last 12 months is something to which Yugoslavs are unaccustomed; far from being generated within the sport, it accurately mirrors the rapid disintegration of Yugoslav society itself.

The moral standing of Yugoslav football has been in a state of bankruptcy for years, blighted by the kind of match-fixing, corruption and political interference common to the one party states of eastern Europe. Provincial politicians who saw success on the soccer pitch as a handy barometer of regional prestige were adept at manipulating local networks of power and influence in order to achieve it.

For many in the sport, nobbling the referee has become the most important part of the game. It has always been customary (and fairly legal) for clubs to make sure that visiting referees and linesmen are more than well looked after on their arrival at the ground. Yugoslav hospitality being what it is, this often extends into the hazy area of present-giving, accompanied by the unspoken but fully understood expectation that the referee will perform various 'services' in return.

With gifts ranging from hard-to-come-by consumer goods to free holidays and even (in the case of key fixtures, it is rumoured), blank cheques, clubs and their backers compete in making increasingly outrageous offers just to keep up with each other. This puts the referees in an impossible situation: by allowing yourself to be bought, you at least secure the gratitude of the home club; by being honest, on the other hand, you end up being hounded by everyone. Some referees are made so nervous by all this that they simply end up making bad decisions, tarnishing their profession yet further. With Yugoslavia's regionally decentralized media eagerly joining in any criticisms of officials who appear to have discriminated against 'their' team, any objective discussion of refereeing standards becomes completely impossible.

Match-fixing, although common knowledge, escaped investigation until it became so blatant that it could be avoided no longer. Both the 1986 and 1988 seasons ended in uproar when a whole series of somnambulant performances on the pitch made it clear to everyone that many of the final weekend's results had been agreed upon in advance by the participants. Debates about punitive sanctions dragged on for months. Whenever disciplinary action was attempted, delegates on Yugoslav football's ruling body remained true to their regional masters and merely vetoed any decision which might have tarnished the reputation of their local team. This unedifying spectacle was a particular cause of concern to UEFA, who were never quite sure whether Yugoslavia's representatives in the various European competitions had qualified for them legitimately or not.

On the terraces, football has always been followed with an almost Mediterranean intensity and passion. Matches between the big four clubs, Dinamo Zagreb, Hajduk Spilt (both from Croatia), Red Star Belgrade and Partizan Belgrade (both Serbian) have always attracted an extraordinary degree of rivalry – ethnic differences providing Serbs and Croats with an endless supply of insulting songs and taunts. Old enmities didn't always spring from nationalism, however.

Bitter rivalry goes back to the immediate post-War years, when the newly-formed Partizan was considered to be the team of the new regime's security police (hence the nickname of *grobari* or 'gravediggers'). Their political opponents flocked to watch Red Star (despite the ideological content of the name), who increasingly became associated with the kind of renascent Serbian nationalism that the regime had long tried to suppress. Self-styled hooligans modelled themselves with endearing naivety on their Western counterparts; hard core Red Star supporters called themselves 'Ultras' in imitation of those in Spain and Italy, while Dinamo Zagreb fans opted for the moniker of 'Bad Blue Boys' as a mark of respect for the enormous (if highly dubious) reputation enjoyed by Chelsea fans all over the continent. Before 1989, outbursts of aggro were strictly on a toy town level. The only major unpleasantness was at a UEFA Cup fixture between Hajduk Split and Marseille in November 1987, when home fans earned their team a three-year ban from European competition after throwing tear gas canisters into the crowd.

The sudden and dramatic increase in football-related violence that ensued came about as a direct result of Yugoslavia's worsening political situation, as the Communist leaders of the country's republics began to resort to chauvinist demagoguery in an attempt to maintain their hold on power. With a newly vociferous Serbian leadership increasingly at loggerheads with their Slovenian and Croatian counterparts, it was only a matter of time before football fans began to respond to the verbal hooliganism of their elders and betters.

The start of the 1989-90 season coincided with attempts by boisterously chauvinist politicians in Serbia to destabilise the political leadership of Croatia, raising a series of complaints about the treatment of the Serbian minority living within Croatia's borders. In an atmosphere of increasing tension, football stadia became a prime venue for mass displays of national sentiment. When Red Star visited Hajduk Split in September, Serbian fans made their way to the coastal resort to demonstrate their support for much more than just a football team. Bloody confrontations on the sea-front and a burnt-out railway carriage were the results.

Things hotted up again in the spring, with multi-party elections in the offing in Croatia, vote-seeking politicians were regaling the public with ever-descending levels of nationalistic rhetoric. On March 18th Dinamo Zagreb played away at Novi Sad, a mixed town only recently brought back under the control of the Serbian authorities. Large contingents of Serbs travelled up from Belgrade, parading up and down the pitch before kick-off in an intimidating show of strength. When some foolhardy individuals from the visiting end ventured forth in response, they were punished mercilessly by riot police. This timely intervention was praised fulsomely in the Belgrade press the following morning, while Zagreb newspapers offered an altogether different story of police brutality and victimisation.

Doubtless this sensitivity about the role of the police contributed greatly to the fiasco of May 13th (a date which, in a bizarre touch of irony, is marked by national policemen's day in Yugoslavia). Unwilling to be portrayed as partisan, riot control units played a waiting game as columns of Serb supporters moved through the Croat capital, breaking windows, attacking cars, and destroying anything bearing the portrait of newly-elected Croatian nationalist leader Franjo Tudjman. On entering the stadium fans began ripping up advertising hoardings and trashing seats, only to be met by a hail of stones thrown by home supporters in a neighbouring stand. Only now did the police intervene, turning the stadium into a confused multiplicity of localised battlegrounds as they were set upon by yet more home supporters eager to defend 'their' boys. The two teams had at this stage just emerged on the pitch ready to start the match. Red Star quickly retreated back down the tunnel, to be evacuated subsequently by military helicopter. Some Dinamo players, however, stayed where they were, apparently trying to calm things down; a befuddled and ill-fated attempt which culminated in the club captain and international star, Zvonimir Boban, repeatedly drop-kicking a policeman in the stomach.

Police authorities in Zagreb tried to defuse a potential political row by hastily arranging an enquiry which put the blame fairly and squarely on their own supporters. The fans themselves, however, are unlikely to forgive and forget that easily, and with nationalist passions still rising, the continuance of football next season looks increasingly in doubt. For the record, Red Star Belgrade finished the season as champions with Dinamo Zagreb nominally in second place; but the latter must await a potential points deduction and a possible European ban. ○

Revival of the Fittest

Every magazine in the world had sent reporters to the World Cup in Italy. WSC correspondent Phil Tanner, however, had to make do with an all-expenses paid trip to... Wales

WSC No 42, August 1990

"THERE WERE BUT FEW SPECTATORS... IN THIS GAME, AS IN CRICKET, THE inhabitants of Newport display but very little interest and are generally conspicuous by their absence."

That was in 1868, when the local rag reported a game of something called 'football' against a team from Abergavenny. Times change. Twenty two years on, Newport supporters have made up anything between 80 and 99 per cent of the gate at away matches, and the home average is probably more than that of our six closest rivals taken together. The snag, of course, as anyone knows who can read or enjoys *Saint & Greavsie* – not the same people, you mutter – is that home games have been played 75 miles from Newport at Moreton-in-the-Marsh.

Just imagine it in the context of football in your town – dropping straight from the Third to the Conference, a bogus take-over, and a collapse in a flurry of bouncing cheques. A group of enthusiasts set up a new club, but are betrayed when the council withdraws an offer of a ground at the last minute. Help is at hand, but the Good Fairy insists upon a two-hour drive to home games.

Nine months on, those of who were incredulous at the venture are wolfing humble pie. Newport AFC, with no big money behind it and rarely playing less than 50 miles from its home town, has run off with an established feeder league, awaits a cup final and – perhaps more importantly – has organised itself brilliantly behind the scenes. The club logo, designed in a competition, captures a local landmark (Reading FC take note). The board has even laid out a hard-earned £8,000 to buy County's title from the liquidators and prevent that club's last regime, more candidates for *That's Life* than *The Match*, getting their grubby hands back on it. The club's rapport with its fans is second to none, and I mean none, because essentially the fans are the club. My brother rides a motorbike from Plymouth to watch them.

For supporters who not long ago saw the County squander a three-goal lead at the Baseball Ground, and who had entertained Steve Bull and Co less than 18 months earlier, the Federated Homes League was a mystery. Where's Pegasus? How much is a day return to Supermarine? Might we run into Rupert Bear in Shortwood? But at least we had a team to follow, and you could sense something big was stirring when nearly 600 watched the first match. This in a league where gates go as low as a dozen and visiting teams always take more players than supporters. We were reassured to find the great John Relish in charge and there were some familiar names on the staff – lads thrown in too young as the County disintegrated, one or two older lags fondly remembered from better days. Among these was Brian Preece, The Man Who Scored the Last League Goal At Workington, thicker in the waist than in 1977, possibly a bit shorter, but even more crafty.

So what's attracted getting on for 400 people on a 150 mile round trip to home games? What's life been like down in the Federated Homes

League? First you have to find your fixture. The national dailies virtually ignore it, the names of two of the 18 Premier clubs give no clue to their whereabouts and three have only second call on their home grounds. Add a rule dating from the time of the Black Death which gives the many county cups precedence and you have numerous last-minute switches and a travelling fan's nightmare. The table runs like one of those fairground horse racing games. A club can build up a huge lead and then lose it as it stops dead and some team back in the pack wins six games-in-hand in succession.

The big surprise for Cardiff City supporters in five years' time will be that, though some are very pretty, the grounds are about as basic as you can get in a league taking gate money. The only two you could call stadia are shared with bigger clubs – Sharpness at Stroud's inappropriately named 'The Lawn' and Pegasus at Edgar Street, Hereford. It's hard to imagine any others being passed for promotion, though most clubs would collectively crap themselves at the thought. There is hardly any cover, few lights, and the only decent seats in a non-shared ground are on the blasted heath of Ruislip, where the wind has ripped off the stand roof. The hosts did likewise to visitors, charging £2 admission.

It's best to move the decimal point where stated capacities are concerned – you might get 200 premature babies under cover at Swindon Athletic but not 200 Newport supporters; you can fit exactly 7.5 spectators into Supermarine's stand.

We spent part of the season chasing Bicester Town, who have taken 100 years to get where they are but whose pitch is still fenced on two sides only and just roped on the others. With rugby and hockey matches just over the touchline, three whistles competed for the players' attention. My particular favourite was Kintbury, where the surface was like the Somme but with deeper trenches, and the atmosphere that of a village fete/bonfire party. They had to wipe the barbecue sauce off the ball before returning it to play from one end, and massed ranks of badgers gathered behind the hedge as the game finished in pitch darkness.

All the clubs publish programmes but you can count the tannoys on the nails of one finger. Inside you'll find some choice names – Clint Gobey, Jason Delicata. Imagine booking a player who says his name is Kent Drackett. You'd think he was really Spiderman, or that he'd got it from a Black and Decker catalogue. Mind you, two of our best players are postmen called Pratt and Parselle.

Apart from Jarvis and Lilygreen, the Tynan and Aldridge of the

Cotswolds, few players can be relied upon not to panic in front of an open goal. Surprisingly few have League experience, which may account for a healthy commitment to attacking play. The obligatory Fat Defender rules out the offside trap for most teams. The standard of goalkeeping is very high, the best being one Johan Gunst, a Dutch navy chef (seriously) playing for the dirty, foul-mouthed no-hopers, Ruislip Park. Ruislip wouldn't beat the Doncaster Belles, but Johan single-handedly kept us to eight goals from 15 chances one week and two from ten the next. The Kintbury midfielder gesticulating wildly at his colleagues proved to be wearing a hearing aid.

Like my daughter, when the referees are good they are very, very good and when they are bad they are horrid. We heard one free kick explained with the words 'he kicked him when he was nowhere near the ball' but the pencil stayed in the sock. Most refs seem to distrust their linesmen utterly, and with good reason. Many of these are very easily intimidated, right up to letting players yell "fuck off" to their faces and taking no action. One wore sunglasses. Another, plainly unnerved by paying spectators, ignored the play to conduct a running argument with Newport supporters at Bicester, culminating in "if you want the flag, you can have it". And if Sue Townsend wants to track down Adrian Mole for permission to write another book about him, he appears to be running the line in the Federated Homes League.

You might think from all this sneering that we can't wait to get out of this league. Yes and no. The drive to village grounds is often delightful. You can park and you don't get searched by some would-be Burnside on the way in. The atmosphere in the club-houses is terrific. When you can find an opposition supporter you can have a friendly conversation, and his grandsons won't beat you up on the way home. Despite the pitches you can see some excellent football, though I wouldn't travel far for Headington against Bishop's Cleeve on a wet day. You just have to make the mental adjustment and accept that most clubs are social clubs with football teams attached, rather than vice versa. You end up feeling a bit sorry for teams which put up competent, enterprising performances in the complete absence of vocal support.

It's been a season to warm the cockles of your heart and what really counts is that the League and Moreton Town took Newport AFC in when the council and the Welsh FA turned their backs. They deserve the record attendances, cup final atmosphere wherever we play and massive bar receipts. The portents are right for a rise up the pyramid once the ground is sorted out. At the time of writing the club is seeking a short lease on Somerton Park – which has long looked as likely to become a Beazer Homes ground by being built on as by hosting football again – but has an alternative share organised at Gloucester City.

The triumphant first season ended on a note of farce when the cup final was drawn and Abingdon crapped out of the replay at Moreton despite it having been agreed weeks before and printed in the programme. The management committee, panicking like the Ambridge over-sixties and desperate to keep the cup in Oxfordshire at all costs, re-arranged the replay for mid-June. Many AFC fans – well, four of us at least – think they should be told to stick the trophy. Newport are back! Which junction for Bilston? ○

Beneath the Surf Ace

During his playing days, Craig Johnston was probably the best known footballer to have come from Australia, but he didn't impress everyone in his homeland, as Ian Sherwood explained.

WSC No 42, August 1990

HE LOOKS LIKE ANY OTHER AGING YOUNG MAN WHO GROWS HIS HAIR LONG AT the sides as apparent compensation for a receding hairline, but Craig Johnston has a mission. He was recently seen on the panel for the live coverage of the FA Cup final, which showed that a career in football is not necessarily good training for making articulate comment about the game. He was also on a TV comedy show in a red wig, false breasts and a polka dot dress, which showed that he could trap a ball just as well dressed like a woman as dressed like a Liverpool player. It may well be a slight exaggeration to say that Johnston is engaged in an orgy of self-promotion and self-advancement.

Back in Australia after his ungracious parting from Liverpool he was soon a sports anchor man on Channel 9 television. One of his first assignments was the Adelaide Grand Prix. He was apparently under the impression that he could be a photographer by buying a very expensive camera and the television piece was of him taking photographs at the race. He would have got just as good results with a box brownie.

Craig thinks that there is nothing that Craig can not do. Anxious to be noticed as a home boy hero he was shown in the press pursuing his "first love" of surfing. You cannot be much more Australian than that. As a youth he spent "every spare moment" playing football. To show he was returning home to Newcastle, he joined the local Steel City Malibu Club and promptly went off to live in the wealthy Sydney suburb of Point Piper, 100-plus kilometres down the road. Newcastle is not an attractive or fashionable city. He showed, however ,that he had not lost his command of 'waxhead' (surfie) slang. "When I was a grommet off Nobby's Beach... where all the grommets hang out, every grommet had a chick. Through all those grey days in England I never forgot those surfing days. They were magic."

The grommet can also be seen in advertisements encouraging the purchase of health insurance and is a keen believer in self motivation. His "basic philosophy is that the talented come second and it is those with some ability who work harder than anyone else who come out on top." Insurance companies have hired him to motivate their staff as have BMW Australia and the Bond Corporation.

Johnston has many ideas for succeeding in business by trying really hard but "I can't tell anyone exactly what my ideas are because somebody will steal them. But I know they are absolute winners." Arrogance and paranoia motivate Johnston. At Liverpool "I lived in constant fear of rejection. My paranoia was such that I felt I had to put in a Pelé-like performance just to stay in the side... (in business) I feel so much hostility. I have achieved already and I'm walking into someone else's territory and they want to see me fall on my face. They smile to my face and stab me in the back. But they are not fooling this kid. I left school when I was 14 and went to England when I was 15. Nobody is going to put me down."

In all this it may perhaps be easy to forget that although a grommet and business motivator, he was also a footballer. Fear not, for he is planning a comeback in that sphere too. Recently he submitted a 40-page programme to the Australian Soccer Federation. He has declined offers to become involved in Australian football on a lower level but now feels ready to "put something back into the youth of this country and why not start with the game which has given me so much?"

Why not indeed. The question may be asked: if he wanted to put something back into Australian football why did he not wish to play for his country? In Australia, as Johnston knows well, you can never go far wrong by quoting patriotism and singing to the flag. It is received as well by the public here as in America. So patriotic was Johnston that he touted himself around the Home Countries' international sides rather than play for the land which gave him Nobby's Beach and a surfboard to call his own.

The main features of his scheme, which he wants to be funded by private enterprise, are threefold. Firstly there would be a thirty minute coaching video which "extols the virtues of a healthy lifestyle and good diet for a successful career". Produced by Johnston this will be available to schools at "budget prices". Secondly, a soccer education kit to be distributed to schools and thirdly an annual overseas tour by a national under-15 team funded by sponsorship whose coach is to be, yes, the shy and retiring Mr Johnston himself.

With typical modesty he is sensitive to even a veiled hint that he is not a qualified coach. "As far as I'm concerned I'm the best coach in the world because I coached a 14-year-old from Lake Macquarie to play for Liverpool, not because he had natural ability but because he worked harder and smarter than everybody else."

It is difficult to escape the conclusion that these proposals, like everything else he does, are for no other purpose than furthering the career of the man with an ego the size of Bobby Robson's persecution complex and lower lip combined. It is difficult to tell where his ambitions lie if they are inside football. Whatever happens it will not be done quietly or far from a mirror. There will always be someone who loves Craig Johnston. ○

Back to the Future

English teams had been readmitted to the European club competitions but not everyone was happy about it.

WSC No 43, September 1990 – Editorial

UEFA's decision to re-admit English clubs to European competition certainly came as a surprise to anyone who had read a newspaper or watched a TV news programme during the month of the World Cup.

The media appeared to be intent on dutifully reporting every incident of hooliganism in terms of the detrimental effects it was likely to have on the case for re-admitting English clubs. It reached the point when we expected to be gravely informed that a bit of pushing and shoving between commuters piling onto a rush hour train was also likely to have a negative influence on UEFA's judgement.

The fact that Manchester United and Aston Villa will now be competing in Europe this season can probably be attributed both to UEFA's basic keenness to bring the five-year exclusion to an end and to the effect that England's progress during the tournament had on the British government's attitude.

Throughout the duration of the ban, UEFA had stressed that meaningful discussion about the return of English clubs would have to be prefaced by their receiving "certain assurances" from the British government.

In effect, they wanted to be told that anyone with a record of causing trouble at football matches would be prevented from travelling to the continent. UEFA could then have disclaimed responsibility for any violent incidents that might have occurred and instead transfer all blame onto the UK authorities for failing to carry out their promises. Given that, for a variety of reasons, the government was unlikely to strain itself to help the cause of English football, it seemed that Football League teams would never be re-admitted while conditions were imposed on their return.

Obviously, England's exploits during the tournament provided a succession of positive news images which were broadcast around Europe and, just as importantly, at home. It appeared that everyone in England, including the usual lighthouse keepers, night-watchmen and hermits unearthed by news reporters on such occasions, watched the semi-final against West Germany. Politicians of all parties whisked off messages of goodwill to the team, in some cases evoked the "Spirit of Dunkirk/Battle of Britain/Falklands," and afterwards spoke of an "honourable defeat" which had "restored national pride". After all that, no rational politico (let's not even think about David Evans) will dare revive calls for action to stamp out the lawlessness and thuggery which we have often been told stalk the land every Saturday during the football season. Not for a month or two anyhow. For the time being at least English football is a cause considered to be worthy of support.

Prior to the start of the World Cup, UEFA president Lennart Johansson made encouraging noises about re-admission. The implication seemed to be that a blind eye would be turned to any minor skirmishes that occurred. UEFA could scarcely fail to be aware that incidents of hooliganism seem to be on the rise in other countries. Punishments for crowd misbehaviour had been imposed on individual clubs (Ajax, AEK Athens,

Hajduk Split) but no other blanket ban had been introduced comparable to that applied to the English League. It now seems reasonable to suppose that the European authorities decided beforehand that the behaviour of England fans would have to be substantially worse than that of their German, Dutch and Italian counterparts in order to be able to justify maintaining the ban.

In the event, as we all know, there were a few incidents which ended in multiple arrests, and one infamous mass deportation. There were also a couple of deaths believed to have been brought on by gang-fights. However, the scenes of mass carnage anticipated with barely-concealed glee by sections of our national press (and, no doubt, by the government) did not materialise.

The Italian police seem to have received a lot of credit for this, indeed their heavy-handed methods have been unstintingly praised by both UEFA and the British government. The prevailing view suggests that equally forceful methods of deterrence will have to be adopted by other police forces around Europe whenever English fans turn up to watch their team. But what possible good can come from the forces of order in every town on the continent where English clubs are to play being psyched up for a pitched battle before the fans have even arrived? It is also surely a fact that the intimidating atmosphere prevalent on Sardinia over the summer – England fans kept locked in for a long time after games and then being escorted away by armed police – only helped to increase the likelihood of trouble flaring up.

In this context, the declarations by the chairmen of Manchester United and Aston Villa, that they don't want their supporters to travel to away matches on the continent, are just plain stupid. The implication is that anyone who defies their club's request is utterly irresponsible and deserves whatever treatment is meted out to them. Surely the best way to prevent violence occurring is for the clubs to endorse trips made by large numbers of responsible fans? Their large numerical superiority over the hard-core fringe would help to defuse tension and reduce the prospect of a direct confrontation with local police. If English clubs are to compete in Europe on a regular basis, they must learn to trust their own supporters. If they can't, how the hell can they expect the rest of Europe to? ○

Better Late Than Never

Not everyone who watched England's 1990 World Cup matches will have understood what they were seeing. Luckily, WSC's resident ideologist, Tim Megone, was on hand to explain all.

WSC No 43, September 1990

ONE OF THE GREAT BONUSES OF THE WORLD CUP IS THAT LARGE NUMBERS OF the population who profess to despise our great and glorious game wake up every four years to realise that watching football is their sole mission in life. Those of us who had to suffer their ignorant sneers could feel entitled to an overdose of self-satisfaction.

The less attractive side of the coin is that this new breed of fan doesn't understand what the game is supposed to be about. These people don't stand in the pissing rain or get frost-bitten toes watching uncoordinated full backs slicing the ball into the stand or attempting to understand referees' penalty decisions. They don't have to tolerate their side getting knocked out of every cup competition at the first hurdle year in, year out. This is because they are not real supporters: they are fickle, fairweather fans, who sit in their armchairs and demand to be entertained. Worst of all, they choose to inflict upon the rest of us their views on the World Cup.

Nowhere did this become more apparent than in their comments on England's progress in the tournament. The first game against Ireland was the prize example. Some of us expected a gruelling battle of honest sweat and endeavour, a tactical war of attrition with an element of endearing incompetence chucked in, and England somehow chiselling a result from the proceedings. Which was more or less what we got. The response was as predictable as it was depressing: the treacherous turncoats wittered on about England being the worst side in the competition, and incapable of playing football, while the slimy purists in the press trotted out the age-old bollocks about English football living in the Dark Ages.

Bobby Robson, during one of his more coherent spells, had warned against "fluffy hearts" and these may have contributed to the occasional hiccup in England's opening performance. But anyone who expected to see players nonchalantly knocking the ball around and making triangles deserved to be disappointed.

The armchair hangers-on would have been happy to harp on about

Holland as the saviours of football, but events denied them. Only bad finishing and bad luck, notably Van Breukelen's unsuccessful attempt to get a foot to Stuart Pearce's goalbound indirect free-kick, prevented a handsome England victory.

This would have been virtually enough to secure qualification in itself, making the game against Egypt irrelevant. Instead a win was needed, the pressure was on and the whinging critics were ready to pounce. Anything less than a stylish 10-0 triumph would have had them wittering again.

England's response was a suitably scrappy 1-0 win. This was ideal: at such an early stage in the tournament, it would have been foolish to waste more goals than necessary. The lily-livered traitors refused to listen to reason as they stormed back out of the woodwork. England had no place alongside the might of West Germany, Italy – who had performed so convincingly at home to the footballing titans of the US – or even the free-scoring Irish.

In the next round, our wickedly powerful Belgian opponents ran the midfield for long periods, and the fairweather fraternity reckoned they were unlucky when the post appeared to deny them twice. They were wrong: on the first occasion, Shilton had the situation well in hand as Ceulemans' shot, probably assisted by a freak breeze, harmlessly rapped the outside of the upright. In the second instance, Scifo might have been a trifle miffed to see his evil, swerving, long-range effort come back off the inside of the post, but unlucky he wasn't. A crafty deflection by the referee played a major part in the move that led to Scifo's chance.

This was only one of a number of examples of the conspiring freemasonry of officials attempting to foil England at every turn. Key penalty decisions went against us in the matches against the Republic of Ireland and West Germany, when Chris Waddle was brought down in the box on both occasions. But the worst of all was the disallowing of John Barnes' clinically taken winning goal in the first half against Belgium. Though eventually it was Platt's blistering volley in extra-time that saw England through and denied us the dubious pleasure of watching Waddle hoof his penalty into the stratosphere two game before he did, the game should never have gone beyond 90 minutes.

Amid the celebrations, the dissenters continued to mutter that our EEC partners had been robbed. Cameroon presented them with an even greater cause for complaint. Despite their achievements in defeating Romania and Columbia, the African challengers were still being written off. The sight of England wobbling over the precipice against impertinent underdogs would have the detractors in raptures. Then the World Cup would be left to the technically gifted nations – like Argentina.

England teased the watching public by allowing themselves to be overrun by the Indomitable Lions, before taking control (relatively speaking) in extra-time and staggering majestically through. The Fifth Columnists were foaming at the mouth by now: the better side had lost and England would be well stuffed in the semi-final.

Clearly, they had forgotten, or more likely never been taught, the essence of cup-tie football. Against Cameroon and Belgium, England had showed character (in contrast to the European Championships capitulation) and snatched victory in the face of adversity, sweating and bleeding through extra-time. A series of glossy performances of the kind expected from Brazil in every World Cup could not be half as satisfying.

The semi-finals arrived with the entertainment junkies looking forward to a West Germany v Italy final. Argentina predictably buggered up proceedings by going through deservedly 1-0 against Italy (Schillaci's goal was offside and the penalty competition therefore irrelevant). So it was left to England to complete the process. While not quite achieving this end, they effectively silenced the moaners with an heroic performance. Unfortunately the penalty farce that has marred previous World Cup finals went into overdrive with both semis being decided by the 12-yard travesty that has as much to do with football as the game of bagatelle. But amid the grief, there were consolations to be had. The malevolent meddlers were finally subdued: ignorance had been stifled.

Football needs friends. Casual fans should be encouraged, but they must be educated. I would suggest the lower reaches of the Vauxhall Conference and the early rounds of the FA Cup as starting points. There they would learn the finer points of tedium, toil and tactical unpredictability. They would also learn about cup fighting spirit and determination. A lot of them wouldn't want to know, in which case they should be lined up against a wall and shot. ○

Joe Public

Andy Lyons paid tribute on the death of former Man City and
England manager Joe Mercer.

WSC No 44, October 1990

"I NEVER WANTED THIS BLOODY JOB IN THE FIRST PLACE." THAT WAS JOE
Mercer's succinct opening remark at his first team meeting as England's
caretaker manager in 1974. He must have been delighted by the opportunity to be involved with the international side, albeit only on a
temporary basis, but to have made a public display of the fact would have
been contrary to his unassuming, cheery persona.

Mercer was a natural optimist, incapable of the introspective
gloominess which seems to afflict many football managers, particularly
in late middle age. He was a purist, rather than a puritan, undoubtedly
more interesting than Stan Cullis, perhaps not as intriguing as Alec
Stock. Like the latter, he seemed to represent all that is decent, invigo-
rating and, in the right sense, wholesome in English football.

His image as a manager rests on that comparatively short period in
charge at Manchester City. As he had been a famously successful player
too, one might be led into imagining that his entire working life amounted
to an effortless procession of triumphs. This is not the case though. Prior
to his arrival at Maine Road, Mercer experienced mixed managerial
fortunes with both Aston Villa and Sheffield United, presiding over
relegations from the First Division in both cases. It was after Villa took the
plunge in 1961 that he received the famous telegram from a Sheffield
United fan which read "Congratulations Mercer, you've done it again."

At Villa Park at least, he is acknowledged to have inherited a sinking
ship. At the time of his dismissal the club were bringing through a clutch
of bright young players, most of whom, with the exception of the doughty
Charlie Aitken, subsequently failed to fulfil their teenage promise.

He was not a great coach. The evidence provided by his honest but
bland autobiography *The Great Ones*, written before he took charge at
City, suggests that he was unable to effectively transmit precise tactical
ideas to his players. He didn't have any technical qualifications before
becoming a manager and could hardly be said to have moved seamlessly
from playing career to manager's office. He was in his grocer's shop,

boning bacon, when the summons came from Sheffield United.

Pictures of Mercer as a player offer proof of the contention that people aged twice as quickly in pre-war times as they do now. He never appears to have been less than 53 years old. He was born into a footballing family in Ellesmere Port. His father had played for Tranmere alongside Birkenhead's most famous citizen since Lady Hamilton, the colossal Billy (never 'Dixie') Dean. Mercer junior was subsequently Dean's teenage sidekick at Goodison Park (he ran errands, collected his mentor's mail and borrowed his golf clubs). He became Everton captain and, therefore, team tactician in the days when the club secretary was nominally in charge of affairs. In the 1938-39 season they ran off with the League title, Tommy Lawton scoring the goals with Mercer offering bandy-legged promptings from his customary wing half position.

The successful Arsenal teams of the immediate post-war years were marshalled in the art of the counter attack by their rather elderly captain, written off as an old crock after the war by Everton, who rued their mistake for years afterwards as they slid into Division Two.

Mercer's early City sides were a bit on the packed meat side – combative, cautious, certainly not inclined to free-form expression. Sturdy George Heslop was the totem figure, a world removed from his successor, the ample Frannie Lee. They snarled their way to promotion and were then magically transformed, partly by the arrival of the gangsterish Malcolm Allison. The era when Allison was a successful practitioner of his craft now seems even further off than Joe Mercer's playing days. Allison's career seems to have paralleled those of a few pop musicians, Ray Davies springs to mind, whose arrival was marked by a stunning burst of creativity but who then lost the plot completely, dabbing about here and there in an embarrassing fashion but, oddly, always able to find someone prepared to pay them large amounts of money.

The City team which won the championship in 1968 is still regarded as a benchmark, one of the most entertaining sides of the post-War era. Their all-out attacking style took opponents by surprise, but they were rumbled all too quickly. The team were prone to error in defence which hadn't mattered too much when Lee, Bell, Summerbee et al were in full flow, but when smothered and deprived of possession, the rearguard was liable to be overrun. No matter. Manchester was one of European football's hottest spots in 1968 – in the eyes of the press, George Best was busily supplanting his namesake Pete as the 'fifth Beatle'. Yet City made do with Tony Coleman, who had a face like an ashtray, topped by a dense, dirty blond fringe. Romantics can find reassurance in the fact that under Uncle Joe's guidance, Coleman, signed from Doncaster and destined for Rochdale, was, briefly, a star.

Allison rather charmlessly manoeuvred himself into the managerial seat shortly afterwards, but he was less than a decade older than most of the players, wore the same clothes and, unlike Mercer, was crucially unable to take a detached view of their faults and strengths. A clever bit of business by Jimmy Hill led to Mercer's appointment as general manager at Coventry where he made a mark by unloading the lumpen Jeff Blockley onto Arsenal, using the cash to buy Colin Stein and, more importantly, Tommy Hutchison.

It was one of his last moves in the transfer market – but, of course, he wasn't entirely finished with football, as his Indian summer with the England team testified. He championed several causes, some (Frank Worthington, David Nish) perhaps more worthy than others (Alec Lindsay), but at least he always followed his own judgement. Partnership with Jimmy Hill was renewed through a stint on the BBC's 1974 World Cup panel, where he revealed a considerable, though by no means unique, talent for mispronouncing 'Cruyff'.

He had been in retirement for several years, making the occasional TV appearance, usually in sad circumstances when an old colleague died (he was sitting next to Dean when the latter had a fatal heart attack at Goodison Park).

Mercer's appeal was neatly summed up in a Granada TV programme about football managers broadcast a dozen or so years ago. Crusty old curmudgeons like Shankly and Busby were asked to recall favourites among the players they had worked with. When it came to Joe's turn, he reeled off a list of names, extolled the virtues of City's Holy Trinity, Bell, Lee and Summerbee, then, voice quivering as he reached a crescendo of excitement, he triumphantly declaimed "and oooh... Glyn Pardoe!!" That roly-poly Glyn Pardoe should have sprung to mind at that moment speaks volumes about his former manager. Uncle Joe Mercer, a gent and a product of a bygone age. ○

Zion Filings

Mark Rivlin, our man in Israel, had news of odd goings-on in Jerusalem involving one of Britain's biggest publishers.

WSC No 44, October 1990

THERE'S A CAR STICKER IN ISRAEL WHICH READS, "MAXWELL, PLEASE BUY ME." In pure Israeli style, the proud bearers of the message can't handle being left out of the commercial circus Cap'n Bob is administering here. At the beginning of the year he bought a 40 per cent share of the country's second biggest-selling paper, *Ma'ariv*. Not content with that, he expressed financial interest in other Israeli businesses and in June, while everyone was glued to some second-rate tournament in Italy, he dropped the bombshell: he offered to buy Jerusalem's two football teams.

Offered is the right word. For the plight of the two Jerusalem teams would make a worthy cause for a Barnardo's collection day. Despite their presence in the Israeli First Division, both teams are about £2 million in debt. With the players' wages firmly on hold and the prospects of starting the season remote, to say the least, the patrons of both clubs went cap in hand to Uncle Bob, who had revealed what a committed Zionist he is by his previous purchases and who was never one to refuse a plea for help.

What he failed to realise is that football in Israel is run on similar lines to the UN General Assembly, with the game taking a very uncomfortable back seat to the parties that administer it. Making an offer for the two Jerusalem clubs, Hapoel and Betar, is like trying to buy the Conservative and Labour parties. When he realised just who he was dealing with, he was out of the deal quicker than a pork butcher from a bar mitzvah.

Hapoel belong to the trade union Histadrut sports federation, play in red and are seen as the team of the Labour Party in every city in which they are represented. Betar are part of the right-wing Likud organisation, play in blue and are followed by the Jerusalem equivalent of Hackney's Trowbridge estate. Both clubs share the tiny YMCA ground (capacity 6,000; TV coverage from a second floor balcony on line with one of the 18-yard boxes, only if the resident family moves out for the day). The pitch is so bad you are guaranteed six postponed games a season.

Never mind. Jerusalem mayor Teddy Kollek, after years of bargaining with the religious-minded in the city, finally got the go-ahead to build a new stadium to house 15,000 football-hungry Jerusalemites, whose enthusiasm for the game has led both clubs to rank among the top four best-supported sides in Israel. Derby day at YMCA may not be Liverpool or Manchester, but the tension could be cut with a Black and Decker power drill. Football is the religion of Jerusalem and don't let them kid you otherwise.

Maxwell agreed to help out to the tune of £4 million on condition that both clubs merge into one team, to be known as Jerusalem United. Apart from the inappropriateness of the name – imagine a senior league baseball team owner buying Barnsley and calling them the Oakwell Bruins – the idea was about as popular among the football fraternity as starting a team for the PLO. Managers, players and fans were against the merger but the clubs' patrons, desperate for a quick-fire remedy to solve their financial bungling, accepted the offer. Jerusalem was to be United.

Meanwhile, as the Italians, Spaniards and French were buying anything that moved in the World Cup, all was quiet on the Maxwell front. No money had arrived, the players were itching to start training but were on strike until their back pay was settled. Then, in mid-July, the faeces hit the fans. Maxwell sent some of the money "to be frozen until the Israeli Football Association gives its go-ahead for the merger".

Maxwell had assumed that the IFA would simply stamp the cheque, name the new stadium after him and plant a few trees on his behalf. Instead, they blocked the deal by refusing to renege on their own standing orders which explicitly state that any new club entering organised football in Israel must begin life in the Fifth Division. The said Fifth Division is akin to the Ilford Jewish Taxi Drivers Sunday Morning League, so the prospect of waiting at least four years before Jerusalem United could scale the heights of our First Division was not exactly pleasing to those in favour of the deal.

The IFA further stuck to its guns by adding that if one team disbands and the other continues, no more than three players could be transferred from the defunct to the new club.

Everything came to a head on July 29th when the IFA said they would look into the possibility of changing the standing orders during the coming year, thus finally dooming the possibility of the merger happening in time for the new season. To rub salt into Maxwell's wounds, IFA deputy chairman Azrikam Milchen singled him out for abuse, saying that he didn't like the idea of "foreigners dictating terms to the IFA". Fair enough, but the saga has left a bad taste in the fans' mouths because Milchen and Co did not vote against the merger for purely footballing reasons, but rather from ulterior political motives. As part of the Maccabi (liberal) faction on the IFA, he and his colleagues were able to veto the two-thirds majority needed to get the deal through. Maccabi wanted to 'put one over' on their hated rivals Hapoel and Betar.

Maxwell was outraged. In a formal letter retracting his offer, he bit back at Milchen in true Milton Friedman style. "Mr Milchen will quickly learn that the dictation comes not from a foreigner but from the basic laws of economics. There is no independence in bankruptcy," he wrote. When asked on Israeli radio whether he had been looking for a way out of the deal after seeing early on that it was not viable, he said that the question was unfair and that he never wanted to be interviewed by them again. Shame.

The fans, ever optimistic, are delighted. Hapoel are training, there's talk of transfers in the air and hopes are high that they will get some money together. Betar, on the other hand, are considering the economic realities of life. No money, wages or training. But as one of their fans said recently, "I'd rather have no team than half of theirs." ○

Frank Account

Hinckley was awash with non-League football fervour and now, to cap it all, a tall, dark stranger strolled into town. Geoff Veasey was on the case…

WSC No 46, December 1990

THE ACCOMPANYING CHORDS TO A SPAGHETTI WESTERN ECHO EERILY through the hosiery factories of south west Leicestershire. Spurs jingle confidently on the wooden sidewalk outside the *Hinckley Advertiser*. Tumbleweed drifts across the deserted M69, completely obscuring the Burbage and Sapcote turn-off.

Why? Because Big Frank is back in town. Hinckley Town, to be strictly accurate. It's Frank Worthington we're speaking of here, partners, he of the electric hips, slicked-back Grecian 2000 and deadly sideburns.

Hinckley (pop. 29,325) is strictly Border Country. Some of the population support Coventry City, from nearby Warwickshire. Slightly more are haplessly following David Pleat's relentless pursuit of Third Division status, a few miles away in Leicester. The remainder dither between the town's three non-League clubs. They are, in ascending order, Hinckley FC (smart name eh?) of the Scoreline Combination, Hinckley Athletic, of the Banks's Premier League and Hinckley Town, now one tier above their rivals in the Beazer Homes League, Midland Division. The three of them have access, via the Pyramid system, to the Football League, once they have overcome the slight obstacle of the Vauxhall Conference. This means that, technically, fabulous Frank could be playing against Arsenal again by 1994.

And don't think he wouldn't try. He's a mere boy in current League terms, just into his forties. Frank's arrival has stirred up some rancour in the town, and sent more than a few hearts a-flutter over at Filbert Street. There's even talk at Highfield Road of an exchange deal involving the kid Speedie, who's thought to be a bit juvenile for a midfield currently sponsored by Phyllosan.

Town won the Banks's Premier championship in May. It was the climax to a heady rush from Leicestershire League football which took less than a decade. It was the first title match I'd seen since Coventry City beat Wolves to secure the Second Division championship, some time before the Crimean War broke out. Town's doughty performance endeared them to me greatly.

Maybe not quite the same atmosphere as when City and Wolves fans filled Highfield Road with almost 52,000 on that memorable day perhaps, but passion was just as high at Leicester Road. Victory there would see Town promoted on goal difference, as long as their ground passed the acid test of not looking like something out of the First World War. Promotion would mean lucrative derbies against Leicester United and Nuneaton Borough. With Newport up also, the prospect of 600 exiles from south Wales thronging the grassy tussocks behind a goal made fans positively salivate.

All of which explains our excitement and a failure to inspect the side of the car for cow dung before leaping in. A change of trousers was definitely not the best way to ensure getting to the kick-off on time. It was going to be one of those nights. Fuel gauge on red, credit card in garage on the blink, nowhere to park... got the picture? Most of Hinckley, except die-hard Athletic fans, had gathered to watch some history. By the time we got into the ground, the programmes were sold out and we had missed Town's opening goal. The turnstiles were white-hot. And I do mean both of them.

A break in play gave some breathing space to take in the hastily tidied-up stadium. Portakabins had sprouted everywhere, with labelled doors proclaiming 'Directors' or 'Officials'. Town were taking it seriously, then.

I'm still not sure if Halesowen Harriers were. The buzz around the ground was that they had an important cup tie coming up and that one or two key players were being rested. (This would account for the rotundity and advancing years of one of their full-backs, and the schoolboyish looks of the goalkeeper – though in fairness both players gave it everything they'd got.) We actually managed to see Town's second goal, but their third one also eluded us. Deciding to change ends before half-time, they scored whilst we were walking behind one of the assortment of stands which had erupted casually around the ground.

With Town 3-0 up at half-time, and us ensconced behind the goal they were playing towards, a massacre, it seemed, was on the cards. Halesowen had other ideas. Their pungent cocktail of age and great tonnage had everyone checking watches. Was this going to be the second trouser-change of the night, one wondered? Fortunately not. At the final whistle, jubilant fans ran on to the pitch to salute their heroes. The last pitch invasion I saw was at Highfield Road, celebrating another relegation escape. Mounted Hussars from the West Midlands Police swathed through the crowd on that occasion. I studied the faces of the two special constables anxiously, therefore, before piling on to join in the fun.

The highlight of the celebrations for me was a spirited rendition of a song called *A Man Without A Woman Is Like A Ship Without A Sail* belted out not by the fans but by the players. They treated us to two verses of this fine ditty, at a volume which would have any rugby team quaking in their jockstraps. Quite what relationship the lyrics have to winning the Banks's Premier, I'm not sure. It was the kind of display of individuality and eccentricity Frank would adore.

The thought of seeing Town v Athletic derbies one Boxing Day, to decide who goes top of the Fourth Division, is a truly delicious one. Rumour has it that if Frank stays, Athletic are putting in a bid for Eusebio and Hinckley FC have pencilled in WG Grace for appointment to their board. It's all happening in the land of the Triple-Hemmed Overlocked Support Garment. ○

Bully for You

Does Steve Bull amount to much more than a decent haircut
and a superb Black Country accent? Ed Horton thought so.

WSC No 46, December 1990

IF STEVE BULL'S INTERNATIONAL CAREER ENDED RIGHT NOW, IT WOULD BE
possible to argue that his major contribution was demonstrating that the
national stadium doesn't need to be moved to the north or the midlands.
Pick a player who inspires sufficient loyalty, and half the population of
Wolverhampton will follow him anywhere.

It would be a shame if this exceptional loyalty served to obscure the fact
that Bull really does seem to be a player whose particular characteristics
inspire a unique admiration far beyond the Black Country. Mainstream
journalists usually regard Steve Bull with a combination of fastidi-
ousness and amusement; reservations about his style seem almost to
outweigh appreciation of his achievements. Some of us who view the
game from a fan's, rather than an art critic's perspective, consider Bull
the most admirable of England's leading players.

What excites the admiration where Steve Bull is concerned? Think
about what everybody knows about him. His hair is close-cropped,
evoking memories of National Service and its era. His style is brisk and
direct. He scores, oh, loads and loads of goals. He plays for his local team,
outside the First Division. And he doesn't want to leave. Put them
together, images and facts, and what do you get? Throwback.

Not throwback in the Neanderthal sense, though this is the tone with
which our Premier Analysts approach the man, not to mention his
devoted followers. What I mean is that Bull appears to embody the
virtues of a different age – virtues which are magnified by time and the
belief that the vanished age was a better one than this. It wasn't, of
course. But its virtues were virtues nonetheless, particularly as they're
ones which are understood and celebrated by the ordinary football
supporter more than the Pundit.

The most expensive pub in Oxford (and my God there's some competition) displays on its wall an old cigarette card collection. I try not to sit
over there: it kills the conversation if I'm forever staring at forgotten
players from the Thirties. Most of them look a bit like Bull: broad-

shouldered with a minimum of hair, they emphasise the physical aspect of the game rather more than its essential subtlety. Personally, my hair is shoulder-length and talk of 'a man's game' leaves me cold. But Bull's cigarette-card image is worth preserving for the same reason we prefer older kits, not disfigured by designers' whims or degraded by sponsorship. It's simple; it's honest; and it doesn't aspire towards a false and disposable glamour. For that reason it quite properly appeals to ordinary people who follow the game for a lifetime in order to celebrate its ordinary virtues.

It's the same simplicity that I find most appealing about his style. Graham Turner is supposed to have remarked: "People say his first touch isn't good, but he usually scores with his second," which was pretty apt as a description as well as a rejoinder. He gets the ball, he runs towards goal, he shoots – the fact that then he does usually score is justi-fication enough. It's a basic style, not a crude one, and it always seems strange to me that the same critics who praise Liverpool for showing that 'football is a simple game' are unable to extend the same courtesy to Bull. Again, the image is one that evokes memories of newsreel football: the heavy ball and clumsy boots enforced a game of strength and early shooting, nostalgia for which can be assuaged at Molineux.

But the most substantial part of Bull's attraction is his apparent intention to carry on playing for his local team for as long as they want him. Those who wonder why a Tottenham player is so keen to celebrate the Tyne are quite old enough to understand that players move on, they get transferred, they want a higher standard of football and a higher wage.

Having said that, there's still something special about a player who plays for the same club for years, not least because outside the ITV teams this almost always entails periods of failure and relegation as well as the good times. Such players are invariably able to summon forth a little more determination than their colleagues: their relationship with the supporters is a mutually supportive one, and even in their decline they can be forgiven their mistakes. Frequently they stay in the area after their retirement. It's a different set of values than the world of tabloid transfers, two year deals with Juventus and so on.

It becomes all the more admirable when the long serving player is local, whose passion for his team is an accident of birth, growing from childhood, and thus is the same for the performer as for the audience. Paul McStay is such a player: Steve Bull another. His apparent content-edness with scoring his goals at, say, Vale Park irritates the hell out of writers whose backsides never sit in a Second Division press box, but it's a considerable source of pleasure to me. What can I say? I hardly mind if he scores against my team.

Of all teams, it would have to be Wolves. Champions in the Fifties, just as Nat Lofthouse went out, just before George Best came in, just previous to the end of National Service and the maximum wage. Wolves were a great team in the period of Maximum Nostalgia: led themselves by a long-time player and manager. Most importantly, Wolves are a provincial team who will never again (like Bolton, Huddersfield, Sunderland) achieve the constant success they once took for granted. In the days of the Big Five and the Big City, watching Wolves is an act of nostalgia in itself. We would all prefer it if a lot more teams had the chance to succeed, but we can't really do anything about it – but it's as if Steve Bull is trying.

He's a local lad, playing, it seems, for the love of it, in a style that, in form if not ability, is like football most of us watch. His club isn't Liverpool but a team, like ours, that's failed far too often. He's not a bought man, and he could just as easily be scoring goals for the team you support. No wonder he's so widely admired.

The terrible irony, of course, is that the Wolves side struggling towards the play-off zone is patently inadequate in half a dozen positions, the common result of a rapid rise through the divisions. And while it struggles, it lets him down as well: relying on him for the regular miracles, providing him with less of a service than he deserves. It would be quite easy for Wolves to put right the faults that keep them out of the First: by selling their centre-forward they could raise the money to buy first rate players in every position that they need.

And I don't think they'll do it, because I don't imagine the fans will let them: and I'm not going to say they're wrong.

But it might make Bull a regular England player, which he deserves, but which looks at the moment like it may not happen after all. Good thing too, say the purists. Well, Graham Taylor must do as he thinks is right. The rest of us can only dream of picking the team. But who can deny that Steve Bull is the dreamer's choice? O

It Don't Mean a Thing

Tony Christie railed against the monotony of the modern football song.

WSC No 47, January 1991 – Ranters' Corner

WHEN I WAS FIVE YEARS OLD MY FATHER TOOK ME TO SEE THE ARSENAL. THIS was in the days of the incomparable Alex James. That afternoon the North Bank greeted every jink, swivel and body swerve from the little magician with the spontaneous rendition of "There ain't nothing like a James," stomping their feet as they sang and moving up and down the terraces, arms akimbo, in perfectly choreographed mimicry of the sailors in *South Pacific*.

The Gunners' stopper at the time was a large, ponderous man. He had a dreadful game. Once, after he had made a frightful bish of a simple clearance, 20,000 fingers pointed at him and the grandstand shock to a thunderous burst of "I'd Like To Put You On A Slow Boat To China".

Alas, such delightful songs are now absent from the terraces (so too is the wit. Bearded do-gooders may well poo-poo the suggestion, but isn't the decline in terrace humour a direct result of the removal of Latin from the schools' syllabus? I believe it is.) Nowadays the tunes behind the chants are a monotonous diet of *Bread Of Heaven, Fly The Flag* and

Guantanamera (a song which is infinitely easier to sing than it is to spell, I can assure you). Where is the spirit of musical adventure that once led thousands of Teessiders, doubtless under the influence of John Coltrane's *Dolphin Song For A Cerulian Carpet*, to attempt an atonal improvisation on the nodal structure of "We've Got Willie, Willie, Willie, Willie Wigham In Our Goal, In Our Goal"?

Gone. Gone as the great songsmiths are gone. For there is no doubt in my mind that the poor standard of modern chanting is mirrored by the appalling cacophony churned out by the modern day 'popstars'. The showstoppers of Rogers and Hart, the toe-tapping tunes of Barney Kettle and his Rhythm Syncopators may well by dubbed 'square' by present day 'beatniks' with their 'Happy Mondays' and 'Tony Orlandos', but at least you could chant along with them! Try attempting that with *Theme From Twin Peaks* or Viv Anderson's *O Superman*.

No, as far as terrace chants are concerned, things, if I might purloin a phrase from someone a bit more 'with it' than myself, ain't what they used to be. ⭘

Opening a Super Market

The seeds of the Champions League were being sown by the big European clubs. It was time for UEFA to take a stand. They didn't.

WSC No49, March 1991 – Editorial

THE EUROPEAN SUPER LEAGUE IS A BIT LIKE THE ABOMINABLE SNOWMAN. Everyone has heard of it, but no-one knows what it looks like. We all have our theories though. Indeed, a full-scale, papier mache model of the QE2 could be knocked up from the newspaper reports predicting its imminent creation. Now, finally, there has been some action.

A meeting of UEFA's executive committee in April will discuss a proposal for re-organising the European Cup. The quarter-finals of the competition would be replaced by two mini-leagues, each containing four teams who would play one another home and away with the two groups winners qualifying for the final.

The idea under consideration was apparently conceived by the Real Madrid president Ramon Mendoza, but it seems slightly odd that it should have been formally proposed by the English and Scottish FAs, neither of whom are exactly renowned for a willingness to embrace new ideas.

It may be intended as a compromise, designed to placate the advocates of a breakaway league who might otherwise press on with plans for a new competition. However, it would obviously serve as a means of gauging the commercial potential of a larger competition. If UEFA willingly move halfway to the Super League's ultimate goal, they may find it difficult to stop.

Entry to the European Cup is currently restricted to the national champion, but if the mini-league is a financial success, UEFA would come under pressure to expand the competition. In fact, this would be even more likely to happen if it was a commercial flop. There would be demands to include more clubs from countries that can guarantee big TV audiences and interest from commercial sponsors, and possibly, to exclude those that can't. Western clubs have no compunction about buying up players from the former Soviet Bloc countries, but until the 'eastern European Berlusconi' emerges (though, God forbid, Robert Maxwell is already depressingly big in Bulgaria), they are not too interested in playing teams from that region. Impoverished clubs in eastern Europe also seem to have the happy knack of knocking out wealthier opponents from the west, as the ardent Super Leaguers in the Ibrox boardroom could confirm from recent experience.

Under the present seeding system, which classifies teams according to their performances in Europe over a five-year period, there is no guarantee that all the representatives from the major western European nations will avoid one another in the early stages. For example, neither Arsenal nor Liverpool have played in Europe in the past five years, so they could be drawn against the champions of Italy or Germany (or Scotland) in the first round.

From the perspective of the businessmen-turned-fans who can't help but see football teams largely in terms of commercial opportunity, a knockout tournament leaves too much to chance. Big clubs, especially those who dominate their domestic leagues, budget for success and so face serious financial problems if they either fail to qualify or are eliminated early on. PSV Eindhoven, for example, calculated that they would lose over £1 million in revenue as a consequence of losing to Montpellier in the first round of this season's Cup Winners' Cup.

However, clubs such as PSV are wealthy to an almost impractical degree and tend to generate financial problems for themselves. They create inflation in the transfer market by spending absurd amounts of money on players, and often accumulate needlessly large first team squads simply in order to damage their domestic rivals' chances by reducing the number of good players in circulation.

As the co-ordinating body for all the football associations within Europe, UEFA should be working in the interests of a majority of their members and should not be expected to yield to pressure from a handful of wealthy clubs.

UEFA should reject proposals for a reform of the European Cup because its proponents will not be satisfied with a half-way measure like mini-leagues. No-one has yet produced a specific blueprint for a Super League, chiefly because they are hoping that UEFA will do their job for them. There isn't space here to go into the reasons why a Super League wouldn't work in the long-term but UEFA should call the bluff of Berlusconi, Tapie and their associates. If they want a new international competition, they should be forced to go it alone. ○

Coach Trip

Kevin Donnelly revealed all you'd need to know about the coaching courses run by the Scottish FA.

WSC No 49, March 1991

YOU ARE STANDING NEXT TO YOUR COURSE INSTRUCTOR FACING AN OPPONENT who is holding a football in his hands. As the instructor shouts, the ball is thrown over your head and you turn to collect it. Suddenly there is an extreme pain in your Adams apple. As you sink to the ground it dawns that the cause of this pain was, in fact, your instructor's elbow. Is this an SAS training routine or some middle management survival course in the Lake District? No, it is an SFA coaching course and the wily old pro of a coach has just shown you how to take out a centre half if you are playing up front and the ball gets played over your head. This tactic of course could only be used in an amateur game because, in the words of the coach, "If there's a linesman, you've no got much chance of getting away with it".

This is one of the methods used by the Scottish Football Association to ensure that all the coaches who are fortunate enough to gain the 'C' licence are fully equipped to preach the gospel of pure football and fair play. The 'C' licence represents the first step towards on the road to gaining the highly prized 'A' licence which enables its holder to apply for jobs from East Kilbride to East Africa.

The only person I know who has taken the 'A' certificate found it very hard work. His chances of passing were not helped by the antics of one of the Scotland youth players who was helping with the course. A certain Ralph Milne, now proving that Alex Ferguson doesn't need to spend a lot of money to get a bad player into a Man Utd jersey, practised a particular joke on unwary souls. His party piece involved folding an ear into the side of his head so that it seemed to disappear. Such was his amusement at this uncanny ability that he practised it at every opportunity, pretending to be deaf and pointing at the side of his head where his ear should have been.

I took the 'C' licence course in the summer of 1987, which entailed spending a week at the University of Stirling, utilising its superb football pitches. For years the *Sunday Post* has been telling its readers that Scottish football must be held in high regard overseas as people were coming from all over the world to take these courses. With some doubts regarding charter flights of football pilgrims winging their way to the football Mecca of 6 Park Gardens (the SFA equivalent of Lancaster Gate), I was surprised to find that an American and two guys from the United Arab Emirates had journeyed to Scotland with the express intent of gaining a certificate. The American, Billy, once volunteered to retrieve a mishit shot by saying "I'll go and shag the ball". Not understanding why everyone had cracked up, he told us that he always shags the ball if required and that ball-boys in the States are called 'shaggers'.

Approximately 40 people took part in the course, split into two groups of 20, each group supervised by two coaches who had gained the 'A' licence. Three of the four tutors had played professionally for a considerable time, and one was assistant manager at a Premier League club at the time. The pitfalls of a coaching career were highlighted on the second day of the course when he was sacked from his job.

Over the next five days they held classes on various aspects of play, such as setting up attacks, defending at set pieces and simple basics, such as passing and moving off the ball. I had expected most of the course to be given over to pure instruction, but practical involvement meant that everyone was forced to coach other students through a routine at least once a day. Once you had done this you would then be taken aside by a coach who would go over the strengths and weaknesses of your performance.

Nothing commands respect on the training ground as much as pure footballing ability. The people on the course came from a variety of backgrounds, some of which, such as teaching, gave them an advantage in putting across the message. If, however, you actually cannot make a ten-yard pass to another player, all the teaching ability in the world is not going to provoke much of a response from your players.

Anyone who has played semi-professional or full-time football for a certain number of years can take a 'B' licence without having been on the initial course. The SFA seem to believe that exposure to football at the highest level will provide any individual with enough insight to coach at a basic level. However, anyone who has had the misfortune to see a team from the lower reaches of the Scottish Second Division in training will know that the players' exposure to 'coaching' is kept to a minimum.

On the last afternoon, every participant is awarded a certificate of attendance to have at least something to show for the week's endeavours. Six weeks later a brown envelope dropped through my letter box, the contents of which informed me that I was now a qualified 'C' licence coach, and that without a blackboard or magnetic wall chart in sight. I had originally gone on the course in the belief that it might give me greater insight into what the likes of Brian Moore refer to as the 'technical aspects of the game'. More fool me. What the course did give me was an idea of how to get players organised on a training field and how to convey a specific idea, be it the timing of a run into the penalty box or the holding up of an attack if you are the last defender.

One got the impression that most, if not all, of the participants would get the coaching certificate. The SFA's coaching scheme is self-perpetuating in a way, because if most applicants do not gain the 'C' they will not be able to move up to the 'B' and 'A'. Participants pay for the pleasure of taking part in these courses, so they would be unlikely to fork out year after year if they were getting nowhere.

My one disappointment was that we were not visited by the man who offers living proof that you do not have to be a great player to be a coach. Sadly, Andy Roxburgh did not turn up to give his coaching prodigies a pep talk prior to our leaving to pass on the SFA's footballing vision to the world.

I attempted to put over the message with a Sunday league team, but found my pearls of wisdom went unheeded. Having ignored virtually all my detailed instructions, they found themselves at the top of the league playing a style of football more reminiscent of Wimbledon under Harry Bassett than the Dutch team of 1974, whom I had used as a role model. At the end of each training session, I was left with little more than an acute sense of frustration and a sore throat.

The elbow applied to my throat during the course proved to me that the people in charge were clued in about typical footballers' behaviour. It would be interesting to find out if the more advanced courses were similarly in touch, not only on the field but off it. If so, have they picked up any handy hints from direct experiences with the international squad and do they insert these as part of the course curriculum?

To get the 'B' certificate, pupils may well be required to decide on the action to be taken against two national team players who have drunk lots of champagne in an Italian bar, then refused to pay the bill. To make the 'A' licence into a real test, participants might be asked what they would say to the media when a player failed a drug test in an international tournament. Hopefully no-one would have to stand on the banks of the Clyde trying to get a pissed Jimmy Johnstone to row himself back to shore so he can play in a match that afternoon, but with the SFA, as with the team itself, you never know. ○

Cottage Pyre

With the future of Craven Cottage still in doubt, Neil Hurden explained why many Fulham fans were unhappy with the board's manoeuvrings.

WSC No 49, March 1991

IN ANY POPULARITY POLL CONDUCTED AMONGST FOOTBALL FANS, THE NAME OF Jimmy Hill is unlikely to be up there elbowing aside the likes of Gazza and Platty. Not content with winding up Terry Venables and the vast majority of the TV audience with his 'idiosyncratic' post-match analyses, he has now become the scourge of Lancastrian ball-girls, too, after the notorious Blackburn own-goal affair. Scotland fans take the most positive approach to this media phenomenon and indulge in healthy doses of ridicule. For Fulham fans, though, there is considerably less to laugh about.

For one of the game's widely acknowledged friendly clubs, it is remarkable quite how unfriendly relations have been in the Craven Cottage boardroom over the last twenty years or so. It now seems highly likely indeed that, after a process of gradual decline and periodic high drama, Jimmy Hill will be the man who leads us away from our ancestral homeland.

This whole sorry tale has been shaped by a succession of different influences, but Hill may have played a crucial role in the final episode. Hill's public persona is very much that of the politician. He thrives off publicity, but is also liable to fall prey to it. He also has a characteristically well-developed immunity to criticism and abuse, and continues to stride stoically on to the pitch at half-time, after another particularly inept performance, ready to bellow out the names of the month's lottery winners as the chorus of "Hill Out!" resounds around the ground.

In a sense, it is difficult to feel too concerned about the sensitivities of a man who did not shrink from the reflected glory associated with the battle to save Fulham from extinction during the merger crisis of 1987. The famous programme cover, promising "Happy days are here again!", shortly after he had taken over as chairman from David Bulstrode, was acceptable in the euphoria of the moment, but to have his face staring out from the cover for the whole of the following season was a definite sign that the club had become a little too closely identified with the chairman.

Because of the labyrinthine maze of deals involved in this saga, people both inside and outside the club inevitably look for a simple explanation for Fulham's plight. And, of course, there he is, standing bashfully in the centre circle in his sheepskin, sharing his thoughts with us via the public address system at a volume that would put Motorhead to shame.

However, there are some points to be made in his defence. The riverside at Fulham is a highly sought-after piece of real estate. This has meant that the club's survival is more closely linked to the ownership of the freehold than is the case with any other League club in the country. Hill's defence for everything he and his board have done in relation to deals with Cabra Estates is that he has never had any control over this freehold, and this is indisputable.

In January 1985, Ernie Clay, Fulham chairman since 1977, bought the freehold from the Church Commissioners for less than £1 million, most of which was loaned to him by the Manchester-based property company, Kilroe. Just over a year later, however, after the then-Conservative controlled local council had rejected Kilroe's plans for a partial development of the site, Clay sold the whole thing to SB Property Company, a subsidiary of David Bulstrode's Marler Estates plc, also owners of Chelsea's ground. Bulstrode paid roughly £9 million for this – £5.5 million for the club's shares, and the rest to pay off the club's creditors, including Kilroe. Ownership of the freehold subsequently passed on from SB to Cabra Estates and Ernie Clay walked off with his share of £4 million to resume his entrepreneurial activities from a hotel in the Algarve.

If we are looking for villains, therefore, the key figure should be Clay, scourge of the football authorities in his day, rather than the nation's favourite TV pundit. Special mention should also be made of the man whose role in our gradual decline is still immortalised in the name of our main stand. Sir Eric Miller, who committed suicide in 1977, not only left the way open for Clay, who had joined the board just a year earlier, but bequeathed debts on the stand so damaging that they would not have been paid off even if it had been full for every match between then and now.

At a meeting of the board and the various supporters' groups two weeks ago, Hill, aided by Wilson (a former fullback of the early Fifties, who is now chairman of one of the city's top surveying firms), resumed this line of defence, and explained the latest stage in the club's dealings with Cabra Estates, the current owners of the freehold.

Perhaps the most notable feature of this meeting, apart from the ludicrously small room it was held in and the fact that Tom Wilson looked disturbingly like Robert Robinson, was the revival of some degree of understanding, if not full harmony, within the club.

Relations with the supporters began to deteriorate after the first Cabra deal, signed early last year, which stipulated that Fulham FC should receive a series of payments in exchange for vacating the ground. This agreement also committed the board to adopt a neutral line over Hammersmith and Fulham council's compulsory purchase order bid, which sought to deprive Cabra of its ownership of the land.

A confused situation was certainly not helped by the existence of legal covenants which prevented the directors from expressing their opinions as freely as they and we may have wished. In the autumn, the atmosphere worsened further with the dismissal of the popular club secretary, Yvonne Haines, which led in turn to the resignation of the programme staff.

Rumblings about the new management style on and off the pitch, and the disturbing performance of the team, especially away from home where we have taken traditional generosity to ridiculous extremes, merely added fuel to the 'Hill Out!' campaign, led by the terrace Ultras.

Hill has clearly been following a policy of co-operation with Cabra. He appears to have tacitly recognised that Fulham will have to leave the Cottage, but has tried in the meantime to gain as much money for the club as possible. We have now heard directly from the horse's mouth that the only way he could envisage us staying at the Cottage would be the sudden appearance on the scene of a 'white knight'. And, as we all know, there is about as much likelihood of a genuine Fulham supporter galloping up Stevenage Road, swerving round the massed ranks of local BMWs, and slamming £20 million or so on the boardroom table, as there is of us getting promotion this season.

Nonetheless, many supporters still have lingering doubts about the board's policy. Whilst Hill has been co-operating with Cabra, Ken Bates has, characteristically, been doing exactly the opposite. In taking Cabra to court, it seems that he is trying exploit their current financial vulnerability, and damage the company so badly that Chelsea FC will be able to resume full control of its own destiny.

Admittedly, Bates has always been in a stronger position than Hill, because of Chelsea's option to purchase their freehold, but many Fulham fans would rather our board had taken a more aggressive approach from the start, given the weakness of property developers in the current financial climate.

As Cabra did not adhere to the strict timetable of payments laid down in the first deal, Fulham could have enforced a penalty clause entitling them to receive £10,000 per day. Instead, fearing substantial legal costs and delays, the board concluded a second, more lucrative agreement, which will bring in an immediate payment of £3 million as soon as Cabra's bank gives formal guarantees. It may be, as Hill maintains, that this more cautious approach will give the club a better chance of survival. However, to those supporters for whom Craven Cottage is the home and not just the site of Fulham Football Club, this policy of co-operation rather than confrontation does not suggest that the board is quite as desperate to remain at the Cottage as the vast majority of the fans are.

Here again, Jimmy Hill's own publicity and background give rise to further doubts. The man who negotiated freedom of contract for players, and built an all-seater stadium for Coventry, has always been keen to portray himself as a visionary. Now that football is largely committed to enacting the recommendations of the Taylor Report, Hill might even set an example for others to follow by leading Fulham to a sparkling new stadium within spitting distance of the M25.

CORRUPTION

If everything works out for the best, might a new Fulham emerge, ready to greet the new era with the backing of sackfuls of money from Cabra Estates? The answer is most probably 'no', given the way in which the money we have already received has been used. It is an open secret that the club has been living beyond its means over the last year, supporting an over-sized and underachieving squad on perhaps the highest wages in the division, and there is every reason to believe that this approach will continue over the next year. The directors do face real difficulties in finding a new site for a stadium, but with only two years remaining on the lease at Craven Cottage, no viable alternative has yet been suggested. Jimmy Hill initially did a deal with Cabra because there was a real danger that we would have been made homeless in May 1990. The way things are going, we could still face exactly the same fate in 1993. ○

Postscript: This phase of the struggle over Craven Cottage ended when Cabra went into liquidation in November 1992. It got much more complicated after that.

A Bad Draw

Olly Wicken had a disturbing tale to tell about a League Cup draw. Prepare to be shocked.

WSC No 49, March 1991

IN MANY WAYS, THE FOLLOWING NEWS DESERVES BANNER HEADLINES ON THE front page of a national daily rather than an article hidden away in *WSC*. But you read it here first.

The draw for the semi-finals of the Rumbelows League Cup, filmed by ITV on January 16th 1991, was a fix. The whole thing was rigged: the participants had already decided which teams would come out of the bag in which order. If this sounds like a scandal, that's because it is. Let me tell you how it happened.

On the evening of the 16th, I happen to be looking into an executive box at Stamford Bridge after the Chelsea v Spurs game (which had been recorded for later highlights). As I looked on, I could see TV sound engineers and lighting cameramen setting up the room for the imminent next round draw. The room was tastefully decked out to mimic the holy portals of Football League headquarters, except that the wooden panelling was 'panel-effect' Vymura, and the imposing table was a Formica-topped trestle.

At ten o'clock (forty minutes before *Midweek Sports Special* was due on air), three men in suits sat down and began the draw. I witnessed the representative from the Football League introduce Arthur Sandford (chief executive) and Peter McParland ("formerly of Aston Villa and Wolves"). The green velvet bag lay draped tidily across the Formica, and within a minute the draw was over: Chelsea or Tottenham versus Coventry or Sheffield Wednesday, Southampton or Manchester United versus Leeds.

But immediately afterwards, as the three men sat there in simulation of a closing freeze-frame, the producer's voice rang out: "I'd like to do a second take of that, please. Can you all try and look happier? Be more animated... think of the funniest thing that's happened to you in the last week. One more time."

What?! Imagine my disbelief: they were going to re-draw the Rumbelows Cup semi-finals.

Let me interrupt myself for a moment here to discuss the magnitude of this, because there are a number of perspectives. There's the perspective of morality and ethics; financial implications for clubs involved; simple fair play. But perhaps most acute for the genuine fan is the perspective that cup draws are sacrosanct. They are our equivalent of being vouchsafed the eternal verities by the Goddess of Fortune herself. (Just as the Ancients, awe-struck, learned their destiny from sacred oracles, we fans learn ours from wrinkly old committee men pulling out their balls.) No one should be allowed to tamper with divine pre-determination – and especially not some TV producer who has decided that a miserable-looking Arthur Sandford hasn't prefaced his calling of the numbers with a chuckle, a theatrical double-take, an "Ooh no, missus", or a fully-choreographed 'dying swan' plunge into the velvet sack.

I watched on panicking but powerless. The committee replaced the numbered balls in the bag as it lay flat on the table. Were these people really going to change the outcome of the semi-final draw?

Time seemed to stand still. Until – thank God! – I realised that they were carefully positioning each number so it could be found to re-draw as before. My relief was beyond description. They weren't actually re-drawing, just re-enacting. Celestial pre-ordainment would not be changed but just jollied up for the camera.

CORRUPTION

They went through the motions of the draw again. Exactly the same motions, and actually no more happy or animated than before. The teams came out of the bag in the same order, but I still found it hard to believe I was watching such a charade. It was a fake draw. These upstanding independent arbiters of Fate were sneaking looks into the bloody bag!

You probably think I'm over-reacting: the draw turned out as it should, after all. No harm done – just a bit of tidying-up for the slick presentation standards of TV. But play-acted cup draws challenge the precepts of Truth and Good which have been bred into us by years of 'going over live' to Bryon Butler at Lancaster Gate.

As I see it, cup draws should be part of important committee meetings. These meetings should be so important that even the great Bryon Butler has to wait patiently outside the room until the appropriate 'next item on the agenda' is reached.

Furthermore, these meetings should even be so important that the cup draw is only item six on the agenda. (For years I've tried and failed to imagine what could be so important that it would precede the draw on an agenda.) But the only items on the agenda before this latest mockery of a draw would have been to stick down the corners of the Formica table-top with chewing gum, and to clear away the plastic coffee cups. The shame of it.

And, as I see it, draws must be live. Being a fan means you can't possibly wait for news: how many times have you ruined *Sportsnight*'s highlights for yourself because you couldn't bear not to find out the score as soon as possible? And draws must be real. What if there had been 64 teams in the bag to be re-drawn exactly as before? It could have taken months attempting to pull out the teams in exactly the same order. Imagine it: three years later, an ageing Arthur Sandford finally gets the 63rd name out in the correct sequence and at last cracks a smile of relief (the producer exclaiming "That's it, lovey, hold that grin!") when, suddenly, Peter McParland noisily expires and they have to start all over again.

So isn't it time that we fans stopped being messed around and insulted by TV? They know we want highlights, but they give us live games. They know we prefer watching all the divisions, but they give us the Big Five clubs. They know we've got brains, but they give us Emlyn Hughes. And now they are committing the ultimate act of blasphemy by profaning our oracle of righteous Truth and Good – the cup draw.

You know who to write to. And don't forget his real name's Roger. ○

Coming Back for Seconds

Courageous beyond the call of duty, Ed Horton ventured into that parallel universe commonly known as the reserve team fixture and survived to tell the tale.

WSC No 50, April 1991

WHEN I TURN UP THE PLAYERS ARE READY TO KICK-OFF, AND THE KIDDIES ARE already playing kiss-chase on the Beech Road terrace. It's only at reserve games that you can actually get a pie and a cup of stodgy water without missing most of the first half, so duty is done before I go to see who's made it this time, and slag off whoever hasn't.

The Fat Boy's there, chewing gum and telling us about all the bands he's seen that week. It's usually eight o'clock before he thinks of one the rest of us have heard of. His 'uncle' Kevin's there too, handing out Polo mints. On a normal evening at the stiffs, one or two of the others from the youthful cynicism crew are hanging around, talking about away games they're going to go to, and the one they didn't go to last Saturday.

When the first team plays, the kick-off is the peak of an emotional crescendo: at the reserves, it takes a while to filter through that the game's in progress, like the dinosaur that doesn't realise when it's dead. Anyway, the game doesn't really begin until the first offside decision goes the wrong way, and Thick Glasses gets his first chance of the evening. "Rubbish, rubbish," he bellows, then changes down into a sneer and a baffled shake of the head. His followers shake with him.

Thick Glasses is a popular and influential man, and a better reason for watching the game than the game is. We always reckon he must be from one of the villages, with his burr and his unsophisticated manner, and his short sight is easily explained away as a result of centuries of country village inbreeding. He's hardly unique, every terrace has one, but like your average local pub band, he's a reliable act. We know what we're getting, and it's not long till we get it – "Oi, Frankie!", he shouts as Paul Byrne fails to trap an elementary pass. "Do that again and you'll be in the first team!" The acolytes chuckle.

Tonight, a couple of scouts have obviously got lost and come here instead, to judge by the cheerful coterie of notebook-handling gentlemen behind me. Sometimes I wondered why people become scouts, watching not just dross, but unfamiliar dross – now I know. They're nostalgics pining for the days when the police would let you bring a vacuum flask into the ground. This being the reserves, they're all right tonight, and the coffee looks warmer than I feel. They do not offer me a cup.

I try to look at what they're writing, but they've deliberately squeezed (well, ambled) to the back of the terraces just to frustrate nosey bastards like me. The only course left is to sabotage their operation, so we think about shouting, "Beauchamp, you're useless!" and "Get off the pitch, Byrne!" to put them off the scent. But it's too embarrassing, even for a reserve match. Somewhat to our surprise, we score midway through the first half: a bad goal of course, someone nipping in after the keeper – Perry Digweed as often as not – fumbles a ground shot. We jump – once – and clap for six or seven seconds. Then we argue about who scored.

It's a curious thing, but, even though the view is clear and unimpeded, it's always harder to recognise the players at reserve games. Possibly that's because you don't have the crowd to chant, "Go on, Simmo!", or – what do we find to chant these days – "Go on, Simmo!", or possibly it's because you don't recognise the players' style in a lacklustre reserve game, especially when they're out of position. Phillips out wide. Jackson in the middle. Penney on the pitch. Poor old Penney, what a waste. Not a waste of talent, just a waste of an unused headline. **Black Day for Penney. Bad Penney. Penney Dreadful**.

Just before half-time, the Fat Boy goes to the food hut for his Mars bar and congealing coffee. A couple of minutes early, more out of Saturday habit than Wednesday necessity. Just a couple of minutes, but like Andy and Fergie, an annoying couple. I hate it when people leave early. One day, I want to get that terrace organised, so that the moment his head disappears down the steps, we all take a breath and simultaneously shout "GOAL!" That should put a stop to it.

The players troop off and some desultory pop music comes over the PA. Kevin hands out some more mints and I stroll over to the Main Stand to see how many footballing celebs have come to watch the game. None. You surprise me, I think to myself, half-consciously waiting for the half-times to be read out. Then I remember that they won't be, because I wrote a letter to the programme asking them to stop doing it. It was either that or lose the gripping tension of *Midweek Sports Special*. Although they did break the rule last season when we were 2-0 down to Tottenham, breaking in halfway through the second half to announce: "A latest score we have is Tranmere two, Spurs one."

Phil Collins comes on to do *In The Air Tonight* and the players jog back on. The referee comes on, they kick-off, play proceeds, and Phil carries on singing. Thick Glasses emits displeasure, the rest of us just snigger. Eventually there's a small commotion towards the top of the stand, and a nasty scratching noise. We talk about what more appropriate song Phil might sing at United games. *I Missed Again* suggests the Fat Boy. When we remember there's a game on, there's a through ball, and a chase cut short by a foul. The ref waves play on. Thick Glasses is apoplectic. "Rubbish, referee, you're rubbish!" he shouts, leading his group in the chorus.

The thing is, he is not wrong, give or take a large exaggeration or ninety. The refs really are pretty dreadful in the Combination. Last season, I saw play waved on with two balls on the pitch. I assumed it was one of Havelange's lunacies being tried out on the quiet. This season, a goalkeeper dribbled the ball outside his area, then back inside, then picked it up. Not a word or a whistle. Paul Tomlinson lost a League Cup quarter-final for Bradford doing that.

Not unusually, the problem is solved by a senior player taking over from the inexperienced ref at critical junctures of the game. More than once, I saw Gerry Armstrong take a game under his control when a referee failed to meet his standards. Billy Whitehurst tried the same manoeuvre, which was carried out as well as his manoeuvres are. Funny bloke, Billy. "Not a footballing town," he said of our fair city. In that case Billy, I should think you were our kind of player.

Eventually the opposition equalise and their lone supporter on the terrace reveals himself by shouting about it for ages. We look at each other and wonder what he's doing here. Probably a student. We look at him. We're mad mate, what's you're excuse? No-one tries too hard in the last ten minutes, vital League points being exactly what's not on offer. I did see Micky Hazard try hard in the last ten minutes once. Honest – what he was trying hard to do was get himself sent-off. Two unprovoked fouls, kick the ball away, abuse the ref after the booking, Bob's your uncle. What a craftsman.

Nine-twelve, the whistle, nobody looks at the Combination table or discusses the performances. Even Thick Glasses contents himself with a couple of wicked glances at the departing linesmen. Phil comes back on and we walk a little faster.

I get into work the next morning, listen to the telly talk, say "Oh yeah, forgot that was on, missed it." So where was I instead, then? For five or six seconds, I really can't remember. ○

Gone by the Board

Neil Reynolds rued the day West Brom replaced Ron with John.

WSC No 51, May 1991 – If Only…

SEVEN YEARS AGO, WEST BROMWICH ALBION WERE A LITTLE BELOW HALFWAY in the table. The First Division table, that is. They were through to the fifth round of the FA Cup and had got the draw everyone wanted: home against Third Division non-entities Plymouth Argyle. A measure of the speed of the club's decline is that in 1984 that situation was considered unsatisfactory – lower half, but in no serious danger of relegation – and on the eve of the match manager Ron Wylie was sacked, and Johnny Giles re-appointed. The timing was such that the board must have considered the cup-tie a mere formality, little more than a bye.

And so it proved. Complacency off the field was transformed into utter confusion on it, and Tommy Tynan, veteran of several million games who joined Plymouth Argyle shortly after Francis Drake left, duly scored the only goal as Argyle coasted to victory. That defeat marked the end of Albion's proud cup traditions, and they have subsequently been eliminated by Third Division Orient, Fourth Division Swansea, and non-League Woking.

Giles bored opposing fans and players into submission in his first spell as manager, taking Albion to promotion with a goal-glut of seven 1-0 wins, five 1-1 draws, and six goalless draws. Unfortunately, he could not re-capture the magic second time around and cleared off within two years. The rot had firmly set in, and Nobby Stiles, Ron Saunders, Ron Atkinson and Brian Talbot did little or nothing to stop the plummet from grace.

If Wylie had not been sacked Albion would have beaten Plymouth, disposed of Derby at home in the sixth round, stuffed Watford in the semis and humiliated Everton again in the final. The money earned would have ensured that they remained one of the world's leading clubs. Woking would never have happened.

I will never forget February 18th, 1984. It was the Beginning Of The End. It was also my seventeenth wedding anniversary. That bastard Giles ruined my wedding as well: on February 18th, 1967 I spent *Match of the Day* in tears as Leeds beat Albion 5-0. ○

League of Their Own

The roar of the oncoming Premier League was deafening.
Andy Lyons and Bill Brewster tried to make themselves heard.

WSC No 52, June 1991 – Editorial

HEARD ABOUT ANY GOOD PREMIER LEAGUES LATELY? SO FAR, THE ONLY definite proposals are in the interim report from the FA, which form part of a 26-point plan, the *Blueprint for Football*. This will be released on June 29th at the FA Council meeting at Torquay. The details are set out in the table below.

– An 18-club 'Super League' to begin 1993-94 season, with a new First Division of 22, a Second Division of 24 and a Third Division of 24 teams.
– Agreed requirements for clubs in the 'Super League'. 1) Minimum of 20,000 all-seater stadia; 2) Financial guarantees; 3) Levy on transfer fees for stadia redevelopment; five per cent is recommended.
– Mandatory postponement of League matches before World Cup and European Championship games.
– A possible panel of professional referees.
– Procedure of two clubs relegated and two promoted.
– Each of the member clubs in the Premier League to be given a seat on the FA Council.
Source: *Mail on Sunday*, April 14th, 1991.

The proposals that have been released so far are clearly only a basis for negotiation, and not even necessarily a cause for alarm. Of course, there is no guarantee that common-sense will prevail. There are several reasons to be fearful.

If the FA are intending to maintain links between their new competition and the rest of the League, why are they so keen to come up with a new name for the First Division? What is it about those two words that would make sponsors recoil in horror? They didn't seem to bother sponsors such as Barclays Bank, the *Today* newspaper and Canon, all of whom lent their name to the League in the past.

Cosmetic marketing terms seem to be widely employed when League reform is under discussion in the press and on TV. Everything is 'elite', 'super', 'premier'. Why not go just a little bit further and begin to extol the merits of the Hyper League or the Supreme Set-up or the Utter Division? All those irritating phrases that were bandied about three years ago when the 'Super League' was first proposed are back with a vengeance. Once more, we are being told that that 'football is part of the modern leisure industry' and 'if clubs can't compete they will go to the wall'.

Beneath the bluster, do we detect a keenness to reflect what we might as well call, for the sake of simplicity, the Thatcherite agenda, that combative attitude towards football so prevalent in the (very) dim days of our last prime minister?

As an example of the sort of comment we're referring to, here's the *Daily Express* on April 9th:

"The premier clubs have carried their smaller brethren like an increasingly heavy yoke while they in turn do nothing to help themselves." Surely these are not the same clubs who have produced eleven of the current England squad, including the universally-admired Lee Sharpe? Who are the 'premier' clubs in any case? If they are defined as teams who have been constant members of the top division for, say, a decade or more, then Chelsea, Manchester City, Leeds, Aston Villa and the two Sheffield clubs would not be among them, yet in terms of their support, they would all be placed among the top 18 clubs in the country. No team has an inalienable right to a particular position in the League table. They are all tenants, not landlords.

Admittedly, whatever the League spokesmen say, the existing, top-heavy structure was never likely to be trimmed voluntarily.

Derby's managing director, Stuart Webb, has been quoted as saying "I am all for progress... but it should be achieved by democratic methods within the structure of the Football League." Fine sentiments, but would he hold the same views if Derby were top of the First Division now, rather than on their way down? We strongly suspect that many people involved in football would be perfectly happy to endorse the creation of a streamlined First Division if their team was to be guaranteed a place. The interests of the majority of the League members become uppermost in their minds only when they realise that they are to be overlooked.

And surely no-one is likely to be impressed by Bill Fox's belated attempt to pose as a man of the people? He was quoted in *Today* on April 9th, referring to, "The man in the street, the man who pays football's wages," who "must now be appalled at what is going on in his game." Odd to see the interests of "the man in the street" suddenly being brought up by the League president, when fans are so often treated with contempt by the complacent and small-minded clubs for whom Fox is the ideal spokesman.

It is vital that playing performance alone should be used as the basis for Premier League membership. Football, as we are endlessly told, is a business, but it is also still first and foremost a sport. Opportunities to progress have to be taken solely on the basis of sporting criteria or the instincts of the ordinary fan would be grossly offended.

With this in mind, what is to be made of the interim report's recommendation that all members of a stream-lined Premier League should have all-seater stadia with a capacity of at least 20,000? On the face of it, this appears to provide a means of excluding smaller clubs. According to the most recent figures available, there are 19 teams in the top two divisions whose ground capacity would fall below 20,000 if they were to replace all the standing areas with seats. What would happen if teams likely to qualify through League position either do not have room to install the number of seats required or cannot afford to construct a new ground from scratch? Provided the stadiums are safe, why should capacity matter at all? Perhaps it is simply an extension of the thinking behind the membership card scheme – instead of supporters being required to hold a licence to attend matches, it is now the clubs' turn to justify their existence.

Additionally, clubs might have to spend enormous sums on equipping themselves for a Premier Division with stringent capacity requirements, only to find these efforts wasted if they were relegated after one season. The money lost in such circumstances might quickly lead to pressure for an ending of the promotion/relegation set-up, particularly given that relegated clubs will be excluded from a new TV deal.

This attitude towards ground capacities is symptomatic of football's attitude to the Taylor Report, whose recommendations seem to have become a quasi-legal imperative rather than an issue for discussion. This is in sharp contrast to the situation in Germany, where proposals for making Bundesliga stadia all-seater are in the process of being defeated in the face of opposition from clubs.

Despite Europe's more sceptical attitude towards all-seaters, there still seems to be a widespread belief here that the Europeans have 'Super Leagues' of their own in place already, a view exemplified by the *Independent* leader, again on April 9th, which argued for the creation of a "continental-style, Premier League". Which country did they have in mind as a benchmark? Might it be France, which has a First Division of 20 teams with two automatic relegation places and promotion/ relegation play-off? Or perhaps the Italian *Serie A*, with 18 teams and four relegated? Or Spain, where four Second Division clubs are in with a chance of promotion each season, with the top two going up automatically?

Each of these league systems permit the local equivalents of Wimbledon, Oxford and Luton to gain promotion. None serves as a suitable model for the 'Super League' advocates. Certainly no other country in Europe has a 22 team First Division, but they have properly integrated leagues with a substantial number of regionalised divisions in various formats. Apart from Holland (where league football is primarily semi-professional in any case), nowhere else is there a distinction made between 'League' and 'non-League'.

The interim report appears to make no mention of the relationship between professional and semi-professional football. Yet the FA is responsible for the administration of the game at grass roots level, and must be aware of the damage that could be done if the League were to exist in a vacuum with no connection to the lower leagues.

Instead, they seem to envisage 70 teams staying in the re-structured League, below the Premier Division, which would mean five clubs dropping out. Surely they ought to be considering ways in which to open up the League, rather than close it off? They also appear content to leave all such considerations in the hands of the League, which would presumably still be run by the same people who agonised for so long before consenting to the minimal contact that now exists between the Fourth Division and the GM Vauxhall Conference.

An 18-team First Division is certainly a good idea, particularly if it were to be accompanied by a decrease in the superfluous cup competitions hogging space on the football calendar. (We have a particular tournament in mind – four words, begins with 'Zenith', ending in 'Cup'.) It would lessen the physical demands made on players and allow more time for international teams to prepare prior to matches. But from the big clubs' point of view, the overriding appeal of a smaller First Division lies in its attractiveness to sponsors and television. At present, the top clubs are clearly resentful of the fact that revenue generated by the televising of matches is spread throughout the League.

Liverpool and Everton voted in favour of a return to the 22-team First Division that will be inflicted upon us next season, because they wanted to regain the two home fixtures lost when the First Division was reduced to

20 clubs. But a smaller Premier League opens up even greater commercial possibilities, so they have changed their tune and now appear to be backing the FA's proposal. For the big clubs, money is everything.

Yet, according to the *Daily Express,* "What the FA want, what the 18 clubs want and, most importantly, what the public want is a national team to take on the world." Who really believes that the chairmen backing the FA's proposals are primarily concerned for the future well-being of the England team? As far as we can recall, the over-riding factor influencing moves towards a breakaway league in 1988 was that it would bring about a lucrative new TV deal with all the money being shared among the handful of clubs involved.Talk then was of a dozen teams playing each other four times a season, which would have provided even less opportunity for national team get-togethers than is the case now.

We doubt if the big clubs' priorities have changed significantly in the past three years. They may be prepared to reap the profits of a successful World Cup campaign by England, in terms of increased attendances and the media's new-found enthusiasm for 'positive' football stories, but they don't give a damn about the international team. If further proof were needed, just consider the number of players withdrawn from national team squads due to injury who then miraculously recover in time for their club's next game.

Most fans still place club before country and will often turn up at international matches to support specific individuals, as was the case when 4,000 Wolves' fans journeyed to Wembley to cheer on Steve Bull.

The most striking thing about the Premier League saga is that it has demonstrated once again that the FA and the League are incapable of acting in unison. In fact, they appear to be seeking opportunities for confrontation, having fallen out over the bid to bring the 1998 World Cup to England and again over the decision to return to a 22-team First Division. Bill Fox's pathetic performance at the League's press conference, mumbling about how shocked he was, summed up its inactivity. And what has happened to the enigmatic Arthur Sandford, whose arrival as new League secretary was greeted with what now appears to have been naive optimism a few months back? In recent weeks, he has been about as forthcoming as Howard Hughes. We're beginning to wonder how he fills in his days.

The FA, in turn, seem quite prepared to hand over control of the new Premier League to the big clubs, given that their blueprint calls for each of the 18 member clubs to get a seat on the management committee of the new League. However, now that the splutters of outrage have subsided, the two bodies must get together and try to thrash out a compromise proposal that can be satisfactory to all concerned. Both groups have things to be gained from working together. If they are incapable of finding common purpose, the new 'atmosphere' surrounding English football, aided by the end of Thatcher's reign, will dissipate.

Although the remainder of the League may be justifiably suspicious of the motives of the bigger clubs, it would not be in their interest to be intransigently opposed to restructuring. In 1988, the FA were opposed to a 'Super League' and were able to threaten dissenting clubs with a ban from the FA Cup and international competitions. This time round, the opponents of reform don't have the same sort of leverage. It is inconceivable that the FA would support a move towards a complete breakaway, but if the bigger clubs are thwarted now, they would only try again in a year or two. To prevent more wrangling in the future, every effort must be made to tie them into a binding agreement now. ○

Least Said Souness Forgotten

After the dust had settled, Graeme Souness' controversial tenure at Ibrox was assessed by Graham McColl.

WSC No 53, July 1991

IF YOU CAN IMAGINE SPENDING FIVE YEARS WITH AN OVERGROWN CHILD clambering about in your attic, then you'll have a fair idea of the impact Graeme Souness has made on Scottish football. Hard to ignore, noisy, and a bit of a character whether you like him or not.

Many were subjected to the Souness verbals at one time or another – from the high hats at UEFA all the way to the tea lady at St Johnstone. Acts of savage brutality became commonplace on Scotland's football pitches. Rangers, and Souness, managed to become even more unpopular – a spectacular feat. Despite all this, his departure for England was an occasion for great sadness. There is no question that Souness is best viewed from the rear while travelling at some speed in the direction of a distant horizon. It's just that he had an opportunity to do great things for the game in Scotland and, on the whole, failed to come up with the goods.

If Souness were to be regarded as simply a glorified public relations officer, then only the most churlish would dispute that his record is flawless. Simply by joining Rangers as player-manager in 1986 he managed to double the crowds immediately. A continuous feed of new signings and pronouncements from Souness kept interest high, particularly for the 20,000 or so souls who, it would appear, had managed to survive without football pre-summer 1986. This could go a long way towards explaining the lengthy periods of silence during matches at Ibrox nowadays: they're still trying to get a hang of the rules.

Certainly, in terms of sponsorship deals and such-like, Rangers have been propelled on to a level previously unknown by any Scottish club. It would have been nice for their followers, and for followers of the game in Scotland, if this could have been matched by a similar jump in playing standards. However, once all the cash has been counted, and the Rangers team is looked at long and hard, it leaves a lot to be desired. When Souness arrived at Ibrox, it was mostly kick and rush stuff which he managed to replace with the slow build-up from the back. Unfortunately, this was also accompanied by a slow build-up from the front.

Like most people, Souness seemed to realise that winning the Scottish League whilst paying out massive transfer fees and inflated salaries was small beer. Soon after arriving at Ibrox he gallantly insisted that he be judged on his record in Europe. Oh well, if you insist, Graeme.

His fifth season in charge saw yet another brave tilt at the European Cup. Rangers' efforts at cutting through the Red Star defence were as crude as any employed under Souness' predecessor, Jock Wallace – a man who appeared to build his teams with reference to First World War military texts.

Sadly, all five of Rangers' European ventures under Souness collapsed as soon as they met semi-competent opposition. Still, Rangers always went out with some style. A bad-tempered tussle with Borussia Mönchengladbach saw Davie Cooper sent off. A bad-tempered tussle with Cologne saw Ally McCoist sent off. A bad-tempered tussle with Steaua Bucharest saw Souness himself reach a zenith in a career devoted to taking opponents 'out', with what appeared to be an attempt to amputate Rotariu's leg above the knee using only studs and willpower.

It is difficult to see how Souness, for all his European experience with Liverpool and in Italy, has upgraded Rangers' reputation on the continent.

They have won the Premier League consistently but it's usually been a painful process. The 1990-91 season was no different, as Rangers stumbled towards the title with all the elegance and panache of Rab C Nesbitt demolishing a fish supper after closing time. Whenever those little European stumbles happened, Souness would usually harp on about the standard of play in Scotland hindering his side's chances of developing a sophisticated, continental mode of play. The likes of Terry Hurlock and Gary Stevens were being knocked out of their stylish stride by the unsophisticated tartan rabble who didn't know how to treat such distinguished guests.

On his arrival at Ibrox, millions of pounds were placed at Souness' disposal. A club which had regularly lost players to the South was about to become one of the biggest paymasters in the UK, to the point where they had the best-paid footballer in Britain by 1991. They had the most modern stadium in Britain, frequently one-quarter full for matches before his arrival, but which became magically full when his name was breathed.

Most significantly, the team had been a shambles for the best part of a decade. Five years later, Rangers face Celtic in the Scottish Cup. Resembling a park side, Rangers are outfought by a Celtic team so poor their manager would be unceremoniously sacked two months later. To top it off, Rangers became the first side since the hackers of Atletico Madrid in 1974 to have three players sent off at Parkhead. The following week, another Rangers player is sent off against the same opponents in a league match.

Again, they were comprehensively beaten. It suddenly seemed as though nothing had changed in five years. Souness was rich when he arrived at Ibrox. His livelihood didn't really depend on Rangers' results. Swamped with money to spend on big-name players, he never needed to develop a keen managerial eye and when things got difficult, he was not under pressure to analyse the team's tactics. All he had to do was dip into the considerable funds made available to him.

It seems strange that, having spent £17 million on players, Souness should have been unable to impose a particular style on a league where most of his rivals are restricted to budgets which were strictly Third World in comparison. Of the many Englishmen who arrived at Ibrox, only a few could really do tricks: Mark Walters, Trevor Steven and Ray Wilkins. Most of the Anglo signings were simply big, strong and fit with little else to recommend them.

In overlooking Scottish players Souness did at least encourage his competitors to do the same. As a result almost every Scottish Premier

Division club now has at least one exotic continental in their line-up. This would have been unimaginable just a few years ago, and for that Scottish punters should be genuinely grateful to Souness.

Just before leaving in a cloud of dust, Souness made a stream of mysterious comments which conveyed little apart from the fact that he was seething inwardly.

Things had happened which convinced him he had reached the limit of what he could do at the club. He seemed convinced that certain people were determined to give Rangers less than a fair deal, saying: "I feel I have gone as far as I'll be allowed to go." He declined to say any more in case it got him into trouble. To those unschooled in Souness' ways, this could have seemed like creeping paranoia. Either that or he was about to set himself up in a lucrative sideline making up clues for cryptic crosswords. At Liverpool he is surely beyond the clutches of the Scottish football authorities and he should be encouraged to speak out directly.

If, for example, the recent Scottish League reconstruction was a motivating factor in his leaving, it might be instructive to those who voted through this change if he were to say so. After all, the reconstruction came about almost as a direct result of Souness' spell in charge at Ibrox.

After he arrived, the Premier Division became the only place to be, the place where the money was. Clubs in the First Division developed full-time staffs and attracted medium-sized star players as they attempted to muscle their way into the top division. Excitement and crowds grew and for most of the 1990-91 season the First Division was far more interesting than the Premier.

That wasn't enough for certain club chairmen, though. At a stroke they managed to devalue both divisions by increasing the Premier by two teams and eight fixtures a year. If Souness were to declare this to have been a major factor in him leaving, he would be doing the Scottish game another service.

The grief with which the Rangers chairman greeted his manager's departure suggested that he thought Souness had done a fine job. Certainly, Rangers have attracted the levels of support necessary to compete in this European League they feel they should be part of. But as far as the football is concerned – it had everything Souness had as a player, except for the style. ○

Beaten Hearts

Knowing that you support the twelfth best team in Scotland would be enough to drive anyone to tears. Roddy McDougall was no exception.

WSC No 55, September 1991

I'VE NOTHING AGAINST MOTHERWELL. I DON'T BEGRUDGE THEM THEIR Scottish Cup victory at all – especially as they hadn't won anything since 1952. It's just that it made me sad and a little envious .

You see, in winning at Hampden in May, Motherwell have, in my eyes, joined a select group of Scottish teams who all have one thing in common. There are eleven of them: Celtic, Rangers, Hibs, Aberdeen, Dundee, Dundee United, Dunfermline, Motherwell, St Mirren, Kilmarnock and, for heaven's sake, even Partick Thistle.

And what dark secret do they all share? Most, if not all of the big names in Scottish football are there. But look again and you'll see that one club traditionally numbered among the Scottish elite isn't: Hearts. And therein lies the answer. All eleven clubs have managed to win either the championship, the Scottish Cup or the Scottish League Cup during the last 29 years. Hearts haven't. Not since 1962, when they beat Kilmarnock 1-0 in the League Cup Final, have maroon and white ribbons adorned anything worthwhile in the world of Scottish football.

And before you pedants write in, I haven't forgotten us winning the First Division championship at Arbroath, or taking the Tennents Sixes in 1985 and 1991, all of which are listed in the 'honours' section of the official programme. They don't count. We may be getting desperate, but Hearts' fans aren't at the stage when we'll demand that the victorious Sixes squads clamber aboard an open-topped bus and wave to us along Princes Street. Not yet, anyway.

But, I hear you say, Hearts are a big club, one which is always mentioned whenever there's talk about a breakaway British League. And one which has its fair share of European campaigns and Hampden semi-finals and finals. So why not be content with that? After all, it's a position that many clubs, even some of those in that group of eleven at the beginning, would gladly be in today. Except, of course, that it's the expectation that comes with being a big club that makes Hearts' record such a sorry one. And which leaves many supporters misty-eyed when the Scottish Cup is paraded round places like Paisley and Motherwell.

Over the 24 years of what has become an increasingly masochistic pastime, I've often wondered whether it's better to have won the League Cup, for example, and then been relegated in consecutive seasons, or never to have won the League Cup at all but to have remained on a fairly even keel? In the end, I suspect, it's irrelevant. Once we've started supporting a club, for whatever reasons, we don't change just because our lot are incapable of winning anything. If you'd come up to me when I was at my first Hearts game in 1967 and told me they'd win bugger-all for at least the next 24 years, I'd probably have burst into tears, being a fairly sensitive seven year-old who'd been told not to talk to strangers, but it wouldn't have made me support anyone else.

In more philosophical moments, I've consoled myself with the thought that Hearts aren't alone. Look at Sheffield Wednesday, I'd think. Big club, large support, no trophies since 1935 – a full-scale drought which makes ours look like an overnight hosepipe ban. Except they won the Littlewoods Cup this year. Then there was Tom McKean, the Scottish middle-distance athlete whose ability to perform spectacularly badly on big occasions prevented him taking any top individual titles. Perhaps Hearts were football's equivalent. Except this one went out of the window in the summer of 1990 when McKean finally won the European Championship 800 metres. And there was also consolation, of sorts, in The Clash. A big name who had never troubled the people who compile the Top Ten despite releasing umpteen singles. Except, of course, the re-release of *Should I Stay Or Should I Go* meant the end of this one, too. Consolation from outside has gone. Are we alone after all?

Don't get me wrong, I'm not looking for sympathy. Hearts' position at the moment, despite their precarious financial state, is actually better than at many times in recent history. The late Sixties and early Seventies saw mediocre teams at Tynecastle which, had it not been for Jim Cruickshank in goal and Donald Ford at centre-forward, would have seen us relegated for the first time long before the trap-door finally opened in 1977. During that period we suffered the ignominy of a 7-0 defeat on New Year's Day by Hibs, made even worse by Hearts' fans chanting "Easy, Easy" at the Hibbies after an encouraging first ten minutes. This was later broadcast during BBC Scotland's evening highlights to further compound our embarrassment.

Between 1977 and 1983, we yo-yoed between the Premier and the First, with some of the worst players ever to wear a maroon jersey making appearances. The nadir was undoubtedly 1982 when, challenging for promotion, we lost 5-2 at home to Dumbarton and faced the final two matches with a long list of players out because of injury or suspension. As a result, we had to re-sign a player who'd been released earlier that season and who was then playing in the pressure-pot of the Edinburgh Midweek League for the Bank of Scotland. Not surprisingly, we didn't go up.

We did in 1983 and, since then, have generally hovered around the top half of the Premier League without – apart from the famous 'double' season of 1985-86 ever really threatening to win it. Our own version of Dundee United's 'Hampden hoodoo' has seen us produce some of our worst performances there. In fact, we have only beaten Morton, Dumbarton and Dundee United in eleven appearances at the so-called national stadium. In Europe, we got as far as the quarter-finals of the UEFA Cup before going out gamely to Bayern Munich.

We did have some pretty tough luck in 1987, though. According to the recently-published *Ten of Hearts* – the official history of Hearts from 1980 to 1990 – we lost to Dukla Prague on 'goal difference', possibly the only team ever to have been eliminated under a rule normally only applied to league competition.

Ah, goal difference! What a large part it's played in Hearts' misfortune in recent times. In 1965, we faced Kilmarnock on the last day of the season in a head-to-head contest for the title. Anything better than a 2-0 defeat would leave us champions. With a certain inevitability that would be echoed 21 years later, we lost by exactly 2-0, thereby losing the title on goal average. Had goal difference been used to settle the tie, then Hearts would have won. On Hearts' prompting, the Scottish League agreed to use goal difference to settle such situations in the future. This wasn't needed until the final day of the 1985-86 season, when, with uncanny coincidence, Celtic pipped Hearts to the title, on goal difference. Had goal average still been in operation, then, you guessed it, Hearts would have been champions.

Those last few weeks of the 'double-that-never-was' season still come back to Hearts fans like a bad curry. The side wasn't a great one. It was a team with a decent blend of youth and experience, many of whom were playing to the best of their abilities that season. They gained confidence from an unbeaten run that started at the beginning of October and continued, almost but not quite, to the end of the season, 31 matches in total.

The fans were confident, too. I can remember leaving the ground at the end of our penultimate league game against Clydebank and saying that I hoped Celtic managed to beat Motherwell in midweek because, having waited so long to win something, I didn't want the anti-climax of winning it and not being at a match. Even on the morning of the Dundee match, when Celtic had to win by four goals and hope that the unthinkable happened and we lost for the first time in seven months, we were confident. The parties were organised.

It was only when Celtic started running amok against St Mirren that doubts began to surface. As the famous 'tyranny men' passed on the ominous news of four Celtic goals by half-time, you could sense the nervousness begin to spread out from the fans onto the park. But as long as we held on at 0-0 we were champions. With seven minutes to go, Dundee's Albert Kidd hooked in a shot, that still, on the odd occasion I've forced myself to watch it, enters the net in the slowest of slow-motions. His second didn't really matter, as Celtic were by this time winning 5-0. We were sunk and they were champions.

I will never forget the sight that greeted me as I stumbled out of Dens Park before the final whistle that afternoon (masochism does have its limits, you know). Hearts fans were lying on car bonnets, in front gardens, against garden walls or bus shelters, seemingly unable to move or even talk coherently. It was as if a cloud of nerve gas had suddenly descended on the area, resulting in a massive communal muscle seizure affecting all those wearing an item of maroon. There was an old woman who had just done her shopping picking her way among the inconsolable mass of Hearts support, looking quite bewildered by the whole thing.

That night was one of the most miserable I have ever had. The following morning, Hearts' fans by the dozen phoned into Radio Forth's open-line, commiserating with the players, saying they were still behind them and they should pick themselves up for the Cup final the following week. A Hibs fan phoned in as well and I remember thinking: this is such a national tragedy that even our traditional enemies have been touched by the occasion. What a poignant moment in Scottish football. This moment was somewhat spoiled by the Hibbie going on to say that he'd been listening to the Hearts game and wanted to say something about Hearts' misfortune: namely that it had been the happiest day of his life.

Of course, the following week, we blew the Cup final against Aberdeen and another opportunity was lost. Since then we've not had a sniff of a trophy – though leading Celtic 1-0 with two minutes to go in a Hampden semi-final and still getting beaten 2-1 is surely deserving of some *hara-kari* honour.

Now into my 25th year of supporting Hearts, I do actually have serious doubts that I'll ever see them win anything. It would be nice to think that a trophy is just around the corner. If only on the 'Buggin's turn' scenario, we must be due something soon. Or perhaps St Johnstone, Falkirk and Airdrie are ahead of us in that particular queue... ○

Postscript: Airdrie (twice) and Falkirk have lost in finals since, but Raith Rovers came through the pack to take the 1995 League Cup final. Hearts are still waiting.

Private Hull

No-one has yet managed to break the code of silence that exists on Staircase Y, in the West Stand of Boothferry Park. One brave soul tried and failed, as Chris Herman recalled.

WSC No 56, October 1991

AN UNUSUAL THING HAPPENED AT BOOTHFERRY PARK, HULL, ONE SATURDAY afternoon last season. No, don't tell me – more than 5,000 people turned up? Hull retained their manager after the game? The 90 minutes passed without a single Hull supporter mentioning the name Ken Wagstaff? Nothing quite so improbable, of course. But in its way the actual incident was more sinister, more shocking and more profound: somebody in the 'Best' stand actually became emotional enough to get out of his seat and shout.

I should perhaps explain to the 99.9 per cent of readers who are not veterans of Staircase Y of the West Stand at Boothferry Park that it is not a place for loudmouths. Well, it's not actually a place for mouths at all. Until that fateful Saturday, nobody in there had raised their voice much above a confidential whisper (usually "They're going down, you know") since, well, Ken Wagstaff put City two up in an FA Cup quarter-final against Stoke in 1971. It is, rather, a place of peace. A quiet haven for unfortunate souls, where watching a uniquely underachieving football team as it drifts down the divisions has a special charm all of its own. The atmosphere is a heady cocktail of boredom, disbelief, mild amusement and seemingly endless tolerance. To have a seat in Staircase Y (or, these days, a whole row) you must accept the rules of the house. As our regular steward warns any unfamiliar face who wanders unknowingly in – "If you want to whinge and complain, go and sit in Staircase Z. If you want to watch the football and get all excited, go and stand on the terraces."

But back to that Saturday. If my memory serves me right, City had just gone 5-1 behind in a Cup match to a Notts County side that looked frankly world class to me. Mind you, I did have my head buried in the new Jackie Collins (the book, that is), and couldn't swear to catching all their goals. It must have been the fifth, though, because my brother had just completed the 'concise' crossword in the *Guardian*, and it usually takes him just over the hour. Well, we were just admiring for the umpteenth time the handiwork of the rather unusual young man who sits, and knits, to our left – you can't miss him, whatever the weather he wears a pair of his own rather fetching black and amber mittens with 'Wagstaff' sewn into the cuffs – when the bombshell struck.

A middle-aged man rose slowly from his seat about five rows in front of us. This in itself prompted several regulars to glance at their watches and mutter, "Is it that time already?" and "He won't get a Bovril now, surely?" As the man gathered himself to his full height, we all recognised him. He had once amused the whole staircase with rather a good George Formby impression during a four-goal capitulation to Middlesbrough. My, how we had laughed. But now his face was a rather alarming purple, his eyes were bulging and both his arms had started to flap uncontrollably. Someone said, "Oh look, he's doing his George Formby again". As a result he had our undivided attention, thus causing us to miss Hull's consolation second goal. I think the man saw it, but it did not put him off his stroke. With a supreme effort he brought his arms under control, pointed one of them at the pitch, and opened his mouth.

For what seemed an age, he stood there open-mouthed, arm outstretched. I glanced behind me. The whole staircase seemed to be in a state of shock. Husbands covered the ears of wives. Mothers covered the ears of sons. I covered the ears of my brother (aged 38). For it seemed certain that the impossible was about to happen – finally, somebody was going to complain, to give vent to emotions bottled up for season after season, to rant and rave against the fortnightly humiliation. Staircase Y would never be the same again. The spell would be shattered. But wait.

The tension was broken, ironically, by something that happened on the pitch. A Hull midfielder, in seeking to execute a simple square pass in the centre circle, inexplicably struck a wildly overhit ball which threatened to take the head off the City substitute, who was doing half-hearted warming-up exercises on the touchline. At the last moment, the sub looked up, nonchalantly took the crazily veering ball on his chest, and killed it stone dead. He allowed it to drop, under perfect control, onto his right instep. From there, in a majestic display of footballing skills not seen from the home team at Boothferry since Wagstaff's 'slim' period, he flicked the ball to his forehead and nodded it a couple of times before handing it to an unimpressed Notts player for the throw-in. To wild applause, he resumed pretending to touch his toes.

As the ovation died reluctantly away, the middle-aged man looked around him in desperation. Criticism in the face of such wizardry was clearly unthinkable. But he had to do something. Finally, he found voice. "That's the spirit, City. Come on you Tigers!" he cried, loyally, and sat down. Waves of relief washed over the whole staircase. All right, he had shouted. But he had not complained. It could have been a lot worse. Sheepish grins were exchanged. Books, knitting, newspapers were taken up once more. It had been a genuinely nasty moment, but it had passed. The rest of us could resume our unquestioning, silent vigil. We could go on handling our grief in our own private ways. One of us had almost cracked, but we would forgive him. ○

Flaming the Fans

Lance Bellers explained why Millwall's keenness to appear on TV had a disastrous, long term effect on the club's image.

WSC No 56, October 1992 – If Only...

MILLWALL CAN BOAST THREE MAJOR 'IF ONLYS...' SINCE THE DAYS OF POSSEE and Weller. If only Leyton Orient had beaten Birmingham in 1972 the Lions would have graced the First Division and undoubtedly been The Team of the Seventies. If Only Millwall had kept their heads for those astonishing seven minutes at Brighton last season. And If Only there hadn't been a firemen's strike on November 14th 1977...

The BBC's *Panorama* were scouting around for a likely documentary on football hooligans. They found a certain degree of resistance. Several big clubs turned shy at the thought of bad PR and bad karma all round.

But not, of course, Millwall FC.

Gordon Jago, the manager at the time, welcomed the TV cameras, confident that the previously unruly fans had calmed down and that the BBC would present a balanced view of the club. At the end of the programme, a slot was allocated to present the positive community-based side of the club that Millwall so proudly continue into the 1990s.

At the eleventh hour a national firemen's strike flared up. Millwall's right-to-reply on *Panorama* was booted into touch to make way for a report on the boys in the yellow helmets. The result was a major public image own goal for the Lions.

The hooligan documentary itself re-inforced every prejudice that existed at the time against the common football fan. Long hair, big boots and limited IQs. And it was spiced up with some extraordinary anti-heroes in the guise of Harry the Dog of F-Troop and the cheerful lads in their 'treatment' masks. People who had previously amused themselves with these silly games suddenly took it all seriously.

A full five years later I found myself to be the only Millwall-supporting student at Coventry Polytechnic, witness to a violent sub-culture that had built up around video UVC 316 – number one in the Poly library's video chart for years. The *Panorama* programme had been added to the section for Social Sciences, and boy, had students done some studying. People knew the entire dialogue off by heart (as if afflicted by the same disease as fans of the *Rocky Horror Show*) and it was commonplace at most parties to find Rotherham and QPR supporters miming out the most obscure sections of the programme in an utterly impossible version of charades.

Gordon Jago left soon after the BBC had paid its visit, fed up with the problems on the field and the image nightmare off it. His successor, George Petchey, reasoned that *Panorama* had cost Millwall £1 million in lost gate receipts and sponsorship. And the next time the BBC cameras paid a visit to The Den they recorded scenes of vicious rioting as Millwall lost narrowly (6-1) to Ipswich in the sixth round of the FA Cup. Could these visits by Auntie Beeb be in any way connected? I think we should be told... ○

Cape of Good Hope

South Africa was agog at the prospect of a return to international competition after the enforced exile of the Apartheid years. John Perlman reported on the turbulent state of the country's football.

WSC No 56, October 1991

FOR PEOPLE ACCUSTOMED TO OPENING THE MORNING PAPER AND READING "WoodsSeamanMartynDixonzzzz..." it's probably difficult to imagine getting excited at the announcement of a national squad. But throughout September, South African football fans and players will be talking about nothing else.

You see, we've never really had one before. There have been representative sides – President's XI v League XI, that sort of thing – and 'national' teams that played against Tottenham and others in the 1960s. But you had to be white to play in those. And we did play against Rhodesia in the late 1970s, when no one else in the world would share a pitch with either of us.

Next week, national coach Geoff Butler – a former Football League defender – will select his first party of 24. Over the next month, he will shuffle the pack a bit, calling up new players and resting others for training sessions on the first two days of every week.

On the fourth Monday of September, Butler should be able to walk up to his charges and say: "OK boys, we're in." At the same time, a delegation of officials will be winging their way back from Cairo with membership of the Confederation of African Football secured. That means a November date for our first ever real international, almost certainly against Cameroon, and a place for our clubs in the African Champions' and Cup-Winners' Cups. Hopefully it means a place in the December draw for the 1994 World Cup, even though FIFA – which expelled white South Africa in 1976 – will only ratify CAF's decision next March.

South African soccer's exclusion from the world game has generally had the support of the game's administrators, players and fans, and attempts to organise rebel tours usually ran into political opposition – for a first-hand account, ring Jimmy Hill. Black players always say this was a sacrifice they were prepared to make. "There were people who died during this time," says Mike Ntombela, a skilful left-back who four years ago would have captained a national team. "What I did wasn't much."

But as the national squad gathers for the first time, a couple of extraordinary talents for whom the changes came just too late will surely feel a pang. There was Patrick 'Ace' Ntsoelengoe, a smooth-moving brooding midfielder who could pass like he was fitted with radar, and Nelson 'Botsotso' Dladla, the nimblest of wingers – Botsotso is township slang for drainpipe trousers which is what Dladla's legs resembled. Dladla could reduce defences to shreds and stadia to helpless laughter with his dribbling.

The late Seventies and Eighties were their golden years. At least the greatest South African player of that era, striker Jomo Sono, will still play a part in the international future. Sono plays occasional games, the fact that he now resembles George Foreman being offset by the fact that he owns a team. But nobody in South Africa has a shrewder eye for talent – Roy Wegerle had a spell at his club, Jomo Cosmos. He will start as Butler's assistant and will probably end up in charge.

The sight of Sono at the first training camp will do more than just remind the 24 young hopefuls of how precious their opportunity is. It should also call to mind the very best traditions of South African soccer: the verve and dash of Sono, Ntsoelengoe and Dladla, the players whose names they took on as youngsters in countless games on township streets.

Ironically, South African soccer will need a strong whiff of nostalgia as it steps out into the world. The game is currently low on self-esteem and wracked with problems. The most obvious of these are in administration.

South Africa's 'Mr Soccer' used to be Abdul Bhamjee, the National Soccer League's public relations officer, a man whose taste in gold jewellery made Ron Atkinson look ascetic. Bhamjee was to gold watches what Imelda Marcos was to shoes. He would direct a torrent of words at anyone who looked vaguely in his direction – potential sponsors, journalists, passers-by – a mixture of stock expressions like "world-first" and "blockbuster", and phrases that nobody had ever heard before, like "all over the bar shouting".

All over the bar shouting – that is where a lot of other soccer officials were while Bhamjee blustered and bustled. He wasn't just South African soccer's praise-singer. He managed to secure massive sponsorship for a sport that had hitherto lived on scraps. He was the fuel behind a dream that led to the building of soccer's first real home, an 80,000-seater ground on the edge of Soweto. The days of bowing and scraping to government officials for a place to play were past.

But Bhamjee, it seems, is history, too. Last month he was arrested and charged with fraud totalling R7.4 million, all of it soccer-related. The league's general manager, Cyril Kobus (a man who would say, "Notification will be by means of human performance emanating from the GM's office," instead of "My secretary will call you"), was arraigned on similar charges soon afterwards.

Others have stepped into the gap, but it's been a real body blow, coinciding as it does with real decline on the pitch. The fans have simply stopped coming – three years ago, upwards of 90,000 would pack into a stadium for cup ties, often staged as double headers with two matches on a day. No more.

There is no single reason for the fall-off. Money in the townships is tighter than ever, so a fan who sees three dreary matches in a row starts picking his games. Add in the fact that he can see two local games on TV, plus a Sunday night highlights package, plus Everton v Aston Villa on Saturday, plus Inter Milan v Sampdoria on Sunday (both live), plus highlights of Italian, Portuguese and Spanish first divisions midweek: the local game needs to be a lot more compelling than it is.

The plunge in playing standards has been coming for some time. For a start a first division of 24 teams is way too big. Good players in poor teams lay off passes to team-mates who are yards and seconds behind and eventually stop bothering. Good players in good teams come up against hackers in empty stadiums and don't bother much, either.

The game has become hopelessly regionalised around Johannesburg with the big Durban clubs, Amazulu and Bush Bucks, crumbling around administrative incompetence. The same thing's happening in Bloemfontein, where the local team, Celtic, were playing the country's best football two years ago. There is a dearth of decent coaching – the same mediocre bunch have been playing musical chairs for years. And the season which runs from mid-January to the end of November, with four knock-out cups, is way too long. Add in the fact that players are unorganised and hopelessly exploited and it's a bit of a mess.

But enough of the bad and the ugly – South African soccer is still possessed of riches. For a start, the game is played everywhere and by everyone, and we will never have to lament the death of the street game, because it isn't going to die. The poorest rural villages will still find money for jerseys, split poles for posts, a truck with sagging axles for away games.

Where else would you see an amateur cup game between Sheffield Sunday and Argentina? We have Ashton Villa, Brains Milan and Rainbow Juventus. We have Oscar Hotspurs, Kelvinator Arsenals and Pele Utd Brothers. We have AC Gullit Stars, and they are just a netball team. Soccer here, for all its crooked referees, one-eyed supporters and whip-swishing security guards, is still incredible fun.

But that doesn't means the fans won't expect Butler and his men to approach their tasks with deadly earnest. Italia '90, the first World Cup ever televised here, left fans in no doubt of the mountains we still have to climb, not least in Africa against teams like Cameroon. It was a timely dose of reality. The fans still save their wildest cheers for the guy who beats an opponent then beats him again for good measure. But the players have a better idea of how little time and space there is at the top.

The choice of Butler as coach is surprising. For some time there has been antipathy shown towards English coaches, whose methods some see as contributing to the de-skilling of the South African game. But Butler has been in charge of the country's biggest team, Kaizer Chiefs, and taken them to a cupboard of trophies, mixing attractive short-passing football in midfield with speed and ruthlessness on the break.

He has coached in Zambia and in Egypt, where he took club side National to the African Champions' Cup. He has credibility and popular support. Most of all, he clearly believes in the skill of South African players. His task will be to teach them teamwork, patience and tactics, without encouraging them to be too cautious and scared to strut their special stuff.

Butler has some marvellous players with which to work. To name but four: Zane Moosa, 23, is a fleet-footed midfielder with league champions Mamelodi Sundowns, possessed of extravagant ball skills. Sundowns were playing Soweto giants Moroka Swallows at the end of the season and needed a point to clinch the title. With ten minutes to go and his team just holding out, Moosa suddenly stood on the ball. First he flipped his arms at the fans of Swallows, known as the Birds. Then he turned to the Sundowns fans, whose slogan is 'The Sky is the Limit', and pointed at the sky, still on the ball like a footballing Billy Graham. The place went mad; Butler might string him up for that.

Then there is Phil 'Chippa' Masinga, 20, a tall lean striker who plays for Sono at Jomo Cosmos. He started the year with seven goals in three games including two hat-tricks, then missed a chunk with injury. In his last three games he has scored seven more. He is strong, quick on the turn and scores with a mix of bicycle kicks and headers.

August Makalaklane, 26 this month, is another from the Cosmos stable, who is currently playing in Switzerland for FC Zurich. He plays wide in midfield, and his great skill, pace and international experience – which is more than any of his team-mates have had – will certainly count.

And lastly, lest it seem that we will field five in midfield and five up front, there is Lucas Radebe. At 20, Radebe, a sweeper, has the sureness on the ball of a redirected midfielder. He's fast and tall, strong in the tackle and in the air.

When they run out in South African soccer's colours of gold, black and white on that November afternoon, many a cheer will first have to get past a lump in the throat. Will Radebe be good enough to keep Cameroon out? Will Moosa and Masinga get through at the other end? I haven't the faintest idea. But we're going to have the time of our lives finding out. ○

School Daze

Have you received personal coaching tuition from one of British football's major personalities? Neither has Andy Korman. But he did get to meet Ian St John.

WSC No 57, November 1991

"But be not afraid of greatness: some men are born great, some achieve greatness, and some have greatness thrust upon them (though not many attend the Bobby Moore Soccer Skills Coaching School)."
                                                            Shakespeare, *Twelfth Night.*

MANY YEARS AGO, MY GRANDAD DECIDED THAT £30 WAS A SMALL PRICE TO PAY to keep me out of what was left of his thinning hair for one week of the school holidays. He booked me into the Liverpool branch of the Bobby Moore Soccer Skills Coaching School. A green and callow youth of some eleven summers, I nevertheless convinced my mother that I was sufficiently mature to take the 18c bus two stops to the ground on my own without being arrested, molested, or seduced by the delights of cigarettes and drink.

On arriving, I discovered several huge piles of bibs and cones, no doubt left over from the mother of all cycling proficiency tests, and some footballs made from genuine imitation leather, ie real plastic. I also discovered that my bunch of skinny kids was to be coached by an amiable Jocko short-arse by the name of Ian St John. Some poor sods in another group were being yelled at by Ron Yeats, a man with a face so red and belligerent it looked like his neck was exploding.

Warming up consisted of a raggedy trot round the pitch's perimeter, while St John tested out the alignment of the goal posts by leaning against them. As the temperature was only just into the 90s, we were obviously in need of increasing our body heat, but I was secretly rather pleased not to be in the care of Yeats, who was leading his lads out of the gate, heading for Speke.

Over the next few days, St John earned his money by husbanding his energy and inventing nicknames for us all. Stretching his imagination to the limit, he came up with 'Hafnia man' for me, no doubt inspired by the name of the Danish canned meats company emblazoned across the Everton shirt on my chest in letters three inches high. I had earlier silenced the derision this kit had caused in my fellow students, bedecked in the favours of Liverpool, Real Madrid, Brazil etc, by claiming that I didn't actually support Everton but Andy King was my uncle. (This blatant lie has tormented me ever since, and convinced me that the team's total lack of success for the following seven years was divine retribution. Lads, I'm sorry.)

We did, however, find time to smooth the rough edges of our footballing ability and, in fairness, have an all round good laugh. The one black spot occurred when a 'professional referee' (sic), one N Midgeley, came to give us a talk. When he offered to clear up any area of the rules that confused us, I asked him why Joe Corrigan was booked for pacing out the distance to the penalty spot on that muddy pitch. He told me that was a stupid question. I bet he didn't know.

When Friday arrived, we were obliged to pass aptitude tests in the skills our coach had taught us, such as shooting, heading, tackling and the like. Since there was, apparently, no category which involved sitting around in the centre circle lying about what a good player you were in the Sixties, I feared that even the bronzest of awards would be beyond me and I would have to settle for a career with Lincoln City rather than Inter Milan.

Luckily, Uncle Ian was to be our examiner, and he brought all the zeal of his old teaching to this new task.

Shooting was first. From a distance of 20 yards, each student was required to hit the target with at least five shots from ten attempts. Positioned barely outside the six-yard box, we timorously side-footed the ball along the ground towards an unguarded goal. Even when we missed, St John employed all the refereeing strictness of John Virgo in Big Break. Yeats' lads, performing ostensibly the same exercise, were somewhere near the centre circle peppering a hockey goal defended by Big Ron himself. While our chipping test degenerated into an orgy of carting the ball over the bar as hard as we could (sometimes, I am ashamed to say, out of our hands), the Yeats elite had to make the thing spin backwards on landing.

I passed these trials easily. As one of the abler traffic cones could have done the same this was little to shout about, but I did manage to partner the best player in the one-two exercise. Since the Saint had described this lad as "the new Peter Ward" (which, looking back, must have been some sort of compliment, I suppose), I raced through and on to the next problem, heading.

This was, and always has been, my footballing Room 101. I would now be required to score a few goals, as opposed to glaring at the ball in fearful anticipation before performing the complicated feat of jumping out of the ball's way while appearing to hurl myself towards it. I needn't have worried, however, for our coach had surpassed himself. Not only did we eschew our regular target in favour of a rugby goal, but this in turn was defended by a goalkeeper of quite alarming brevity of stature. His shirt sported the legend 'Sefton Boys AFC', and indeed he may have represented his district, but only if Subbuteo had marketed a .00 scale replica of the team.

In the final exercise, St John tackled with all the animal ferocity of Duncan Mackenzie, while one youth was seen running away from a guffawing Yeats, tears streaming down his bloodstained face, and issuing empty threats involving his big brother.

I graduated, then, with a certificate and octagonal patch, each bearing a somewhat Cubist representation of Bobby Moore, a sun-tan that made me look like I was wearing a white T-shirt when I got into the bath and an enduring incapacity to beat a goalkeeper from outside the penalty area.

One moment from this week of what may loosely be termed 'coaching' has provided me with years of undiminished pleasure. Each

Saturday lunch time during the football season, I tune into ITV with the quiet satisfaction that the cheeky Scottish imp playing straight man to Jimmy Greaves was once smacked squarely in the testicles by one of my free kicks. ○

Something Slightly Amis

Bill Buford wrote a celebrated book about his experiences of football hooliganism, Among The Thugs. He was very pleased with it and so was his chum, Martin Amis. Ed Horton thought they were both wrong.

WSC No 58, December 1991

I WAS GOING TO REVIEW BILL BUFORD'S *AMONG THE THUGS* FOR *WSC*. THIS is, apparently, an account of how the editor of the literary magazine *Granta* spent some time hanging out with the least acceptable elements of Man United's support, seeing at first hand all sorts of exciting thuggery and violence. Slumming it. I decided to give it a miss, though, for three reasons – first, I'd rather spend my £14.99 on a couple of football games; second, who's heard of Bill Buford anyway?; third, the *Independent on Sunday* carried a very interesting review of the book by Martin Amis. And everybody's heard of Martin Amis. Let's talk about Martin instead.

Amis nearly won the Booker Prize this year for his novel *Time's Arrow*, about the Nazis' extermination of the Jews. His earlier *Money* was critical of Margaret Thatcher's money-grabbing ethic when yuppiedom was at its height. He is concerned about nuclear weapons and other important issues. He is no reactionary – in fact it's common to contrast his attitudes with those of his misanthropic old man Kingsley. It's important to realise that if we're going to explain how his review came to be a poisonous display of ignorance and bigotry, aimed at the scum of the earth – you or I, the football fan.

I do not exaggerate. Get this: "At my last football match, I noticed that the fans all had the complexion and the body-scent of a cheese-and-onion crisp, and the eyes of pitbulls". If that didn't cause you a sharp intake of breath, see how Amis continues, explaining the motivation of the Crispy One: "What I felt most conclusively, above and below and on every side, was ugliness – and a love of ugliness."

A remarkable way, you may feel, to talk about our passion for the game. Skill? Teamwork? Courage? Character? Pride? Not a whisper of these in Amis's review. He comes up with a different list entirely. Do you stand in the Shed in Stamford Bridge? Well then, this is you: "The solid mass of swearing, sweating, retching, belching sub-humanity."

This is truly offensive stuff. When writing about football hooliganism, or any other area where a small proportion of otherwise peaceful citizens cause serious trouble (for example inner-city crime) it is considered normal to use terms like 'some' or 'a tiny minority', thus exempting most of the relevant public from your strictures. Amis does not do this – in fact he is careful not to do so. How else to explain "above and below and on every side"? Or "the solid mass of sub-humanity"? This is the authentic voice of prejudice. Even when criticising Buford's ignorance, calling the bar a "post", and 'equalise' "tie the score", he calls these errors "thug solecisms" – that is, football language is thug language. A bigot doesn't care who he offends – in fact he *wants* to offend us, and thus the silly comment about the cheese-and-onion crisps. Or, possibly, he doesn't believe any football fans actually read the *Independent on Sunday*, or not the review pages anyway.

So Amis thinks we're a bunch (a very large bunch) of smelly, vicious beasts. But why are we like that? One might expect the progressive and enlightened author to take pity on us – not for him the Kenneth Baker-like invocation of sin and wickedness. Perhaps we come from broken homes and deprived environments. Not so. Why do young males cause trouble at football, he asks? Answer: because they like it.

He approvingly quotes a character in *The Firm*, who, watching a television sociologist refer to hooliganism as "a search for meaning", responds scathingly: "Why don't he just say we like 'itting people?"

For the purposes of this review it doesn't really matter *what* the causes of football related violence – or any other violence – actually happen to be. We just need to observe that Amis plumps for the *right-wing* explanation. This is where his prejudice leads him – directly away from his habitual, liberal position.

Why? Why should a thoughtful and concerned writer, particularly interested in social issues, adopt such a position when it comes to football? Among the intelligentsia, there are many who are disgusted by the poverty, offended by the racism, sympathetic to the victims of society. There are many fewer who will accept a strike, still fewer a mass picket. What's this got to do with football? *The intelligentsia fear and despise the crowd.* This is a class snobbery: when accusing QPR fans of "a love of ugliness", Amis comments with surprise: "This was in the stands!"

God alone knows what horrors must have been visible on the terraces, then! Amis makes it quite clear that he expects a higher standard of behaviour from the stands. I can think of no reason for this other than the fact that those in the stands, in general, are from a slightly higher social group than those on the terraces. Amis certainly will make this assumption, and attach it to his belief that you can't expect the plebs to behave.

Social concern is fine, but let the masses get involved and they might get out of control. Privileges might be threatened and decisions might be taken by ignorant people *who haven't got degrees.* The intelligentsia, therefore, have terrible difficulty distinguishing the *crowd* from the *mob.* In fact, usually they don't bother. Amis unwittingly makes this clear when, in fishing around for the 'explanations' dismissed above, he suggests Colonel Kurtz in *Apocalypse Now*, who says: "Nothingness is what you find there [in a crowd]." Or, as Amis phrases it himself: "He liked the crowd, and the power, and the loss of self."

For football fans these are crucial ideas. Much of the appeal of football is unimaginable without the crowd. The noise, the passions of the mass, and so on. If we accept Amis' thesis that the crowd *by virtue of its existence* is violent, ignorant and bigoted, then must we abandon football itself as a social evil?

Fortunately, we need not do so, since Amis' nightmare is far from our actual experience. We need not take seriously a theory based on the negation of facts. Bigotry is not in the crowd, but in the distaste for the crowd's components. It would be interesting to know what Salman Rushdie, Amis' literary contemporary, thinks about this, as he writes sympathetically about his native India while observing that you cannot think of India without thinking of the crowd.

Perhaps I shouldn't dismiss the literary crowd so readily. The novelist Julian Barnes is a genuine fan of Leicester City; we all know about Albert Camus. The point remains, though, that because of the intelligentsia's distaste for the ordinary people in numbers, it is possible to find the most offensive attitudes towards football supporters in the most surprising places.

One ludicrous example a few years ago was the television review page of a progressive, 'quality' paper, in a week which featured two programmes about Millwall – one a documentary which interviewed actual, real-life Lions fans, the other a ridiculous play invoking tabloid fantasies of deaths and organised gangs. The function of the 'quality' paper, you might think, is to rise above tabloid fantasies by searching out the truth. But the writer's fear of the mob got the better of him, and he managed to dismiss the documentary, *No-One Likes Us*, while praising *Arrivederci Millwall* as truth! A lovely journalistic self-parody, but still an offensive one.

And yes, Amis brings Millwall into it: "As Buford starts sampling the London grounds, we start re-experiencing their squalid exoticism. 'The Den on Cold Blow Lane opposite the Isle of Dogs.' Now that's really good." Amis could have commented on the attractiveness of The Boleyn Ground, White Hart Lane, Craven Cottage. But he prefers to look for squalor where none exists. How dare this man accuse us of "a love of ugliness".

Just a word about Buford. Apparently he got beaten up in Sardinia, as the riot police attacked football fans with impunity. I wonder if he saw the irony in this? 'Informed' public opinion will not tolerate prejudice against black people, thank God, which is why Ron Noades got the humiliation he deserved. It will not accept discrimination against women. But it still finds it acceptable to brand the readers of *WSC* as sub-humans. This cannot but make it easier to keep us in cages, to make us stand in the rain, to arrest us without good reason, to subject us to body searches... well, you know the rest. But if we're really that bad, don't we deserve it? I hope Buford was delighted as the truncheon descended.

I have learned to get angry about this sort of thing – Hillsborough was a watershed in that respect. Are we serious, that it must never happen again? If we are, then we must understand that Hillsborough wasn't a fluke, it happened for reason, and among those reasons were the attitudes presented with glee by people like Martin Amis. Did you read his review that Sunday, and were you as disgusted as I was? And if you were, did you write to the editor and let him know?

And as for Martin Amis – I suppose we could always not buy his books. He could scarcely complain – he'd probably be surprised that we can read. And look on the bright side, Martin isn't going to football any more: "Every British male, at some time or another, goes to his last football match. It may very well be his first football match."

For many, many football fans, women as well as men – don't let Amis get away with a feminist gloss on his prejudice – the last game they go to is on the Saturday before they die. May this be so for all of us. But if I go to football for another seventy years, it will never be a matter for regret that, of all the strange and ordinary, young and old, mild and dangerous people that I meet, not one of them will ever be the great novelist and bigot, Martin Amis. O

Thugs and Kisses

Everyone was talking about hooliganism as though it were going out of fashion. Always keen for a barney, John Williams assessed the prevailing trends.

WSC No 59, January 1992

NOW, SURELY, IT'S OFFICIAL. THE END OF HISTORY. A CHERUBIC VINCENT JONES, scrubbed and dinner-jacketed, beams down from the yuppily glossy *Esquire* magazine. Can this young squire really be the same man who roared, spat at, and generally slagged opponents for lacking 'bottle'; the man who released his grip on Gascoigne's lower end only to hiss, "Don't move, fat boy, I'll be back"? The same destroyer who vowed to make Chelsea "'orrible", and who, according to this feature, "came to represent all the elements that, pre-Hillsborough, were deemed to be destroying the English game"? In short, asks ace journalist Gordon Burn, fresh from exhuming a neo-fictional Alma Cogan, "is football's psycho a softie?" Vinny, an icon of football's very own 'New Times'?

The evidence is persuasive. Jones turns out these days to be an anti-racist, converted ex-knife carrying terrace troublemaker. According to the Wimbledon Wonder, "whereas it used to be admiration for the geezer doing the steamin' in, now it's 'Look at that prat'." Blimey! Next thing you know, people will be talking about Leeds United getting a creche and a family stand and kicking out the racists... Convincing, or what!

The fact is Vinnie, circa 1988, does seem something of a throwback these days. He was a couple of leg tattoos lighter then, but the Popeye biceps and fiercely bizarre haircut were still a bit of a give-away, and watch him on the video when he retreats to launch the long throw into defensive airspace. He steps back for momentum towards a kind of metal grille which seems to be used for keeping the punters at bay. Seems hard to imagine now, but our major grounds used to look like that. Ugly. Carcereal. Fatally dangerous. A fitting venue for the man's taming of weaker, more talented, opponents, and for the intimidation in the seats and on the terraces from his violently well-dressed mates. If what Steve Redhead in *Football with Attitude* calls the "rebirth of soccer spectatorship" goes back to the post-Heysel explosion of spectator agitation through the FSA and the fanzines, Hillsborough painfully brought the beginning of the end of the brutalising incarceration which led to Popplewell describing English grounds in the 1980s as resembling "mediaeval fortresses". More importantly, perhaps, Hillsborough, and the Taylor Reports which followed, finally brought to the fore the long-overdue debate about modernising the British game.

The positions here were nicely summarised years ago by correspondents to *Foul!* magazine as the struggle between the pleasurably forbidding masculinity of the terraces – "Hitching, getting pissed, shouting, standing, pushing, pissing on your boots or the boy in front's legs" (obviously, good) and the numbing boredom of the seats in the "spotless concrete bowls lined with thousands of little plastic seats, lots of clean toilets, a restaurant, a sports complex" (clearly, bad).

Writing in our recent book, *British Football and Social Change*, Ian Taylor urges fans to see the present moves to seats less as an ineffective anti-hooligan device than as part of a wider programme of radical modernisation for the British game, a move which distinguishes progressives from the inert, reactionary nostalgia of some club administrators – and fans. He's surely right (isn't he?), but that's likely to be cold comfort for those 'traditional' fans who may be forced out by the prohibitive costs of ground modernisation, especially at a time when imaginative and rational ground sharing seems about as popular in Britain as Arsenal's away strip or Sky television. On this, Fynn and Guest's *Heroes and Villains* seems sensibly hard-headed on the European aspirations of both Highbury and White Hart Lane.

Of course, you don't have to buy the story of the metamorphosis of the hoolies into football's 'new wave' (post-modern?) fans – millions of pot-smoking, baggy, blissed-up, Cameroon-supporting, Pat Nevin clones – to realise that something good has been happening inside grounds over the past few years.

The ubiquitous Tony Wilson may be greeted with wild-eyed stares when he claims that the game's hooligan element have become the 'new hippies', and Pete Hooton of The Farm might, himself, be dragged off to the drugs depot for arguing that, in Liverpool, "it isn't the robbers that go to the match anymore. It's about working class culture and that's the beauty of it," but there's no doubt that going to the match has changed. This is one of the reasons why Bill Buford's well-observed, but untimely adventure, *Among The Thugs*, has been so summarily dismissed as a piece of literary opportunism. Mind you, even Buford has to conclude in the end that 'the lads' hearts are just not in it anymore'; they're as likely to end up discussing the new James LP as they are a good ruck at home or among 'the enemy' abroad.

So, what has been going on? The Manchester and music thing has been important, but it has also been overplayed as were the original 'London' origins of the skins and hooliganism. (Has Adrian Sherwood really re-oriented the whole assessment of football, popular music and youth culture? Is this what 'the lads' are into now?) The music/rave/warehouse party scene has been important, too, for rather more prosaic reasons. The loss of Europe to English football cut into the profit around the spectator scene – clothes, tickets, flags and hats, etc. Much of the international stuff on sale in the streets in Italy last year came from above a video shop in Wakefield.

The party economy, by way of contrast, provides opportunities for making serious money for those with the street knowledge and muscle to match. At the same time, inroads by the police into some of the major hooligan firms inevitably had its effects. In the end, it didn't matter that some of the main investigations collapsed, or even that doubts were raised about whether the claimed police infiltrations had actually taken place or not. Ten years (or more) in prison 'for football' was a very serious thing to contemplate, especially when there was still plenty of action elsewhere and without the attendant risks. These days, named hooligan gangs are bad news and high risk.

Added to these effects have been changes to the material and cultural contexts within which the game is played. I have already mentioned the dismantling of the fences and some of the general changes inside grounds. Hooliganism now seems out of place as well as out of order in the game's new future. The post-Italia '90 optimism helped, too, though it must also be said that the Italians found hosting the English little fun and at least part of the 'success' of the venture depended upon draconian restrictions and arbitrary intimidation by the Italian security forces. Maybe, too, we brought back a little more vision about what out new grounds might look like, cash and imagination notwithstanding. The Aston Villa and Manchester United European excursions were also encouraging, but then we didn't always ransack the Continent, even in the 'old times'. Everton fans behaved as blamelessly as Mancunians did in Rotterdam in 1985. Will our London colleagues also, please, note and cooperate?

Of course, the fanzines' and supporters' movements have also played an important role in the contextual shifts which have occurred over the past few years. It seems to me that the fanzines and what they stand for are as close as we are likely to get in this country to the cultural role provided by the Ultras in Spain and in Italy, and the 'Fan clubs' in Germany. At the very least they have challenged, on their own terms, the ageing respectability of some supporters' clubs and the more violent and racist aspects of the hooligan repertoire.

The FSA, particularly in England, has also offered an alternative vision of the game and its future from that proposed by the hooligans (the struggle over the terraces) or by many major clubs (the high spending family audience). In short, the nature of the dialogue and debate around football is no longer obsessed with the struggle between the police and 'the lads'.

The result of all this? Arrests down 30 per cent last season, police forces beginning to talk about getting the balance right between security and safety and about customer service(!), and small signs up and down the country of fledgling democratisation within the game. Talk of fan representation of various kinds from Blackpool to West Ham and 'strange' ideas like a women's committee at Sunderland; courses at the local poly to train stewards in crowd management and opportunities at the University in Liverpool to study something called 'Football Science'. (Vinnie is reputed to be considering an application.)

None of this implies man-fights-man is going to go away too quickly. Those with fewer options are going to have it out whether it's on the Meadow Well or in the Gallowgate End. And the bad boys haven't disappeared, though curiously the press might sometimes give that impression. Finally, we could also be hosting Euro '96, with thousands

of German, Dutch and Italian fans *in situ*. There's big money in security. Don't hold your breath, but big football could be coming this way with all its attendant paraphernalia and continental challenge. Then we'll see how far we've come. ○

Beck to Square One

Potential Premier Leaguers Cambridge United were not widely popular in 1991-92. Godric Smith, however, offered an impassioned defence of John Beck and his likely lads.

WSC No 59, January 1992

THE PINNACLE OF JOHN BECK'S PLAYING CAREER – SELECTION IN THE INFAMOUS 'Revie 80', the huge squad of players called together for a weekend chat with The Don shortly after his appointment as England manager in 1974, was widely held by critics to reflect the declining state of the English game. Safe to say there must be a fair sprinkling of *déja vù* with the family Beck cornflakes as they peruse the morning papers with Cambridge United top of the Second Division for the first time in their history.

United's playing style has now comfortably outstripped Jeremy Beadle and the Poll Tax in the unpopularity stakes. 'It's killing the game', cry the critics, 'It's not football', 'A monstrous carbuncle', 'The boil on the backside of the beautiful game' (sorry, getting a bit carried away). Unsurprisingly, the good folk of Cambridge are paying about as much attention to this as London Underground to its public relations. Better to win without friends rather than lose with elegance, or, as John Beck would say, "Last people don't come nice."

If Steve Harrison is the Roger Mellie of the football world, then John Beck must be the Roger Irrelevant. What do you make of a man who peps his team up with the war cry, "Zigzag to the onion bag"? Tormented genius or a man two sandwiches short of a picnic?

At the Abbey Stadium it's no contest. This man is the psychologist supreme – Mr Maximum Framework of Probability himself. The sudden growth in conspiracy theorists is living testimony. We beat Swindon, according to Micky Hazard, because the grass was too long.

Middlesbrough were dumped out of the FA Cup last season because they were not given any tea at half-time if Colin Todd is to be believed, whilst Reading suffered a similar fate in this year's Rumbelows because they warmed up with balls that were under-pumped. It must be true. Mark McGhee said so.

Cambridge's success surely rests on the fact that they recognise, above all other clubs in the League, that football is a team game. Beck believes in his system and the team believe in him. If they don't, they don't play – simple as that. Consequently, the midfield tackle like Mickey Skinner on acid, the wide men could outrun Ballyregan Bob, and Dublin, Claridge and Taylor do more hounding than the Quorn Hunt.

The riposte to those who carp that a rigid playing pattern strangles individuality and spontaneity is simple. The team that took the field at Ipswich last month (November) contained seven free transfers, one YTS trainee, and three players signed collectively for just over £100,000. The same team could now fetch well over £2 million on the open market, so there must be a vestige of individual talent. I can say with confidence that it won't be long before the likes of Richard Wilkins and Dion Dublin are playing European football either at Cambridge or elsewhere.

Maybe Beck should sign a public relations company. For, as he himself commented, when Glenn Hoddle plays a 60-yard ball out of defence to feet, it's pure genius; when the likes of Danny O'Shea do the same, it's football at its crudest. A straightforward problem of perception. Beck will try anything once to get the team going – cold showers, 'ferret of the week' awards, full-scale training sessions 15 minutes before kick-off, or organised snowball and splatter paint fights in training.

The slogan is a particular favourite. Take the crunch promotion clash with Bolton last Easter. Beck was up at the crack of dawn fly-posting the ground with the legend "Be Bold, Be Brave, Be First". The players couldn't even go to the toilet to escape. The result – a below par United scraped a decisive 2-1 win seemingly on self-belief alone.

It's all a far cry from the days when Cambridge were falling through the divisions breaking all the wrong records as they went. Manager John Ryan drove all the team to Newmarket for a jolly day out – or so they thought. On arrival he told them all to walk the 15 miles back to Cambridge as punishment for yet another inept performance. Mind you, I think Barbara Woodhouse could have trained the team better than the unfortunate Mr Ryan.

In a game where loyalty and integrity are not exactly common currency, Beck is also something of a curiosity. In the close season he turned down

untold riches to go and manage Leicester – a deal which at the time would have made him the best-paid manager in the Second Division by quite some way. Instead he preferred to stay at Cambridge for a considerably slimmer wad.

One reason – simply that he felt there was something at Cambridge which only came along once in a lifetime, and he could not turn down the opportunity to make history by achieving three consecutive promotions. When the news hit the streets there was not a dry eye in the town. And it's a decision which has certainly given him the edge in contract negotiations with the players!

Have no truck with the latest Beck yarn that "we've no chance of promotion to the First Division". It's apparent we've every chance, and the manager knows that better than anyone. If we do, maybe we will finally win the nation's hearts. Because isn't this what football is all about? A team which just seven years ago broke the League record for games without a win (a jaw-dropping 31), a team which just two years ago was bottom of Division Four, playing the likes of Liverpool and Leeds week in and week out. What better proverbial two-finger salute to Graham Kelly and his so-called Super League? ○

Postscript: Cambridge finished fifth and lost 6-1 to Leicester in the play-offs. Wilkins and Dublin never played in Europe – but Steve Claridge did.

Spit and Polish

As Graham Taylor's squad sneaked through to Euro '92, Philip Cornwall reflected on the trials and tribulations of being an England fan abroad.

WSC No 59, January 1992

IT IS A LONG WAY FROM LONDON TO POZNAN. LOOK IT UP ON A MAP TO GET some idea, but for the full effect, may I suggest that you make the journey on a coach? And that at the half-way stage of the four-day round trip, you stand on a bench in a football stadium watching England trail Poland, surrounded by the odd alcoholic, several vandals and a few hundred individuals who react to a chant in support of Jack Charlton's less-than-Fenian Ireland with a swift chorus of "No Surrender To The IRA"?

Following England abroad hurt. Not the cold, the lack of sleep, the hour and a half march from the ground escorted by the runners-up in the 1980s' 'Riot Police of the Decade' championships. But the knowledge that thousands of Poles had their impressions of this country heavily influenced by watching the deliberate destruction of parts of a football ground as a form of celebration.

When England scored, the fellow countryman to my left concentrated not on singing the praises of Lineker, but on standing on his left leg and stamping down with his right on the join between the slats of his bench and the support. In time he succeeded in demolishing his bench and came to share mine. Others broke theirs. Some were foolhardy enough to pick up the planks and whirl them around. The police moved in to remove those within easy reach. But at the end I held my breath as some of those furthest from the visored lines hurled the broken furnishings onto the margins of the pitch. It was hard to tell if the aim was to strike the officials and press gathered in front or just to throw down a sort of 'come and have a go' challenge to the police. The police considered it. They'd have had to plough through the rest of us, though, and thought better of it. Another reason to be grateful for the death of communism, perhaps.

I was probably most outraged by the chants of "Where were you in World War Two?" directed at the Poles. Answer: stuck between Germany and the Soviet Union without 20 miles of water to stop the tanks rolling. There seemed little point in reminding my tormentors that Britain went to war in 1939 in defence of Poland.

On the pitch, of course, we had Messrs Sinton and Gray to follow. As I scanned the team sheet I found it hard to recognise a plan, a system designed to get that vital point. The decision to throw in a couple of dodgy debutants into a match of such importance numbed the mind even more than the cold. Given the team and the nature of the loudest elements in the crowd, I pinned my hopes on a 0-0. I couldn't see them scoring many, and that way we wouldn't have to 'celebrate' any goals. Mabbutt's misfortune left me in a quandary: could I make common cause with those around me whose attitudes to life seemed to be based on a copy of *The Sun* Book of British History that had a few too many pages missing? And was it realistic to expect one of those chances England did create to fall to someone capable of putting it away?

Gary Lineker provided the answer to both questions. If ever I meet him, the first question I'll ask will be whether he finds it embarrassing to hear his name chanted alongside the kind of xenophobic rantings that would have warmed the heart of Sir Oswald Mosley. The second thing will be whether he minded being interviewed on the pitch afterwards while the remaining Polish fans kept up a chant of "Fuck you, Gary, fuck you".

When a Pole went down and stayed down, Gary tried to pull him up, and the referee agreed with him that they should get on with the game. That was the only time he took out his frustration on anyone else, but the lines on his face were like one of those Easter Island statues. While others squandered chances, Gary kept on going. He wanted it so badly. However little the likes of Gray and Sinton deserved success, Lineker, Rocastle, Platt and even Geoff Thomas did not need the humiliation.

Failure to support those players who deserved our cheers would have amounted to surrendering the right to support the side to those 'fans' who do most to tarnish the team's name – even though I could see that their behaviour would probably reach its nadir with an equaliser. It is not Lineker's fault that some of the support regard England's overseas matches as an opportunity to continue the worst excesses of empire. He deserves better. And to me this meant the nearest to positive action that I could manage under the circumstances.

Swing Low, Sweet Chariot, however nauseating you might find the sudden popularity of a rugby song, is infinitely preferable to choruses of *God Save The Queen* with the words 'no surrender' tacked on the end of the third line and the widespread use of the right arm in what frequently looked like an imitation Nazi salute. Some people certainly knew that that was how it looked. And one of my fellow-travellers commented afterwards on how odd I sounded screaming "For Chrissake stop! Don't be so bloody stupid!" at those who tried out their Steve Backley impersonations at the end of the match. Just as the surest way to combat racism on the terraces was for those around to make their objections clear, so with the national team, it's not enough to just stand by these days.

My prediction of mindless destruction when Lineker scored came true. But mindless destruction by a tiny minority of those watching, even if the percentage was higher among those attending. And so I shouted and I sang when Lineker scored – but for joy not hate. And the more of us who do so, who go to England's games because they love their national side not because they hate the other nations', the less likely it will be that the scenes in Poznan will be repeated.

As rallying cries go, this one's a bit limp. England aren't that bad – 799 Germans were arrested in Brussels before and after the Belgium v Germany game. The English did not, unlike a couple of groups of Poles, attempt to warm themselves up by setting fire to parts of the stadium. Some of the Poles reacted to Lineker's goal by lobbing fireworks at those England fans within range. UEFA have praised England's anti-hooligan efforts as being a good example for other countries. But the ideal is no arrests, no damage, no chancing of arms to see how much the foreigners can stomach.

The Second World War probably did more to enhance other countries' view of Britain in general and England in particular than any other event – it is ironic that those in this country who seem most obsessed by it are those who do most to destroy that hard-earned reputation. The crowd is not by its nature violent, ignorant and bigoted, but at England's games the fight is still on for its soul. We must avoid the path of Bill Buford, the American intellectual who took on its worst characteristics and give Gary a support worthy of his reputation. See you in Stockholm? ○

Afrique Occurrence

Andy Lyons saw more Strange Things than goals during the African Nations Cup finals in Sénégal.

WSC No 61, March 1992

ZIGUINCHOR, SENEGAL, THE THIRD DAY OF THE AFRICAN NATIONS CUP Finals. A man races across a football terrace babbling heatedly into a telephone. It is not connected. Periodically he stops, cackles, makes a high-pitched bleeping noise, rams the earpiece into the face of a startled spectator and bellows "It's for you!". He was supporting Congo ('Les Diables Rouges') and seemed blissfully unconcerned by events on the pitch in front of him, where his favourites were on the verge of losing to the Ivory Coast ('Les Eléphants'). Whenever the football got a bit dull during Sénégal '92, and God knows it happened more than once, the fans came bounding to the rescue.

Apart from the final and the third place play-off game (conceivably the most pointless encounter in international football history), all the matches in the tournament were double-headers, played more or less back to back in one of two stadia. As a result there were usually four sets of supporters present for both games, some in fancy dress, others with face paint and colour co-ordinated t-shirts, all armed to the hilt with drums, whistles, trumpets, flags and, in the case of the Ivory Coast, an immense air horn on wheels powered by a gas cylinder, which emitted a terrifying honk like a walrus with a sinus problem.

Followers of Les Eléphants (led by a rather gruff witch doctor called Denis), massing outside the stadium in Ziguinchor to run through some of their more robust chants, gleefully greeted the smaller groups of Congolese, Ghanaian and Zambian fans with the equivalent of 'Is that all you take away?'. Given the distances, and heartache, involved (which in some cases meant slogging 3,000 miles across Africa to see your team fail to get a single shot on target), it seemed remarkable that so many supporters should have turned up. Stranger still that some should sway and chant in perfect synchronisation while paying little or no heed of the action on the pitch. It transpired that many teams were egged on chiefly by local Sénégalese, paid to make up the numbers by the football federations of the relevant countries. (The Algerian FA must be stuck for cash at the moment, because they seemed to have just the one supporter who popped up at each match, gamely waving the right flag for all he was worth, which must have been a couple of quid at least.)

Sénégal's first round games were witnessed by raucous capacity crowds, but, aside from those who were being paid to become honorary citizens of another country for a couple of hours, local fans largely shunned the remaining matches in Dakar. Some were put off by the terrace ticket prices, roughly one-fifth of the weekly wage, while others may have been discouraged by the fact that even when they were allowed in for free to fill up the spaces opposite the TV cameras, the soldiers patrolling the stadium concourse often demanded to see tickets and openly laid into people who couldn't produce them. From the semis onwards some troops carried bazookas. Thankfully, we never discovered why.

Two facts were conclusively established during the first games in Ziguinchor. Firstly there would be little danger of a spectator nipping out for refreshments and missing a goal. The first shot in the Ivory Coast v Congo game arrived after ten minutes. If they had been playing rugby there would have been a line-out near the corner flag. Players had plenty of opportunities to practise the standard gesture of exasperation common to footballers world-wide: stand with hands on hips then slowly extend both arms, with palms open, to indicate that you were in a much better position than the team-mate whose stratospheric punt has just been skilfully trapped by a ballboy. Even the best match of the tournament, the semi between Ghana and Nigeria, was afflicted by Shocking First Shot Syndrome, the ball making a beeline for the players' tunnel, narrowly escaping the flailing dive of a policeman.

Secondly, our first sight of Ghana established that they were a quick, skilful, potentially thrilling team lumbered with the worst goalkeeper seen at international level since Brazil's Felix wobbled through the 1970 World Cup finals. Edward Ansah made two good reflex saves during the tournament that stood out in the memory simply because everything else went wrong. During the Congo game he prepared to gather a tame shot in his arms, then finally opted to punch it. With his nose. If a cross needed to be collected, he would hop about on the goalline, hands clamped behind his back, while a simple back pass rolled along the floor would be leapt upon melodramatically as though he were a chocoholic preparing to do business with an immense Walnut Whip.

The only consolation to be drawn from Ghana's defeat on penalties in the final was that at least Ansah didn't make a trophy-winning save which would have elevated him to undeserved stardom, a 1992 version of Sergio Goycochea. There was a small army of players' agents in Sénégal, eyeing up the considerable playing talent. A Businessman of the Year award awaits the man who can persuade a European club to snap up Ghana's No 1. (Then again, stranger things have happened. Allen McKnight is still drawing a wage).

For the first four days of the tournament we were based in The Gambia, which as a result of a colonial carve-up, occupies a chunk of what ought to be central Sénégal. The Gambian national side has made little impact at international level, but some of the best ball control we saw during our entire stay was produced by a group of under-12s who ran rings around rapidly tiring white legs during a beach kick-about. Their inexact grasp of economic bargaining ("I like your shirt. Give it to me.") proved conclusively that they would slip seamlessly into the freebie-festooned world of the Football League professional. (Best to gloss over the other match defeat suffered by our party against a Sénégalese college team, except to say that it was 9-1, "but could have been 50," and that the victors didn't bother to celebrate any goals after the first.)

During the course of the tournament, acres of newspaper space was given over to attacking refereeing standards, with the Japanese official in charge of Sénégal's quarter-final defeat against Cameroon being unfairly singled out for a hammering for no obvious reason other than local frustration at the result. As ever, the referees were almost wholly taken in by theatrical dives, though they rarely allowed trainers on to the pitch. They may have been wary of doing so after an incident with a Ghanaian player who appeared to produce a plume of smoke from his leg while undergoing treatment. Either the cut was so deep that it required the use of a soldering iron, or else the physio had been having a sly fag which dropped down a sock.

There was no such obvious explanation for a bizarre outbreak of injury-feigning during the Nigeria v Zaire quarter-final when, over a 15 minute period, a number of Zairians flung themselves to the floor and lay completely still, faces down, arms over their heads, as though suddenly in the grip of a traumatic childhood memory. Within a few seconds they'd spring to their feet as if nothing had happened. Something in the pre-match meal, perhaps? Or had the Nigerians sneaked a hypnotist into their opponents' camp with instructions to plant a trigger word which would cause them to blank out? Another tactical option for Graham Taylor to mull over, anyway.

Usually, whenever someone thumped to the ground as though deceased, a team of stretcher-bearers in sinister black uniforms, conceivably on loan from the Animal Liberation Front, would rush on, scoop up their prey and cart him off. Most miraculously recovered within seconds, but it was rumoured that others were never seen again...

Overall, the level of officiating was no worse than would be seen in any World Cup finals, though several refs were afflicted by a sort of galloping madness whenever they ran the line, the chief crime among many being a tendency to flag for offsides in the future tense, pulling up a player who might stray offside at some point later in the game.

Some officials spent an inordinate amount of time remonstrating with coaches who dared venture from the dug-out even if only to flick fag ash on the running track. Things came to a head during the final, which was momentarily enlivened by a superb dust-up involving the Ivorian boss, Yeo Martial, who was banished to the stands after storming up the touchline to demand that the suspended Abedi Pelé be removed from the Ghanaian bench (though he may simply have taken exception to the latter's dangerously loud crimson jacket).

There was little doubt that Pelé, recently elected African Footballer of the Year, was the most influential figure in the Ghana camp. (He was made captain at the start of the tournament largely because he could speak French and would be able to communicate with the Francophone referees. Ironically this proved to be his downfall, because the first of the two bookings that were to keep him out of the final was for dissent.) It was strongly rumoured that he picked the team. Somebody had to, if one is to believe the welter of stories about the nocturnal habits of the nominal coach, Otto Pfister, who is supposed to have spent each poolside evening amassing an enormous haul of empty whisky bottles.

Most of the journalists, and all the teams apart from the Sénégalese, were staying at the same hotel where players circulated around the lobby proudly displaying an impressive range of spanking new club shirts: Arsenal seemed to be popular with the Congolese squad, Anderlecht with the Zambians and Liverpool's old grey monstrosity with some of the Ghanaians, through Pelé, keen as ever to stand out from the crowd, swanned about in full Barcelona kit.

Because the teamsheets distributed before each match invariably listed some names that weren't even on the substitutes' bench, identification of the players during matches was a daunting task. That said, there was still little excuse for the Nigerian journalist who insisted, in the face of overwhelming evidence to the contrary, that his country's centre forward, Rashidi Yekini, was a dead ringer for Tony Cascarino.

There was a highly partisan atmosphere in the press area throughout the tournament due in part to the fact that some fans had craftily acquired press passes under false pretences, first prize for ingenuity going to a Sénégalese group who set up a newspaper, produced one issue, collected their press cards and then closed the paper down. The most animated member of the press corps was an Algerian who berated his team for their abject elimination in the first round while simultaneously filling us in on his complex stomach problems (communicated by a mimed explosion and vigorous nod). Journalists of all nations were a-quiver with excitement before the final on hearing that Bobby Charlton would be ensconced in the VIP Enclosure, almost within touching distance. He was in Dakar to collect an award for being 'The Best Bobby Charlton of 1991' or something similar, and doubtless managed to shift a few tickets along the way.

All in all, a fascinating tournament, the final word on which should be left with a senior official of the Ghanaian FA who, when congratulated on his team's performances, replied, "Thank you, but I'm a golf man really". It's a global game all right. ○

Sense of Loyalty?

If you consider yourself to be a loyal supporter, happy to follow your favourites come rain, wind or shine, Ian Plenderleith thought you ought to find something better to do.

WSC No 61, March 1992

IT'S OVER 20 YEARS SINCE I FIRST SAW THE SIDE I'VE SUPPORTED ALL MY LIFE, Lincoln City. All the usual crap applies – I always look first for their result, had a replica kit at school in the face of ridicule, once travelled 400 miles with pneumonia on a bobsleigh on a December Monday evening to watch them draw 0-0 with Aldershot in the preliminary round of the Autoglass Trophy. And all the other excruciatingly tedious anecdotes that obsessive losers with nothing better to do with their lives than follow a sad Fourth Division football side tell you.

Loyal fans are seen in settings such as the following: a couple of years ago I watched Lincoln away at Gillingham. They were 1-0 down with a minute to go, having created nothing and having packed ten men in defence the whole game, then broke away and equalised with virtually the last kick. Objective observers would have declared Gillingham moral and footballing winners. Down in the away end they didn't care and went apeshit. I, too, was pleased, but unlike my fellow fanatics I had the benefit of an extra insight to temper my joy – I knew that we were crap.

I further began to suspect that I was not really a loyal supporter when I was caught by surprise watching *Sportsnight* one Wednesday evening near the end of the season. I was just dozing off at about a quarter to midnight (just before the boxing and about three hours before any football highlights from Scotland), when there was a special report from Sincil Bank. I jolted to life like I'd received an enema of pure caffeine. New boys Barnet were at it again, and anyone still awake was rewarded with the sight of Lincoln defenders sprawling farcically about their penalty area as they went down to an ignominious 0-6 home defeat, a new club record. Anyone in my living room would have been rewarded with the sight of me spread-eagled in a state of hysterical laughter as mistake followed mistake, own goals were sliced home and City players received shiny red cards.

There's clearly something wrong with my attitude, I thought, as my flatmates picked me up and strapped me to my bed. Barnet have, after all, been Lincoln's main rivals since the club's single non-League season that culminated in them regaining League status by leapfrogging Barnet on the second last Saturday of the campaign. But my lack of sympathy for the side of my youth's 6-0 humiliation perhaps emanated from the shame of finding out, in a very roundabout way, that the Lincoln back four had spent the whole of the home fixture that Conference season racially abusing a black Barnet forward. Disappointment at numerous losses since has always been offset against the thought that they really deserve it.

Where common sense ceases, loyalty begins. I have stood on the North Bank at Highbury and been surrounded by the adulatory cheers that have greeted the sight of Nigel Winterburn successfully executing a hamstring stretch during the warm-up. So the club thinks it can get away with increasing ticket prices from £6 to £8 in one swoop. Still the supporters come. Eight pounds to stand for 90 minutes of football? Against Wimbledon and Luton and Coventry?

And I've met many seemingly sensible people who hailed Wimbledon's Cup final victory over Liverpool as a great day for football, when what they meant was that for years their side had been outplayed by Liverpool. How can anyone prefer a side of kickers, thumpers and sub-Neanderthal thugs against a team who for almost two decades have played beautiful, flowing, passing football, who've played the game properly?

I don't really care if Lincoln drop out of the Football League again and go bankrupt if they don't have players who can pass properly. I don't care if Wimbledon continue breaking post-war records for First Division attendances until nobody turns up at all, while they keep belting the ball down the middle of the pitch. And I'll stand and applaud Tottenham, Arsenal or West Ham if they furnish my vision with quality, passing football, irrelevant of their shirts' colours and the mindless hatred spawned not from rivalry but ignorance.

You could argue that 'rivalry' is harmless, even humourless. But if it was harmless then fans would no longer have to be segregated and terrace prices could plummet thanks to savings on policing bills. And when was the last time you heard a humorous terrace chant aimed at a rival side? The stunning wit of "We are the Arsenal haters" and variations thereon don't exactly result in echoes of raucous chortling across the nation's stadia.

Loyal fans are lauded as the grass-roots saviours of football, but in reality they're a pain in the arse. They know sod all about football because they're blind to the qualities of any side but their own. If they support a bad side they jealously resent the skills of their classier opponents. They'll pay anything to see their team and show surprise when the club fails to acknowledge their loyalty with medals of allegiance. They're as single-minded as born-again Christians, as dogmatic as bellowing Trots.

Why should I be loyal to my team just because I was born near their ground? Why should I continue to let them insult me with full-time footballers who can't play football? Why should I accept 25 per cent price increases like a doe-eyed lapdog? I don't care, I'll watch someone else, I'll watch it on telly, I'll cheer Ryan Giggs one week and Dennis Bailey the next. Then, when Lincoln beat Manchester United in the third round of the Cup I'll deny every word. But I think I'm safe. ○

My Beautiful Career

The indestructible Diego Maradona had wandered into one of his periodic new leases of life by appearing on Argentinian television. James Hooke took up the story.

WSC No 64, June 1992

EARLIER THIS MONTH, IN FRONT OF A LIVE ARGENTINIAN TV AUDIENCE, DIEGO Maradona – banned by FIFA until August for cocaine use – was up to his old tricks. With his back to goal twenty yards out, surrounded and hounded by three lunging opponents, a back pass looked the only option. A split second later, having executed an exquisite drag-back and backheel to nutmeg the nearest of the mesmerised defenders, he spun around and released himself like a hare from a trap.

Bearing down on the exposed goal, leaving the three goons trailing in his wake, he drew the hapless keeper, before slotting the ball into the empty net. He turned and raised his fist to salute his delirious public before being mobbed by ecstatic team-mates. For the remainder of the game the gibbering commentator could barely be heard above the raucous, chanting crowd, "Ole... ole,ole, ole... Diego, Diegooool!"

On this showing it was clear he has turned back the clock and redis-covered his full repertoire. Lambasting the referee for an unseen shirt pull, wagging his finger at the left back after being brutally hacked on the edge of the box and dancing around the pitch with the ball glued to his left foot.

But where on Planet FIFA has the former Argentinian captain and greatest player the world has ever seen escaped his global ban? The answer is a sad one, as this pathetic spectacle is just a 20-minute feature on the country's most tasteless TV show, *Ritmo de la Noche* (Rhythm of the Night), Argentina's equivalent of *Russ Abbott's Madhouse*, but worse.

The plastic pitch is the centrepiece of the enormous, sprawling set. Twenty yards long, with barely enough width for a Ray Wilkins square pass, its dimensions are quaintly marked out in miniature, even down to the corner arcs, and it contains those grotesque DIY goals frequently seen in suburban gardens around the home counties.

Diego approaches from a 'tunnel' under the audience, bedecked in garish fluorescent pink, whilst scantily clad cheerleaders gawp moronically into the cameras' zoom lenses. After a ten second warm up, the two four-man teams line up to be announced. Opposing Maradona as captain is some recent has-been from the local scene – Alberto Tarantini, Daniel Passerella etc who attempts to add a smattering of footballing talent.

The rest of the teams are drawn from the world of entertainment (sic) – washed-out gameshow hosts, soap opera stars and even the king of the one-liners, President Carlos Menem, who proved that you can still score far post headers with a hair weave and a face full of collagen. While the hysterical nation is in raptures over the weekly appearances of its favourite son, outsiders scoff at his craving for the limelight. Rumours about his inability to kick *La Coca* are inevitably linked to this shameful farce.

Not that Maradona is the only parody in this silly circus. Former national team colleague Ricardo Bochini – architect of Liverpool's 1984 World Club Cup final defeat in Tokyo – is another stool pigeon left with egg on his face. Independiente directors failed to see the funny side of his childish clowning in a recent appearance and promptly sacked him as coach.

Meanwhile Maradona is hoping that when the circus shuffles out of town in August he'll ride the applause all the way to a lucrative contract with his beloved Boca Juniors – now a necessity given the understandable refusal of US Immigration to issue him a work permit.

Another man for whom the joke is falling flat is diminutive young playmaker Diego Latorre – worried sick about having his Boca limelight stolen by his old idol. Publicly, Latorre claims to be thrilled at the prospect of a 'Diego Duo' spearheading next year's assault on the league. Privately, however, he's frantically seeking a European move that would allow an escape from Maradona's sombre shadow.

Regardless of the fate of these players come August, of one thing we can be sure: until then, *Ritmo de la Noche* will continue to soar in the TV ratings. Perhaps the BBC could learn a trick or two from an old adversary and cease the tired old formula of boozing-up old heroes before hacking them down with a derisory interview. Instead, let's dress up Georgie Best, Stan Bowles and Dennis Law in the Arsenal away kit and enjoy seeing them rifling in a few penalties past Wogan, Parkinson, Aspel etc *ad nauseam.* ○

Sky's the Limit

At last, a TV deal that promised some diversity — but at a cost.
WSC No 65, July 1992 – Editorial

THEY HAVE BEEN SHAMELESSLY MANIPULATED BY THE GREEDY BUNCH OF backsliders in charge of the Premier League, but Hell will freeze over before we feel even the slightest twinge of sympathy for the ITV sports department.

It is particularly ironic that ITV should have failed to secure the rights to exclusive coverage of the Premier League, because they played a crucial role in its creation through their elitist approach to the televising of English football over the past few years. Criticism would be rebuffed by claims that the size of audience necessary to keep their advertisers happy could only be guaranteed by serving up a regular diet of the Big Five and, occasionally, one or two of their medium-sized chums. Market research would be brandished to back up their argument.

Mindful that statistics can be made to prove anything, many fans remained sceptical. It was bad enough that their intelligence should be insulted by the tawdry populism of *The Match*; more alarming still was the thought of the influence that such highly selective television coverage might be having on the next generation of potential football fans, those not yet old enough to attend matches on a regular basis, who may have absorbed a false image of English football, revolving entirely around a handful of clubs with whom they are encouraged to identify.

Unfortunately, the First Division club chairmen, peculiar organisms that somehow manage to combine a mile-wide conniving streak with a naive, trusting nature, swallowed the story whole. It was to be survival of the fittest. To its founder members, the principle appeal of the Premier

League was that all the money gained from a future TV deal would be kept by the participating clubs, with none filtering down to the rest of the League as had been the case with all previous television agreements.

The FA momentarily hoped that they might be able to engineer the creation of a streamlined division whose reduced fixture list would be of benefit to the England national team and might improve the quality of matches presented to the paying spectator. The illusion didn't last long, however, and we have been left with a new competition containing the same number of clubs as the old First Division, the critical difference being that its creation has substantially widened the gap between the wealthiest clubs and the rest. (Of course, now that clubs stand to make so much money from the BBC/BSkyB deal, who would bet against concerted efforts being made to prevent the Premier League being reduced to 20 clubs, as is supposed to happen at the end of 1993-94?)

The pitiful financial state of many smaller clubs, likely to be made worse by the financial commitments imposed upon them by the Taylor Report, provided a pressing reason for hoping that ITV might be out-bid. The Football League simply can't afford to do without revenue from television. The various ITV regions already transmit highlights programmes, in many cases showing almost all the weekend's matches involving League teams within their catchment area. The BBC, however, has virtually no regionalised sports coverage in England and it seems unlikely that they would have taken up the option of covering the remainder of the League had they failed to secure rights to the Premier League.

It was no surprise that ITV should seek to gain some mileage out of the fact that live matches will now be seen by a much smaller audience. There has been talk of 'overkill', but the owners of satellite dishes are the only ones who will see substantially more football than is currently available on the terrestrial channels. Anyone prepared to spend a couple of hundred pounds on a dish is hardly likely to be the sort of floating fan who might lose interest in football through over-exposure to it.

A more genuine cause for concern is the issue of pay-television. So far, all that has been established is that in the first year of the new deal, Premier League matches will be transmitted 'free'. In the second year, viewers will be expected to pay a subscription to a football channel. Thereafter, they will pay for each game watched. It is understandable that BSkyB should want to recoup some of their huge amount of money invested in the Premier League. However, they should at least give some indication of how much the subscribers' channel will cost. That they haven't yet done so suggests they will wait to see how many dishes are sold in the first year, with subscription charges being hiked up if sales fall below expectations.

Another way of making up the shortfall would be to increase admission prices for Premier League matches. Either way, fans will be fleeced. Which is, after all, what the Premier League is all about.

The plan to stage live matches on Monday nights met has been vehemently criticized by a number of club chairmen. Their principal complaint, that it may oblige teams involved in European competitions to play twice in the space of three days, is easily resolved – it ought to be possible to arrange the fixture list so that no team due to play on Wednesday would have to turn out two days earlier. Far more objectionable is the imposition placed on travelling fans. Supporters are an integral part of a football match. The smaller crowds likely to result from the Monday night scheduling will only diminish the game as a spectacle. It might serve as an ominous warning of what is to come if Silvio Berlusconi succeeds in his ambition of launching a European League funded entirely by corporate sponsorship and viewers' subscriptions.

Given the low calibre of people holding positions of power within English football (Gordon Taylor honourably excepted), there was never any likelihood that the television contract could have been worked out in a way satisfactory to a majority of football fans. BSkyB have muscled in largely because it seems the BBC were not prepared to share coverage with ITV, a consequence of the feud which can be traced back to 1988 when the commercial network bought up exclusive rights to League football. One horror show is over, another may be about to begin. ○

Courtney Pine

George Courtney wouldn't feature heavily in a poll to find Britain's most popular man, but he would get Jeffrey Prest's vote.

WSC No 67, September 1992

IF THE UNTHINKABLE EVER OCCURS AND FANZINES BECOME 'ESTABLISHMENT', there will be those who claim the slippery slope started here. I come in praise of referees. Just one, in fairness: George Courtney. Southampton fans should read on for the twist before handing my name to the death squads. Old Father Time having just seen off George's name from the Football League list, it's an apt moment to pay homage and to open the debate on what makes an otherwise stable human being save his applause and paper snowstorm for the last man onto the pitch.

I plead parochialism. Courtney and I both hail from Spennymoor in County Durham, a town vaguely famous for having a football team which used to be vaguely famous, courtesy of various sorties in the FA Cup and FA Trophy. The corners are starting to curl on those memories now, but it's never really mattered. For the last 19 years, thanks to George, my home town·has featured on the finest stages the game has to offer, from FA and League Cup finals to three European finals and two World Cups. If yours is a town like Spennymoor, you'll realise we're talking big vicarious ego-trips here.

He caught me during my impressionable 'teens, whenever he showed up with his mates in the crowd at Spennymoor Utd's ground. Parking myself within eavesdropping range, I found the game becoming a blur as he spread tales of First Division life around the gathered throng like crumbs from Olympus. Northern League football had little to offer when George was outlining the joys of going eyeball-to-eyeball with Graeme Souness over a disputed corner.

I was hooked, and have rooted for him ever since. The proudest day was May 10th, 1980. A hundred students crammed into a college TV room in Nottingham to watch West Ham play Arsenal in the Cup final. Muted murmurs of approval as cameras homed in on the Gunners during the kick-in, a process repeated with the odd tentative cheer as West Ham's players came into shot.

"... and today's referee is Mr George Courtney from Spennymoor in County Durham."

"YEEEEEEEEEEEES!!!" boomed a lone voice at the back. I was young, homesick, and proud as hell, all of which cut little ice with the sea of faces turned in my direction. "What a tit" writ large across all of them.

Yes, it's perverse, but supporting officials is not without its perks. Referees, after all, never lose. They don't go down on goal difference, nor do they get knocked out of anything 'just 90 minutes from Wembley'.

While the masses scream for his head, ref-fans enjoy that 'Condor'-like serenity which comes from following the king-maker instead of the heirs apparent. I can also testify to the unaccountable satisfaction of watching the cream of British footballers brought to heel by someone who uses the same post office as you do.

On some locals, however, such sentiments are wasted. My father, who enjoys first name terms with the great man, brings back occasional reports from Spennymoor health centre which prove that prophets are indeed without honour in their own country. Having picked up his prescription, George has been known to face a waiting-room gauntlet after an iffy showing on TV, ashen figures hitherto at death's door heaving themselves forward on crutches to score cheap points over the offside law.

They know not what they do. Not only is Mr C a legend for having carried my town's name to unimaginable heights, he is also pretty sound at his job. Not flawless, mind: I have blurred memories of Match of the Day being at Old Trafford in the Seventies to see United allowed a gem of a goal scored directly from a free kick; the effect being a tad marred when George was caught by the action reply with his arm aloft like an incontinent first-former...

Such rare blemishes, however, did nothing to prepare me for the horror of January '91. Forget Hendrix and Morrison, no one flirted with the self-destruct button like George Courtney did in January 1991.

Leeds v Barnsley, FA Cup. Interpreting the professional foul rule so liberally even Lord Longford may have cried 'wimp', Courtney flashed a yellow at United's John McClelland when the latter was probably already trying to recall where the soap was kept.

I squirmed in front of the TV, little knowing that this was merely *hors d'oeuvre* to the year's principal refereeing controversy a fortnight later, when George sent off Southampton's Jimmy Case at Old Trafford for the 'foul' that in retrospect didn't even amount to a caress. Courtney's transition to Mr Hyde was complete and Saints were out of the Rumbelows Cup.

And the twist? I am also a Southampton supporter.

How someone from County Durham comes to say this is a long and faintly ridiculous story. Suffice it to say that on that awful winter's night I faced an emotional conflict akin to watching your dearest friend drive your Ferrari off Beachy Head. This was my George, putting my Saints to the sword. I was conscious of my mouth opening and closing but no sound coming out.

At Highfield Road for Southampton's next game, indigenous supporters had no such difficulties. "Are you Courtney in disguise?" was the chant around me as the ref dished up his first howler. "Geordie bastard," muttered the man in front reflectively ("Dunelmian bastard" is actually more precise, though the metre not quite as favourable). I went with my fake New Zealand accent for the full 90 minutes.

There's probably a moral here about clutching vipers to the bosom, but I have no regrets. Spennymoor may play host to Rothmans ciggies and 'England's most northerly vineyard', but these will never stir the blood in quite the same way as George swanning around Wembley, swapping quips with the stars. There is, thank heaven, no 'Big Five' mentality when it comes to refereeing: any town or village can find itself shaping football destiny as long as there's some masochist with a whistle on the electoral roll.

Like all good things, however, it doesn't last. For 'George Courtney' on the next season's list, read 'Kevin Lynch'. Take a bow, Lincoln, your time has come. ○

Hit and MISL

Another football competition bit the dust in the USA. David Wangerin charted the fall of the Major Indoor Soccer League.

WSC No 67, September 1992

NOT MANY ARTICLES WHICH HAVE NOTHING TO DO WITH FOOTBALL EVER appear in *WSC*, but here's one. It's about the Major Soccer League, which has about as much to do with the game as Beethoven's Fifth Symphony.

I must confess I am no expert on the MSL. I only ever watched a handful of its games and only then on television as an alternative to *Knots Landing*. I didn't even understand its rules; after hearing something about an "illegal three-line pass" and seeing a referee show someone the blue card, I gave up trying. All I know is that I hated it. Hated it worse than cricket purists hate the one day game, worse than rugby union folk despise the league code. Maybe even worse than some of you hate certain types of music – although I'm not sure about that.

For 13 years, the MSL tried to persuade my countrymen that they were actually offering us soccer. They took what the rest of the world took nearly a century to build and turned it upside-down, inside-out, and back-to-front. It was Madonna to Marilyn Monroe, an unabridged Eddie Van Halen solo to George Benson playing *Last Train to Clarksville*. Take an ice-hockey rink, cover it with a plastic pitch, make the goals a bit bigger and hey presto – 21st century football. De-simplify the rules to satiate the American thirst for complexity, allow unlimited substitution to maintain an air of familiarity, and throw in a red day-glo ball instead of that wimpy white thing... ugh – must I go on?

The Major Indoor Soccer League was the misbegotten child of one Earl Foreman, fleeting owner of NASL's Washington Whips in the late Sixties who quickly turned his interests to professional basketball. As the Seventies drew to a close, and his basketball team went nowhere, Foreman returned to soccer. He was intrigued by the impressive crowds which were beginning to turn out for certain NASL contests, but the near-total lack of interest shown in the sport ten years earlier convinced him that if America was really going to take soccer to its heart, the game had to be re-invented.

I have visions of how the MISL was born: would-be big wheel sports owners gathered in some posh north-eastern hotel whilst specialist sports management consultants scribbled down ideas for their new game on flip charts. Increase scoring! Keep the ball in play! Let players kick each other! Give teams weirder nicknames!

In 1978, soccer's bastard child was born in the shape of a six-team regional league playing during the NASL close season. The New York Arrows became the league's flagship franchise, with the outspoken and near-famous Shep Messing tending goal for them when he wasn't telling anyone who would listen how the outdoor game would never succeed in America. The Arrows won the first four championships, with a Yugoslav named Steve Zungul scoring goals like they were going out of style. Which of course they weren't.

Sadly the MISL proved no one-season wonder. It soon expanded to the rest of the country, securing the all-important nationwide cable television contract for extensive exposure. Word got out that an MISL contest was the next best thing to a riot. Players were matter of factly bundled into the dasher boards. Well-padded goalkeepers bravely threw themselves in front of anything that moved. The ball was almost an after-thought. When a goal came, it was the 4th of July – sirens, spotlights, organ fanfare, and a demented public address announcer screaming out the scorer's name in his very best Caesar's Palace voice. Soccer Hell had arrived.

The NASL began to take notice. Its beloved New York Cosmos may have been attracting bumper crowds, but other teams were struggling at the gate. Were they playing the wrong sport, perhaps? Their traditionally informal indoor league put on a more serious face in 1980, when it opted to go head-to-head with the newcomers. All of a sudden, nearly every major city in America found itself with an indoor soccer team. Some, like Chicago, even had two.

In many respects, this may have been responsible for the NASL's demise. The San Diego Sockers, for example, the MSL's most successful team, started life as an unassuming franchise in the NASL. Hugo Sanchez even spent a couple of seasons with them. Outdoors the Sockers were no match for the likes of baseball's San Diego Padres (which was really saying something). Indoors, on the other hand, Socker crowds came closer to filling the stands to capacity.

By 1982, the MISL had festered to 14 teams and gone coast-to-coast, providing its growing legion of fans with an abundance of dry ice, laser shows, and organ music. Foreman's views seemed unassailable. While MISL flopped in some cities, in others it was big business. The Baltimore Blast, St Louis Steamers and Cleveland Force (no, honestly, I'm not making these up) could boast crowds on a par with professional ice hockey or baseball teams. The same could not be said for the San Francisco Fog, Phoenix Inferno, and Hartford Hellions, who quickly folded.

Goals came quick and fast at an average of about eight a match. Amidst the mayhem, tactics had developed and stars were being born. The Brazilian Tatu made a name for himself with the Dallas Sidekicks, scoring on average a goal a game and infuriating the club's equipment manager by insisting on removing his jersey and throwing it into the crowd each time he scored.

In 1985, the NASL went belly-up, leaving the MISL as the only game in town. American players wishing to continue after college now had no choice but to forgo the green, green grass of the great outdoors in favour of the carpet and plexiglass of Soccer Hell. Just about anyone who was anyone in American soccer wound up in the MISL, as well as a few British players (step forward Chris Whyte). It has remained more or less that way ever since. Regional outdoor leagues, including the American 'Professional' Soccer League have sprouted up. But these, operating on shoestring budgets with matches held on high school playing fields before phone-booth sized audiences, are professional only in name.

If the MSL succeeded in achieving anything, it was in blurring the distinction between 'indoor' soccer and the real thing. This culminated in the odious decision in 1990 to remove the word 'indoor' from the league's title, making the MISL the MSL. Most of the nation's media – and the United States Soccer Federation – were already refusing to make any distinction between it and the outdoor game, so in a perverse way, this made sense. Hell, the NFL got away with it for 70 years.

But indoor soccer, thank the Lord, proved to be just as much of a fad as the NASL. Perhaps it just took the MSL longer to realise it. The New York Arrows folded in 1982 (not long after their fourth consecutive title), and the game never really caught on in the markets it needed to. Teams from Tacoma, Washington and Wichita, Kansas were making up the numbers instead of Los Angeles, Chicago or New York. By 1991, entries had dwindled to just six. Financial problems had led to the Cleveland Force being reformed into the Cleveland Crunch, and the St Louis Steamers into the St Louis Storm. And when only four clubs confirmed their interest in a 1992-93 season, there was little option but to fold up the circus tents and send the clowns home.

What of the MSL's legacy? Instead of inspiring the development of an outdoor league or two, all it did was encourage a few more leagues of its type to sprout up at a regional level. The best-known of these is the AISA, with sides like the Milwaukee Wave and the Canton Invaders. We're no closer to the formation of a big-time professional outdoor league than we were when the NASL folded, not even with World Cup '94 on the horizon. The MSL is dead – long live indoor soccer. ○

Architecture and Morality

Bill Brewster found the state of stadium design suffering from a lack of money and imagination.

WSC No 69, November 1992

NOBODY COULD HAVE FAILED TO NOTICE THAT IN CERTAIN GROUNDS ON matchdays there are almost as many bulldozers as there are fans. Equally, many may have noticed that some of the stands and stadia currently under construction owe a lot to the early Sixties 'flared-trouser' period of architecture when tower blocks began to blight British skylines. The most striking examples of this new trend are in Scunthorpe, Walsall and, latterly, Chester: stadia that more resemble edge-of-town industrial units than cathedrals of football. Fans appear to have very little influence at the planning stages of these buildings: their buildings.

As a result of pressure applied by supporters and local residents, Arsenal look set to produce a fine new replacement for the North Bank at Highbury. However, if the club had had it all their own way, the outcome would have been somewhat different. Charles Sands, an architect living near to the ground, decided to form the Group for the Alternative Arsenal Stand and, although eventually defeated, helped to ensure that there would be vast improvements in the design and function of the stand.

Says Sands: "I don't suppose you can blame the club for what went on. Neither us nor the local community ever had anything against Arsenal, but their whole approach to life is fairly basic. All they really care about are their 12,000 seats. At least all the hassle we went through eventually produced a decent design. That was a major achievement in my mind."

Simon Inglis, author of *The Football Grounds of England and Wales* and a member of the Football Licensing Authority, was fulsome in his praise for GAAS. "They deserve a medal for the pressure they applied. I never liked their own designs, but in the end Arsenal have decided to put money into providing extra facilities which not a lot of other clubs have bothered to do."

Are aesthetic considerations being thrown to the wind as a result of the pressures of the Taylor Report? Inglis points to its impact: "It's revolutionised attitudes; changed everything except for one point: the majority of clubs are still run by people for whom aesthetics are unimportant. The other side of the coin is that not many of our stadia had much architectural merit to begin with. We only grew to love them because we got used to them."

But perhaps we're being churlish. Fans of Chester are no doubt grateful they've even got a club to support: if that means such nancy-boy stuff as aesthetics going out of the window, then it might be a price worth paying. Can interesting buildings be built cheaply or do we have to sacrifice aesthetic considerations for expediency? Inglis feels there's a middle road: "It often doesn't cost more to make something look good as long as the right people are hired to do the job. Timing is crucial too. One thing I'm always critical of the Taylor Report for is that I fear that clubs in the new First Division are going to be rail-roaded into temporary solutions.

"What Chester had before, for example, was a conglomeration of buildings – an accidental mixture of mundane structures which combined to form what we call a football ground. Other people would just call them a mess. In that sense there is more merit in the overall concept at Deva Stadium than Sealand Road, but you can't call it architecture. The people behind the crop of new stadia are in danger of ignoring what it was that made football grounds special. But the difficulty – and this is where you have to sympathize with clubs like Chester – is the cost."

With verve and imagination in seemingly short supply, we were surprised to receive a phone call from GMW, a respected firm of architects in London, who are working on an 'Every stadium'. Ali Ozveran is in charge of the project: "Having attended a number of seminars and exhibitions on stadia design I concluded that the proposals being put forward fell into two categories. They were either overambitious, fantastic designs which were unaffordable, or they were ugly, cheap-looking, almost temporary structures."

GMW have been involved in stadia design in the Middle East, and were also engaged by Wimbledon as designers for the Wandle Valley stadium (which failed to get planning permission). Can this design be put to practical use by large and small clubs? "It's a design system which could be adapted to suit differing ambitions and financial capabilities. Imagine a giant Meccano set relying primarily on a series of prefabricated standard components. It is a concept, it is not even a prototype design. We believe it is suitable for all clubs and all site conditions."

Meanwhile, on terra firma, Huddersfield Town have been hatching perhaps the most ambitious scheme of all. Inglis is hopeful that this may point to better times ahead. "They are planning a brand new stadium next door to the existing site which is going to be shared with the local rugby league club. They've got a tripartite agreement between themselves, the rugby club and the local authority and have chosen a design based on something called Stadium For The Nineties. It's a very imaginative, futuristic stadium which, if built, would be one of the most advanced in Europe."

Inevitably as the conversation turns to football grounds, the word 'Italy' tends to crop up. Are comparisons with them erroneous? Simon Inglis: "We only see the nice Italian stadia. There are a lot of awful, run-down Italian grounds. I was at Cosenza, a *Serie B* side, and the stadium was falling down. There's no way it would have been given a safety certificate in this country.

"It's not all hunky dory in Italy or in France even: Bastia are a Second Division club and look what happened there. I agree that we're not very design conscious, but I would rather watch football at Ipswich than at

Bari and I think, given the choice, most Bari supporters would as well.

"Italian stadia look great, but they're just shells. Places like Arsenal, Aston Villa, Manchester United and Norwich are bloody nice little stadia. You don't lose your love of them just because they're not terribly imaginative. We have a British style and we've got to find ways of designing new British stadia, not clones of their Italian equivalents. What we have to do is not emulate the designs so much as emulate their imagination."

Jonathan Glancey, the presenter of *Et In Stadia Ego*, a programme on football architecture due to be screened as part of Channel 4's *Without Walls* series, agrees. "What the film says is that although recent work in Italy and France – and coming up in the United States in 1994 – is superb, many people have voiced the feeling that these things aren't a perfect fit for British football. It would be terrific if we could resolve that, but it does require clubs to be a lot less pompous and for the state and cities to treat sport more seriously by helping clubs get the best."

Eric Cantona's contribution to the programme – in speech as elegant as his football – best sums up the perverse attraction of British stadia: "Although French stadia are more modern, they are used for other things such as athletics. But I prefer British stadia. I prefer the atmosphere here. You are closer to the public. It is warmer, there is room for love."

A combination of the ever-diminishing returns of the smaller Premier and Football League clubs, the customary stupidity of the clubs' owners, and a distinct lack of interest from central government, means the prospect of seeing new stadia springing up throughout England is rapidly disappearing up the players' tunnel. What seems more likely is a continuation of the rash of hi-tech bike sheds that have risen out of the ground from Kingston to Chester. Of course, the clubs are not helped when spectacularly obstructive local councils join the fray. A number of stadia proposals have been ditched simply because councillors have made it clear that they don't want a football club on their patch.

Inglis' conclusions are a reminder that the sea-change in attitudes supposedly engendered by the Taylor Report is still some way off: "We'll be lucky now if we get four or five new stadia: Blackpool, Sunderland, Wrexham, Southampton and Huddersfield. The tragedy is that Maidstone could have got the ball rolling if they'd been given planning permission. I think a lot of people would have looked at it and said, yeah, we want one like that. Unfortunately, they're now looking at Scunthorpe and Walsall and saying, yeah, we'll have one like that." O

Yeboah's Witnesses

Did you see Ghana's World Cup qualifying tie against Algeria in 1992? Neither did James Mayers, but he came pretty close.

WSC No 72, February 1993

WHEN THE GOING GETS TOUGH, THE WEAK GO BERSERK. THIS WAS THE *Liberian Observer*'s analysis of the 1989 encounter in Monrovia when Liberia put history behind them and ejected Ghana from the World Cup qualifiers. The goal damage was done by the then little-known George 'Oppong' Weah, one of the very few Liberians to have had a pleasant and lucrative time since then, as a striker first for AS Monaco and more recently for Paris St Germain.

In honour of the epic win, Liberian President Samuel Doe, later to have sundry parts of his anatomy sliced off before dying in a civil war completely unrelated to football, declared a two-day national holiday. I was working in Monrovia at the time and I kept a chicken for which I had great breakfast-egg-laying hopes. The first day of that celebration was the last I saw of my chicken. Since then, Ghanaian football has not taken things lying down. The Black Starlets won the under-17 World Cup in Italy in 1991 and last year national sides were pipped in the final of the African Nations Cup and the semi-final of the Olympic Games.

Whilst the club game continues to wither as players with talent flock to Europe, there remains a fierce hope that the glory days of the past may return for the national side. (Following the meandering lead of Stanley Matthews who dribbled his way around the country in 1957, the Black Stars won the African Nations Cup in 1963, 1965, 1978 and 1982.) But already in late 1992 the team had lost their opening World Cup qualifier away to the Burundi Swallows so there was a lot at stake against Algeria's Desert Warriors on December 20th.

The night before the game, the British monarch's much reported bum year took another turn for the worse when the New York 'consciousness rap' outfit Public Enemy, headlining at the climax of a week-long Pan African cultural extravaganza in Accra, admonished the assembled masses to, "Fuck the Queen". The rappers were similarly unfriendly towards the Pope and were none too fond of Father Christmas.

The group went on to praise Ghanaian leader JJ Rawlings for doing a great job, despite widespread public depression following iffy election results. And by the time they came off stage at two in the morning they had still failed to mention the major cultural event of the year – the Black Stars' footy encounter with Algeria only hours away. The audience was unimpressed and largely unconscious.

Unlike me, however, most of the audience had foregone sleep, because by the time I reached the stadium, a considered three hours before kick-off, they had all crossed the road from the gig site and had filled the place to bursting. "The stadium heaved to its very seams." as the *People's Daily Graphic* put it the next day.

There had been no advance ticket sales and the 35,000 capacity ground had been technically closed for two hours. To get in you needed to find a scarce touted ticket from amongst the peanut and Abedi Pelé yoghurt sellers, and you needed sufficient 'dash' (ie cash) for at least three security guards and police.

With the high price of the former having used up all the latter, my three Ghanaian friends and I tried flattery, elaborate promises, Freudian word association games, and in my case a desperate "But I'm Terry Venables". But we were silently repelled, and at one point tickled into retreat by a policeman wielding a palm frond and riding a horse the size and construction of an ironing table.

We stood in awe, and fear for the potential consequences for the over-packed stadium, as three fat women squeezed through.

Later the roof of the VIP wing caved in under the weight of the fans who had climbed there. One man died and at least six people were hospitalized, including the national coach of the Ivory Coast. Many people leaving the ground after the game agreed, however, that Accra was very lucky not to have hosted a disaster on a much grander scale.

The match finally got underway and, as the *Ghanaian Times* reported, "with over 80,000 voices roaring hoarse and melodious for them the Black Stars realised they had a duty to perform".

The first half was lively, although individual Ghanaian talent rarely gelled into effective teamwork. The 1991 and 1992 African Footballer of the Year, Abedi Pelé (Olympic Marseille), and current *Bundesliga* goalking Tony Yeboah (Eintracht Frankfurt) looked like the jet-lagged Euro-heroes they were. The next day's *Sports Star* saw things more descriptively:

"Displaying dextrous (sic) footwork and astonishing perspicacity, Pelé unfolded just a flash of his genius when he outwitted a couple of Algerians and laid on a glorious pass to CK Akonnor whose quixotic attempt to put the rotund leather in the path of bulldozer Tony Yeboah, was cheekily brushed aside when an Algerian defender cleared the ball to safety."

Yeboah got his chance later – "As if a whiff of fresh oxygen had been sniffed by the striker, he took the pass with glee and in a characteristically mazy manner went past a couple of Algerian defenders, but his glider was kicked by Warriors' goalkeeper Acimi Redà to corner."

The Algerians meanwhile were fit and fluid passers of the ball who never quite looked like scoring but could have passed for ballerinas. Soccer's leotard men punctuated the match with Duriesque flourishes, twirling to the turf with élan.

Ghana's win came from well struck goals from Prince Opoku's boot in the 24th minute and from the head of Pelé's younger brother Kwame Ayew in the 70th. A netted punt from Yeboah in the last second of the game was judged offside as the crowd erupted. (**Terrible Senegalese Ref Robs Ghana of a Classic Goal No 3 by Tony Yeboah!** – *Africa Sports* headline).

Meanwhile, the local aluminium smelting magnate had agreed to pay at the last minute for televising of the game. I watched it at home with a cool beer and an eye on my chickens. ○

Goals on Film

Anyone who thought Escape to Victory and Gregory's Girl were football's principal contributions to the history of the cinema has been cruelly misled, as Phil Crossley explained.

WSC No 73, March 1993

WHAT DO THE FOLLOWING WELL-KNOWN FILM DIRECTORS HAVE IN COMMON – Anthony Asquith, Peter Yates, Wim Wenders, John Schlesinger and Blake Edwards? What was the subject of Rex Harrison's first feature? What has provided the all-time low in the acting careers of Ian McShane, Richard Harris and Michael Caine?

The answer to all of the above questions, rather unsurprisingly since you are reading *WSC*, is football.

Most of us, when pressed, can come up with the names of a few of the best known football films: *Escape to Victory* (Caine), *Yesterday's Hero* (McShane), *The Arsenal Stadium Mystery*... It gets more addictive when you reach the point where you are trying to remember the title of the one where Arthur Askey throws a pie at the referee.

The bug caught hold of me many years ago when I spotted a name-check for my beloved Blackburn Rovers in a feature film. That film was *A Kind of Loving* and the Rovers are mentioned by Alan Bates' window cleaner – they are to be the tough opposition to the local club in their next match. The mere idea of the Rovers as tough opposition gave me an unexpected frisson in those far off, pre-Walkerian days. Enthused, I set out to compile a list of films containing references to Blackburn Rovers. After several years of energetic enquiry I had reached the magnificent total of... two.

At this point a couple of things became obvious to me:

1) Collecting cinematic references to Blackburn Rovers was not a very fulfilling hobby;

2) I needed to go off in a new direction.

Obvious Thing No 2 led to me deciding to widen my net and become less exclusivist. Why not try to track down every film which includes football? In a matter of moments I had sailed past my previous best score and was taking the first tentative steps along the road that would eventually lead me into the bizarre world of football on film, a world inhabited by such strange bedfellows as Julio Iglesias, Pelé, Kent Walton and Omar Sivori.

It is the world of the crap team name – Burnville Utd, Stockford FC, Oldchester Utd and Bestham Vampires. Best of all, of course, it is the world of the match-winning last minute goal, the brilliant dribble and the triumph of good over evil as the lads refuse to accept instructions from on high to throw the match.

From the outset you have to accept the fundamental flaw inherent in all soccer pictures – the actual match footage is always, but always, utterly inept. There are two basic ways of trying to overcome this problem. One is to use large chunks of a real match, but even then you have to use cut-ins of your talentless heroes to sustain the narrative drive.

The second option is the *Escape to Victory* gambit – hire a squad of professional players to act out your match sequences. Even this attention to detail is doomed to failure, as exemplified in the trailer (sadly, all that survives) of the 1926 British film *Ball of Fortune*. In this, the great Billy Meredith beats five players with effortless ease down the right touchline, and still manages to look like a complete wally. I'm sure Meredith did beat opponents with ease, but the point is it must be believable.

I suppose the key is spontaneity – something which simply cannot be created to order for the benefit of the cameras. Pure artistry on the pitch, as enjoyed from the terraces, turns into shoddy artifice when viewed from the one-and-nines at the Roxy. In the world of huge camera crews and naff directors with the same scenes being re-shot 29 times, spontaneity, one of the magic ingredients of football, simply cannot survive. Not that any of this ever stopped them from trying, of course.

There were lots of early silent films which centred around japes and high jinks with a football – *Pimple on Football* (1914) starred music hall comedian Fred Evans as Pimple, a white-faced character whose speciality was the comic pastiche of popular melodramas and epics of the day. Unfortunately, as with so much early cinema, no copy of this short comedy is now known to exist.

A similar fate befell *The Footballers' Honour* (1914), advertised in the trade press as "having hit the popular taste... dealt cleverly and scientifically with the story of a young player's victorious struggle against temptation". Could have been re-made in the 1960s, I'd have thought.

Many other silent soccer movies were made as football and the cinema assisted in each other's coming of age. One of the most famous of pre-First World War football films, probably because it is one of the few which have survived, is *Harry the Footballer* (1911). This one real melodrama from the Hepworth Studio was the first to employ the plot of kidnapping an ace centre forward on the eve of a big game. As one might have expected, the dastardly plan is foiled, and Harry gets to the match in time to score the winner.

As football spread around the world many other nations saw the possibilities offered by the excitement and action of the game. Italy, Argentina and Brazil led the field by the 1940s, with the USSR and other east European states not far behind. In the UK football seemed to have fallen from grace, usually only appearing as background item.

An exception was *The Arsenal Stadium Mystery* (1939), Britain's most lavish soccer production to date. Some would argue that it has never been surpassed. Thorold Dickinson's comedy-thriller took a ludicrous murder plot and offset it with superb action sequences. Dickinson used 14 cameras to shoot a First Division match between Arsenal and Brentford (May 6th, 1939, Arsenal 2, Brentford 0).

At a later date the Arsenal players turned out for close-ups, playing against a team made up of Oxford and Cambridge University players. According to the records, the Arsenal players were paid seven guineas per day's filming and the Oxbridge side three guineas – I suppose filming doesn't count when it comes to jeopardising amateur status. George Allison, the Arsenal manager, played himself and carried the job off rather well. Other nice touches included the Gunners' training-session involving a game of head tennis, and a fake newsreel film which neatly introduces players and actors to the audience. During this sequence the commentator gives us the priceless information that Bremner of Arsenal "was born with a silver football in his mouth". I'd still rather listen to him than to Jimmy Hill, though.

What *The Arsenal Stadium Mystery* did was to take to its logical conclusion a trick first used in *The Great Game* (1930) – that of incorporating real match footage into a fictional format. *The Great Game* (Rex Harrison's first film) told the story of true love thwarted and then reconciled, played out against a football background which culminated in a sequence showing the Cup final of 1930, when Arsenal beat Huddersfield Town by two goals to nil.

Of course, for every soccer triumph on the silver screen there are ten or 20 dead-on-their-feet turkeys. Where does one begin to plumb the depths? Perhaps with *Small Town Story* (1953), a British Z-movie starring Kent Walton. (Yes, *the* Kent Walton, grapple fans).

Kent is the ace centre forward for Oldchester United, who are promised a small fortune if they win promotion to the Third Division. Kent is kidnapped by dastardly rivals... heard this somewhere before? All ends happily and along the way there are appearances by Arsenal (again!), Millwall and Hayes FC. The baddie is played by Alan Wheatley, who was the Sheriff of Nottingham in the TV version of *Robin Hood*, so they must have known something was up.

This is not to say that the British hold the copyright on making rotten footy movies. I feel duty bound to say a few words about *La Vida Sigue Igual*, made in Spain in 1969. This is the pic in which Julio Iglesias starts as a goalkeeper thwarted by injuries sustained in a car crash when on the verge of stardom with Real Madrid. Multi-talented being Julio's middle name, however, he goes on to make a full recovery and stars a career as a singer-songwriter.

Escape to Victory (1981) is perhaps the best known of recent soccer movies. Proving once again that soccer players can't act and actors can't play believable football, it was actually shot in Hungary to save money. Even with "soccer plays designed by Pelé" as the credits record, there was no way of making Michael Caine's stomach look the part. Much more interesting are two of *Victory*'s antecedents, *Tretiy Taym* (USSR, 1963) and *Ket Felido a Prokolban* (Hungary, 1961).

Tretiy Taym, or 'The Last Game', was based on a true Second World War story and has a Soviet team in occupied Kiev forced to play a match against a German side. The Soviets are under strict instructions to lose the match, but on the day find they cannot betray their compatriots who make up the huge audience. They win the game and, rather than melting away into an adoring crowd, as in *Victory*, are led away to face a firing squad.

Ket Felido a Prokolban ('Two Half Times in Hell'), is a similar story but was not as well received by the critics. In this field, the Hungarian team are mown down on the pitch and the final image is that of a solitary football.

A footnote to these two thought-provoking pictures is that Gennadi Yukhtin, who played the Soviet goalkeeper in *Tretiy Taym*, was considered to be so good at the part that he was later offered the chance to play the game professionally. What chance of Premier League club scouts turning up at Pinewood and Elstree? Why didn't someone make a similar offer to Sly Stallone?

My guess is that we will not be given the opportunity of seeing

Appuntamento a Liverpool (Italy, 1987) in this country. This is a second rate revenge story involving an Italian girl whose father was killed in the Heysel disaster. She dreams that she knows the killer, and heads off to Liverpool carrying a gun. Tacky or what?

Another Italian picture which misses the mark, although not by as much, was *Ultra* (1990) directed by Ricky Tognazzi. This is one of the very few full-scale features to deal exclusively with soccer violence; Tognazzi hoped that the film would be the starting point for dialogue about the problem of hooliganism. The violence in the film is not brought off particularly well, but a convincing sense of the powerlessness of your average football fan is created. Principe, the central character, calls a TV phone-in to complain about problems we are all too familiar with: being ignored by the club, exorbitant ticket prices, and all the rest.

We also see Principe and his mates barred from watching their team at a training session for no apparent reason. Football is never seen during the film, which concentrates purely on scrapping, with a fairly poor love-interest sub-plot.

Tognazzi is on record as saying that since he made *Ultra* (which tells the story of a group of AS Roma fans) he has been criticised by: Roma fans who say they aren't hooligans; Roma fans who say they are hooligans and are much harder than portrayed in the film; and Lazio fans who are aggrieved that he didn't make a film about their hooligans. *Ultra* tries hard, but ends up not getting anything like the best out of its subject matter.

In a hymn to national identity, the protagonists of *Pervaya Lastochka*, or 'The First Swallow', form a football team and gradually become experts at the game. The finale consists of a stuffing handed out by a team of visiting British sailors (played, incidentally, by visiting American sailors). As the victorious Brits sail away, the initially despondent home side join together in a hearty rendition of their national anthem, suggesting that they are well aware of the value of a good drubbing as regards their learning curve.

There is so much more – football films from China, from Hong Kong, from Tunisia and Vietnam. There are even Swiss ones, for God's sake. And they are still being made, *Nordkurve* from Germany being the latest not very impressive contender. There are feature-length World Cup documentaries, the TV films... To think it all started with a casual mention of the Rovers in *A Kind of Loving*. Which reminds me that *AKOL* actually had a sequence shot at a real football match – only it's Bolton Wanderers at home to Sheffield United on November 4th, 1961. Bolton won 2-0. I wonder if they got paid seven guineas per day...? O

How Can I Love You Moore?

England had just lost its finest ever defender. Cris Freddi paid tribute to the man Beckenbauer described as "a football idol".

WSC No 74, April 1993

SPORT MAKES SOME MEN HANDSOME. REPHRASE THAT: WHEN YOU SEE CERTAIN players in repose, it comes as a surprise that they're not really good-looking. Glenn Hoddle, Günter Netzer, Bjorn Borg. Bobby Moore was probably top of the list.

An opening paragraph like that shows how much I'm struggling. Looking for an 'alternative' view, all I could come up with was that he had a bit of a podgy face and difficult hair. Pitiful. Almost wished he had nicked that stupid bracelet: might've proved he was human.

All right, yes, we know about the failed country club, the mixed success at Oxford City and Southend, the confidence-bordering-on-arrogance that was just shyness in disguise, the break with Tina – but none of this is any of our damn business. Concern yourself with Moore the player and it's hard not to agree with everything that's been written.

Weaknesses? Well, leave him man-on-man with the very best and he'd struggle at times. In only his second game for England, against Hungary in the '62 World Cup, Lajos Tichy dummied him to score the opening goal. He let a long ball go over his head for Dzajic to knock us out of the European Championships semi in 1968. When Sigi Held ran at him he gave away the penalty that put West Germany 2-1 up in Netzer's match at Wembley in 1972. In Katowice, his famous attempt at a drag-back let Lubanski in for the goal that effectively knocked us out of the '74 finals (Mooro had scored an own goal in the first half). A week later, in his record-breaking 107th international, he was standing on the goal-line when Anastasi's shot went between his legs.

But most of this was at the top 'n' tail of his career. From 1963, when he became the youngest England captain ever, to about the end of 1971, he was everybody's idea of the greatest defender in the world. Voted best player of the '66 World Cup, he made two of Hurst's goals in the final, the first slyly (taking a free kick before the whistle), the second probably to needle Big Jack who was screaming at him to kick it into Neasden, each one with perfect long passes through the air. In 1970 he was even better:

those famous tackles, never a mistake you can remember, no ill effects from heat, altitude or Colombian shysters.

Did it all the right way, too. In the semis of the 1968 European Championships, he might have handled the ball before it reached Dzajic, but wasn't sure he was outside the area, "and anyway that's not my way". He could've kicked pieces out of Pelé like they did in '66, but "it would have been an insult to myself". He kept faith with that through the Hunter-Storey era, for which we're all grateful; it's England's loss that his style of play didn't start a trend. We've been saddled with the double whammy ever since: Watson-Thompson, Butcher-Fenwick, Adams-Pallister, Keown-anybody. A pairing of Mooro and Des Walker would match anything produced by any other country any time.

When dear old Walter Winterbottom gave Billy Wright 105 caps, for some reason it smacked of favouritism, sentimentality (this is being unfair to both, but you see what I'm saying). When Sir Alf gave Bobby Moore 100 (out of 108), it seemed the right, hard-nosed decision.

Two compliments sum it up: Brian Clough was desperate to sign him even when he had Colin Todd ("I'll put him at right back and tell him to learn from the master"); and the one thing any Scottish, Irish or Welsh player wanted to do, even if England won, was to put one over on Bobby Moore, or at least make him break sweat. So all right they managed it once or twice. So show us your World Cup medals.

He was a red rag to a bull in parts of England, too, especially on freezing nights up north when Ron Greenwood sent them out with mittens on. But even then he looked a class above anyone else – and that's the main thing when you're trying to decide on his place among English defenders. There are no other contenders.

Perhaps Neil Franklin, though he didn't play in quite the same position, came closest in terms of style and dominance. To mention anyone else in the same breath – well, try it: Flowers, Hughes, Phil Thompson, Mark Wright...

And yet, come on, isn't it true that Bobby Moore was never quite the national folk hero he should have been? Respected, sure. Much appreciated when Pelé and Tostao were striking matches in Mexico, thanks very much. But while unspeakable anti-footballers like Stiles, Hunter, Holton, Tommy Smith and Tony Adams have been given cult status, Moore must have played it a little too cool for English tastes, too posh. Strange really, because he was as hard as any First Division defender in an era of very hard ones (ask Geoff Hurst, Shankly, anyone), and he liked a shandy or two: witness the Blackpool affair and the expert, J Greaves, who credited him with hollow legs. Kept his accent, too. So we called him Mooro, we grieve loudly now he's gone – and we mean it – but as a player he wasn't quite loved.

Except, for what the hell it's worth, by the likes of me. We thought he was bloody wonderful, one of the very few reasons for being proud of English football at the turn of the Seventies. We'd watch him take the ball off Jairzinho's toes, hear the commentator say "Moore, again", and get a genuine shiver down the back, a physical thing, to think that in a World Cup lit up by Brazilians, Germans and the odd dazzling Peruvian, the very best defender, by a street, was ours. I'm pleased as Punch I got his autograph.

His death seems, for want of another word, symbolic, the end of someone so closely connected with the Sixties a decade looked back on with amused tolerance now, but one of the better ones: full employment and so much downright fun. Did Labour really lose the election because Germany knocked us out of the Cup? Probably. For us, it was the end of the world. ○

Double Booked

A prior engagement kept Nick Hornby from attending the 1993 FA Cup final replay, but, as anyone who watched will know, he didn't miss much.

WSC No 77, July 1993

I WAS ENTIRELY CONFIDENT THAT ARSENAL WOULD WIN TWO CUPS THIS season. And if anyone had asked me last August who would score the winning goals, I would have gone for Morrow and Linighan – I've always felt that they were cruelly underrated, those two – without any hesitation. I could even have predicted that Tony Adams, in an exciting variation to the Wembley tradition, was going to keep a firm grip on the trophy and drop the player instead. If you had told me, however, that on the night Arsenal won their first FA Cup in 14 years I would be sitting in the Savoy stuffing my face, I would have laughed in yours.

It was all very unfortunate. My book *Fever Pitch* was shortlisted for a prize – the £25,000 NCR award for non-fiction – and I had already accepted an invitation to the ceremony before I realised that there was going to be a disastrous conflict of very major interests. (Why was the replay on a Thursday? Thursday is usually the one day of the week I can pretend I'm a rounded human being, with a plurality of relationships and interests.) I only made the connection a couple of days before the Saturday game, and wasn't too worried; I was not then aware, however, of the new FA rule that bans Cup finalists from having more than one goal attempt per team during the game.

If Lee Dixon had lobbed Seaman from 30 yards – and he's done it before – during extra time, I would probably have stood on my backless, £30 seat yards below the pitch at the Arsenal end and wept with relief. (For me, it's not the winning or the losing, but the taking part.) As it was, the two teams contented themselves with aiming long balls carefully at their friends, wives and hideously crippled colleagues in Row B. The Doomsday Scenario was upon me.

For two days, I agonised about what to do. Wembley has long ceased to be the Promised Land for most of us – I had been three times in the previous month, and hadn't seen a decent through ball in five hours of football; on the other hand, there is this residual fear that each time my team appears in a final, it could be the last one during my lifetime (Chelsea fans will understand this better than most).

But how many book prizes could I realistically expect to be nominated for? There was no way of finding out beforehand whether I had won the dosh or not – I could only find out by going to the dinner.

In the end, it was the award organisers' guarantee of a TV set that swung it. I bought an Arsenal bow-tie from the World of Sport at Finsbury Park, put my Dad's old dinner jacket on and went to the Savoy. The TV was just outside the main dining room; a small table had been placed in front of it, so I could eat my dinner in front of the box. It was just like home. For form's sake, I started the meal with the other guests, but I had only just squeezed my lemon over the smoked salmon when a waiter tapped me on the shoulder. "Excuse me, sir, but you may care to know that Ian Wright has just scored for Arsenal." I raced off to see the replay.

Things continued in this vein until half-way through extra time, when the judges began their summing up. I listened to Margaret Jay rave about Peter Hennessey's *Never Again* and Michael Palin say kind and amusing things about *Fever Pitch*. But just as Diana Rigg was giving her considered assessment of Lewis Wolpert's *The Unnatural Nature of Science*, I got another tap on the shoulder – Linighan had scored for Arsenal. I reached the TV just in time for the final whistle.

There wasn't time for me to see Tone go up to lift the FA Cup, however: my partner came racing in to tell me that David Puttnam was about to award the prize. I opened the door to the dining room and the bearded movie mogul (and, disturbingly, Spurs fan) announced that the winner was Peter Hennessey even before I'd had a chance to get back to my seat. I felt like the man who had won the Cup and lost 25 grand in the same evening. Hell, I was the man who had won the Cup and lost 25 grand in the same evening.

The next morning I got married. We are poor but happy. ○

The Final Frontier

Roger Titford explained why the world's oldest knockout tournament is in decline.

WSC No 77, July 1993

ANDY LINIGHAN'S LAST-MINUTE GOAL MAY HAVE WON THE CUP FOR ARSENAL, saved the final from penalties and put him into the quiz books for the next century – but it won't do anything to reverse the steady decline of England's premier football fixture.

The FA Cup final, sadly, is not what it was. In retrospect we can see its modern heyday lasted from the advent of mass TV and radio coverage in the 1950s until the mid/late 1970s. But, like that other great fixture of yesteryear, England versus Scotland, it is beginning to fade away.

The TV audience was less than 10 million at kick-off time on Saturday. The replay attracted a 'meagre' 62,267 at the stadium (but a creditable average of 15 million on the box). However, the whole event seemed to be treated by some of the media as an unwelcome grind, just another Wembley match to be accommodated and consumed. We were spared the degrading outrage of penalties this time, but one day soon that will be the way the competition is ended. Then we will see more clearly how far the final has fallen.

In the 1950s and 1960s the FA Cup final had an immense hold on the public imagination and a festival atmosphere that was more religiously observed than most religious occasions. The back pages in the preceding week exhibited the likely heroes of the day dressed as highwaymen, policemen and jailers. The injury to Liverpool's Gordon Milne in 1965 was treated with all the high-profile anguish that now seems reserved for the Queen Mother's throat.

On the day, the nation gathered before its TV sets. Those, alas, at work were presumed missing, glued to transistor radios. A 1973 TV documentary featured the utterly deserted streets of Sunderland on Cup final afternoon. I'd always imagined everywhere was like that then, but I haven't been out since the age of six to check.

All (ie both) TV channels offered six or seven hours coverage. Jokes about the TV breaking down or men having to get married on Cup final Saturday were standard comic fare. It genuinely seemed like a whole different kind of ball game then. The sapping turf, the cramp, the Wembley jinx, the possibility of extra time, the fact of being the only live, televised, domestic club football match and virtually the only one at Wembley all added to the sense that this was a game like no other, famed for ultimate endeavour and lasting legend.

And at Wembley there would be exactly the blessed 100,000. Always the perfect round number. Nobody ever failed to turn up, according to the press. Interviewed beforehand by the likes of David Coleman as to how they had come by their precious ticket fans told of incredible feats of perseverance and ingenuity. No sacrifice seemed too great to be present at such an experience. When the BBC bestowed a pair of tickets on two ticketless unfortunates on the Wembley concourse, it was as if a miracle had been performed.

Inside, the presence of senior royalty (when did the Queen last attend the final?), and the singing of *Abide With Me* gave a sense of congregation, to be shared by the TV millions. This is an exhibition of national togetherness. It matters not so much who wins but that the occasion is properly honoured. There would be best behaviour. It was difficult to get booked and impossible to get sent off.

And afterwards the hero of the hour, clutching his post-match pint of milk, not quite believing he had written himself into history, said his piece, first to one channel then the other, the high point of the season was reached, the credits rolled and football was over for another four months.

Now the Cup final slips in between the League play-offs and the

Autoglass final whilst exhausting participants in the World Cup qualifiers. Would Bill Shankly have Ron Yeats flown back from Sweden the day before the Cup final?

The FA Cup final's high tide mark was probably the Chelsea v Leeds replay of 1970 watched, according to some calculations, by 32 million viewers, the biggest TV audience ever in this country for a single event. But that year also marked the turning point, the time when the Cup final, and its much delayed replay 18 days later, started to become a nuisance rather than a celebration. It was getting in the way of the World Cup and of Leeds' European Cup ambitions. By 1977 it was the minor element of the Treble Liverpool didn't get.

There was a certain inevitability that the pre-eminence of the FA Cup final would decline as the mass society that was Britain in the post-war period fragmented into more media choice and more leisure pursuits. But, despite far more diversity in the USA, the Superbowl now has at least as strong a position in the hearts and minds of it own people.

The Superbowl has not had to suffer from being partially obscured by a cluster of new events of the sort that have sprung up around the FA Cup final in recent years (like FA Cup semis at Wembley, an April League Cup final, the Autoglass final, the play-off finals, the Anglo-Italian, the European Cup Winners' Cup all in the last two months).

Nor is it seen as a means to an end. It is slightly depressing to hear victory in domestic competitions like the FA Cup talked about so often as a prelude to Europe, especially when in recent seasons 'Europe' seems merely to involve rolling over some Cypriots or Finns before flailing hopelessly against the first Italians or Germans encountered (Man Utd being the honourable exception). In these circumstances, the last thing the Cup final needs is to become yet another sponsored bauble with permanent Wembley semi-finals. Unfortunately there is no reason to hold out hope on either count.

Over the past couple of decades the neutral or uncommitted fan's focus has come to rest increasingly on the England team, and in particular on its performance in the finals of international tournaments, rather than the FA Cup final. This fits better the modern idiom of watching football: to participate by active support for your side rather than to spectate and appreciate other teams. While some Cup finals leave the neutral mystified as to who to support, international tournaments offer fairly clear guidelines.

The massive TV audiences and public debate are more inclined to centre on England v West Germany or Sweden than Liverpool v Sunderland or Arsenal v Sheffield Wednesday. The mundane nature of the last two finals have not helped. More than ever, Wembley needs its stories and surprises – headlines like **Gazza's Knees**, **Wright's Return** and **Dons' Shock**.

The demise of the FA Cup final as a truly major national event is part of the growing internationalisation of our football culture. As far back as 1945 and the Moscow Dynamo tour George Orwell spoke out against the mixing of politics, sport and internationalism. His prophecies may be judged too gloomy now. There is, however, a more selfish reason for dismay. The FA Cup final came around every May bringing national football drama in its wake. With England as the focus instead, it's not going to be quite the same. The international matches that will be the equals in media terms of the old Cup finals cannot, of course, be guaranteed to happen...

Shortly after Waddle stepped up to the spot in Turin, leant back, gambled everything on the top left corner and missed, someone nearby groaned "that's it for the next 20 years". The blood froze. O

Fear and Loathing in Pontiac

David Quantick travelled from Illinois to Michigan for the England v Germany US Cup fixture. It wasn't just a bad trip. It was the worst 24 hours of his life.

WSC No 79, September 1993

"SING IF YOU'RE WINNING! YOU ONLY SING IF YEURRGHH EURR... EURR... ON our way to Wembley! We're on our way to eurrggh!!!!"

Surely this is Hell. I am in a coach which is driving from Chicago, Illinois, to Pontiac, Michigan, to see a friendly, a plug-the-1994-World-Cup game between England and Germany and I have been plunged into the inferno itself. The reason for this is not the interminable six-hour drive or even the lack of oxygen on the ventilationless and air-conditioningless coach, it is because I am surrounded by expatriate Britons.

There could be no worse people to be among. With the exception of the driver, one Roger Kirby ("My friends call me Kirby. You can call me

Roger"), and a few Anglophile Chicagoans, everyone on this coach is an ex-pat, blind drunk, aggressive and, worst of all, incapable of remembering more than three words of any known football song. To my left, two brothers from Birmingham splay in their seats, clenching their guts and making a fourth attempt at *The Wild Rover*. Behind me a group of Londoners are being led by a curiously pie-faced physics professor in a chorus of *Nice One Cyril*.

I mean! Jesus! *Nice One Cyril*! I feel like I've fallen through a hole in time. These people are like Japanese soldiers lost in the jungle; they've probably never heard of Thatcherism, punk rock, or even Paul Gascoigne. And this is the sad problem. None of these bastards has been near a British football match in 20 years; they're locked in some kind of football time-warp where Gordon Banks winks and tosses the ball to George Best as the crowd spin their rattles appreciatively. And this, God save me from certain death, is their Big Day Out.

Slowly the coach makes its way across Indiana, dullest state in the Union. Suddenly the pie-faced professor is on his feet, bellowing like a stuck walrus and tossing lager foam everywhere. "Germans!", he screams. The Cockneys scramble across their seats and shout "Bastards!" and "Krauts!" and "Boo! Boo!" at a small car with a German flag on its windshield. The occupants smile and wave. They have a car, they have air-conditioning, they have an economy.

And they are not in a coach with the brothers from Birmingham. The phrase 'Brits on the piss' must have been invented for this bloated duo. Now they seem, dimly, to feel that the coach driver should sing for them, perhaps since he may know more than four words of some songs, and chant "Roger, Roger, give us a song!" ineptly.

Roger, black and tolerant beyond salary, is having none of this. He picks up the intercom mike and declares, "Not all of us sing and dance." This retort goes unnoticed by the Brum brothers, who break into *The Banana Boat Song*. My friends and I cringe. Roger remains sanguine. "Heh, heh, heh," he laughs, proving that sometimes you don't have to spell things out; sometimes you can say "Die, scum bastards!" just by smiling and going "Heh, heh, heh."

Now we are approaching Pontiac, which is just outside Detroit, the Motor City. Like the classic car that bears its name, Pontiac is big, green and smells of petrol. It is a glum place that for some reason contains a vast and beautiful stadium, the Silverdome. Slowly Roger brings the coach past other cars ("Germans! Boo!"), through a quiet and efficient line of traffic police ("Kill the Bill! Kill the Bill!"), and into a car park filled with other coaches, themselves filled with other England fans ("Wa hey! INGERLUND!")

We file into the stadium and watch with some joy as Professor Pie-Face is body-searched, then climb millions of stairs to a bar located some inches below the roof. 'BEER' says a sign. Hooray! "No beer today on account of the soccer game," says a man. "However, we do have a wide selection of non-alcoholic beverages."

It is now that I lose it and spend ten minutes verbally working my way around a theme whose constituent themes are that everyone on the coach is a blind drunk swamp animal, that they have finished all their beer already, and that the only way that the rest of this afternoon would have been even remotely tolerable was if I, too, was a blind drunk swamp animal, but instead I find I cannot get a drink because the Americans are not prepared to let English football fans get drunk in their stadiums.

The match seems brief after the coach journey. Germany are bored and England are boring. The only really entertaining thing I see during the entire game is a T-shirt worn by a girl from an all-female high school soccer team in the row in front of me. Depicting, from left to right, a caveman, an American footballer, a male soccer player and a woman soccer player, it is captioned 'EVOLUTION!'

Through cosmic aptness, the Brum brothers are sitting behind me, exercising their knowledge and their mouths. "Everything to play for!" they shout whenever England are within twenty yards of the German goal. "Donkey!" they shout at anyone who misses anything. "That was offside!" they shout when Germany score. They have all of Jimmy Hill's insight, wit and imagination, without any of the trimness of his little pointy chin.

The match ends, England lose and we file out into the thunderstorm straight out of *Moby Dick*. We quickly find our coach and pile in to wait for the others. After twenty minutes it becomes apparent that Professor Pie-Face has got lost in the short distance between our coach and the stadium. Eventually, he turns up, soaked to the skin, and looking miserable. Hooray!

The coach moves off in damp silence. "Liquor stop," announces the saintly Roger and drives into what is either part of Pontiac, or a disused *Starsky and Hutch* set. We buy as much beer as we can and return to the coach and drink it. Then, after a head count, Roger goes into the store and returns with a passenger apparently too stupid to work out how to leave a shop once he has entered it.

Night falls as the coach makes its way across Michigan. The Brum brothers have remembered some more of *The Wild Rover* but keep abandoning it to sing a song about the sexual perversities of Londoners. The Cockneys at the back of the coach respond with some material about the poverty – both spiritual and literal – of people from Birmingham. It must have been like this in the trenches. We chug lager at speed, but find that it cannot make you deaf.

Now the Brum brothers lose their minds. "In England, right, it's niggers. You go to the shop to buy a jar of coffee and it's shut," one of them is telling someone else through a mush of incoherence and lager stupidity. "Here you can go to the shop to buy a bag of concrete at ten, you can buy a bag of concrete at midnight, you can buy a bag of concrete at two..." Then he passes out. His immobile brontosaurian carcass, beer-stained and huge a mere aisle away from my seat, suddenly makes me think that we have become trapped in *Jurassic Park*. Except here the dinosaurs are inside the coach.

Finally we near Chicago. The bright lights of the city welcome us. Hooray! "Sorry, folks," says Roger. "There's been some kind of accident up ahead. We're gonna be delayed a little while..." A silence falls in the darkness. Nearly everyone is comatose – except for friends and I, who are suicidal.

But here now at least is a brief moment of peace. Even Pie-Face has snuggled up inside his flag, fast asleep and quietly steaming from Pontiac rain. Only one person is still talking, an American near the back, chatting to a friend. Drowsily, I eavesdrop. It is the worst mistake of my life. "This parrot is deceased!" the American chants. "It has ceased to be! Bereft of life, it has joined the choir invisibule! It is no more..." Yes. This is Hell. ○

White Man's Burr Den

It seemed that the sterling efforts of Millwall's Football in the Community project were being undermined from within the club. Jakko M Jakszyk wrote to Millwall's chairman, Reg Burr, to describe events that took place at The Den in February 1993. Below is Reg Burr's reply.

WSC No 80, October 1993

Dear Mr Burr,

I saw you on television the other day on the ITV lunch time news programme. You were discussing the new 'Kick Racism Out of Football' campaign with John Fashanu. Fair enough, I thought, nice to see someone from the Millwall organization standing up to this unpleasant scourge of the game. I was therefore amazed when I heard you say that "Racism has been all but eliminated from Millwall". On further reflection I assumed that maybe racism had been eliminated from the directors box. It certainly has not been removed from the terraces.

Back in February, a friend invited me down to the Den to watch my team, Watford's, away fixture there. Now I have been to a lot of away games and I am not easily shocked. However, nothing could prepare me for what I heard at Millwall last season.

Watford currently have four regular black players in the first team and the abuse coming from behind me was astonishing. What I heard with nauseating regularity throughout the first half whenever one of Watford's black players received the ball was "Kill that black c***", "F****** stab the black c***" and "Burn him, burn the f****** black bastard". No one within my earshot made any comment to the perpetrators other than general encouragement and much laughter.

At the end of the first half we moved to the other side of the terrace and stood in front of what looked like a family group. Admittedly, no one screamed every few seconds, but the words "black bastard" were heard throughout the second half, greeted with the same degree of complicit amusement I had witnessed in the first half.

Maybe I am being naive or maybe the relatively mild nature of the Watford crowd has made me a touch sensitive. Either way, seeing you on national TV paying lip service to the anti-racist lobby while dismissing the problem at Millwall as something you have already dealt with, indeed setting yourself as something of an example to other clubs, was something I couldn't ignore without comment.

There are, I understand, laws pertaining to racist comments during matches. It would have been nice to see the police having a word with someone at the very least.

And if you really want to rid yourselves of this unpleasant element and encourage more black fans to the ground, how about banning the numerous young men openly selling racist, National Front and British Movement literature right outside?

Suffice to say I will not be going to any game at your new ground at the somewhat ironically named Senegal Fields. As it is an all-seater stadium one doesn't even have the option of moving about the ground in an attempt to find a racist-free zone.

Yours sincerely,
Jakko M Jakszyk

Dear Mr Jakszyk

Thank you for your letter of 18 August.

The open space sports ground upon which we built our new stadium is owned by the London Borough of Lewisham and was named by them Senegal Fields. The Borough has the reputation of one of the most efficient and competent authorities in the UK.

I do not think we will miss you at the New Den and I must say I feel sorry for somebody who seems to be as sick as you are.

Yours sincerely,
R I Burr, Chairman

Field of Dreams

Jimmy Armfield offered A Lesson for Youngsters Everywhere.
But, as Paul Miller found out, it didn't help much.

WSC No 81, November 1993

LONG AGO, WHEN NORTHAMPTON TOWN WERE IN THE FIRST DIVISION AND
Mark Hateley's Dad played for Villa, I operated under the sobriquet of
Chalkie. One of my mates at the time was a lad who was even smaller
than I am, called Trevor Paul. In truth, we weren't that close, but we were
united in rivalry as arguably the two best footballers in the school. Ours
was one of those grammars that used to wish it was a public school, and
could kick oiks like Trev and me out. They couldn't actually ban us from
playing soccer in our free time, they just treated us to the same brand of
discrimination other schools reserved for homosexuals.

Sometimes Trev would be picked first when choosing the sides at
break, sometimes I would. I don't remember either of us being given the
responsibility for selecting the sides. We would just swan about oblivious
to that sordid side of things, a bit like royalty not knowing where the
kitchen is. I have to say, however, that I knew he was better than me.

From the time that I realised it counted as a job, I never seriously
considered any other career for myself apart from that of a professional
footballer. I read and put into practice every word of text-book advice.

I tackled with studied concentration: shoulder, knee and instep all in
an imaginary plumbline. I wore my shirt neatly tucked in and my hose
seams were straight – the model footballer. You played better that way.
Jimmy Armfield said so in *Teach Yourself Better Soccer*, or somesuch.

And I did most of it in secret because it was really rather frowned upon in
our family. We lived on one of those new estates and had aspirations. My
cousins and I were expected to go to university and have careers, anything
less would have been letting the family down. Or at least, that's what it felt
like. I carried on as if I was studying seriously, but it was more important to
me that I didn't go in until I'd bounced the ball on my head fifty times
consecutively. In keeping with Jimmy Armfield's advice, I watched the
professionals: from the beginning of the 1960-61 season until the 1967-68
season, I don't believe I missed a home game Villa played.

I'm a slow learner and hadn't yet realised that experience is a question of quality, not quantity. Pretty well none of it rubbed off on me. Come Sunday afternoon the result of all this for Leomansley United was a player who could juggle a ball endlessly in the warm-up, but who lost his footing when confronted with an opponent who didn't go to his school.

Trev, on the other hand, was cavalier about everything. He was just a natural upstart. He didn't get the Christmas annuals, hardly ever went to the Villa, only played football with other people, and showed not respect at all for his kit. Between matches, my boots would be stripped of their laces, stuffed with the *Sunday Mercury* (after I'd finished my scrapbook) and left it in front of the fire – but not too close – before being dubbined. His caked size fours were simply clouted against the tree under whose shade he changed.

The Pauls lived in the time-honoured traditional domicile for future footballers, a terrace house. Admittedly not a backstreet, but they were pulling all the slums down then. His dad ran a paper delivery service from a shed in their back yard, and was always bollocking Trev for not getting up in time to do his round. It was always noisy round there, and I loved it. I wanted cobblestones, and not being able to afford a ball, so that I had to play with a cotton reel. I wanted the advantages Matthews, Finney and Lofthouse had been brought up with.

With the onslaught of puberty and teenage passion, I discovered Willie Anderson at about the same time that Trev discovered girls, and with the same alacrity. Willie was my inspiration to be interesting at last. Out came the hem of my jersey, up came the twisted hose to my knee, and over came the sleeve cuffs. My elbows adhered to my waist and my Roy Orbison pompadour flopped in front of my eyes.

A Villa scout sent Trev for trials. For one whole season I suppressed a desire to talk to Trev (much) about what it was like to train with the Villa after school. I remember the effect it had on his game: he learned how to tap ankles, pull shirts and control the ball with his hand. What's more, he learned it all with such innocence that even opponents didn't take exception.

If only someone had realised that Trev should have taken the field in elastic-sided Cuban-heeled boots, he'd have made it. He was one of those little shits defenders hate, who twist and squirm and then fly over the ground for ten yards. By then he'd got the space to do one of those curling chip crosses that were his speciality, and which were probably a bit of a pain for onrushing forwards, who would have preferred a lower trajectory.

In the end it just petered out. I never heard it as official that he wasn't at Villa anymore, but he wasn't. A bit lightweight probably. He was back on Beacon Park and had done better than the rest of us, without trying much. My game went to Hell. I was worse at nineteen than I had been at fifteen. I grew a beard, long hair, and a donkey jacket. The last time I saw Trev he stopped to give me a lift in his lorry as I thumbed my way home from Stafford Art College. The spirit of self-assertion Trev's brush with the professional game instilled in him didn't go to waste however: he has elbowed his way from driving a lorry to owning a big new golf course near Lichfield and – a typical Trev flourish – employs an ex-manager of Walsall. ○

Celtic Soul Brothers

After the gloom of recent years, would the arrival of Lou Macari, and the possible removal of the current board, signal a return to good times at Parkhead? Graham McColl had his doubts.

WSC No 83, January 1994

CELTIC MAY BE POVERTY-STRICKEN THESE DAYS, BUT THEIR MUCH-CRITICIZED board clearly haven't forgotten that the club was founded as a charitable institution. Not only did they spend the first few months of this season gently grooming Stoke's new manager, Joe Jordan, but they are currently helping the Potteries club out with £80,000 towards the big man's salary.

That £80,000 is the fee Celtic have generously given 'little' Stoke as compensation for approaching and poaching Lou Macari for the post of manager at Parkhead. Celtic's actions are a bit like a down-at-heel aristocrat distributing alms to the poor and then returning home to a supper of bread and water. Stoke must be wondering what they have done to be singled out for such generosity.

After all, there's been no real explanation on the part of the Celtic board as to why they waited and waited and negotiated and negotiated for weeks until they finally ensnared Macari.

No-one else was approached, no-one else was considered. Not even

Jordan, apparently, who was good enough to be brought in during the summer as assistant to Liam Brady, but who didn't merit consideration for the manager's post when it became open.

On the day Macari was appointed, chairman Kevin Kelly came out with a statement that was a study in saying nothing at great length. "It's a new era. We've tried other things (that's no way to talk about Liam Brady), but they didn't work (that's almost slanderous). Lou was the only manager outside the club that we looked at. He was the man we wanted." Why?

"There's been something missing in Scottish football and some thought it was the Italian influence. There was a feeling that we should look at this and we thought the combination of Liam Brady and Joe Jordan would do the trick. Unfortunately it didn't work out."

And so, when the Italian influence was finally abandoned, Luigi Macari was brought in. It's good for Celtic to have a manager from Scotland's sizeable Italian community. And Macari is proof indeed that Italian people are well integrated in Britain: the football his previous clubs have played has been about as Italian as a supermarket tin of spaghetti bolognese.

From his time at Stoke, Birmingham, West Ham and Swindon, Macari brings with him a reputation as a long-ball merchant. Early Celtic matches under his charge have already seen defenders 'getting rid' of the ball as constructively and thoughtfully as wooden table-footballers.

Some of the possible signings being suggested, such as West Ham's midfielder Martin 'Mad Dog' Allen, are so alarming that it might, in the future, be more pleasing on the eye if Macari's sides did, indeed, miss out the mini-Bosnia that Celtic's midfield would surely soon become. The long-ball, muscular game just isn't good enough for Parkhead, though, and if Macari knows his stuff he must realize it's not on, mainly because of Celtic's traditions and their supporters' expectations, but also when examined in practical terms.

If Celtic try to muscle in on Scottish football's prizes, they're always likely to lose out. Rangers, in particular, have decades of experience of doing just that, they've become very good at it, and they can afford to spend massive amounts of money on defensive bouncers. It's also the type of game that's certain to extend Celtic's almost Thatcherite avoidance of serious involvement in Europe. When the Celtic board first paraded their prize catch at the end of October, much was made of Macari's connection with the Stein era. At the press conference, Lou was strategically placed underneath a painting of a stern-looking Stein, so lifelike he appeared ready to reach out and clip Macari round the ear.

Macari make the expected noises about Stein's greatness, but whether Stein would have been enthusiastic about the new appointment is another matter. Macari had barely established himself in a very good Celtic side before he began looking for more money or a move. On leaving Stein to join up with Tommy Docherty at Manchester United in 1973, he appeared to be signing up for a manager more attuned to his way of thinking.

For the remainder of that decade, Macari frequently offered the opinion, often couched in bizarrely bitter terms, that Scottish football was dying and that he certainly wouldn't be coming back. So the much-trumpeted line that Macari is a Celtic supporter finally returning home seems rather hollow.

Macari's appointment was described, on the day it happened, as a "PR stunt" by one Fergus McCann. McCann was the figurehead of the romantically-titled 'rebel' group, a collection of well-fed, besuited businessmen with money, who wanted to replace the bunch of well-fed, besuited businessmen with money who currently have the keys to the Celtic boardroom.

McCann and Co, who appear to have backed down after an attempt to prove that the existing board don't have the club's best interests at heart was defeated in court, weren't averse to the occasional stunt themselves.

They threw their considerable collective weight behind those Celtic fans who chant British football's 1993 chart-topper, 'sack the board', at every opportunity. Sometimes, as the fans chant in the car park outside Parkhead's main entrance, they would be rewarded by a thumb's up from one of the 'rebels' inside the comfortable surrounds of the main reception suite. Sometimes, one of the 'rebels' would even come among the people, who provided a good backdrop to an interview in front of the TV cameras.

The pressure on the current board, from the fans, the 'rebels', and certain members of the media is now immense. The more the board members dig their heels in, the louder the cries for their removal.

It's understandable that the Celtic fans should become emotional about the arrogant manner in which the club is being run, but if the current board members had been replaced by McCann's group there would have been a real likelihood of huge anti-climax. The 'rebels' would have given the new manager £5 million to spend, yet Liam Brady effortlessly wasted even more than that, and still complained that he was skint. McCann and Co would have also let the fans buy shares in the club – in five years' time.

The supporters ought to have asked themselves, as they stand in the wind and rain chanting 'sack the board', why they should be expected to wait so long to get tangible reward and a say in the running of the club. If the club is so short of money, it seems strange that the 'rebels' didn't want to look for a massive public cash injection straight away, rather than at some vague date close to the 21st century.

"When Celtic came in for me, my father said 'If you want to learn football, that's the best place to go'," said Kenny Dalglish, explaining why he, a Rangers supporter as a boy, joined Celtic. The modern Celtic Park must still be a hugely attractive place for young professionals – if their chosen field is corporate finance or creative accountancy. ○

Livingston, I Presume?

In 1994 Meadowbank Thistle relocated to Livingston. Colin McPherson was among the many Thistle supporters alarmed at the prospect.

WSC No 85, March 1994

THESE ARE SAD DAYS IN THE CONCRETE LAVVYPAN WHICH MASQUERADES AS home to Meadowbank Thistle. The few zealots who remain have watched a slide from First Division respectability to the spectre of relegation for the second successive season (with a little help from league reconstruction). Edinburgh's third team has been engulfed in a web of treachery and turmoil, which has shattered this formerly user-friendly club.

Gone are the salad days of Terry Christie's enterprising management, when the Scottish League's youngest club was denied a place in the Premier Division (with a little help from league reconstruction), when players were sold for profit to bigger clubs, average gates were on the up, peaking at 900 during 1988-89, and the club was run with a gentle, if arcane, bonhomie by an ageing but well-meaning committee of directors.

Every silver lining has its dark cloud. In Thistle's case it was more like a permanent eclipse. Over the horizon strode local self-made businessman and self-appointed saviour of Meadowbank Thistle, builder Bill Hunter. If this is sounding familiar to legions of fans throughout Britain, wait! Here is a tale of monstrous behaviour which would put even a South American *junta* to shame.

The Great One's acts of barbarity have included seeing the club being dragged through the courts by Terry Christie after he was deposed in a bloodless coup. This in turn alienated long-serving directors and supporters, the final straw being the imposition of a new constitution and a first ever share issue in which Hunter and his hand-chosen cronies gobbled up two thirds of the shares while denying ordinary supporters a chance to stake a claim in the club's future.

All this can usually be attributed to the typical egomaniac behaviour of a greedy director on the make. But then the board surpassed even themselves by unilaterally declaring that Thistle were going to re-locate in Livingston, a sprawling, and rather poor, new town 20 miles west of Edinburgh. Of course, with £4 million being promised by the local authority to build a brand new stadium, a builder could in theory profit from such a venture.

With the cash seemingly already promised by the soon to be disbanded Livingston Development Corporation, the chosen few have been promised our very own Nirvana. And with that achieved, it's on to the highest reaches of Scottish football (they've actually set a target date) under the banner of Livingston Football Club – well, they insisted we change the name once it was their cash. Hooray! Trebles all round!

If ever there was a case of a man believing his own PR, this is it. Paul Daniels may allegedly be a fabulous magician, but he would never dream of trying to pull 1,500 fans out of a hat, which is what the proposed new club would require to survive. To become Scotland's 14th best supported club (from position 36 with an average gate of 200), in a town where unemployment is bad and the local economy isn't even strong enough to sustain a cinema, would be a miracle of loaves-and-fishes proportions.

Although the deal has yet to be signed and settled, the Harbinger has trumpeted its merits to all and sundry. Dissent from within has been ruthlessly stifled. The programme editors have been sacked; players and officials have been forbidden to speak to *The Thistle*, an excellent fanzine which has studiously and relentlessly tried to publish the truth about boardroom shenanigans during the past two years. Supporters protests, such as they have been, were dismissed as irrelevant in a hail of expletives by a board whose paranoia is matched only by its ineptness.

Meanwhile, the team which began this season so well, started pirouetting downwards as soon as goalkeeper Jim McQueen was offloaded because the club were supposedly broke. The price? £8,000. The result? The team that had conceded just one goal in eight games (and that a penalty), went into free-fall, culminating in manager Donald Park resigning followed by a costly Cup exit to a dreadful Montrose team. Former boss Park has remained tight-lipped about his departure, but it is believed that he had major disagreements on policy with Hunter & Co who, amongst other things, demanded a bigger say in team selection.

All the while Mr Hunter continues a recruiting drive in Livingston aimed at establishing his franchise successfully in war-torn West Lothian. Spearheaded by the club's new PR man, a former referee detested by Thistle fans for his on-field aberrations, the regime has attempted to induce hapless locals with free transportation from the sticks to Meadowbank for specially selected home games. Ironically this treat includes a guided tour of the ground they are so desperate to leave.

I mean, we know that an athletics stadium isn't ideal for football, but it never stopped Bayern Munich winning three European Cups. Probity would dictate expending similar energy in prosperous old Edinburgh, thus truly establishing the club in the city and staving off the 'inevitable' bankruptcy we are told is imminent without Hunter's largesse.

Tempers are fraying on both sides now. The directors stormed out of Jim McQueen's testimonial dinner after fans booed the idea of moving to Livingston. After a barrage of unfavourable comments following a stupe-fying home draw with Cowdenbeath, Mr Hunter rampaged through the orange tip-up seats to manhandle and harangue a young fan who had been shouting the odds at him.

Subsequent matches have culminated in angry Meadowbank fans (there's a thought), chorusing their disapproval and pleading with the board to resign. But they won't. Chants of 'sack the board' may have become a cliché in Scotland recently, but it only serves as an indication of the annoyance felt by supporters everywhere at the antics of the people who claim to be running Scottish football.

Like any internal strife, to the outsider this whole sorry episode may seem trivial, but it is our club and it really hurts. To be dictated to is unpleasant. To be bullied, lied to, dismissed as an irrelevant nuisance after spending God knows what percentage of my GDP following Thistle around, really, really hurts. Unlike Aldershot, Newport or Bradford Park Avenue, if Meadowbank Thistle die, and by that I mean moving away and changing their name, there will be no coming back.

At the present time we are on the gallows awaiting our fate. We are condemned and have no choice. Only one question now remains. Will it be heaven or hell? Or worse, Livingston? O

Stars and Gripes

Scarcely a day went by in 1994 without someone criticizing the decision to hold the World Cup in the USA. Rich Zahradnik had had enough. The fightback started here.

WSC No 85, March 1994

IT WOULD BE HARD TO AVOID NOTICING THAT FOOTBALL FANS OVER HERE ARE worried about what the USA is going to do with and to the World Cup, the globe's biggest sporting event. In an attempt to back this concern up with some evidence, a British TV news programme asked some Americans about the tournament. The soundbite answers were all ridiculous, inane or arrogant; most of those interviewed didn't even know what the World Cup was. It is not funny but nor is it accurate.

Soundbite journalism can convict anyone of anything. Combine that with the standing order from every British editor and producer to their team in the USA – "bring me those wacky Americans" – and the picture reported back is of a nation of imbecile serial killers and fast-food freaks. In fact, now that I live in the UK, I'm convinced my friends and family are all busy killing each other down at the local McDonald's. My mom denies it. But she would, wouldn't she?

I'm getting used to defending how we're going to handle the World Cup. I do it in pubs. I do it after football matches. I've even had to write to a fanzine for the side I support – Nottingham Forest – which went on for an entire page blaming Americans for the word 'soccer'. To set the record straight, the word was borne of the politics of language and the politics of sport right here in England.

During the last century, had someone here seen fit not to let two sports run around calling themselves football (association football and rugby football) and had someone English not referred to association football as soccer, we wouldn't have these problems. Because then, when gridiron evolved in the US, out of rugby *football*, it wouldn't have picked up the second name and kept it. Proof we Americans had our hearts in the right place?

Back in 1912, when two organizations sought recognition from FIFA, they applied using the names the American Football Association and the American Amateur Football Association. Unfortunately, once the

American sport with helmets and pads caught on, it was too late for the word football. But soccer wasn't our word in the first place.

Perhaps the complaints about Americans and football arise because, as Pete Davies wrote in *All Played Out*, "The English always need to cherish the superior feeling that Americans can't play football with a particular intensity – because they have always to rub from their minds one of the greatest upsets in the history of the game. In 1950... they went to Brazil for the fourth (World Cup) tournament, and in Belo Horizonte the USA beat them 1-0. USA 1, England 0 – a fact like that, it shakes and grinds at the very roots of your culture. It's *unthinkable*."

Let's for a moment set aside why people write the way they do about football in the USA. The fact is, 57 per cent of American respondents to a recent poll by London's Sponsorship Research International said they expect to watch some World Cup matches on TV. That may not match Brazil's 93 per cent score, but it's a long way from apathy towards the big jamboree. Where do all these people come from? Well, for starters, 15 million people participate in football in the US; it is the second most popular team sport with kids under 12, third with kids under 18. Unless I miss my guess, my countrymen – as alternately thick and enthusiastic as they can be – are not doing all this just to be involved with "a bit of eccentric, cute European nonsense," as Nick Hornby described the US perception of football in a recent *Modern Review* piece.

Journalists here have expressed concern that World Cup matches will be played in stadia that are three-quarters empty, and those there will make noise in all the wrong places. Yet the offering to the US public of first round World Cup tickets sold out within hours of ticket windows opening at six of the nine venues. Americans will hold 2.25 million tickets by the time the Cup begins. This autumn, a US friendly against Mexico drew more than 40,000 people to Robert F Kennedy stadium in Washington – not a town noted for its Mexican-American population. We got a 1-1 draw out of that one. (As I understand it, England will now have three years to test public demand for tickets to international friendlies. Be interesting to see how that works out.)

The US side, however, wasn't even involved in the international match that holds the American attendance record. That was England versus Germany at the US Cup during the summer. Again, England versus Germany. In Detroit. My countrymen bought tickets for the pleasure of seeing two of the footballing world's powers clash. OK, one world power. US perceptions may have been a little dated there, but you get the idea.

Will Americans make noise in the right places next summer? I don't know how many of you watched England v the US last June, but the crowd seemed to have the knack during that match, an occasion when Ian Wright couldn't have put the ball in the net with an RAC map and police escort. He did make some noise of his own, though, to the effect that US keeper Tony Meola would never get a chance to play League football in England again. "And you won't be here next year," Meola told the excitable and noisy Mr Wright.

Also annoying is the widespread belief that we are trying to rewrite the FIFA rulebook. I still spend time defending myself against alleged American efforts to chop the game into quarters, get rid of goalkeepers, play with two balls, widen the goals, shorten the field, or arm defenders with semi-automatics. Just a few months ago, the *Guardian* reported a US TV deal for the World Cup had been held up at the last minute because of the difficulty of squeezing all those commercials in. According to the yellowing, months-old press release in front of me, a deal with ABC and ESPN has been in place for almost a year now – and the 51 full matches to be transmitted will only contain advertising spots during half time.

We now come to the point where a nation of used-car salesmen will probably never agree with a nation of amateur dramatists. I've seen the spectator facilities here up close and personal. I used Craven Cottage's grimy, near-flooded changing rooms when I played in a five-a-side tournament earlier this year. I've pressed myself flat, cheek-to-brick, to get through the turnstiles at any number of English grounds (cattle in the Chicago stockyards have it better). I've waded through the toilets at Wembley during the FA Cup final.

What's with the dedication to crap football facilities in the nation that invented the sport? Let me guess. You've always done it that way. (Possible national motto there.) It helps tighten the upper lip for those moments when you really need it? Dedicated football supporters in this country are getting ripped off in so many directions they must be spinning like tops. Beautiful game, my ass. More like nice little earner. For some.

Americans and foreign visitors will get class treatment in class facilities during the World Cup. As will the teams. Big, clean, supporter-friendly stadia. Toilets that aren't swamps. Motels and restaurants that are good value. For the same reasons you all go to Orlando, any Brit that does attend the World Cup will have an excellent time (barring gunfire, of course). We will run a well-organized, even entertaining show. For that, I'm sure the British press will sniff at us.

For all I've said, I admit Americans understand little of the size and scope of world football. Our own press, outside of a dedicated few, does little to help. I've read quotes lately – particularly by one idiot at a comic-book-cum-weather-map called *USA Today* – which are plain embarrassing. And of course he picked the weekend of the World Cup draw to write his column, understanding little how many overseas journalists would be around to read his drivel. And quote it. Americans need to hear and read more about the beauty of the game. Any volunteers? ○

Schoolboy Wonders

The methods used to coach schoolboy footballers had been attracting hefty criticism, which was long overdue if Matt Nation's experiences were anything to go by.

WSC No 86, April 1994

OCCASIONALLY, HAVING HAD TO ENDURE A BILIOUS DIATRIBE REVOLVING around the downside of Bristol Rovers FC, people ask me exactly why I harbour such feelings of ill-will towards the boys from Twerton. Unfortunately, the answer "Because they're crap and they're not Bristol City", although accurate, never appears to satisfy their thirst for knowledge and reasoned justification. Recently, I've thought about this problem a little more carefully and have hit upon a slightly more acceptable argument: their training methods are completely bloody cuckoo. And I can prove it.

In 1981, the under-13 schoolboy team of which I was a member was trained for a few months by an apprentice from Bristol Rovers, by dint of the fact that his girlfriend worked with the extremely pushy mother of one of my team-mates. Not wanting to embarrass this poor lad or rupture the scar tissue of the wound which is an association with Bristol Rovers, I shall refer to him now as we referred to him then, namely as Keefer. At the time, I was unappreciative of the fact that Keefer sacrificed his Friday evenings to watch a load of cocky pubescents strut around under the impression that they were better than he was, but I never, ever questioned the training methods. Nowadays, I award him full marks and more for his selflessness, but believe, in retrospect, that the training often had as much relation to football as Kenny Burns.

As he was still an apprentice, Keefer was only about 17 years old and still willing to learn, still as hungry and starry-eyed as Paul McGrath at the end of happy hour. His sense of irony, I am certain, had not yet blossomed and any wry humour would have been usurped by the fact that he was probably shitting bricks about not getting a professional contract. Therefore, what now seems asinine to me appeared to be intended in all seriousness by him then. A paragon of earnestness, a youthful version of Sergeant Major Shut Up in *It Ain't 'Alf Hot, Mum*. Bent double with laughter, he may well have regaled his team-mates with stories of his Friday night exploits before South-East Counties matches on Saturday mornings, but if his tongue was in his cheek during those training sessions, the lad hid it great.

The warm-up exercises were the starter for this feast of fatuity. We began by jogging around the tennis courts, clutching our cuffs, puffing out our cheeks and then blowing hard like real footballers do (although the reasons for the last two actions have never been entirely clear to me, particularly as the more slowly a footballer runs, the greater he seems to want to expand his cheeks).

Suddenly, he would lambast us with something like "Last one on his back riding a bike!" A few of us would stand around awaiting the end of the sentence and a couple would chase whichever unfortunate paper boy happened to be passing at the time, but the majority of the team would understand immediately what was meant, hurl themselves backwards onto the asphalt and begin kicking their legs wildly. It was like watching Jürgen Klinsmann taking part in a trench warfare exercise on Salisbury Plain.

After a few seconds, we had to get up, soaking wet and nursing head wounds and a splintered coccyx, to recommence the cuff-clutching and cheek-blowing. Nothing happened to whomever was slowest to react. But nobody ever stopped to think about that.

The alternative to this was "Knees, shoulders, head, clap!" This meant having to run in two parallel lines, touching the aforementioned parts of the body in unison and rounding off the whole movement with a single piece of applause. This exercise was doomed, however, to end in the ridiculous. Being at that age where we had the grace of a Bristol Rovers fan in defeat, it was like watching Tony Cascarino with a severe case of the bends attending his first Morris Dancing class.

After about half an hour of cuff-clutching, there was a quick burst of psyching-up to get through. Each player was asked questions pertaining to his mettle.

"The rain doesn't bother you, does it?"

"Do you clean your own boots?"

"Does your old man pay your subs or do you pay them yourself?"

Once, we were all asked: "Are you a chicken?" Blood running cold at the having been found out, we pulled back our shoulders, puffed our cheeks out to Gary Mabbutt proportions, adopted a hard stare and pusillanimously shouted back: "No, I ain't no chicken!" This continued for a couple of minutes, shoulders becoming wide enough to force us to run in the crucifix position, until one rascal produced what many of us thought the funniest thing we had (or have) ever heard: "Yeah, and I'm a turkey, too." Full credit to Keefer, he did not shout or resort to corporal punishment, he just frogmarched the lad away for ten minutes of block tackling practice.

After about 40 minutes of not a whiff of a football, the "concept" was introduced, which, more often than not, also omitted the use of the leather globe. The "concept" was one of those schemes famously implemented at most clubs in an attempt to vary the monotony suffered by having to play football for money. You know the sort of thing: Clough had his players picking up litter alongside the Trent, Wimbledon have all-in wrestling matches and Steve Foster practises putting one foot in front of the other.

Unfortunately, this malignancy has even spread to Bristol City, where, during pre-season training this year, they rode BMX bikes up and down the beach at Weston-Super-Mare – all except Mark Aizlewood, who, as is his wont, prepared for the season by taking full speed running kicks at the back wheel of his bike from a distance of 20 paces or shouted at it for making him bugger up the offside trap again.

Bristol Rovers' "concepts," diligently and seriously regurgitated by Keefer, were all technique-honing bankers. Once, we had to play rugby. We protested that this would be impossible, as the surface was too hard, it had nothing to do with football and none of us was overweight or had a forename which would cause him to cry himself to sleep at night. To be fair, Keefer relented, demonstrating the fair-mindedness for which his club is renowned: "You play rugby or you're running around that fucking pitch all night!"

The concept most related to football was "only scoring with a header". Once again, a sound enough idea for those with a misguided admiration for Harry Bassett, but it failed to take into account one crucial deficiency in our technical make-up: none of us could cross or chip a ball properly. Thus we could only manage this exercise crouching, on our knees or sliding along the asphalt on the side of our faces, exacerbating the cranium damage received in "Last one on his back" and acquiring facial gravel rash and a complexion resembling the Twerton Park pitch in the middle of February.

Keefer was not to blame for all this. He didn't load the bullets, he just fired the gun forced upon him by his employers. Despite this early setback, he eventually made it to the First Division and, for a short, excruciating while, he made people view Phil Neal, Gary Stevens et al in a completely new light by turning in some of the worst right back performances ever seen in an England shirt. He puffed his cheeks, clutched his cuffs, put it in, wanged it, but he couldn't shake off the Bristol Rovers brainwashing. He wasn't a chicken, but he played like a headless one: his head was like a 50p piece in 3-D. Every game was a 'mare. It was awful.

During the European Championships, in a game against Denmark, I believe, Keefer was left for dead by the left winger. He disappeared from the picture for an over-long period of time as the camera followed the Danish attack, but I spared a thought for Keefer. He may have been flat on his arse, wishing he were elsewhere, having been done like a trawlerload of kippers in front of a television audience of millions. But I prefer to believe he was doing his 50 press-ups, exactly as one should in situations like that, exactly as Bristol Rovers had taught him. Mad as hatters, all of them. ○

Greater Manchester?

After months of uncertainty, Francis Lee finally took control at Maine Road. A relieved Steve Parish looked back over the Peter Swales era at Manchester City.

WSC No 86, April 1994

"BE PATIENT!" CRIED THE REVEREND JIM BURNS FROM THE STEPS OF THE MAIN entrance of Manchester City Football Club. He made the "calm, calm" wrist-clasping gesture from TV's *GBH*, and cried "Frannie will be here!"

Francis Lee, former player, former bogroll tycoon and now racehorse owner, was indeed there, acknowledging the cheers from a desperate Maine Road public. QPR fell under the spell and City won 3-0. However, it took another half-season before Lee was able to secure the deal that made him chairman, and left Peter Swales, the incumbent for 20 barren years, as life president.

Swales might have gone more gently, rather than hang on for grim death, and make City the laughing stock of the League. But his tenacity posed again a question that has often surfaced in the world of football: "Who rules?" The people who own the club, or the fans whose loyalty is taken for granted? *Foul*, the great forerunner of the fanzines, was asking that when Swales took over in the early Seventies.

On paper, City were making profits, though a total valuation of the shares at £10 million suggests the finances may be more complex. Corporate entertaining and rock concerts substantially boost the income from gate receipts: the directors could probably get a better return from not having a team at all.

Nothing new in this. Clubs like Fulham and Chelsea with valuable real estate are tempted by property deals to sell out, and the development value of the pitch as collateral is the only thing that keeps banks from foreclosing on many clubs' overdrafts. But no-one accused Swales of not wanting a successful team. His decisions were no worse than those of other football club chairmen, and probably better than most. He had been the fans' champion: the cheapest entrance fees in the League, season tickets for standing customers, and the innovative and much copied Junior Blues Club for young supporters. He also led the opposition to all-seating while other chairmen were calculating the extra revenue from higher prices for the scarcity value of reduced-capacity stadia.

But by his own declared ambitions, let alone those of the fans, he had failed. And the fans were furious. Not just frustrated at City's present plight, but really angry. United winning the League took away the longest-running joke in football. Until the last couple of years, City fans could claim for all the money poured into United's team, City were as good. The kudos of a 5-1 victory over the Reds lasted for three years. The United factor is necessary to an understanding of the campaign against Swales. He has presided over City's slump from United's equals (at the least) to the running joke of the League.

Swales might legitimately plead some bad luck – managers walking out (to add to those he sacked) and serious injuries to Colin Bell in the 1970s and to Paul Lake, City's classiest player of recent times, but Maine

Road has gone from being a place where it was cheap to watch good football, to being simply a cheap place. The new Kippax Street stand would leave a maximum capacity of only 32,000. The ambition to make City the number one club has given way to a dismal settling for mediocrity on and off the field. And there had been some 'cheating' of the fans. Trevor Francis played one brilliant season at Maine Road, was used by the club to advertise season ticket sales for the following season, then – with the ticket money in the bank – Swales sold him to Sampdoria. Even the economics looked wrong: Our Trev was putting 5,000 on the gate every time he played: enough to pay his wages and the interest on his £1 million transfer fee. He felt badly used and so did the fans. The rot had set in.

It's difficult to pin down exactly when managerial and team failures began to be blamed on the chairman, but reporters began to record the point in each season when the first "Swales Out" chants were heard. In 1990, Howard Kendall resigned as manager, aided by a 'get-out clause' (ostensibly so he could take the England job if offered) which he used to return to his old club, and we wanted to know how City could have agreed to such an arrangement. Peter Reid was appointed player-manager and City finished fifth two seasons running, but were playing some turgid stuff: the big boot up the middle to Niall Quinn wasn't what the fans liked. Sam Ellis was Reid's appointed assistant, and the long-ball style seemed traceable to him.

After the last match of 1992-93, a 5-2 defeat by Kendall's Everton, the first egg landed on the chairman's back. In a league with poor standards, City could still play well at times but the overall feeling was of going nowhere. Swales may still think himself unlucky to get the blame for City's failure under Reid, but it was the way in which Reid was dismissed which killed any sympathy for his employer.

Faced with mounting criticism of the handling of the club, and with a record of not keeping managers long, Swales appointed a general manager, John Maddock, an ex-sportswriter, who within a few days had sacked both the manager and his assistant and replaced them with an old buddy, Brian Horton from Oxford United. Under Horton, there were glimpses of real football again, and if City had kept a 2-0 lead over United, a lot would have been forgiven. But City lost 3-2, won only once in the next ten games, were defeated by Forest in the Coca-Cola Cup and were doing worse than under Reid. A ridiculous injury list afforded Horton some excuse and several players seemed to be slacking, though it did not look like they were part of a subversive movement to oust Swales.

The media, who needed the club's goodwill to do their job, briefly latched on to the supporters' campaign but then settled into sniping at the fans' tactics. Allegations about death threats became "revelations", a story about fans invading the nursing homes where Swales' aging mother lived did not bear investigation but was given credence, while the "two-minute hate" directed at Swales at each match was voluntarily curbed by the fans. But apart from gentle intimidation, what other power does the ordinary loyal fan have? I knew I couldn't take much more, and despite the offer of a 1994-95 season ticket for the new all-seater Kippax stand at early discount prices, I left it late, until the Lee deal seemed sown up.

Why did Swales try to hang on? I asked a psychiatrist friend why someone would willingly suffer such abuse, knowing they could just walk away with a few million pounds for their shares. "Just an ordinary obsessive," he said. But I'm the addict, not Mr Swales. Perhaps he really believed he could make City successful, and that to give up would be to acknowledge failure.

Still, with the 'consultancy fees' Swales has been getting, and the £1.5 million he received for half his shares, he has not done too badly out of the deal (though a fifteenfold increase in the shares over 20 years cannot be seen as a brilliant investment). The receivers will not be called in; the players are worth perhaps £20 million, though you'd hardly know it at times, and it's a long while since City have had to sell a player to please the bank manager. The Lee consortium may want to restore City's fortunes, but they would not be taking risks with a club on the rocks. They're not addicts, either.

But nor are they carpetbaggers looking for just any club to run. Lee and his main partner, Colin Barlow, are former players, with memories of the good times, wanting to restore some of the friendly atmosphere that used to reign at Maine Road. And in the end, I suspect that's where Swales went wrong. City were known as a happy-go-lucky club, and Swales wanted to change it, to bring efficiency off the field and the killer instinct on it. Instead, efficiency lost to bad luck.

Lee's final accession means dancing on the terraces, what's left of them. The slump into the bottom three may take some turning around, but City fans can walk tall, for we've won a victory few other supporters have managed. 'Sack the board' chants may suddenly take on a new vigour around the country. You can't sack the board who hold the shares, but by gum you can make it uncomfy for them. ○

The Ron Way to do it

Piers Pennington reminisced about a certain Ron Atkinson, who amply filled Oxford United's midfield in the 1960s.

WSC No 87, May 1994

LONG, LONG AGO, IN THE DAYS OF HALF-BACKS AND OUTSIDE-RIGHTS, WHEN Ramsey's wingless wonders were but a twinkle in his eye (well OK, in 1965), a Mancunian lad (me) was cruelly parted from his beloved City and forced by misguided parents to live in Oxford.

Surrounded by southern softies and with nothing to sustain him but his devotion to football, he had little choice but to find out what was on offer at the Manor. Just promoted to the Third Division, United had two players that instantly caught the eye. The first was a loony left-winger called Colin Harrington who would race down the touchline until brought to a crunching halt either by the right-back or the boundary wall beyond the goal-line; and the second, a sandy haired, chunky inside-forward with abundant skill and an obvious footballing brain, who went by the name of Graham Atkinson.

The team was captained by Graham's older brother Ron; a definite family resemblance but thinner on top, thicker in the middle and sporting the alarmingly scarlet legs which in others are a sure sign of early defensive talent on the wane (the names and thighs of Steve Redmond and the late, lamented Tommy Caton spring to mind). In Ron's case, however, it seems that this was as good as he'd got. Squeezed into the No 4 shirt with evident difficulty, it was hard to know quite what the point of him was. I suppose you would describe him as a midfield ball-winner – a kind of Nobby Stiles and David Batty in one pair of shorts. Opposing forwards were not so much tackled; it was just that Ron managed to get in the way.

Through some genetic quirk he shared Graham's positional sense even though he had failed to acquire his talent; and many an inside-left found what he had thought to be a clear run on goal suddenly impeded by something large and yellow. There were two possible outcomes to such encounters: either the forward would be panicked into passing the ball without looking, giving the Oxford defence the chance to clear, or, more commonly, make a pig's ear of it; or else there would be a kind of squelching noise as the poor sap discovered that trying to sidestep Ron, with or without the ball, was neither a good idea nor indeed a possibility within the confines of the space-time continuum.

Every now and again the ball would finish at Ron's feet, whereupon he would embark on a storming run upfield while the ecstatic crowd chanted, "Tank, Tank, Tank," until, after 15 yards or so, he would run out of steam, welly the ball in whatever direction he happened to be facing, and stand there looking modest.

When not immediately engaged in his defensive duties, the Big Man would indulge in the art of captaincy, which seemed to involve a lot of shouting, some clapping of hands and occasional pointing. Nobody seemed to mind much.

Never a particularly dirty player (he didn't need to be), the only time I remember seeing him genuinely upset was at the end of a cup-tie with Southampton. With Oxford poised for one of their periodic giant-killing feats, keeper Jim Barron unwisely tried to waste time with short passes between him and his defenders. Inevitably they lost the ball; and Ron Davies headed the injury-time equalizer. The other Big Ron was rightly furious; and straight from the kick-off he launched himself at a totally innocent Southampton player (probably an oxymoron even then) and landed him in the Beech Road Stand. Quite out of character, but we all knew how he felt.

I can't actually recall seeing Ron score a goal, though the record books assure us he claimed a few. But it's easy to imagine how it might happen. Not a great header of the ball (he'd connect with no problem if it came at him at head-height, but jumping was out of the question), he would occasionally amble into the opposing penalty area for free-kicks or corners purely for nuisance value. It must have happened a few times on the law of averages: the ball swung in, the unstoppable first-time clearance from the defender encountering the immovable object and the keeper left helpless.

As the years went by, Ron became even larger and slower; his face during games became as red as his legs; and Welsh international Dave Roberts claimed the No 4 shirt. Ron drifted away into non-League football as player-manager of Kettering and quietly vanished from the public gaze. Perhaps he took up birdwatching (he would often look up at the dawn chorus of jackdaws during his winter training runs on Shotover and remark, "Early daws!"). But he will be remembered as a typical lower division pro; trying hard, no particular talent, no evident ambition and happy to stay with one club for almost all his playing career.

Where is he now? O

Comic Relief

There was a time when it seemed Graham Taylor would never work in football again after the ridicule heaped upon his performance as England manager in a TV documentary. But it turned out that any publicity was good publicity.

WSC No 87, May 1994 – Editorial

So, Graham Taylor's back, as manager of Wolves. It's almost as if he hasn't been away. In fact, he hasn't; if you've watched a few commercial breaks on the television at any time over the past month, likely as not you will have seen him making a fool of himself for quite a lot of money, a process he may now repeat at Molineux. Not that we expect him to fail, after all, Wolves reacted to the news of his appointment with a 3-1 win, but the swiftness with which he was appointed to another high pressure job has set us thinking.

With players, it's all too easy to understand why they're on the pitch and we're not. If, in a fifth dimension, we could simultaneously stand on the terraces and play on the pitch, we'd be shouting for our own substitution after a minute. Professionals are more skilful and faster than us, and spit further than we could ever hope to. With managers the case is far less clear-cut. We have to believe that the reason why managers have their jobs is because they have accumulated a store of special wisdom about the game, insights which the fans will never have, and that as ex-pros (mostly) they command the respect of the players.

Of course, partly this is a necessary delusion – we want to think that magical spells can be worked to halt a downward slide or that a team two goals down at half-time can be miraculously revived with a few well-chosen words, rude or otherwise. On the evidence of the now legendary documentary about Taylor, it appears that his perspective differs very little from that of the average fan – he doesn't appear to communicate with the players in a way that is discernably different from how they might be addressed by a supporter plucked out the crowd to take the half-time team talk. Players were seen muttering under their breath at one of his spectacularly embarrassing press conferences, and Carlton Palmer gave his best performance in an England shirt when impersonating Taylor telling Gascoigne that he was dropped. Did Taylor command the respect of his players then? And what will the Wolves players, most of whom must have seen the programme, think of their new boss?

Any of them reading this who still haven't seen *An Impossible Job* will be pleased to know that an extended version is coming out on video shortly, bringing more seemingly unwanted attention on the greatest failure in Taylor's career. Yet in spite of all of this, he has landed a lucrative contract to manage a club owned by one of the many wealthy men who would like to emulate Jack Walker.

So how to explain an appointment that seems to have dismayed a large number of Wolves fans? The answer probably lies in publicity. Far from shying away from his status as a comic figure the world laughs at rather than with, Taylor has shown himself to be remarkably keen to promote the caricature image of himself created by the programme. In an indecently short space of time since England failed to qualify for the World Cup finals, he has appeared in a Yellow Pages commercial sending up one of his own strange non-sequiturs, done a newspaper advert for cider and, most bizarrely of all, written a column in the *Sunday Express* applying Edward Gibbons' analysis from the *Decline And Fall Of The Roman Empire* to modern Britain.

Like Alex Ferguson, Jim Smith and Howard Wilkinson among others, Graham Taylor would once have been seen as an old-fashioned football professional, who painstakingly built up a reputation as a good club manager, having had an unspectacular playing career. Now, however, he has a lot more in common with the ever-swelling collection of ex-government ministers who re-invent themselves in a desperate bid to stay in the limelight. The packaged Taylor is a good-natured journeyman who strayed out of his depth and is happy to acknowledge his own presumption in doing so. There is not the slightest hint of style or dignity and no apparent sense of the damage he is doing to the public standing of own trade. Children who would once have told careers advisors that they wanted to be football managers when they grew up will now dream of becoming fly-on-the-wall documentary makers.

But it is working for him. Club owners want high profile personalities who will attract regular tabloid headlines. Even if they hover around the middle of the First Division, Wolves' name will stay in the papers for the forseeable future because the team is being picked by a comedy character. If Taylor gets the chance to spend £20 million like Kenny Dalglish, he could make a go of it. Who knows, the England job might become vacant again in 1996 – as he said himself, there aren't many other people in the English game at the moment with a comparable amount of international experience. If the worst happens and he flops at Wolves, all that TV work will keep the money rolling in.

And there's always a panto at Christmas. ○

Wrong Time, Wrong Place

The Germany v England match scheduled for April 20th, Hitler's birthday, was called off. Mike Ticher examined the circumstances that led to the cancellation and pointed the finger of blame squarely at the German FA.

WSC No 88, June 1994

IT PROBABLY WOULD HAVE BEEN A TERRIBLE GAME ANYWAY. BUT AMONG ALL the accusations and recriminations in the aftermath of the FA's decision to pull out of the international against Germany in Berlin on April 20th, the last thing anyone wanted to talk about was the football. Even those most insistent that the game should take place didn't risk making themselves look ridiculous by pleading that 'politics should be kept out of sport'. In this particular context it was barely possible to separate the two at all.

The reaction in Germany was predominantly, but by no means universally, hostile to the FA's decision. Although some responses were predictable (for the *Sun*-equivalent *Bild Zeitung* it was "a black day for Berlin"), the political battle-lines were far from clearly drawn. The liberal *Berliner Zeitung* called it "a goal for Adolf," but some traditionally conservative publications, like the *Frankfurter Allgemeine*, drew the opposite conclusion.

Three theories were repeated endlessly by the critics of the cancellation. First, it was "a capitulation in the face of violence" (*Hamburger Abendblatt*). Second, it gave Hitler's birthday a prominence which it had previously lacked. The president of the DFB (German FA), Egidius Braun said: "Hitler died in 1945. He should be dead for us all. I can't understand why people now want to make his birthday into a day of remembrance." Third, scapegoats had to be found. The most popular were "fringe groups" (Berti Vogts), "minorities" who had "left football and sport open to blackmail" (Reiner Gentz, Berlin FA). Interestingly, it was often left vague whether the accusers were referring to the neo-Nazis, or the left-wing groups who campaigned against the match, or both.

All but a few of the responses, on both sides, betrayed a certain amount of woolly thinking. (Not just in Germany. Bert Millichip showed his complete grasp of the situation by sympathising with the DFB – he found it difficult to remember the birthdate of British war leaders, too, he admitted.)

On the one hand, those who agreed with the cancellation, like Franz Beckenbauer, not normally known for his radical left-wing views, based their arguments on the fact that there were simply going to be a lot of very nasty people around and so inevitably someone was going to get hurt.

German neo-Nazis were certainly coming – they promised 10,000. The English too, according to Searchlight, including the Combat 18 group (18 standing for Hitler's initials). The strong left-wing scene in Berlin would certainly be there to protest and, if possible, defend foreigners and themselves from Nazi attacks. Then, of course, there would be your regular hooligans, who don't much care who they lay into, as long as it's someone.

No doubt there would have been trouble. But if it was just a case of random hooliganism, the occasion would have been different only in degree from many other big matches, including those in Germany in the 1988 European Championships. What made this one exceptional, and why it was right to call it off, was the heaven-sent political opportunity it afforded the German far-right.

It wasn't the easy targets of the "minority" groups who were responsible for setting this inviting stage. It was the DFB. Yet apart from the fan groups themselves, whose slogan 'Wrong Time, Wrong Place' made exactly that point, very few commentators pointed the finger directly. One was *Der Spiegel*, which said the cancellation of the match was "the result of a lack of political sensitivity in the DFB". And that was putting it extremely politely.

The crucial point in the story was the DFB's reaction to the decision of the Hamburg authorities in January to decline the chance to stage the match. With the significance of the date already an issue and neo-fascist groups encouraging their support to attend, the potential for conflict was already clear, and the Hamburg decision only confirmed it. Yet rather than defuse the situation by calling off the match then, or trying to arrange another date, the DFB instead inflamed it by accepting Berlin's hasty offer to take the game.

The move to Berlin added several political/historical elements to an already volatile cocktail. The game would now take place in the Olympic Stadium, with its bad memories both of the 1936 Olympics and the infamous match against England two years later, when the English players gave the Nazi salute.

Furthermore, Berlin's sporting authorities were still smarting from their humiliating defeat in the bid to hold the 2000 Olympics, and desperately wanted a big event to restore some lost prestige. With the city's highest-ranking clubs, Hertha and Tennis Borussia, currently second-last and last respectively in the Second Division of the *Bundesliga* and facing relegation to the regional leagues, Berlin's pride as a major sporting venue was at stake.

Lastly, Berlin's new status as the capital of a reunified Germany makes it a focal point for the extreme right – not in the sense of an organizational stronghold, which it isn't, but as an object of conquest. Again, this had clear historical parallels, which the DFB must have been aware of.

Berlin was never a Nazi bastion, indeed, Hitler had a personal loathing for it. The torchlight procession through its streets the night after he was appointed *Reichskanzler* in 1933 was not only a celebration of the Nazis' political triumph, but also of the victory of the south over the north, and over Berlin in particular. So the threats from extreme right groups that "the capital is calling us – and we're coming" for the England match had an especially dark historical resonance.

The instincts of the DFB first to take the match to Berlin and then to stick so stubbornly and disastrously to it cannot be understood without reference to its own political history, some of which has been detailed in the book *Rassismus Und Fussball* (Racism and football), published last year. It showed how the DFB co-operated with the Nazis so willingly when they seized power that its leaders were allowed to remain in office after 1933 and throughout the entire Nazi period.

After the war, its president, Peco Bauwens, resisted denazification. So much so that following Germany's 1954 World Cup victory, he stopped the train taking the team home in Austria so that they "could receive signs of the loyalty of the Germans in the enclave [ie Austria], which is no longer allowed to be united with the Fatherland".

Bauwens' most famous successor, Hermann Neuberger, allowed a former Nazi, Hans-Ulrich Rudel, to visit the team camp during the 1978 World Cup in Argentina (while denying access to Günter Netzer, who was there working as a journalist). Rudel was a leading figure in the far-right German People's Union (DVU), whose newspaper also printed a flattering obituary of Neuberger himself on his death in 1992.

That the same spirit is not yet dead within the DFB was demonstrated in startling fashion as recently as January of this year. Commenting on the threat to Germany's reputation abroad if the England match led to violent confrontations, its spokesman, Wolfgang Niersbach, said: "Eighty per cent of the press in America is in Jewish hands. Any events in Germany will be noted there in minute detail." The *Washington Post*, he said, "had printed a series of articles marking the 50th anniversary of the Second World War, which were a daily slap in the face for Germans."

It's against this background that the DFB's characterization of the cancellation of the match as "a defeat for democracy" should be seen. To choose England as opponents for a match on Hitler's birthday could charitably be regarded as unfortunate, or in *Der Spiegel*'s words, insensitive. To then move it to the Olympic Stadium in Berlin, however, was more than mere ineptitude – it was gross and wilful political culpability.

As for the DFB's claim that April 20th should be treated just as any other day, it should have been aware from previous years that such an attitude amounts to turning a blind eye to far-right violence, which has often found its expression at football matches. Playing the England match on that day, far from detracting from its status as a rallying point for extreme right activity, could only have massively reinforced it. In fact, the furore over the match has already done so.

The decision to cancel the match may not have been taken for the right reasons – the FA's concern was clearly with violence of any kind rather than with denying the far right the perfect political stage. But nevertheless, they deserve some credit for taking the responsibility which the DFB and the Berlin authorities, with their delusions of grandeur, so shamefully declined. The fan organizations in Germany who bombarded them with faxes and the usual suspects in England (ie Gordon Taylor) clearly played a significant role in persuading them.

Instead of playing England, the German team had to make do with a warm-up match in the United Arab Emirates. Berlin's consolation prize was a promise from the DFB that it will host one of next year's European Championship qualifiers, probably against Georgia. Given the shambles which its government and football authorities helped to perpetuate, you can only say that that's about what they deserve.○

Brother's Grim

Joel Cantona doesn't paint or write poetry, and his football skills are open to question, too. Dave Epsley described how Eric's younger brother failed to make an impact with Stockport County.

WSC No 89, July 1994

CANTONA, ONE OF THE MOST EVOCATIVE NAMES IN ENGLISH FOOTBALL AT THE moment, conjuring up images of inventive Gallic industry, spectacular goals by the hatful, and stamping on opponents' heads. If you're a Stockport County fan, however, the name conjures up a rather different image. Instead of the brooding, flawed genius with the upturned collar and the stylish sidies, it evokes an image of a smallish dark individual with very bushy eyebrows and an absolutely massive hooter, whom your average footy fan outside Peterborough or Stockport would have great difficulty recognising. Joel Cantona to be precise, and, yes, he is the brother.

Hands up those who saw a small filmed report in the skateboarding parrot slot on the news a couple of months ago, in which it was revealed that Eric Cantona's brother was being given a trial at Peterborough? Yes, we did, too. And how we all smiled to ourselves when the Posh saw through him, declining to offer a contract. Trading on the family name, you are, matey. Sur votre bicyclette. Two weeks later, Danny Bergara had signed him for Stockport County.

Well, here was a turn up, and no mistake. Not only had we signed a player who had appeared for some of Europe's top teams (well, one of the middling teams in actual fact, but we have a differing view of life down here in the Second Division), but he had a famous brother, too. And the famous brother had an inspired football chant, which certain sad County fans saw fit to utilise at the earliest possible opportunity when the French one made his debut, coming on for 15 minutes of a game we had long since lost, being 2-0 down at home to Bournemouth at the time.

Sadly, however, although given every encouragement from a large majority of the County faithful, Joel's debut 15 minutes were not very good ones. It was impossible not to feel a little sympathy for him as he chased around, willingly enough, without realising that 2-0 down at home, and promotion slipping away, the ball was destined for the head of Kevin Francis at every opportunity, and back-heels, flicks or overhead kicks, no matter how imbued they were with *je ne sais quoi*, were most definitely not the order of the day. Not everyone was as fair minded, however, as Joel's quarter-hour performance was enough to elicit more than one cheeky waggish shout of "Get him off, he's shit". By heck, that friendly northern hospitality.

Strangely, Joel has only been allowed three fleeting appearances as a substitute, despite County's end of season form plummeting us from promotion favourites to fourth place in the final table. He's obviously not quite as short tempered as Eric, as he would undoubtedly have been at least booked in that period of time, and quite probably sent off as well. He did, however, score what was reported to be a fine goal in his first appearance with County's reserves, and it is widely thought that this is what led to his being offered a contract at the end of the season.

One or two unkind souls, though, have suggested that his signing was nothing more than a marketing ploy, aimed at shifting a few T-shirts at a quiet time of the year.

For Joel's trial game, he, not unnaturally, wanted an interpreter nearby, although whether anyone alive could actually translate into French the particularly colourful version of pidgin English which Danny Bergara employs remains open to debate. Nonetheless, Joel wanted his man in close attendance. Such close attendance, in fact, that the fellow donned full kit and joined him in the starting line-up. Regardless of any linguistic abilities, said interpreter then proceeded to impress with the ball, so much so that he was promptly signed as well. (The fact that he was actually a fellow professional, who had played with Joel at a previous club only serves to spoil a good story.)

County's seeming willingness to sign players in such a cavalier fashion lent weight to a worrying rumour which persisted around this time. The story was that Manchester United were actually paying Joel's wages, as Eric had insisted on some filial company whilst away from the bosom of *la famille* Cantona, and Joel had thus been shipped in to provide just such companionship for as long at Eric stayed at Old Trafford.

As he was also known to 'do a bit with the ball', he was sent down the M63 to Stockport, to keep his eye in, as it were. Such rumours have been strenuously denied by the County management, but they would, wouldn't they? And just whose nose was spotted jutting out of Eric's side as the TV cameras showed him sitting out his suspension at Maine Road the other month. Rewind your tape of the *Sportsnight* review of the Premier League season. Yup, that's Joel. Game, set, and match to the conspiracy theorists.

County's retained list hasn't, at time of writing, been published, as we have a season prolonged, yet again, by the play-offs. Whether Joel will be on that list or not I wouldn't like to say. He signed at roughly the same time as American international Bruce Murray (90-odd USA 'caps', ie about three in real money), who has just been shown the door after impressing, it has to be said, far more than the Frenchman.

Some cynics might say that whether Joel appears in County colours next season depends on whether Eric is still turning out for United up the road in Stretford. I'll reserve judgement. Suffice to say, that if Eric's *wanderlust* should take him to, say, Chelsea, in the near future, Fulham fans would be well advised to start practising their French. ○

Yesterday's Hero

To mark the death of former Wolves and England captain Billy Wright, Cris Freddi looked back over his career and explained why he symbolized a long-vanished period in English football.

WSC No 92, October 1994

HE'D BEEN ILL FOR SOME TIME, SO THE VALEDICTORY ODES WERE PROBABLY lying there waiting, but there's no reason to doubt their sincerity, especially as they all said much the same thing: Billy Wright, one of football's gentlemen, was much loved and is greatly missed.

You can't argue with that – no bookings in an eighteen-year professional career, not an enemy in the world – and wouldn't want to. But when they say he was as great a bloke as he was a player, treat it as strictly the stuff of obituaries. He was much greater as a bloke.

Before circumstances moved him to centre-half, Billy Wright won 59 caps as (whisper it) a very average wing-half. It's true that Puskas (despite his two goals at Wembley) said, "he made my life pretty tough on the field," and Walter Bahr (despite the USA's 1-0 win) called him "the world's greatest defenceman" – and they had a point: those tree-stump legs went right through a man. As an out-and-out defender, Wright was international class.

But half-backs of his day were expected to link up as well as dig in, and Billy wasn't particularly clever at that. Years later, Stanley Matthews mentioned his habit of leaving the opposing inside-forward free when he went up to join the attack: it caused England all kinds of trouble (Wolves were so strong it didn't usually matter). And no-one wrote home about his passing.

Still, Walter Winterbottom liked him enough to make him captain in ninety internationals. No great tactician, he led by being a kind of all-round good egg. Unfortunately, alongside the similarly limited Jimmy Dickinson, he led England into a few embarrassing places.

The mourners have been calling it the golden age of English football, but it's not true. For the national team and clubs in Europe, it was a time of self-doubt, when all the divine-right certainties were being questioned by Hungarians and Spanish club sides, one traumatic match following another. And Wright and Dickinson played in most of them: England's first home defeat by a country from outside the United Kingdom (Republic of Ireland 1949), the USA in 1950, the Hungarian humiliations (6-3 at home, a record 7-1 away). Some classy players came and went (Shackleton, Bentley, Barlow, Ronnie Allen) but the wing-halves stayed and stayed and the holes kept appearing in England's shape. Under Wright's captaincy, they failed to qualify for the quarter-finals of two World Cups and lost to a nine-man Uruguay in the other. The drag-back which left him flat on his back as Puskas scored his first is probably the most pertinent image of the decade.

What saved him (his place throughout the Fifties, his footballing reputation now) was an injury to Syd Owen during the 1954 World Cup. England hadn't found a centre-half worthy of the name since Neil Franklin went looking for a working wage in Colombia in 1950. Owen, who was given a severe going-over in the group match against Belgium (centre-forward Pol Anoul scored twice) made way for Wright, a temporary replacement who stayed for another five years.

By default, but by right, too. Not tall for a stopper, he made do with his hard tackling and determination in the air. Once Dickinson had given way to Duncan Edwards, England went 16 matches without defeat (1955-57), beating Brazil, Scotland, Spain 4-1, Yugoslavia 3-0, world champions West Germany 3-1 away. Edwards and Johnny Haynes bossed the midfield, Matthews and Douglas provided from the wings, Tommy Taylor headed the goals. At the back, Roger Byrne, Jeff Hall and Wright looked the part in 17 consecutive matches together. But for Munich, who knows what might have been achieved.

"I was lucky," said Billy Wright. "Ten years before or ten years after, I wouldn't have got a place" – which was typically modest, but not falsely so. In the early Forties, he'd have been kept out by Britton and Mercer, in the Sixties by Peter Swan and Big Jack, perhaps even Maurice Norman. As it was, the fact that a 5ft 9in 35-year-old could play centre-half for England indicates there wasn't a surfeit of central defenders – and that Walter Winterbottom was a one-man man.

Would his golden boy have won 105 caps under any other manager, or very many today? No-one really believes it, especially as it's hard to know what his best position would be. But that's hardly the point. More than anyone who immediately comes to mind, he was a player (by all accounts, a man) of his time, which was nominally the Fifties but actually a kind of endless pre-war, which lasted deeper into the Sixties than the usual David Bailey images lead us to believe. The big shorts and white shirt with the collar and buttons and rolled-up sleeves, the hair someone should have told him about – Billy Wright looked like what he was: a grown man who lived for football in the days of the maximum wage (no smoking, drinking or girlfriends, years on end in the same digs, the "making rugs at home, embroidering tablecloths or table-runners" he listed as hobbies) – and if we find him harder to mourn than his contemporaries would like, it's because the past is another country all right, and we don't want to live there.

Still, when they call it a fitting memorial if we beat the States, we'll go along with it as if our opinion mattered. One generation can't force another to believe its footballers were great players, but everyone under-stands what's gone when a great footballing man dies. ○

Another Pointless Winger

Simon Kuper welcomed Bryan Roy to the City Ground, but had an inkling it might all end in tears.

WSC No 92, October 1994

FRANK CLARK HAS OFTEN SAID THAT SIGNING BRYAN ROY WAS A "COUP" FOR Nottingham Forest, by which he means, "God knows why this chap wants to play for us". Let's agree straight away that Nottingham is one of the hippest towns in the midlands, and that Forest are one of the most creative teams in Britain. Roy, however, is one of the most fashionable people in the world. It's as if Princess Di had suddenly decided to go and live in Stoke.

Consider. Whereas even Jürgen Klinsmann is a baker's son from a small town in Swabia, Roy grew up hip in Amsterdam. He was a male model as a teenager (photographers still love him because he poses so professionally). His father was an accountant. He more or less finished school. He has a flash, American-sounding name. Johan Cruyff thought he would be the best Dutch player of his generation. He is married to a well-known actress (even if Dutch films are the worst in Europe). In short, this is not a man who belongs in British football, let alone in the midlands. When he signed for Forest in June, his first question to English journalists was how long it takes to drive from Nottingham to London.

As a child, Roy never used to dream of being a famous player; he pretty much knew he was going to be one. From the start he was the quintessential Ajax player. They tend to be teen geniuses, who consider trying too hard a bit plebeian, and who have good, short haircuts. When the villager Peter van Vossen joined the club, his new team-mates swiftly persuaded him to get rid of his working-class mane.

The Dutch team is run by a few Ajax players and a lot of former Ajax players (Roy, Marco van Basten, Wim Jonk, Ronald Koeman, Dennis Bergkamp etc) who have their own in-jokes and who don't talk much to players who aren't from Ajax. Ed de Goey, the Feyenoord keeper with the bad haircut, is not really at the centre of team social life. Roy loves the Dutch team.

At Ajax, he made his brilliant goalscoring debut at 17 (a club ritual), and went on to spend years messing around on the left wing. He would dribble past a few provincial defenders and then lose the ball, or watch with interest as his marker forayed into the Ajax box. Every couple of months or so, he would hit a 40-yard lob over the goalkeeper and then run around making aeroplane gestures with his arms. Ajax managers who had to deal with Roy used to put together sociological theories about how kids who grew up rich don't have much of a killer instinct. (The obvious solution was to impoverish the Netherlands.)

Finally Louis van Gaal became manager of Ajax. Van Gaal used to be a schoolteacher, and he was probably never a very popular one. He is gangling and flat-faced and likes lecturing journalists on complex tactical systems. Rapidly, Van Gaal spotted that Roy was of little use to Ajax. The general reaction in Amsterdam was, "So what?" Everyone knew that Roy was pointless. Wallpaper is pointless too. Rinus Michels, as manager of

Holland, once told the Dutch press that Roy hardly ever scored, crossed the ball, or did anything decisive at all. Having got that off his chest, Michels picked him for Holland.

Eccentric wingers who were pointless were part of Ajax tradition. Jesper Olsen, who played for the club in the early 1980s, was by Ajax standards hopelessly result-oriented. More typical was Tscheu la Ling, a tall Chinaman of the late 1970s who never scored or crossed but who did a quite beautiful step over the ball. Hundreds of Amsterdammers would turn up to games strictly to watch him. They would sit in the stand by the right touchline (it soon became known as the Tscheu la Ling Stand), and when Ling was substituted (as occasionally happened) they would all go home.

The time would invariably come, usually after a defeat to Feyenoord, when the Ajax manager would grow fed up with his eccentric winger and would try and get rid of him. For months (the parting was always lengthy, because it was hard to find another club that wanted a pointless winger) fans would bring large banners to the ground pleading for the player to be retained. Eventually he would be sold and another pointless winger would emerge. Roy stood in a long tradition.

Van Gaal placed himself in an equally long tradition by booting him out, and Roy had to go to Foggia, a side from the southern Italian provinces. Roy describes flying into Foggia on the chairman's helicopter, and seeing lots of desert and a small town in the middle. It turned out that Foggia was one of those charming places where everyone knows everyone and nothing ever happens. Roy was disappointed. His mate Richard Witschge, also kicked out by Ajax, had got to go to Barcelona and later to Bordeaux, glam towns both. Foggia (the Southampton of *Serie A*) was definitely a comedown, and Roy found his new teammates gauche. He hated the way they would go volubly crazy at the sight of a woman. But he never told the Italians this, because he is polite, tolerant, and clever.

He did very nearly his best in Italy, and was often sweating by the end of the match. He even began to score goals, something which he had never seen the point of at Ajax. At the end of last season, or so the word goes, Inter, Parma and Napoli were trying to sign him. But he turned them all down and went to Forest instead.

A perfectly logical decision, I am sure. Roy's explanation is that he has always been in love with British football. The Dutch press thinks he went to England because his wife missed being in terrible Dutch films, and wanted to live in a city that was only an hour's flight from Amsterdam.

Maybe the real reason was that he had lost a bet with Frank Clark. Whatever, Roy signed for Forest, went on holiday (four weeks lounging about on Florida football pitches while World Cup games were played around him) and then turned up in Nottingham.

By a happy chance, he scored one of his lob goals in his very first match, and Forest beat Ipswich 1-0. After that game he told the Dutch press that he liked England because he didn't have to worry about being chopped down from behind all the time, and because he no longer had to play on the wing. The Nottingham crowd took to him; all seemed dandy.

Forest might be the English club most likely to put up with Bryan Roy, and he certainly wouldn't last more than about seven minutes playing for George Graham, but let's get his new club's character into perspective. Roy comes from Ajax; Forest have spent years employing Stuart Pearce. Roy has probably never met people like Stuart Pearce before. Maybe he didn't know they existed. Imagine Roy's first day at the City Ground. Practice is over, and a kind team-mate says, "Bryan, we're off to spend all day getting smashed in a midlands pub and then maybe we'll bet a hundred quid on the dogs. Fancy coming along?" What possible reply could there be except, "No thanks, my wife and I are going to dinner in Hampstead"? O

Getting Shirty

Joyce Woolridge had a complaint to make on the subject of new football kits, and the people who complain about them.

WSC No 93, November 1994

AUGUST 3RD, 1994; I PUT THE DATE IN MY DIARY AND THOUGHT ABOUT NOT buying the papers or leaving the country altogether to avoid the usual shock horror headlines when Manchester United's new kit went on sale. **Stripped Off**, the headline screamed; I started screaming, too, but for different reasons.

We are invited to share in the sense of moral outrage generated by the fact that these kits cost twice as much as the raw materials and labour required to make them. Am I alone in finding the hype about profiteering from the sale of football strips hypocritical and maddening?

There are two infuriating aspects to the gasps of horror which now accompany the launch of any new strip. The first is that it is so patronising. The subtext which runs through the 'debate' is that the victims of this rip-off haven't the sense not to buy this merchandise. Usually much is made of parents being held to ransom by children who must have the new strip. The 'victims' are obviously once again the feckless working class, unable to exercise any sort of control over their desires or their deviant, untamable offspring. They must be told what to buy, just as they must be told what to eat and what to watch on video. Thus football once again becomes in some way responsible for the decay of British society.

By implication, the middle classes, on the contrary, can spend their money on whatever overpriced, useless consumer items they wish as they aren't stupid, weak or irresponsible. This concern for exploitation doesn't usually extend to all areas of the market. One paper, which was loud in its denunciation of football clubs' greed, had a pull-out special on brideswear, full of helpful hints about how brides (social class immaterial) should purchase only the best on their special day, even to buying underwear designed by the Emmanuels (presumably selling at cost price). Better to get wed in a team shirt, surely, because you can wear it more than once and you can machine-wash the curry stains out.

Isn't it rather the case that instead of being 'victims' many people who buy these shirts do so because they can afford £35: they buy them because they want them. Many like new ones being issued. They are able to make a rational choice. Clubs always emphasize that most shirts sold are XL size. If you've been in the hell which is Rhodes Airport in August at 4 am with most flights an average of four hours late this would seem to be the case. Every male from 14 to 40 appears to be wearing a team shirt, despite the fearsome combination of 32 degree heat and 100 per cent acrylic. They don't all appear either stupid or impoverished.

This doesn't mean that I wish to defend the commercial rapacity of the producers and retailers of football merchandise, but I do loathe the assumptions made about those who buy it. More importantly, it is the second aspect underlying these articles that really enrages me and does generate a genuine sense of moral outrage. This is that tabloid critics, whilst hijacking the long-running concern of supporters' associations at rampant profiteering, take it out of its wider political context and omit the necessary remedy.

Missing is the obvious political point that Alan Sugar, Martin Edwards and Co are not going to turn into philanthropists overnight. We all know football clubs are private businesses and exist to generate profits for shareholders, not to provide role models for young boys or to better society. Why should we express surprise, even horror, when they don't behave responsibly towards their customers beyond that minimum which is necessary to maintain the sentimental loyalty which guarantees attendance?

In a country which commits the obscenity of handing the water we drink over to the charge of people whose main concern is generating income, why get so worked up over the price of shirts? And why suggest that the solution to clubs treating fans in the same way as every other customer is treated by every other business in this country is to try to shame them into knocking a few quid off the prices in their shops?

Committed football fans would never describe themselves chiefly as customers. The nature of the attachment makes them followers, supporters, someone who put something into the club. If the reality is that all we are called to put in is our money, we must either drop this fantasy of 'the people's game' or agitate for radical change. The theme of the hour's rant I deliver in August, and shall, no doubt, be delivering several times this season is thus: don't shed crocodile tears about the symptoms, if you don't intend to treat the disease. ○

Out With the Old, In With the New

Where do you stand on sitting down? A Highbury regular, Boyd Hilton, offered views on the merits of all-seater stadia.

WSC No 93, November 1994

FOOTBALL PURISTS MAY RECOIL AT THE HUGE SIGN OUTSIDE HIGHBURY Stadium announcing that it is the 'Home of Football', but Arsenal certainly becomes my home for a few hours every other Saturday. Football grounds are more than mere receptacles to hold the largest number of people, they are places where fans get to know every nuance of the pre-match build-up, where they feel safe and secure as soon as they go through the turnstiles. So when this home is practically destroyed and slowly renovated in front of your eyes there is the perception that a part of your soul is being tampered with. Just as moving house is supposed to be the most stress-filled experience in life, so attempting to rebuild the very structure which has housed the most exciting and miserable moments of your life can fill you with apprehension.

That is what happened, with much attendant publicity, at Highbury two years go. The North Bank was destroyed. Tears were shed, articles written, books compiled, all replete with memories of the great terrace where millions have watched their footballing dreams played out in front of them. And soon Arsenal became one of the biggest examples of football's new post-Taylor Report era. Bond schemes were also launched, fans grouped together and became activists and Independent Supporters Associations cropped up to fight against the desecration of their footballing homes.

I was on their side. I stood on the North Bank when I was younger. I was there for the last few 50,000-plus attendances, when the atmosphere was incredibly intense. I joined in the irresistible flow of sentimental memories when the last game was played before the old North Bank. But now it all seems like a rather grotesque wallow in a sea of sentimentality. Wipe away the rose tint from my spectacles, and I remember being too short to be able to see what was going on half the time. I remember losing my glasses in one particularly hair-raising crowd celebration and being crushed on many tedious exits from the North Bank.

Now the Home of Football is a state-of-the-art all-seater housing a mere 39,000 fans, a place that lets almost everyone get a great view of proceedings, that is comfortable, with leg-room to spare, that has clean toilet facilities for men and women which don't take half-an-hour to get into, that gives vegetarians a pre-match meal option. Maybe the old, working class, white male fan stranglehold on football is being loosened. Maybe chairmen are deliberately pricing out the traditional fans. Maybe. Maybe Oliver Stone can make a conspiracy theory movie about all the rich owners convincing Lord Justice Taylor of the capitalist advantages of all-seater stadia.

But all that's really happened at Highbury is that someone realized that having to turn the fans' home into an all-seater stadium was an opportunity to make that home as pleasant, comfortable and appealing as possible. Someone realised that football is watched by short, bespectacled, vegetarian, middle-class graduates, too. And we were watching before Nick Hornby put pen to paper, before Melvyn Bragg decided to interview George Graham, before David Baddiel and Frank Skinner appeared on *Match of the Day*.

Perhaps some of us always hated the atmosphere on the old North Bank, when alcohol at the ground was banned, but, ironically, drunken bastards were regularly seen pissing on each other, when good-natured excitement invariably boiled over into frenzied hatred, lashed with casual racism and homophobia. While fanzines bemoan the lack of singing and atmosphere at Highbury 'these days', I remember 0-0 draws under Don Howe when there wasn't much singing, either, apart from the odd, tiresome, nonsensical chanting of "Yiddo! Yiddo!" Don't believe the hype. Anyone who was at last season's Cup Winners' Cup semi-final will testify to the volume raised that night. Even if Jeremy Beadle helped raise it. And I can barely remember any moments of casual offensiveness or barely suppressed violence from the North Bank fans these days, even on such miserable occasions as the one I've just witnessed against Crystal Palace.

Now there are more women, more black people, more children. These are the new regulars whose arrival seems to have coincided with the new, comfortable, safe Highbury with its giant TV screens, smoked salmon and cream cheese bagels and cushioned seats. These are the people who were practically disenfranchised five years ago.

I'm more proud than ever to be an Arsenal fan, despite our reputation, despite our lack of superstar foreign imports (Schwarz does not count), despite the fact that the crowd may be slightly quieter this year during the Coventry fixture than it was in 1987. Highbury feels more like the Home of Football to me than ever. More than that, it's a civilized home, to civilized fans. A home fit for a club of European stature, fit to welcome AC Milan in February for the Super Cup.

Perhaps I'm just getting older and need to sit down a bit more, but I'm sure in the knowledge that those who look back with monotonous regularity to the good old days are wilfully forgetting the miseries of going to matches in the past. Highbury is still the 'Home of Football'... and the future of football. ○

Speak no Evil

In the light of a furore caused by Rangers defender Basile Boli's criticism of his club's tactics, Simon Kuper argued that footballers might play more creatively if they were allowed to express an opinion occasionally.

WSC No 93, November 1994

AS BASILE BOLI HAS FOUND, BEING A PROFESSIONAL FOOTBALLER IN BRITAIN IS a bit like living in Albania circa 1955. You are free to praise your Leader, or the glorious community in which you labour, but if you say anything else you lose your job, or are fined for 'bringing the game into disrepute'. The greatest crime of all is to give your views on tactics, just as no Albanian was allowed to suggest alternative ways of running the economy.

Ryan Giggs knows the rules. For years we waited for him to speak, and when at last he did he said nothing interesting. Giggs, of course, suffers from the peculiar handicap of playing for a man who thinks that if he were allowed to talk he'd become an alcoholic. But the rest of the Premiership sounds exactly like him.

I spent a year travelling around the world interviewing players, and when I came back home a friend said I must have had a pretty dull time, what with professional footballers being cretins. He was wrong. If you talk to players about football and people in football, they are lucid and often quite funny. They did strike me as a touch self-centred, but that is what happens when every day people come to you and ask you how you feel and then write down the answer and print it in a national newspaper. Also, the players knew that whereas we journalists really wanted to be them, none of them had lain awake as children wishing they were Brian Glanville. They were on top, and they treated us like dictograph machines.

But no, they weren't particularly stupid, and yet British footballers say things like: "At the end of the day, we'll just go out there to enjoy ourselves, hopefully." Partly this is because their mates will laugh at them if they sound sophisticated. Though the middle classes loved Gary Lineker, his nickname was 'Goldenbollocks'. However, the main reason why players sound like morons is that they are terrified of saying anything mildly controversial. The only time a British footballer tells all is when he runs out of money and sells his 'story' to the *Sun*.

Open a French or Dutch football magazine, on the other hand, and you will find four-page interviews with players who sound uncannily like sentient human beings. Some, like Ruud Gullit or Marco van Basten, are even a bit brighter than the average human. Alex Ferguson might argue that this only matters to fans: we would like to hear proper interviews with footballers, and it is largely because none exist that *When Saturday Comes* can flourish. But in fact, if our managers let our footballers talk, British football would probably be a lot better.

In Britain, only managers are allowed to talk about football, and when they do they sound like army officers. Take Bobby Robson telling Pete Davies, author of *All Played Out*, about Bryan Robson: "You could put him in any trench and know he'd be the first over the top... he wouldn't think, well, Christ, if I put my head up there it might get shot off. He'd say, 'C'mon, over the top.'" As Brian Glanville has noted, Bobby Robson was obsessed with the Second World War, but he is not alone. Here is Graham Taylor lecturing the press after England's defeat to the USA: "We are in a battle aren't we? It's a battle we'll stick out together." British managers love soldiers, which is why they pick David Batty over Chris Waddle. Soldiers obey their superiors.

Of course, managers like George Graham, Alex Ferguson and Walter Smith do have a point. Because we have no debate, British team spirit is the best in the world. The Dutch seldom manage to take their best players to the World Cup; Klinsmann aside, the German players hate each other, and the whole country knows it; and even in Russia, four players missed the World Cup this summer because of a row with the manager. No one ever refuses to play for England, and we never have any nasty dressing-room rows, not over tactics, anyway.

Yet that may be a problem. Ruud Gullit walked out of the Dutch camp before the World Cup. He didn't like the trendy young Ajax players who sang on the team bus and declined to treat him with the respect he deserved, and he secretly feared that he wouldn't get a place in the team, which would have been unbearably humiliating. But the main reason why he walked out is that he disagreed with Dick Advocaat, the manager, over tactics. Gullit wanted Holland to play quite defensively, partly because he is a realist, but partly also because he wanted space up front to roam, the way he did at Sampdoria last year. To be at his best, Gullit had to play the way he wanted to.

Contrast this with Chris Waddle and John Barnes at the World Cup of 1990. While in Italy, they complained lucidly to Pete Davies that Bobby

Robson would not let them leave their positions. They felt shackled. They told Davies exactly how they wanted to play. But of course they did not tell Robson, and they only told Davies because he was writing a book that would appear months after the World Cup, when Robson would be managing PSV Eindhoven. Perhaps this helps explain why Barnes and Waddle have had mediocre England careers.

Yet in shutting up, they were merely being sensible. "I've got a reputation of having my own opinion, and they don't like that in Great Britain," said Hans Gillhaus, the Dutch striker, after four years at Aberdeen. "As a footballer there you're just a number and you do what the boss says. That's what you call the manager: 'Boss'. At half-time or after the match, it was customary for the manager to swear for a while at a couple of players. Most players accepted it. The Dutch boys would go against it, and there'd be a row."

It's quite hard to think if you're not allowed to talk. If your tactics are quite complex – as they are at Ajax, or at Milan – it helps if you can discuss them. Arrigo Sacchi, as manager of Milan, reported that his three Dutchmen had given him "new ideas and views", and said that it was largely thanks to them that "a new style was introduced that diverged from the traditional Italian mode of thought and style of play." (Later, Van Basten decided that Milan needed an even newer mode of thought, and Sacchi had to go.) At Genoa, one manager tried to make the team play total football like Ajax, and failed. The club's resident Dutchman, John van't Schip, commented: "To play the Ajax system you have to understand it, and especially talk about it a lot."

As long as English players have to shut up, our game is unlikely to become very sophisticated. Nor will we have many playmakers. Ryan Giggs should soon be the best player in Britain. When he is, it would make sense for him to be running the United game, as Matthäus does for Germany or Gullit did for Holland, or even as Cantona does for United. Unfortunately, as long as Giggs is treated like a child he'll probably stay a winger, dependent on lesser players to give him the ball.

One day the Berlin Wall will fall again, and players will talk. Then there'll be no more John Motson interviews, no more ghostwritten autobiographies with titles like The World to Play For, no more books called Gazza!, and no more managers' programme notes. Every footballer will be Eamon Dunphy, and England will win so many World Cups that everyone will start supporting Germany. O

Cobbled Together

Northampton Town had just moved into a ground with four sides. It was enough to make Dave Cross anticipate happier times ahead.

WSC No 94, December 1994

ON OUR KITCHEN WINDOW SILL SITS A PROUD AND DISTINGUISHED POT. INSIDE the pot reside two hunks of grass. Divots wrestled from the turf in euphoric frenzy. Sods that had previously been stamped, ripped and spat on by gods such as... well that doesn't matter, they were gods to me.

The County Ground, the home to too many lacklustre Northampton defeats, had just staged its last football match. I really don't know why I felt compelled to wrench two handfuls of grass up, it just seemed a natural thing to do. Like the sad bloke at the car boot sale we stripped the ground of any potential memento not fixed by a rivet gun and arc welder.

What a farewell. The game had the fastest goal of the day and, more importantly, finished with three points for us. Manchester United's name was on the championship, Northampton were on the council waiting list anticipating rehousing. It may be that the council computer couldn't handle a list with only one name on it. Whatever, instead of moving into the all-seated, sanitized, battleship grey Sixfields, we were destined to return to the County Ground for the start of this season. The official line was that the police box hadn't been finished. Possible, I suppose.

The final home game of last season (v Chester) pulled 6,432, three thousand more than usual. Now you can call me an old cynic if you like, but I can't help but feel that someone at the club recognized this as a money spinner. As such, we continued with more farewells than Status Quo. Fixed up were The Last Home Game II and The Last Home Game (Midweek). Not forgetting Souvenir Programme II (at special souvenir price).

Having just spent two years in Sunderland, I was there to witness the uproar caused by the suggestion that the club leave Roker Park. I couldn't give a stuff about moving grounds. A friend of mine lost his virginity on a verge next to Deepdale and therefore, understandably, has a very strong attachment to the place. I've not even held hands at Northampton. Okay, I've hugged a few people – but only at the end of another goal drought.

If you've never been, just see what you missed: a ground that only had three sides; a pitch that became the cricket club car park annex during summer; a goal placed upon a hump of earth of Quasimodian proportions; a main stand that would do justice to my Subbuteo set; and a team that continually failed to deliver.

I'm not saying that we didn't have our good times. I remember laughter – the Hereford sendings-off in September 1992! I can even recall cheering and singing on occasions. I remember the Town playing actual football once or twice. But something or somebody has to cop the flak, and, since we sack virtually all the team at the end of each season, I blame the ground. The whole place didn't cut it. We sounded, looked and played crap. I'm not old enough to remember the glory years of humiliating First Division defeats, with 20,000 plus crowds, but I bet they were crap too.

If the County Ground was a song it would be *Agadoo*. If it was a car it would be a Reliant Robin . If it was an entertainer it would be Les Dennis. Some people rate all three of the aforementioned things. These people liked the County Ground. Of course I feel bitter. I waved goodbye to the *Crossroads* of football grounds only to then find they've been given another limited-run series. To have finished on a high last season would have been perfect. 1-0. The goal set up by maverick Efon Elad and his happy feet. But no, too perfect, we had to be embarrassed one final time. At least I am as sure as I can be that it's all over.

So what if Sixfields is all-seater? I have had my fill of standing. Yes, I know the argument runs that if you sit people down they stop singing. You know what this means? It means no longer telling visiting fans that we are the "Pride of Anglia", that "We hate Barnet", "Kettering" and "Peterborough". A trade off of atmosphere for points seems to be more than a fair one. I know that the seats will not accommodate my amply portioned frame. I know that the site sits on top of what was a rubbish tip. I know that you can no longer have a pre-match drink in the County Tavern. I know that Sixfields is a really dumb name. And sits in an industrial estate. But I have hope. I now believe in a future. With four points from six I even have faith that one day we will find a replacement for our current sponsor – Carpet Supacentre. I don't want to remember the County Ground fondly – I don't want to remember it at all. I want to dream. Born 1897, reborn October 1994.

On our kitchen window sill sits a proud and distinguished pot. Inside the pot reside two hunks of grass. I forgot to water them over the summer. Like the County Ground, my grass is now dead. ○

World Beaters

With the World Club Championship about to be staged in Japan, Cris Freddi looked back at its X-certificate heyday.

WSC No 94, December 1994

YOU KNEW WHERE YOU WERE IN THE LATE SIXTIES AND EARLY SEVENTIES: THEY gave us a number of constants in football. England under Ramsey were dull but didn't often lose, English clubs always won the Fairs Cup, the shirtsleeves everyone's nostalgic about today succeeded in making even George Best look soggy. Best of all, year after year the World Club Cup was a sparkplug for satisfyingly extreme violence.

It was a great annual occasion, eagerly looked forward to, confirming as it did British football's view of South Americans in general and 'Argies' above all. Swarthy hysterical men with a full repertoire of dirty tricks and Fiery Latin Temperaments probably caused by those unnaturally tight shorts. Calling them animals as Alf did was being unkind to animals. Needless to say, the feeling was thoroughly mutual.

In British memories it began with Celtic against Racing, probably as a reaction to the way Argentina, Brazil and Uruguay felt they'd been refereed out of the '66 World Cup – but the first bad blood had been spilled back in 1963. Milan, 4-2 up from the home leg, led Santos (minus Pelé) 2-0 at half-time, only to concede four quick goals which forced a bad-tempered play-off on the same ground. After 34 minutes, Milan's captain Cesare Maldini, Paolo's dad, usually a very collected sweeper, suddenly entered into the spirit of things with a thumping foul in the area. Dalmo's penalty produced the only goal of the game, Maldini and Ismael of Santos were sent off, goalkeeper Luigi Balzarini carried off, and a vivid tradition established.

In each of the next two seasons, Inter survived hostile crowds to win the cup against Independiente, who had Roberto Ferreiro sent off, as was Pachin of Real Madrid in 1966. But these were just appetisers for the raw meat of 1967.

Celtic, 1-0 up from the first leg, took the lead in Buenos Aires but were dragged into a play-off after losing 2-1. Things were already so bad (goalkeeper Ronnie Simpson had to be replaced by John Fallon when his head was cut open by a piece of metal thrown through the protective fence) that chairman Bob Kelly offered to forfeit the cup, but his team, its collective fuse drastically shortened, wouldn't let him.

Jimmy Johnstone washed the spittle out of his hair after the first half and was sent off in the second, along with John Hughes, Bobby Lennox and Alfio Basile (Argentina's manager in the 1994 World Cup). Then Juan Carlos Rulli was dismissed and refused to leave, as did Bertie Auld. Gemmell should have been sent off for some spectacular premeditation on Norberto Raffo. Celtic fined their players £250 apiece; Racing gave each of theirs a new car. A classic.

Even this, though, was just a preamble to the great reign of terror. Estudiantes were coming. For the next three years their mass defending, clever dead-ball moves and the wiles of Juan Verón won them the Libertadores Cup, while the other side of their game traumatized Europe. Two players, Carlos Bilardo and Raúl Madero, were professional doctors who seemed to use these matches to provide themselves with patients.

In 1968 Bilardo cut Bobby Charlton's leg to the bone; in 1970 Carlos Pachamé broke Joop van Daele's specs after he scored the goal that won Feyenoord the cup. In between, Estudiantes succeeded in provoking Stiles and Best into getting sent off (along with José Hugo Medina, an exchange they regarded as a bargain) and kicking so many lumps out of Milan that the Argentinian president jailed and suspended three of the team. Estudiantes lost two of their three finals but made their name, which is probably still used to frighten young children in La Plata to this day.

Things had reached such a pitch that Ajax refused to take part in 1971 and wished they hadn't the following year, when Independiente gashed Cruyff's ankle so badly it's said he never fully recovered. That was virtually the last straw for Europe: Ajax opted out in '73, Bayern Munich in '74 and '75, Liverpool in '77 and '78, and Forest in '79. The circus maximus left town.

Its remains were preserved by moving them to Tokyo in 1980, where they've stayed ever since, sometimes dull (Independiente v Liverpool 1984) occasionally exhilarating (São Paulo v Milan last year), always diluted. It wasn't pretty before, it certainly wasn't healthy, but it sort of meant something.

Now? Well, enjoy the actual football between Milan and Velez Sarsfield, but it's become an exhibition match. The crowd's neutral, the fire put out (the only player sent off in the last 22 years was Dejan Savicevic, of all people, in 1991), the old truths irrelevant (it's now conceded that South Americans can play) though they were valid enough at the time, at least for a while: in all objectivity, it's hard not to agree that all the worst aggro was instigated by three Argentinian clubs. Sir Alf, for a period of about eight years, was right. ○

You Just Gotta Have Raith

Robin McMillan lives in New York not Kirkcaldy, so he missed seeing Raith Rovers' League Cup final victory over Celtic. Still, at least he saw Partick play Hearts.

WSC No 96, February 1995

THE ALARM WENT OFF AT 1AM – BUT IN MY HEAD, NOT BY MY BED.

Outside my apartment on Manhattan's Upper West Side, the neighbourhood junkies' crack smoking was interrupted only by the occasional knife fight. Inside, I was reading *World Soccer*, the gentle sound of pages turning interrupted only by the sudden yelp of "Shit!" Raith Rovers had whupped St Johnstone 3-1 in the quarter-final of the Scottish League Cup. In Perth, no less. Darned fine result, I thought. We were in a semi-final.

That was when the alarm went off. Sixteen years have passed since I left Kirkcaldy, but I try to keep up with the Rovers. Best I could remember, the last time we'd been in even a quarter-final of anything decent – which automatically disqualifies the Fife Cup – was probably 1979, when Dundee United put us out the League Cup. Before that, 1971, when we travelled to Glasgow to play Celtic in the quarters of the Scottish Cup. I was 14 at the time, already a veteran season-ticket holder. I seem to recall that Raith did get on the scoreboard, but suffered through an unfortunate spell of about an hour and a quarter, during which we gave up seven goals.

But a semi-final? The big time. The rarefied air of neutral territory. I had to find out when it was.

The following day, I called a friend at home. "What about the Rovers!!!" Albert screamed immediately.

"I know, I know," I replied. "When's the semi?"

"Semi?" he roared. "We're in the final!"

He then proceeded to relate how, during the semi with Airdrie, Scott Thompson, our goalkeeper, had been sent off for doing a Gianluca Pagliuca, how we'd played the last half-hour of the second half and all of extra-time with ten men and how a kid named Brian Potter – 17 years old! – had saved a penalty to win it. You know, we had a pretty good World Cup over here this summer, but it never got as good as this.

For a country whose national side plays football about as skilfully as East Fife, the US gets a surprising amount of football to chew on. European and South American games; an English Premiership match repeated two or three times; a few college games; too many damn indoor games; and several highlights shows, the most intriguing being the Greek one on Sunday nights, principally because every game in Greece appears to be played on the same building site.

But Scottish football? Sure. As much chance as Souness joining the clergy. Apart, that is, from a surreal period about a year ago when one show was almost totally devoted to it. One chilly Saturday afternoon last winter I was channel-surfing. A talk show... a cartoon... MTV... wrestling... a courtroom trial... college football... an Iranian variety show... more wrestling... a Clark Gable movie... even more wrestling... Partick Thistle against Hearts.

If I had to list the five things I'd least expect to see on television in the United States, at least four of them would be Partick Thistle. But there they were, sliding around in the rain and mud at Firhill. It transpired that the network had packaged what they had and could easily get, which meant that a typical show gave you a preview of Argentina v Colombia, a portrait of Dennis Bergkamp, followed by highlights of St Johnstone v Rangers and Motherwell v Hibs.

There are other ways to keep track. We rely on the Sunday version of the *New York Times*. The early edition appears around 9 pm on Saturday night which means it goes to press too early to carry results from evening or west coast events. And you gotta fill the columns with something. Cup and midweek league games are another matter, however. If a newspaper

sports editor happens to be Greek, and there's a hole in the page the size
of Hitler's heart, then he might think of throwing in last night's Rangers
v AEK result. But if he's a baseball, basketball, or 'football' fan, forget it.
These people dislike our football with every fibre of their beings.

Which means about the only way I could have found out about the
Rovers v Airdrie result was to have called home to find out when the
game was on, then call again to get the result. Which I sort of did. Now
the tough part: how to see the game.

It was one of those conversations on which marriages are not built.

"The Rovers are in the Cup final on the 27th."

"And?"

"And I was thinking of going to the game. Fly in, fly out."

"But we're going to my mother's that weekend."

"We're coming back Saturday afternoon. I can fly out Saturday night,
fly back Monday morning. I'll be home on Monday afternoon."

Pause.

"You're nuts."

She may be right. But she also doesn't realize that, as a kid, I
occasionally kicked a ball around in our local park with the likes of
Tommy Hislop, Davie Sneddon and Alec Gray; that I often baby-sat for
goalkeeper Bobby Reid; that I once scored two goals in a Boys Brigade
Cup final at Stark's Park; and that for several years I covered both the first
team and the reserves for the *Fife Free Press*.

Nor, for that matter, does she know that the Rovers hold the record for
most goals in a single season (142 in 1937-38); that Alex James, Joe Baker
and Jim Baxter each did time in Rovers blue; or that when the world's
press was singing Ian Porterfield's praises for the job he did with Zambia
in the World Cup qualifiers, I was still quietly pissed off that the Rovers
had sold him to Sunderland in the first place. (Actually, she did know
about Porterfield; I bring it up every so often.)

As the game drew near it became clear that I'd have to watch it on
television. I started to hunt down some place with a satellite signal. I
called the Sporting Club, a multi-screen affair in lower Manhattan that
airs *Match of the Day* live. Yes, they would be showing the English game
on Saturday. But Scottish football on a Sunday? Sorry. Every place I tried
explained that they'd be unable to get someone to come in to work a
Sunday morning. I even guaranteed a crowd. No dice. What was I meant
to say? "You don't understand; this is Raith Rovers..."?

I knew that somewhere in the Bronx an Irish social club would have it.

Ditto Boston, a four-hour drive. And there's a Scottish enclave in New Jersey called Kearny, but the last time I went there – for a haggis, naturally – it took me two trains and two buses and I still could hardly find the place. Besides, I wasn't sure if I wanted to be the only one wearing blue-and-white in a sea of green. Especially if we won.

So I missed it. But I didn't feel too bad. Three people were taping it for me and, in truth, it wasn't my game. It belonged to those back home. So on Monday morning, November 28th, just before 7 am, I stood at my front door, looking down at the *New York Times* that had been delivered, wondering if I should open it up or wait on my tapes. C'mon, I thought, the *Times* never runs anything but Saturday results. So I picked it up and opened it and jumped about 12 feet into the air and made a most unholy noise that stunned my wife, woke the neighbours, and almost gave my daughter's guinea pig a coronary.

"Six-five on penalties! Six-five on penalties!"

And I've been walking a little above the ground ever since, not really caring about the distance between Central Park and Stark's Park (that's Central Park in New York, not in Cowdenbeath). When the walls of my office threaten to tumble down around me, I shrug my shoulders and think, "Big deal – the Rovers won the Cup." And even now I am working on a scheme to make sure that, if I can't be there in person, I will find a way to see Raith Rovers play in Europe.

Even if it does mean a bone-chilling, stomach-pumping midweek flight to the Faeroes. ○

Asian Games

While football is increasingly a multi-cultural sport at professional level, Asian players are mainly restricted to amateur level. Matthew Brown outlined why that might be about to change.

WSC No 96, February 1995

DID YOU KNOW THAT FOOTBALL IS THE NATIONAL SPORT IN BANGLADESH? AND did you know that when Maradona was banned from the World Cup this summer 20,000 Bangladeshis took to the streets in protest? No? Me neither. But then, why should we?

In 1978 Santa brought me *Soccer: The World Game*, a classic of football literature. "Soccer is the World Game," it says, somewhat predictably, in the introduction. "It is now played in virtually every country on the face of the earth." But in 200 scintillating, glorious, glossy pages there is no hint of football anywhere in the Indian subcontinent, or among its millions of descendants – no players, no teams. Of course, that's because Asians don't play football, do they? They play cricket and hockey and squash, some even play tennis, but not football. It's just not their sport.

It's 16 years later. The USA just held its first World Cup and, it's official, everyone loves football. And the new consumer-friendly, commercial game loves everybody back.

Switch to the English Premier League. A cold, drizzly autumn day at Upton Park. Three sides of the ground (the fourth's a building site) rise as a man called Dicks slots home a penalty. Except for three club stewards, the relieved faces have one thing in common – they're white. Outside the ground, Bangladeshi shopkeepers are dealing with the post-match rush. Asian kids play the amusements down Green Street, their mums stand in bus queues. This is their community. But is it their team?

Jamal Mughal is 24. He's been a West Ham fan since 1981. "I love football. We all do," he says of his mates. "But I have to talk people into going to games. Most Asians are still intimidated. We go there to watch these white and black players and then some of the crowd see us and start singing "I'd rather be a nigger than a Paki". It doesn't exactly make you feel welcome."

Football, like much of society, has been doing its level-playing field best to make Asians feel unwelcome for some time now. Ever heard of an Asian player? No? That's because there have hardly been any – not in the top flight, anyway, and precious few lower down. And the lack of Asian faces belies the fact that so many grounds are smack in the middle of large Asian communities.

West Ham is typical. There's an Asian district around Molineux, 40 per cent of the Smethwick area around West Brom is Asian, as is Small Heath near Birmingham's ground and Villa Park is in the middle of a very large Pakistani and Bengali community. Others spring to mind – Leicester, Leyton Orient, Leeds. Yet, although such proximity does not automatically bring active support, the old stereotype that Asian kids are only into cricket and don't care for the true 'world game' is being belted into the far corner of many an inner-city playground- cum-footie pitch by a football-mad second and third generation.

"If you applied the Tebbit test to football we'd all pass," says Jamal. "When England games are on the telly the pubs round here are packed with Asians. I can remember having a huge party at my house when England played Germany in the 1990 World Cup semis. Things are changing."

Loyalties to particular sports, even nations, may be changing but the habits of a prejudiced culture, and the football industry it breeds, seem to stick like a sodden lump of turf between the studs.

"Some of us do go to games," says 31-year-old Jas Bains, a life-long Wolves fan. "Racial incidents are fewer than they used to be, but there's always the threat. I'm a season-ticket holder, but I can still remember feeling very uncomfortable when I went as a kid."

Twenty-five year old Mano Singh grew up near Villa Park. "I could see the pitch from my house but hardly anyone from our area went. In those days my parents wouldn't let us go. They were worried about attacks – football was definitely frowned upon."

Terrace racism is not the only barrier keeping Asians out of the game, though, for there's a subtle strain of prejudice lurking in the boot rooms. There may not be a direct relationship between the ethnic origins of the players who grace the green fields of England and the supporters who habitually witness the carnage, but it must have an effect. Although, the fact that blacks now make up a substantial proportion of pros does not mean that a similar percentage of the fans at grounds are Afro-Caribbean, it would be hard to deny that the game's image in the black community has changed dramatically since the days when West Ham's Clyde Best was the one black player in the top flight.

But then, as many in the sporting world would have us believe, blacks are natural athletes, aren't they? With in-built speed, strength and skill, Afro-Caribbeans were bound to make it into the game sooner or later – "whereas we Asians are seen as physically frail, not strong enough to play," says Bains, once a district player in his teens. Ah yes, 'frail'. Imran Khan, anyone? Kapil Dev? Hmmm.

Of course Asians play – in huge numbers. A Manchester University study in 1991 found that a higher proportion of the Bengali community in Britain played football than any other (60 per cent), including whites (47 per cent), and that 36 per cent of the Indian community and 43 per cent of Pakistanis played, compared with 26 per cent of Africans and 34 per cent of people of Caribbean origin. Now, call me naive, but I would have thought that one or two of those 60 per cent might be able to play a bit, wouldn't you?

Bains and colleague Raj Patel are running a research project to examine how and why such a huge reservoir of talent is overlooked by the top clubs. Called *Asians Can't Play Football!*, after the basketball film *White Men Can't Jump*, the project aims to persuade clubs that they should be doing more to get Asians involved. "No one is going to convince me that we are not good enough because of some mythical physical factors," says Bains. "I played football at town level and I know there's a wealth of talent in the community being overlooked. Scouts never watch Asian teams play and Asian players are hardly ever asked for trials."

Staff at Leicester City acknowledge that the selection system they use discriminates against Asians. "Scouts don't look for Asian players because they have not been regarded as likely pros," community officer Neville Hamilton admitted. "They watch the two or three non-League clubs where we traditionally get pros from, not the Asian teams, even though many of them are very good."

According to Bains, such treatment has been standard fare for a couple of decades. When Asians were first denied access to white or mixed teams, 20 to 25 years ago, they started forming their own, often through temples and community centres. Now there are an estimated 300 teams across Britain playing in local leagues. "But there's a problem with Asians playing in their own teams and leagues," warns Bains. "It feels more comfortable, but they get ignored by the professional clubs because they're seen as marginal to the mainstream talent."

Balbinder Singh, 31, has been playing in Asian teams since he was 18, the last three years for his own side, Singh United, in the Second Division of the Bedworth and North Coventry Sunday League. He thinks the enhanced sense of identity is vital to keep Asians playing. "One of the main reasons for having a team is so we can play in the Asian tournaments at the end of each season," he says.

A federation of Asian teams organizes five or six such tournaments for its 64 clubs each summer. "Some of these have been going for about 30 years and attract huge support," says Singh. For example, a three-day tournament in Birmingham last year drew over 5,000 spectators. It's a sad comment on some fairly tired football traditions that none of those 5,000 were scouts from professional clubs.

Getting shoved to the touchline of the football world is a common experience for Asians at all levels, from school upwards. "We all play you know," says Jamal somewhat disarmingly. "I went for trials for my borough team when I was at school and was told I was too late. A few minutes later three white guys turned up and got picked. I stood and watched knowing I was better than half the people on the pitch."

About 60 Asians now play in semi-professional or top level amateur football, but there have only ever been six professional apprentices. And whether there are any on the books of pro clubs now is hard to determine, for most don't record the ethnic origins of their playing staff – a fact that Bains hopes his project will put right.

Nevertheless, it is clear that on purely economic grounds professional clubs are making a big mistake. In an era when market-driven ethics have dribbled their way into the heart of the game, clubs have simply failed to latch on to such obvious potential revenue. It's not that Asians have accidentally slipped the net, more that the net's got huge holes in strategic places.

In truth the clubs aren't entirely to blame. There's a reticence about professional sport among older members of the Asian community. Although it's something of a stereotype that sport and entertainment are seen as main routes to success for blacks, it's nevertheless true that social pressures and prejudices have pushed many a black kid into pursuing a sporting career. The parallel pressures on Asians are to take up a more 'respectable' profession or take over the family business.

As Davinder Sangha, a coach in the Asian league, puts it: "The problem is that we are prejudiced; Asians are discriminating against football. Our parents cannot imagine a football career for their children because of the public image of the game, which to them is of screaming hooligans, brawling players and so on."

Bains and Patel hope that their project (already with backing from the PFA, FA, the Football Trust, Carling and Leicester City Council) will push some clubs into making greater efforts to root out Asian talent and attract Asian support. Leicester City have started, targeting areas with large Asian communities in the recruitment of youngsters, and backing an anti-racist project amongst their fans. Although they have none on the books at the moment, the club are now encouraging Asian players to go for trials.

And Roger Reid, of the PFA's Football in the Community Programme, is keen that other clubs do the same. "We want to get round those cultural barriers that prevent contact between clubs and Asian youngsters. Many kids often have to attend Mosque after school for example, which is when most clubs hold their coaching sessions."

Like many, he is confident that once one Asian player makes it past apprentice status to Premiership glory, the floodgates will open.

"Hopefully, 20 years from now there'll be as many Asians as Afro-Caribbeans in the game. Ultimately, they can't ignore talent."

By then maybe kids will be snapping up the latest edition of *Soccer: the World Game*, complete with a profile of England's first Asian stars. ○

Woking Class

Woking fan Simon Bell ran a rueful eye over the state of the GM Vauxhall Conference.

WSC No 97, March 1995

S̲o̲ y̲o̲u̲r̲ l̲o̲c̲a̲l̲ n̲o̲n̲-L̲e̲a̲g̲u̲e̲ t̲e̲a̲m̲'s̲ d̲o̲i̲n̲g̲ p̲r̲e̲t̲t̲y̲ w̲e̲l̲l̲, e̲h̲ k̲i̲d̲? C̲r̲o̲w̲d̲s̲ are up, are they? (They're down at the struggling local League side. How odd.) The team's passing the ball and scoring rakes of goals, and on Thursday someone tarmaced the car park and left six pallets of bricks next to the walk-through potting shed that does for a turnstile.

People have taken to asking about results like they're interested, and some even turn up when there's a decent cup draw. The chairman's talking big plans, big money and big names, and the word is all of What We'll Do In The Conference. Nirvana beckons. But what's this? There's a greybeard loon outside the ground this Saturday. He's looking straight at you. And he's wearing a Woking scarf.

Woking were admitted to the Conference in May 1992. OK, so we were a bit late with completing the ground improvements, but no-one seemed to mind much. Funny what gates of 1,800, a good Cup run and an outward show of ambition can do. And those ground-grading documents did get lost in the post. Only a supporter of Cheltenham Town, relegated to make room, would be churlish enough to moan.

Since then the on-field news has been mostly good. There've been some grim massacres, but we've got the FA Trophy under lock and key, the semi-divine Clive Walker has taken over from the abject Trevor Senior as Old Bloke From The League and finishing eighth and third gives the impression of a club in a hurry. Yet the question remains of where we're in a hurry to. It's a question that goes to the roots of what the Conference is, what it should be, and whether it's got a future.

Ambition has its rewards, and at the time of writing we're third, notionally within shouting distance of a League place. But hang on for a dose of the real world. A League place means a new ground, with all the terrors of relocation. The club, with operating losses over the past couple of seasons of at least £130,000, needs to stretch itself still further to grab the Grail. We're told that we need a break-even average attendance figure of 2,000, when most of the rest of the Conference gets by on half that, and the squad, well as they've done, are severely reduced in number as the wage bill gets squeezed.

Looking around the Conference, it's not hard to find other clubs crippled by the outlay required to get up and/or stay up. Yeovil mismanaged their ground move in the late Eighties and now get bank statements that would make a Mexican finance minister grimace. Farnborough (bless 'em) came nigh unto death a couple of years back and Kettering's financial history is the stuff of legend.

The reasons vary in detail, but at the root of all are the ambition for higher status and the way ambition so often exceeds competence. In our case, the need for £300,000 to bring the ground up to the bare minimum Conference standard didn't help. Nor did thinking of a number, doubling it, sticking a pound sign in front and offering it to 'experienced pros' like Trevor Senior *et al* on a weekly basis and right through the summer. No wonder they didn't perform. They were in shock.

To accommodate these newcomers, at least one of whom never kicked a ball in anger for us, some old and well-loved faces disappeared, and a little bit of what had made the club so special over the previous seven years died. Still, that's progress, though to what end still isn't clear.

When the Conference (*née* Alliance Premier) was founded in 1979, its aims were noble enough. Here was a gathering of the non-League elite, the apex of a mighty pyramid prodding the bum of the League, challenging the Masonic rituals of election and re-election.

After promotion became automatic in 1987, four traditionally non-League sides swept into the League (along with Lincoln, Darlington and Colchester, who came, saw and didn't fancy staying). Of the four, only the Buckinghamshire side whose name escapes me have made a real go of it in the manner planned. Their time may come. With the Maidstone and Barnet fiascos, the League manned the barricades. I sometimes wonder if the San Siro will make Third Division standard in five years. Some current inmates sure don't. With the trickle-down effect of such regulations the Conference has become, 15 years on, a pale imitation of the Premiership. It's a ring-fenced clique determined to exclude any club that does not match up to its definition of a 'proper football club', ie one with the potential to join the League one day, while bleating at the League for its intransigence.

Yet with the lower reaches of the pro game increasingly starved of cash, it's not hard to see a day coming when they might come to join us, and the Conference become merged into a regionalized semi-pro league. Then where's the ambition got us, except back to an up-market version of the feeder leagues we all came from?

Of course, League sides will fight such a loss of status while they've got breath, and while the divide remains, almost all Conference supporters crave wet Tuesdays at Saltergate. But not at any price. In 1993, when the St Alban's City-tree furore was at its height, no-one said much about the team who actually won the Isthmian League, Chesham United. Chesham withdrew their application for admission rather than take the huge financial risks which admission would have entailed. They set up a Building Appeal, and decided to bide their time.

I sometimes wonder if the poisonous atmosphere of secrecy and recrimination which surrounds my own club now would have been diminished if we'd done the same. Probably not. There are enough people for whom winning means nothing if it brings only silverware and the knowledge that no-one else was even close. I don't think like that now. I still dream of seeing the Cards in the League (in whatever format) in ten years. But I'd settle for seeing them anywhere. ○

Dons Leave me This Way

Contributing to a series about games that stuck in the memory, Jonathan Northcroft recalled one that encapsulated a brief but glorious period in Aberdeen's history.

WSC No 97, March 1995 – More Than A Match

FOOTBALL MAKES US WEAR OUR ALTER EGOS LIKE SCARVES. SUCCESSFUL, hard-nosed businessmen buy clubs then go all lovelorn and teenage. Stuffy professionals click a turnstile and become ranting nutters for the next two hours. But sometimes, maybe only once in a lifetime, it can effect a change that lasts forever.

It happened to me when I was 11. The New Romantics were flouncing round the Top 40, but I was still stuck at Abba and the novelty end of my cousin's ageing punk collection. Cub camp was my idea of travel and, living in a small village, in my last year at the local primary school, life seemed a pretty cosy proposition.

Aberdeen FC were the same. Though emergent within Scotland's poky Premier League village, St Mirren and Airdrie weren't exactly football's bright lights. The Liverpools and Milans played a different sport. Then, in March 1983, Bayern Munich went and changed everything.

It was the Cup Winners' Cup quarter-final (second leg), a level which already seemed a bit excessive. At school there was a craze for collecting football pennants which listed a club's achievements. Mine, a scrawny, anorexic thing tapered quickly at the 'Europe' section; 'Aberdeen: UEFA Cup second round. 1979, 1981.' Yet here were the Dons, the two huge and toothless Dougs, Bell and Rougvie, the four gawky teenagers, Black, Hewitt, Simpson and Cooper, warming up opposite Breitner, Hoeness, Augenthaler and Rummenigge. And we'd drawn the first leg 0-0.

We were soon reminded of our place. Bayern stroked it around, Aberdeen chased, Bayern scored and stroked it around again. Aberdeen chased again. Neal Simpson scuffed in an obstinate equalizer. Bayern kicked off, stroked it around and scored again.

When Gordon Strachan and John MacMaster lined up a free kick on the edge of the Germans' area with 14 minutes left, things could still have been promising, but what they did next made us all squirm. Throughout that season the Dons, for some inexplicable reason (Strachan? MacMaster? A dream Alex Ferguson once had?) had used this preposterous set piece. The idea was that Strachan and MacMaster would fake a misunderstanding and both dummy the ball, then stand there, blaming each other theatrically. Just as the opposition relaxed, Strachan would suddenly whip it into the net.

It was a fiasco. Defence after defence from Ibrox to Glebe Park, Brechin, would just watch the would-be farceurs with pity, then head the ball clear. But clearly such amateurish tomfoolery was below Bayern's very lowest expectations. Strachan dummied, hammed it then crossed. Alex McLeish trundled past the stricken Germans and headed into an undefended goal. Bedlam.

History (or rather Grampian TV) records only a fragment of the greatest moment of my life; it, like everyone else, was still replaying the goal. Thirty seconds later the ball was again high inside punch drunk

Bayern's box. Eric Black headed, Müller, the massive German goalie parried and it arrived at John Hewitt's feet. A local lad, Hewitt had turned down Liverpool and Man Utd for the Dons, proof at an early stage that, though very gifted, he was also very thick. At 17 he had already been dubbed 'Tadpole' on account of his apparent brain capacity, but he had enough wit to keep his appointment with destiny. Müller had somehow stayed on his feet and looked like an Alp. Hewitt glanced up and popped it calmly through the German's legs.

The last ten minutes were ecstasy. Bayern were sad and beaten. Aberdeen retained possession and we cheered hysterically at each successive pass. Scots aren't the most demonstrative of peoples and Aberdonians aren't the most demonstrative of Scots, but Pittodrie resembled one of those back-to-nature weekends that repressed American men go in for: all big hugs and primordial roars. Dad, not the most touchy of men, was slapping strangers' backs, shaking their hands and ruffling my hair until my scalp hurt. And I, a crappy kid who'd blinked and found his provincial team suddenly outclassing Europe's aristocrats, just stood on my chair and swore for joy until it was all over.

It was my moon landing; my seminal pop record, my first snog. The world was big, exotic, adult – and for the first time close enough to touch. Pittodrie buzzed with unrestraint and looking back I can't believe that any of us there – not on the rainy Gothenburg night two months later, when the now grown up Dons won the cup, not Strachan, not Alex Ferguson, not me or my Dad – ever had it so good again. ○

Over the Top

Eric Cantona's notorious kung fu kick roused the media to unholy sound and fury, signifying – nothing.

WSC No 97, March 1995 – Editorial

ERIC CANTONA'S SOLO CONTRIBUTION TO THE 'KICK RACISM OUT OF Football' campaign has already been examined in incredible detail. The press mimicked him, jumping in feet first; the famed Lineker lips pouted their disapproval; the FA and the police are still sifting through eye-witness reports; and Eric himself has clearly gone into deep shock:

the only explanation, we fear, for his wearing a mediaeval court jester's tunic outside Old Trafford the morning after.

For many in the media, the story seemed to provide the perfect platform to generalize about the French, footballers, and football supporters, so much so that it made front-page headlines and was the first item on the news for days. In spite of the number of trees that have been casualties in the search for 'the truth', many questions are either still unanswered or have been ignored.

In the last few weeks, for instance, both Stuart Pearce and Cantona's adversary, Matthew Simmonds, made racist taunts at a footballer inside a stadium: Pearce got off with having an apology prised out of him, while Simmonds was banned to the end of the season. Without quarrelling with the punishment for the latter, the disparity between the two is startling.

Another irony of the situation is that if he had not been attacked by Cantona, it is highly unlikely that any action whatsoever would have been taken against Simmonds. Yet there were plenty of stewards around. Football clubs' persistent failure to take positive action against racist abuse of players and fans surely contributed to the incident: would Cantona have flipped if the crowd had limited itself to the standard "Off, Off!" or "Dirty Northern Bastards!"?

Life bans have always seemed to be the standard threat against misbehaving supporters, but such measures only treat the symptom rather than the cause. That Cantona and his 'victim' should have received sentences of identical length looks like more than a coincidence. In view of the fact that only two options seem to have been considered on previous occasions – either a life ban or no action at all – the rest of the season seems about right.

Cantona's punishment, likewise, seems fair enough; he might have played his last game in England, but the choice is his. The hysteria for a life ban was ridiculous, especially when contrasted to the usual tabloid treatment of 'have-a-go-heroes' and to the image of the footballing wild man, best typified by Vinnie Jones' finger-pointing column in the *News of the World* in which one of the game's most relentlessly hyped 'nutters' rants on about the day's issues in a manner that we're supposed to accept as unpretentious plain-speaking. Conversely, Cantona's behaviour is portrayed as being incomprehensible: he is often talked about as he were an alien – but from another galaxy rather than across the Channel.

As with Gascoigne, Cantona's erratic behaviour, sudden flashes of temper and moodiness are part of the package. Had it been coached out of him in some way, either on the training pitch or on a psychiatrist's couch, he'd be less of a player. But he knows, too, that he'd have less value as a marketable commodity to companies such as Nike who featured him in a contrived, 'controversial' ad campaign last year that was banned from television. They seem quite happy to keep him under contract and Manchester United plc are unlikely to consider withdrawing the Cantona merchandise from their club shops.

Whatever may have been said to the contrary, the relationship between players and fans has not taken a significant turn for the worse as a result of the events at Selhurst Park; the fabled families that we're told are flocking back to the stadia won't have turned on their heels and fled to the nearest shopping mall. The pundits eager to make that point ought to be aware that as well as costing an arm and a leg, a couple of seats in the family stand of any major football ground on a Saturday afternoon will also provide a crash course in late 20th century vernacular, delivered at a volume that drowns out the tannoy announcements.

For all the fuss, the double-page spreads in the Sunday papers, the **Football In Crisis** banner headlines, it really doesn't signify anything much – players get sent off, spectators have a go at them. Cantona is a one-off, Matthew Simmonds, former BNP sympathiser, sadly isn't. We know which we'd prefer to see in English football. Unfortunately we also know who is more likely to disappear. ○

A Riot Palaver

It was a nasty jolt to everyone when rioting neo-Nazis following England caused a friendly in Dublin to be abandoned. But some were more surprised than they should have been.

WSC No 98, April 1995 – Editorial

THREE WEEKS AFTER THE MATCH IN DUBLIN AND WE'RE STILL STUNNED. AS YOU may have read, or heard on the news, extreme right activists attend international matches with the specific aim of causing trouble. Imagine that. What a shocker. And we always thought that the people who do stiff arm salutes when the national anthem is playing were trying to hail taxis or waving to friends on the other side of the stadium. But no. They are fascists. In our midst. Been going to football for years, apparently, but only now have they come out into the open.

The *Sun* were astounded too, complaining about the "beery, obnoxious... English scum". Their coverage on the day after the match was instructive of the way that tabloid reporters' inability to react in anything other than a frenzied manner mirrors almost exactly the reactions of the people they are trying to condemn. Citizens of a nation shouldn't expect to be held responsible for for the actions of a tiny, fanatical minority of their fellow countrymen. Why then in the aftermath of the Dublin riots did so many tabloid journalists feel the need to declare their shame at being English? Could it be that somewhere deep in their psyche they realize they are part of the problem? We'd like to think so.

Still, the newspaper headlines the morning after reflected one small positive development. If there is one good thing, just one, to have come out of the Dublin riot, it is that blame for the incidents was placed squarely with 'Nazi thugs' rather than that old catch-all, 'football thugs'.

The attention given to the extreme right's involvement with the Dublin riot had one unfortunate consequence, however: it helped to get the FA off the hook. With so much time and space given over to working out who was a member of which neo-Nazi gang, there was little questioning of whether playing in Dublin at this time was a good idea in the first place, with the likelihood of Loyalist groups, known for years to have strong links with far-right in England, using the occasion of a football match in Ireland to draw attention to their cause.

There hadn't been any serious crowd trouble in recent times, largely because England hadn't played abroad for 16 months, so it would seem that Lancaster Gate got it into their heads that football violence had been licked for good, and remained blithely unaware that the conditions in which violence could take place were as prevalent as they had ever been.

It is too easy to place all the blame on 'extremists'. The press have leapt upon the images of the fat boneheads with throat tattoos taunting the Irish police, and hurling around chunks of Lansdowne Road masonry, but they are by no means the sole problem. The fascist hardcore can't do all that fighting on their own. It's a second type, the sheep, those who wouldn't mostly start a fight but who are happy to get involved once it's started, who are the ones that get deported from foreign cities after the police raid bars where drinking sessions have got out of hand. It is they who might be dragged into confrontations with opposing fans at the next

European Championships, and unlike the Nazis they can't be dismissed as psychopaths stuck out on the furthest fringe of society.

Some do get drawn into far-right activity, but most are happy just to hang about in the small groups who spend so much time being interviewed for Sunday supplement features about 'having it off with another firm' that you'd think they hardly had the time to eat, sleep or dress themselves let alone do any fighting.

While there are few serious group fights inside stadia these days, gangs still run around in shopping centres and elsewhere on matchdays in the misguided belief that they are in some way representing their club or their town. Claims that this sort of thing is on the increase have been all over the papers in recent weeks ('It's Back!' should have read 'It's never been away but you didn't notice') and there is a real danger that they can become a self-fulfilling prophecy with football-related violence being made to sound like an exciting thing to get involved with.

There is an element of wish fulfilment about it, too. Hooligans have always made good copy for journalists, like the ITN researcher who rang the *WSC* office to say that they wanted to travel to Bruges with two sets of Chelsea fans, one respectable and one less so, and could we provide them with some phone numbers.

At the slightest hint of trouble, would-be war correspondents can strap themselves into flak jackets and chase around on the fringes of groups that are organized, you're never surprised to learn, "with almost military precision". All this gives the cretins a sense of celebrity they don't merit and encourages others to join them. Thus the cycle of news-notoriety-more news rolls smoothly on.

Fascists have to foment discontent because being noticed, making people afraid of them, is at the core of their self-identity: it wouldn't be worth doing if no-one was frightened. Measures can be taken that would prevent extreme right activists from going to games, here and abroad. But the second level of football-related violence, the gang fights that are addictively exciting for groups of angry, bored or plain stupid males all over this country, is a longer-term problem, one that afflicts football because it happens to be one of the most popular activities in our culture.

In one respect, though, football can be held at least partially accountable for what goes on around it. Clubs often don't seem to care about how badly players behave as long as they perform on the pitch where their aggressiveness can be channelled effectively: the footballer as squaddie, going over the top because his manager tells him to.

Off the pitch, increasingly it seems that players can let themselves down badly and escape censure, not admitting to wrongdoing even when they're caught. When the prevailing ethos in the game is that anything goes provided you get away with it, no-one should ever be surprised that it continues to provide some people with an excuse to give vent to their worst instincts. ○

One Cup Wonders

Aberdeen's defeat by Stenhousemuir ranked alongside some of the great upsets in Scottish Cup history. Archie McGregor dusted off his seismograph and came up with a list of top shocks.

WSC No 98, April 1995

Berwick Rangers 1, Rangers 0 – January 28th 1967
Never has an English victory been greeted with such spontaneous and prolonged celebrations throughout Scotland. Or, to put it another way, it's not just the fact that they won the European Cup in this year that makes 1967 a particularly cherished one in the minds of trophy-starved Celtic fans.

The irony behind this one is that Berwick's triumph was master-minded, if that's the right word, by Jock 'Character' Wallace – the man synonymous with, er, commitment to the Ibrox cause and a string of championship and cup wins in the mid Seventies.

It will come as little surprise to learn, then, that many have attributed the outcome of this tie not to the surprise deployment of a libero or any other imaginative tactical formation by Jock, but to the astounding standard of fitness of his players.

Since taking over as player-manager a few weeks earlier, Wallace had helped bring about the disappearance of large chunks of the Berwickshire coastline by subjecting his squad to regular bouts of his scientifically-developed training routines, consisting of wading up and down sand dunes for hours on end.

Berwick were to be dumped out by Hibernian in the next round. The other Rangers skulked away with their tails between their legs and ended the season with their appearance in the European Cup Winners' Cup

Final against Bayern Munich. Hardly consolation, is it?
Shock Rating: 10

Tarff Rovers 1, Alloa Athletic 0 – December 27th 1969

There is, to be sure, something faintly ridiculous about the suggestion that Alloa Athletic were once the victims of a giant killing. The Wasps' appearances at Hampden are, after all, unlikely to be for anything other than fulfilling League fixtures against Queens Park, and even the prized B&Q Cup has eluded their grasp in recent years. The passage of time has, however, only served to underline the astonishing nature of Rovers' victory.

A collection of villages situated about midway between Dumfries and Stranraer, rather than a distinct place, Tarff participate in the South of Scotland League which, to the game up here, is probably approaching what the Jewson Eastern Counties League Division One is to the elite of English football. By dint of the SFA's quirky rules of affiliation, however, several members of the SOSL participate in the Scottish Cup each season – usually only to be thrashed out of sight in the qualifying rounds. Any which have had the temerity to reach the first round proper are generally severely dealt with – last year Kirkcudbright's plucky St Cuthbert's Wanderers lost 11-0 to Ross County.

Of Tarff's finest hour few details are available – attention was understandably directed towards the more sumptuous ties, such as Montrose v Cowdenbeath. The bald facts are that Rovers' McKnight scored the penalty winner in front of a crowd of 500, no doubt agog, spectators. Strangely, even the Alloa Athletic 60 Year Commemorative Handbook (1921-81) is unforthcoming with further elaboration. Just goes to show – these big clubs can't take a beating.
Shock Rating: 4

Rangers 0, Hamilton Academical 1 – January 31st 1987

It's surely a measure of the gulf that exists within Scottish football that a defeat of one Premier League side by another is afforded the status of a 'shock' result. At the time of this tie the Souness revolution was in full flow. Millions were being spent on English internationalists, with the latest breath-taking capture having arrived only weeks before – Graham Roberts.

The Accies, meanwhile, might have been more aptly named 'Free Transfer and Player-Swap-Deal Anonymous'. After all, who, apart from 250 Meadowbank fans, had heard of Adrian Sprott?

The disparity of resources was reflected in League placing – Rangers battling it out with Celtic at the top, Hamilton clinging to the basement with fearsome zeal. Amongst Accies results that season were a 7-0 gubbing from Hearts and, a mere 21 days before the tie, a 3-8 pasting at the hands of Celtic. Piling agony upon agony, they had also been adopted as Jimmy Greaves' favourite Scottish team.

The tale of this one was 89 minutes of incessant pressure by the home side and a fine finish by Mr Sprott to an Accies counter-attack. Graeme Souness took defeat with remarkable restraint – he was to get plenty of practice at blowing his top after Cup defeats in years to come – while Accies manager John Lambie, who had vowed to remain celibate until Hamilton recorded another win, left with a strange grin on his face.

Shock Rating: 7

Partick Thistle 0, Cowdenbeath 1 – January 9th 1993

The Maryhill Magyars are turned over by the Blue Brazil! Cowdenbeath's diabolical form that season reached such legendary proportions that a Church of Scotland minister was impelled to write a book about it – the Rev Ronald Ferguson and his now famous *Black Diamonds and the Blue Brazil*. By the end of the campaign the litany read – three victories in 44 games, no home wins, over 100 goals conceded and relegation before the clocks went forward.

An away draw against Premier opposition wasn't exactly the dream ticket for Cowden, therefore. The odds against them also appeared to rise appreciably when it was revealed that their team for the day included within its ranks Douglas, Herd and Lamont – all up against Nelson in the Partick goal. In the end, however, the entire Thistle gave the impression of suffering from severely impaired vision as they meekly succumbed to the Central Fife Samba. Henderson won the tie with a penalty; the homesters contriving to miss one themselves.

The Rev Ferguson's sermon the next day undoubtedly featured a lively re-examination of the much loved parable of the 'Boy David who done brilliant'. Meanwhile, back at Firhill it's quite possible that the Thistle manager, none other than John Lambie, was contemplating another spell of sleeping on the living room settee.

Shock Rating: 3

Stenhousemuir 2, Aberdeen 0 – February 18th 1995

According to the media, this was the result the Scottish Cup so badly needed. As usual, they had got it wrong – this was the result all St

Johnstone supporters so badly needed. The fact that there was a two-division gap between the Mighty Warriors and the Dons meant that this one automatically acquired the "sensational" billing, and conveniently nudged 'Muir's even more comprehensive 4-0 victory over the Perth Saints in the previous round just a little bit further out of the humiliating limelight.

The other point on the globe where this result was greeted with unbridled euphoria was, of course, Oslo. For some inexplicable reason, Stenhousemuir were, several years ago, descended upon by a group of Norwegian anoraks – well, at least they can't be accused of being glory-hunters – who have since become some of the club's most loyal supporters.

Confirmation of this comes from the list of player-kit sponsors in the Warriors' match programme – thus we have goalkeeper Mike Harkness backed by the obliging Vanda and Thore Franstrund, Adrian Sprott (him again) by Manfred Larson, and so on.

In what seems suspiciously more than just simple coincidence, the two-goal hero of this match, Tommy Steel (and what a boon he was to headline writers), is sponsored by the Norwegian Film Industry. What a come-down it must be for left-back Euan Donaldson to merely have a "Warriors Die-hard" listed as his backer.

And that's about it really, other than to mention that treble-chasing Raith Rovers were said to be mighty relieved to have avoided Stenhousemuir in the draw for the quarter-finals...

Shock Rating: 8

From Here to Nowhere?

Reflections on the perceived changes in football fan culture in the ten years since the Heysel Stadium disaster.

WSC No 100, June 1995 – Editorial

THIS MONTH MARKS THE TENTH ANNIVERSARY OF THE HEYSEL STADIUM disaster, football's Year Zero, a terrible time for anyone who can remember it. For a while, in the eyes of the government, sections of the press, and even the game's authorities, there were few species lower than the football supporter, someone from whom normal society would have to be protected.

In 1985 it would have been difficult to imagine a time when there would be a feature in a broadsheet newspaper, in this case the *Independent on Sunday* of April 16th, arguing, in pained tones, "that only about half the men in Britain" like football, and yet "the media seem to be convinced that we are one uniform football-loving nation". Ten years on from Heysel, no-one needs to explain why they're a football fan.

Conventional wisdom suggests that the 1990 World Cup was the turning point in the rehabilitation of the game, with half the nation watching the England v Germany semi (though by no means, of course, all supporting the same team). Vital groundwork had been laid, though, in the five years after Heysel, with supporters groups, such as the FSA, and the fanzines working to disprove the old image of the typical fan as a wild-eyed thug who used matchdays as an excuse to fight. (This attitude lingered on in some quarters: four years later concerted attempts were made to lay the blame for Hillsborough on 'hooligans' when it was crystal clear that responsibility lay elsewhere.)

Partly as a consequence of the turnaround in the game's fortunes since the dark days of 1985, football supporters are now much harder to categorize. Fans used to be simply the people who went to the matches. Now, however, a much bigger proportion of those who would lay claim to the title are viewers rather than spectators. (Not that the Premier League should worry, attendance figures these days count for less than TV ratings and the number of bedspreads and table lamps shifted by club shops.)

People who spend money on football without actually attending live matches have every right to consider that they make a contribution to the upkeep of the game, but they are much less likely ever to be up in arms about it. What difference does it make to them if a local club's ground capacity is cut by half, or if plans are unveiled to merge with a local rival: they've paid to be entertained at home, with panel discussions and match analysis and replays of Ian Walker saving from Andy Cole.

The rise of this new breed of fan has set in chain a counter reaction, still developing, which could yet undo much that football fans have achieved on their own behalf post-Heysel. A while back, after the publication of *Fever Pitch*, a number of people from social backgrounds not previously associated much with football supporting suddenly made public declarations of their lifelong interest in the game.

It was harmless enough: some knew what they were talking about, others had simply identified a bandwagon and hopped on. The wave subsided, but left behind a curious by-product: almost every month an article appears in a men's magazine contrasting the maligned 'soccerati' (the sort of people, in fact, who would read an article about football in a men's magazine) with the fan of the old school – usually embodied by the writer – for whom football is the preserve of macho men both on and off the pitch.

The 'soccerati', we are told, would have hated the old days when football terraces were full of groups of lads fighting each other. The violence of the Seventies and early Eighties is re-presented as a golden age, contrasting sharply with the neutered Nineties, a feeling that has even been developed commercially with the creation of the 'Lad' – boorish, pissed and desperate to impress – as a marketing concept. Fighting (or at least talking about it) is cool again, partly because it's what the trendies are supposed to fear most.

Football matches generate intense emotions, and there is always a danger that passion will spill over into aggression: in pre-Heysel times, some much preferred the fighting to the football, so the boiling point was artificially induced, somewhere in or around a League ground, every week. It mostly involved running, back and forth, across a terrace or piece of waste ground. A worrying sight for onlookers, but not, truly, a horrific one, until Heysel.

The Juventus fans didn't die as a simple consequence of their being chased; their deaths were a product of ignorance and complacency on the part of UEFA and the Belgian police. The football authorities here have learned more about the violent margins of football culture in the decade since then, but they still have a lot to catch up on and their first reaction to a violent incident is still the verbal equivalent of a shrugged shoulder – 'it's bad for business, but what can we do?'

This is slightly worrying, because the more fractured football fan culture becomes, the more it splits into irreconcilable groups, the less likely it is that supporters will be capable of holding onto the ground they have won for themselves in the last decade. Enough people still occupy a position between the two extremes set out earlier for their views to be taken seriously – not enough heed is yet paid to what they say, but they are at least listened to.

That position could be undermined in two ways: either by fans becoming passive consumers rather than participants, or by enough of them coming to believe the old myth, being stoked up again, that allegiance can only be proved by fighting. It is still unlikely that the conditions in which another Heysel could happen will be created, but then ten years ago no-one would ever have thought that the biggest match of the season would be preceded by bodies being laid out in rows on a terrace. ○

Arrested Developments

Richard Darn explained why Barnsley fans felt their team had been unfairly treated by the football authorities and the press in a season when they just missed out on the First Division play-offs.

WSC No 100, June 1995

I BET RICK PARRY'S HEART MISSED A BEAT OR TWO AS THE END OF THE SEASON approached. The unthinkable had almost happened. Barnsley in the Premiership? Surely that was against the rules? Who cares about all this pyramid nonsense, anyway? As it turned out, Rick was safe, for true to the club's previous 100 years, Barnsley's fantasy of running out at Old Trafford was just that, a dream waiting for another season.

But what a season it had been. While Derby's chequebook got them nowhere, Barnsley's youth policy continued to flourish (we have won the Northern Intermediate title three times in the past four seasons) re-emphasizing that smaller clubs are far better footballing nurseries than stately-home academies in Shropshire.

Danny Wilson's side played Bolton, Wolves, Sheffield United and Newcastle off the park, all this in the teeth of one those injustices that convince Barnsley folk the world's against them. Not content with shutting the town's last remaining pit, the government also decided to close down Oakwell's terraces to force compliance with the Taylor Report.

It became increasingly frustrating to hit the road with Barnsley and discover that standing was not deemed such a public danger at some other First Division grounds. A number were granted an extension to the 'sit on your bum' deadline. But the poorest outfit amongst these and one with just about the smallest gates, was treated with the utmost contempt. This despite the fact that £2.5 million has already been sunk into the new East Stand and plans were being drawn up for further redevelopment.

In some ways this injustice produced a 'backs against the wall' spirit among players and fans. It also presented visiting teams with a disconcerting backdrop, as nearly all the support was confined to one side of the ground – and, as tradition demanded, southern softies like Millwall (one win at Oakwell in 70 years) folded under the pressure.

The season's turning point came against Middlesbrough, when international week shut down the Premiership and thrust Oakwell into the spotlight. Even Radio 5 chose it as their live game and as Alan Green jocularly put it, "The producer told me that I might be in Genoa on Thursday and Barnsley on Saturday, but I don't mind." Well said, Alan.

Other reporters from the national press variously delighted in the fact that "a howling gale and rain swept down off the Pennine moor" and that "Oakwell was a tip". The last comment came from the *Guardian*, who despite their political pretensions, invariably send their snootiest reporter. No room for Fabianism in his report. The *Sunday Telegraph* perused the surroundings more cautiously and thought this might be a season for the Reds to consolidate. A century out of the top flight sounds more like fossilization to me, but there you go.

The game took place on a quagmire and ended in a predictable, if exciting, draw, effectively putting paid to the Reds' play-off hopes. At least another small club, Reading, benefited. There was also a memorable run-in between Bryan Robson, standing on empty terracing behind the dug out, and a club steward, who told the former England star he was technically on a building site (if not a tip) and should bugger off, get a hard hat, or apply to the government for a Taylor Report exemption. The local constabulary intervened and things ended amicably, despite the fact that the two protagonists "weren't getting along very well," according to PC Plod.

All this exciting footie took place against continuing rumours that the FA were going to inaugurate a Premiership Second Division. This hermetically sealed proto-elite surprisingly didn't include Barnsley in its proposed line-up. Nor were Grimsby or Reading touted as possible high-flyers, despite being near the top of the current division on merit.

Even though the idea now looks unlikely to get off the ground, it's worrying that the notion football should be run on an invitation-only basis keeps resurfacing. Who are the idiots who think spanking stands are more important than having good footballing sides in the League? Why are smaller clubs perpetually having to excuse themselves for their success?

I wasn't the only Reds fan who darkly predicted that on the eve of potentially our greatest triumph someone would pull the plug and bar us from the Premiership because we didn't sell cheeseburgers with relish under the main stand.

Paranoia perhaps, but that feeling harks back to the days just after the First World War. The authorities wanted an expanded First Division and looked to the second flight for candidates. Those in automatic promotion positions pre-war went up. But one more club was required and Barnsley filled the next berth. Some club chairmen didn't like that prospect one bit, and so glanced a little way down the pecking order and saw none other than Arsenal.

Thus by a shabby vote the Gunners were undeservedly elevated and became the old First Division's longest serving member. The Reds were left fuming at the deal and now share a similar distinction for longevity in the former Second Division.

Money has always talked loudest, but surely the recent success of the Reds, Reading, Bolton and Tranmere ought to convince those with fat wallets that footballing spurs should be earned on the field – not off it. Rick Parry be warned: we haven't given up on the Premier League just yet. ○

Hate of Absurdity

Graeme Kaye recounted how two Leeds fans nearly came to blows over Manchester United.

WSC No 101, July 1995

YOU SHOULD TRY TO GET ON WITH THE PEOPLE WHO LIVE NEXT DOOR. I LIKE MY neighbours. This is partly because they like football. And mostly because they have got a Sky dish, which is why I knocked gingerly on their front door at 4 o'clock a few Sundays ago. After my neighbour (lets call him Dean McIntyre, Flat C, 252 Barnston Rd, N16), had said, "Get up off your knees, man, of course you can watch the footy," I scurried into their sitting room, where the West Ham v Man Utd game was about to begin.

I had met Dean a few months earlier in a local pub, where we discovered our mutual passion for Leeds United. Names, matches, cultural references ("Whatever happened to John Hawley, hahahaha?") were all present and correct. "There's a fellow who thinks like me," I decided as I left the boozer.

As we settled down to the first few minutes of the game, Dean's girlfriend, a Red, arrived. "You haven't scored yet, and you're outnumbered now – by Leeds fans!" said her boyfriend, looking over at me with a matey wink. I stared straight ahead for a few seconds then replied: "Er, I want Man Utd to win, actually." Silence. If I had said, "I eat babies," or "Jimmy Tarbuck has proved himself to be an excellent chat show host," I couldn't have been more controversial.

Dean sat still for a few moments, then leaned forward, red-faced. "You can't!" he spluttered. You can't. Can't like that cos you're this... can't like them cos you like those others... if you do like that, you can't like what I like...

"Bollocks!" I said, brightly. Dean glared. "But... but you're a Leeds fan!" I attempted to argue. About how I'd seen the top two play and preferred to hope that other teams, Leeds included, would be influenced by Man Utd's approach rather than by Blackburn's. It was like saying to a man who has just fallen out of an aeroplane, "Hey look, there's a match on down there! What a great view!" Pointless. Eventually I gave up and allowed Dean to say it: "You're not a real Leeds fan."

When someone insults your manhood in this way, you can do one of two things. 1. Hit him (very, very risky). 2. Walk straight out of the door without a word. Or, as an absolute last resort, you can stay and watch the rest of the game because you know you won't be able to watch it anywhere else: the sensible, Douglas Hurd-ish option, which I chose to adopt in the interests of neighbourly relations.

I know what you're thinking. Part of supporting a team means 'hating' your rivals, but really, it's meant to be a bit of a laugh, isn't it? (Even Dean's infatuation with the Super Whites seems to take second place to his love life.) The same jokes, about cowardly, whinging, sheep worrying, and worst of all, lucky bastards, travel up and down the country. Only the name of the team they support changes. And you could cope perfectly well if one of them moved next door to you.

Often, though, it's the part-time haters, those dabblers in tribalism, who get it all wrong ("I saw in this fanzine that everyone hates Man Utd and, you know, I really hate people who come from Manchester, too!"). So what if they'd never been to Elland Road (or Anfield) and couldn't even place their own team's town on a map of the UK? They've suddenly discovered what they are supposed to dislike and now the whole world must think like them. The only good thing about them is that they probably won't be droning on about football this time next year, comedy (or speedway, or cricket) having made a comeback as the new rock 'n' roll.

I hate people who hate people. Is that you? I hate you. It's summer. Just give it a rest. For a couple of months, at least. ○

Robinson's Crusade

Michael Robinson, once of Liverpool, Man City, Brighton and others, was causing a big stir in Spain. Phil Ball could only stand and admire.

WSC No 102, August 1995

BACK IN THE DAYS WHEN YOU COULD AFFORD A FISH AND CHIP LUNCH without the luxury of a six-figure salary, my job, every Saturday, was to bike it to the chippy for fish 'n' chips x 4. I tended to fulfil this weekly obligation at 12 noon sharpish, in order to be back for the start of Sam Leitch's *Football Preview* on BBC1.

To miss it was unthinkable. I would be prepared to forego *Match of the Day* but not Leitch's programme. His plump, articulate, almost deadpan authority seemed vital to the rhythm of the week, a rhythm that first began to stutter when he was replaced by the altogether blander figure of Bob Wilson – the first in the long line of ex-pro presenters that has proved to be the undoing of that enthusiastic English journalistic tradition of TV football presentation, from Pathé News to *Football Preview*.

Twenty-five years on, living in Spain, I can happily report that the days of rushing back from the chippy have been revived, only now it is on a Monday night. I rush back from work in my car, the programme is *El Día Después* (The Day After) and the presenter, bizarre though it may seem, is one Michael Robinson, the centre forward with the 40" bust whom Malcolm Allison once said would play for England (Ireland, actually), and whose chasing of the ball was memorably described as "...rather like the man chasing the No 37 bus."

In Spain, the average working day misses out most of the afternoon, so that most people resume later on and finish around eight o'clock in the evening. *EDD* begins at 20.08, just giving the rest of the country and myself time to make it to the nearest bar to join in with the nationwide ritual of gulping a few vinos and gawping up at the latest antics of the fully-jowled, but thoroughly entertaining, Robinson.

The programme is 75 minutes of pure joy. Robinson has done more for Anglo-Spanish relations in four years than all the accumulated efforts of ambassadors and diplomats since the Armada. His co-presenter, Francisco 'Lobo' Carrasco, a forward for Barcelona in the mid-Eighties, plays Ernie Wise to Robinson's Morecambe, but he is also an attractive character in his own right. Robinson and Carrasco have somehow managed to hone an approach which combines the knowledge of the pro with the dotty enthusiasm of the supporter.

Herein lies the key to the programme's appeal. It's as though they can't wait to get going, to show you everything that happened on the previous Sunday evening, warts and all. In England, though Hansen and Brooking may command a certain degree of respect with their almost donnish, dark-suited approach, they are always distanced from us – they the experts, us the learners. It's hard to believe that they can actually see the game from our side of the fence.

The Spanish are much more adept at watering the grass roots. Spain is a country much more at ease with itself culturally than is England. Robinson, who writes most of the show himself, has tapped into this perfectly. There's nothing more flattering than to have your culture analysed by a foreigner, and Robinson knows just how far to go without offending.

His Spanish is remarkable, delivered with a native accent and peppered with street slang. He takes the piss constantly, out of his co-presenter, the referees, the players and the public, but unlike Greaves, there is no malice, no dodgy political agenda lurking in the background. When *EDD* devotes a 20-minute slot to how the half-blind groundsman of a Regional B club uses his guide dog to pull his touchline-painter in a straight line, you know you're onto something a little different.

The viewing figures are remarkable, so much so that Canal Plus, a pay channel for subscribers, unscrambles the programme every week for the whole country. The format couldn't be simpler. After a round-up of the weekend's goals, Robinson narrates the section 'Lo que el ojo no ve' (what the eye doesn't see), everyone's favourite bit. Roving cameras, dispatched on the Sunday to every corner of the country, simply record what the public and the players actually do – people picking their noses, scratching their bums, snogging, shouting abuse. Players approach linesmen, only for their complaints to be sub-titled on the Monday, ball-boys fall over in puddles, substitutes and managers fiddle nervously with strange talismans, etcetera. Nothing too clever, you might say, but Robinson's narration saves it from Benny Hill and turns it into Jacques Tati.

In another routine, 'Songs and dances', the cameras scour the terraces of Spain recording the various bands, choirs and kops that have begun an elaborate competition with each other for attention on the programme. Because the lyrics and style of these creations tend to be rooted in regional culture, the appeal of the programme has widened.

Fans even sing songs to Robinson, but it's all good friendly stuff. This has defused any chance of too much nastiness in the grounds, because *EDD* has unintentionally become a watchdog of good behaviour. It's also been quick to jump on and expose the baddies – which for the supporters concerned is a bit like being bollocked by the teacher you most admire.

Nevertheless, after an *EDD* exposé of racist graffiti against the signing of the Argentinian Valdano last season for Real Madrid, Robinson allegedly received death threats from a member of the openly fascist Ultra-Sur. There was a public outcry in support of *EDD*, Valdano was signed, and Ultra-Sur have gone sulking into a corner.

The programme remorselessly portrays players' foibles and weak-nesses, right down to a focus on naff haircuts and baldness. Best of all, it shuns elitism by buoying up the smaller clubs, affectionately documenting the sweaty reality of the lower divisions every week – as opposed to the English convention of a single condescending report on FA Cup first round day.

It has helped to sustain a feel-good factor about the game here, despite the eternal monopoly of Barca-Madrid, the appalling refereeing, and the heartfelt inter-regional enmity that squats below the surface of Spanish society. I could go on, but I run the risk of making Spain sound like some sort of paradise. It isn't. The government and the economy are walking the high-wire while the folks down below are getting restless. However, on Monday nights, at least, Michael Robinson, an unremarkable British footballer of the Eighties, makes the Spanish happy for a while. ○

Pitch Battle

As the Fever Pitch backlash rolled on with no end in sight, Nick Hornby addressed some of the criticisms put forward by the book's detractors.

WSC No 103, September 1995

IN THE JUNE EDITION OF THE ASPIRATIONALLY GLOSSY FOOTBALL MAGAZINE *FourFourTwo*, somebody called Mike Wilson wrote a rant (you could tell it was a rant, because it appeared in a section of the magazine entitled

'Rant') about my book *Fever Pitch*, which has apparently, "helped turn football into a fashion accessory". Mr Wilson gets very cross about all sorts of other things, too, but one of the things that makes him most cross is "the reverential hush now surrounding the book".

Reverential hush? I'd give anything for a bit of reverential hush. In the last few months alone, *Fever Pitch* has been blamed for most of the illnesses besetting the world: it was partially responsible for the Dublin riot, according to a (probably mad) correspondent to the *Independent* letters page; more worryingly, it also paved the way for the rehabilitation of Rod Stewart, according to an article in the *Sunday Times*. A contributor to the *Spectator* suspects that I have single-handedly turned Britain into a nation of TV-watching morons; in his excellent new book *The Best World Cup Money Can Buy*, *WSC* contributor Ed Horton worries about "the direction in which *Fever Pitch* has taken us".

A headline on the cover of one of those depressing sub-*Viz* tits'n'football comics asked the question, **Should Nick Hornby be shot?** More or less every single broadsheet newspaper has run at least one piece on the 'gentrification' or 'intellectualization' of football. (I wish someone would show me where the intellectual ideas are in *Fever Pitch*. I can't find any, although I wish with all my heart that I had come up with one.) And so on and on, and on. If that's a reverential hush, then I'm God.

Fever Pitch seems to be taking the rap for all sorts of contradictory effects. It has turned us into morons at the same time as it has intellectualized football; even more confusingly, it is to blame both for the gentrification of the game and for the return of yob culture (*Fever Pitch* is a "lager saga", according to the *Guardian*). Now, I'm quite prepared to believe that I'm guilty of something. But I'm not prepared to believe that *Fever Pitch* has somehow managed to produce a mutant strain of *Guardian*-reading, lager-swilling, Kierkegaard-quoting, Gaultier-wearing hooligans, the bastard children of Sarah Dunant and Paul Gascoigne, simply because I have serious doubts about whether such a strain really exists. So what exactly is *Fever Pitch* responsible for?

My own feeling is that it is responsible for very little, apart from hundreds of articles about what it is responsible for. I certainly don't think it is responsible for the return of yob culture, an accusation made by those who haven't read the book and hate football anyway, so I'll ignore that one and concentrate instead on the charge that it is responsible for a lot of horrible pretentious middle-class gits descending on our football grounds and elbowing out the true salt-of-the-earth cloth cap fan. Well, I don't see that one either.

Just as political correctness only really exists in the negative in this country – we all know how awful it is, because we've read about its awfulness in the papers, but it is very hard to find anyone whose life has been adversely affected by it – the sudden influx to our stadia of bourgeois intellectuals appears to me to be a media myth. I have yet to read an article by a bourgeois intellectual discovering a sudden, unexpected passion for football as a result of picking up my book in the Hampstead branch of Waterstone's; as far as I am aware, no Cambridge dons or literary editors or advertising executives have read *Fever Pitch* and gone scurrying down to the Abbey Stadium or Brisbane Road (or even Highbury) for the first time. Nor would I mind if they had, incidentally – this might not be the right thing to say, but I think that the experience of watching live football is one that everybody, even middle-class sissies, should have at least once.

And this, really, is what the media debate surrounding *Fever Pitch* is about: who is entitled to watch and talk about football? Ed Horton suggests that *Fever Pitch* is responsible for a certain kind of fan (male, middle-class, with media access) being given too many column inches to write certain kinds of pieces (nostalgic, self-deprecatory). And I guess he's probably right. *Fever Pitch* may well have a case to answer here, but it's a minor misdemeanour rather than a war crime, and I'm not going to suffer too many agonies of self-loathing.

But elsewhere, at the more stupid end of the argument, there is a rather repellent reductionism creeping in: an article in a recent issue of Arena suggests that it's not people like me who should be watching games, not even people like you (*WSC* readers are unrepresentative, apparently, due to their liberal views and their intolerance of violence); nor is it women, or children, or old people, or anyone at all, really – apart from the kind of people who caused mayhem in Dublin, invaded the pitch during the Chelsea v Millwall cup tie, and chanted through the minute's silence for Matt Busby. That, the writer seems to be saying, is how we are, and if you don't like it, well, you're obviously not a proper fan, then, are you? You're a yuppy wuss (or, even worse, a girly, or a kid, or an old person).

There is an irony here. The majority of this debate has taken place entirely within the pages of glossy men's magazines and the feature pages of broadsheet newspapers – you won't find much about it in the tabloids, or on TV. Most of the 'proper fans' that the *Arena* writer talks about so lovingly have no idea who or what 'the soccerati' are. So simply to be aware of its existence, even if you demonstrate your awareness with a sneer, means that by definition you are no longer one of the boys: you spend too much time reading the *Independent on Sunday*, or *Granta* (or writing for glossy men's mags) for that, and you have therefore forfeited the right to represent the kind of fans you purport to speak for.

The publication of *Fever Pitch* coincided exactly with the formation of the Premier League, and I know which one I think has had the most bearing on the way that the game has changed over the last couple of years. If there are more families at football now, and more directors' boxes, and more giant screens and less noise, then it is not because I wrote a book and a lot of southern softies loved it; it is because Alan Sugar, David Dein and the rest wanted it that way. Books don't change anything, unfortunately. Money does.

Over a quarter of a million people have bought *Fever Pitch* now, and not all of these people are members of the Groucho Club or distant relatives of Melvyn Bragg. I know, from correspondence and conversation, that many of them are not big book readers and, indeed, that some of them have not read a book all the way through before. And I'm prouder of this than of anything, because it means that the book made sense to a lot of men and women irrespective of their age, class and educational background. "Football, famously, is the people's game, and as such is prey to all sorts of people who aren't, as it were, the people," I wrote in *Fever Pitch*. They're still out there, writing columns in newspapers and magazines. O

After a Fashion

Like the toilets at Wembley, the football magazine market was full to overflowing...

WSC No 104, October 1995 – Editorial

WOTCHER AND WELCOME TO A BRAND NEW FOOTBALL MAGAZINE. WE'RE daring to be different. We're from the street, not a cul de sac, and we want to know what you, Joe Punter, Mr Bloggs, the geezer at the back of the away coach with a six pack and a roll-up, think about the game that Bill Shankly so rightly said that thing about (sub in copy here – Ed). What are the best terrace songs about Bovril and Subbuteo? Who does Jimmy Hill think he is? Why don't you come over here and say that? All these questions and more will be answered each month, or your money back.

Only kidding. If you're flicking through this edition of *WSC* in a shop, well done for finding it (and if we were in the porn section have a quiet word on our behalf). You can hardly have failed to notice – football magazines are taking over the world: store detectives now collar anyone leaving a newsagents without buying at least one magazine trumpeting exclusives on Ryan Giggs' holiday snaps or Alan Hansen's favourite episode of *UFO*.

Over the past couple of years, the market has been pored over by researchers who have discovered more than can possibly be good for them about the likes and dislikes of 18- to 25-year-olds who would pick Le Tissier in preference to Batty, prefer bottled beer to draught and would be prepared to consider buying shinpads endorsed by the 1994 Brazilian World Cup team. The end result is that publishers are now jostling for the attention of every sentient being who has ever been mildly interested in football.

Not that we're complaining. We'd worry about anyone over the age of 12 who found something to hold their interest in the official club magazines, but the last thing we'd want would be a return to the period BGT (Before's Gazza's Tears, that pivotal moment in football history with which only someone who has been in solitary confinement for five years wouldn't be fully familiar).

In those days, anyone wanting a football magazine to read on their way home for school was well catered for by *Match* and *Shoot!*, but purchasers over the age of 16 had fewer options to choose from than the San Marino national coach.

There was a very thin (in content if not quantity) glossy called *Football Today* and one of the many versions of *Football Monthly*, limping along as a shadow of the magazine it had been in the days when it still had Charlie Buchan's name in its masthead.

Fanzines weren't available in shops apart from specialist outlets like Sportspages and a handful of independents – *WSC* had been going for two years before we were allowed over the threshold of a high-street newsagents – and the publishers who are now bursting to tell you about who's hot and who's not in the Premiership were contentedly beavering away on advert-packed doorsteps about cars, computers and yachting.

So, never a better time to be alive than now, though it's anyone's guess what will happen after the European Championship finals. If England have done well and look to be on course for the 1998 World Cup, expect a media frenzy to dwarf even the obsessive level of coverage devoted to the game in the past year: there'll be daily newspapers for each League club, Terry Venables will be in every TV commercial, and Sir Bert Millichip will replace Queenie as Head of the Commonwealth.

But if the tournament is a catastrophe for England, it is possible that the football magazine market will suffer a knockback, too, as publishers' cash is channelled back into trying to turn on car-owning computer buffs who sail at the weekend. The past couple of years may then come to be seen as a brief golden age for football publications.

But, for all we've said about dreading a return to the creative desert of the 1980s, that wouldn't be a true reflection of the way things are: football magazines are piling up on the shelves because a market has been identified and is now being tapped, but there are nothing like as many new ideas as there are new titles, and the seam could soon be over-mined. (The main shaft is jammed up with state of the art drilling equipment; we're crouched in a sidetunnel with a pickaxe.)

It may not be too long before the current trend for conscious irony in magazine coverage of football culture will reach saturation point. There is a limit, after all, to the number of times you can stand being told about *Escape To Victory* and terrible old perms and "There are some people on the pitch who think it's all over..."

Then we'll be back with the complacent conformity in style that the fanzines reacted against in the first place, a circumstance in which the *Football League Review* would come to seem revolutionary. All of which, we don't mind telling you, has given us an idea... ○

More Than a Game

As England met Colombia at Wembley, Richard Saunders explained why the visitors had more on their minds than football.

WSC No 104, October 1995

ON JULY 7TH THIS YEAR, JUAN JOSÉ BELLINI RESIGNED AS PRESIDENT OF THE Colombian Football Federation. It seems the least he could have done. After years of rumours that he was no more than a front man for the Cali drug cartel, police had finally turned up conclusive proof: a picture of him boozing it up with the Rodriguez Orejuela brothers, who head the cartel. A copy of a cellular phone bill belonging to the cartel's number three, which showed repeated calls to Bellini's phone, had also emerged.

The bulk of Colombia's professional clubs indignantly called for the resignation to be ratified. But, as tends to happen in Colombia, over the weeks the atmosphere gradually changed. "It's a matter of stones and glass houses," said Eduardo Gonzalez, a sportswriter with Colombia's main national daily *El Tiempo*. "They can say to Bellini, 'You're a narco.' But he can turn round and say, 'Well, what about this or that meeting you were at.' In the end they'll support him because they all have something to hide."

Gonzalez was right. On August 24th Colombia's professional clubs voted to reject Bellini's resignation by an undisclosed majority. It's an open secret that Colombian football has been a plaything of the drug lords for almost 20 years now. Narco involvement has led to corruption, absurd inflation in players' prices and wages, and ultimately murder. But it has also undeniably been the catalyst for the country's meteoric rise as a footballing power in the last ten years.

Drug traffickers first began to show an interest in the game in the mid 1970s. At that time a number of clubs were passing through a severe financial crisis. The government had hiked income tax and also introduced a 12 per cent tax on money sent out of the country. The numerous foreign players on which Colombian clubs relied at that time were feeling the pinch.

The drug mafia appeared like a host of guardian angels. Miguel Rodriguez Orejuela, the younger of the two Cali brothers, was one of the first in. During the 1978 World Cup in Argentina he sent $550,000 in cash down to Buenos Aires to persuade the Peruvian team to throw their key match against Argentina. The bribe was intended as a favour to his pals on the Argentinean military junta. But Miguel had counted without the Colombian national airline which sent the suitcase to New York instead of Buenos Aires where it was opened by a startled customs official.

"Within two years Miguel Rodriguez Orejuela was the biggest sporting impresario in Latin America," says Ignacio Gomez, a Colombian journalist whose investigative work on narco-corruption of football has earned him numerous death threats over the years.

The Rodriguez Orejuela brothers took over America de Cali which, until then, had been the smaller of Cali's two clubs. Having never before won the title, America were champions in 1979 and then won the title five years running between 1982 and 1986. Their rivals, Deportivo Cali, who refused to have anything to do with the drug trade, sank into oblivion.

The traditional powers of Colombian football, Millionarios and Santa Fe, of Bogotá, were also dirtying their hands. And by the end of the 1980s there was scarcely a team in the country which hadn't benefited in some way.

But it was the marriage of drug money and a brilliant footballing mind at Nacional de Medellín that proved the key to Colombia's footballing development. From the late 1970s, Pablo Escobar, the infamous boss of the Medellín cartel, was pouring money into Nacional, who won the title in 1981. Initially, they bought success in the traditional way – importing foreign players and perpetuating the chronic inferiority complex of Colombian football. But in 1987 Francisco Maturana was appointed as manager. He insisted the club reject the traditional dour, defensive style and develop an approach more like that of the Brazilians, based on speed, touch and accurate passing. Crucially, he decided the club would rely entirely on Colombian players.

In 1989 Nacional became the first ever Colombian team to win the Copa Libertadores, Latin America's equivalent to the European Cup. In that year Maturana was appointed coach of the Colombian national team, applying the same principles he had used so successfully at Nacional. Colombian football was on a course that would lead to the 5-0 victory over Argentina in Buenos Aires in September 1993.

But the adverse effects of drug money were also being felt. Prices and wages went through the roof. And the power of a small handful of drug barons was growing. "There were just four or five individuals who ran everything," says Alvaro Gonzalez, head of Difutbol, which controls the non-professional game in Colombia.

Players came to be owned directly by these men rather than the clubs. "They weren't footballers. They were merchandise," says Gomez. The traffickers ran stables of players, shifting them around at will on loan between their different teams. The cartels were also thought to be heavily involved in underground betting syndicates. "You would have two teams playing each other owned by the same guy, who also happened to own the betting syndicate which was taking bets on the game. Not a good idea," says Gonzalez.

Intimidation of referees became widespread. The Medellín leg of the Copa Libertadores semi-final in 1989 had to be replayed after the referee revealed he had been threatened. And the Colombian championship for that year was abandoned after a referee was murdered.

After the debacle of USA '94 and, more importantly, following the death of Andrés Escobar, it was decided something had to be done. Investigations were carried out into the financing of the professional clubs and new legislation introduced. No one person can now own more than 20 per cent of a club. And no-one can have shares in more than one team.

But the government's efforts have been greeted with indulgent smiles. The Cali cartel is one of the largest and most complex criminal organizations in history. Its greatest genius lies in its money laundering techniques and financial management. It's hard to imagine its accountants won't be able to keep one jump ahead of the Colombian Football Federation.

Drug involvement in football does nevertheless look to be decreasing, chiefly because of the broad crackdown on the drug trade in Colombia. Police have arrested the bulk of the leaders of the Cali cartel in the last few months, including the Rodriguez Orejuela brothers. Just as after Pablo Escobar's death in 1993 Nacional began unloading players, so America de Cali are now looking to reduce their enormous payroll.

But where does that leave Colombian football? The inflation created by drug money is such that few legitimate entrepreneurs have much interest. And the next generation of narcos are unlikely to be tempted into such a business which proved to be less profitable than the Medellín and Cali bosses had hoped.

The game, though, remains strong. Two years on from Pablo Escobar's death Nacional were runners-up in the Copa Libertadores this year. And although the national team continues to carry the psychological scars of USA '94, it remains formidable, at least on paper. The irreplaceable Valderrama is aging but the likes of Asprilla, Rincon and Valencia will be around for France 1998 and there is a host of younger players jostling behind them, the most impressive being Ivan Valenciano of the Junior Barranquilla club, unusually owned by a millionaire businessman who isn't a narco.

"Nacional were saved by their younger, home-grown players," Gonzalez points out. Thanks to the drug money the infrastructure is now in place and Colombia looks as if it can rely on a steady supply of fresh talent in the future. "Between them, Pablo Escobar and Francisco Maturana awakened Colombian football," says Henry Ramirez, doyen of Colombia's sports reporters. "There's no going back now." ○

Down by the Riverside

Harry Pearson wondered whether certain sections of the national press would be able to adjust to the fact that a Brazilian star had signed for Middlesbrough.

WSC No 106, December 1995

WHEN MIDDLESBROUGH ANNOUNCED THAT THEY HAD SIGNED JUNINHO, THE Brazilian Footballer of the Year, the phrase 'culture clash' flashed up on VDU screens in newspaper offices across the capital. Wading through resulting articles, however, I have come to the conclusion that 'cliché clash' might have been a more accurate term.

Many football folk live in a place of national and regional certainties. A place where Germans are disciplined, the French crack under pressure and nobody relishes a trip to Sheffield in February. This mythic place is called Footerworld and in it Brazil is the land of sand and samba, where lithe girls in bikinis shimmy to the sounds of Astrud Mountain. Middlesbrough, meanwhile, is in the north east, cue theme music from *When the Boat Comes In.*

Because their life is based on certainties, the denizens of Footerworld fear change above all. Like Elizabethan philosophers they believe that change results in anarchy. There is a natural order of things and it must not be meddled with. Middlesbrough (medium sized club, no 'tradition') had transgressed the code. First they had snatched Nicky Barmby away from 'glamorous' Spurs, now they had whipped Juninho from the very grasp of the mighty Arsenal. They had brought change to Footerworld. Now they must pay for it. Over the next fortnight Middlesbrough got a good kicking.

The *Mirror* warned 'The Little One' that County Cleveland has the country's highest rate of car crime. If Juninho had signed for Man United, would the same paper have mentioned drug-related shootings? If he had gone to Chelsea, would the journalists have felt compelled to tell him that London leads the way in financial fraud? I don't think so.

There were the usual remarks about Middlesbrough's lack of cultural life – no Opera House, no fringe theatre – which, even if true, demonstrate a confused view of the value system of the modern professional footballer. I mean, how many players have signed for Liverpool over the years because of Anfield's proximity to the Northern Tate Gallery? OK, then, apart from Julian Dicks?

The *Guardian*, meanwhile, sent a man to São Paulo to ask people in the street if they knew where Middlesbrough was. None of them did! Sadly, this gentleman's journalistic colleagues seem to have an equally sketchy knowledge of the real world. The number of times Copacabana was mentioned suggested that many did not know the difference between Rio and São Paulo, while the tedious fallacy that Middlesbrough is a suburb of Newcastle populated by passionate Geordies surfaced yet again.

The most splenetic article of all displayed a similarly cavalier approach to geography. It was written by Michael Herd and appeared in the *Evening Standard*. Herd took as his source my book, *The Far Corner*. He was kind enough to describe this as one of the best books ever written about football, though his enthusiasm had apparently not extended to reading it. One example from many: Herd quotes from a description of Seaham Harbour which he describes as being "just up the coast [from Middlesbrough]". Seaham Harbour is as far from Middlesbrough as Hemel Hempstead is from Piccadilly Circus.

In the end, I suppose, the best revenge on the inhabitants of Footerworld is to live well. We have a brand new stadium, average home crowds pushing 29,000 and Nicky Barmby. As I write we are fourth in the Premiership, and one of the world's most exciting players is a fortnight away from making his home debut. Teesside may not be the prettiest place on earth, but at the moment it has a certain *je ne c'est quoi*. ○

Miner League

James Taylor and Andy Pitchford related how Sparta Prague managed to stay ahead of the opposition when modern football marketing techniques came to the Czech Republic.

WSC No 106, December 1995

THE DRIVE TOWARDS MARKETED MEDIOCRITY CONTINUES APACE IN THE UK, and with the gradual development of the Champions League, the trend is being mirrored across much of the Continent: more and more football spectators are experiencing the same sort of standardised, plastic experience. If, that is, they can afford it.

Even in the old Communist bloc, footballing traditions are under threat in the name of progress. Take the experience of Czech football, long steeped in a history of away days filled with broken travel restrictions, sausages and too much beer. Under 'classless' communism, clubs had become refuges of difference. Bohemians of Prague, for example, have a kangaroo as club mascot, boast a club driving school and bakery, but have no club shop. Slavia Prague, lovable Manchester City-like failures and favoured by the intelligentsia, have their own brand of sweets but remain in the shadow of their bigger, badder brothers at Sparta.

Elsewhere, breweries are the basis of clubs Viktoria Plzen and Viktoria Budejovice, the latter subject to a much resented take-over bid from American Budweiser, whilst the army are responsible for both Dukla Prague, and the fact that they have no away kit but do have Dukla biscuits.

At Sparta and another of Prague's first division clubs, Viktoria Zizkov, a new picture is emerging. Contrast the experience for the paying spectator. Viktoria Zizkov will be familiar to Chelsea supporters, who faced the Czech Cup holders in last year's Cup Winners' Cup. Blues fans actually missed out on a visit to Zizkov's crumbling ground due to UEFA's ground regulations and seething Chelsea officials. They missed a rare taste of the real thing. Built into a hill behind the pitch is a rambling terrace, on which stand the rump of the four to five thousand home supporters.

The vast majority of Zizkov fans are over 45; the resultant atmosphere is predictably quiet but carries a disgruntled edge. A lot appear to go to matches purely to have a good moan, and at times it's hard to convince yourself that you're not actually at Craven Cottage.

At least, that is, until half time. The standard sustenance at most grounds in Prague is the parek, a saveloy served on a cardboard slab with a hunk of bread, and a well-aimed squirt of mustard. Given the immediate need to wash down the taste of this national delicacy, sales of beer are high at football matches, the fact that most Zizkov games kick off at 10 am being no hindrance.

Curious visitors to Zizkov soon become aware of a cluster of young women who spend the entire first half lumping inordinate amounts of parek and beer down their necks. Disbelief at such a view is soon heightened by the realization that they are actually providing the half time entertainment, as they don the red and white stripes of Viktoria and spend ten minutes prancing round the pitch to a selection to the 'latest' Slade singles.

Beer drinking, sausage quaffing, dancing girls in Stoke kits. There is a God.

Having imbibed their elixir, Zizkov connoisseurs are able to roam freely around the ground, taking up their second half positions. Some, meanwhile, spend their break sorting through the selection of lapel bruisers offered for sale by the famous Prague Badge Van, whose wares include a surreal selection of British enamels – 'Arbroath OK', 'Go Partick' and 'Cup Winners Cardiff' to name but three. The tendency for the old eastern bloc countries to produce badges for almost any occasion continues apace, and a whole new tray for individual ties in the Inter Toto Cup is by no means out of the question.

Equally enjoyable are the half times at Banik Ostrava, a club in the industrial north of the Czech Republic. Banik have a lucky draw during the break and offer three spectators the chance to take penalties against the reserve team keeper. The relative quiet is shattered as spectators leap up and down uncontrollably whenever one of the grizzly, pissed-up ex miners hauled out of the crowd manages to fool both himself and the John Burridge lookalike, and get the ball on target.

Looming over Zizkov and Banik with all their eccentricities is the spectre of the new money, exemplified by Sparta Prague. Sparta have traditionally been one of the big three clubs in the capital, and are now at the forefront of the influx of western money and ideas into the rapidly changing Czech economy.

They already have a number of club shops across town, and have also diversified into the travel agency business. Given the difficulties associated with foreign travel from the old Czechoslovakia, Sparta and their fans are unusually well travelled thanks to regular European competition. (For one match in the 1970s, Sparta took 3,000 fans on special trains to CSKA Sofia – the entire travelling support arrived 24 hours late.) The club now use the contacts established on such journeys as they expand their business interests into the holiday market.

At the Letna Stadium itself other more worrying signs are emerging. It currently costs supporters three times as much to watch Sparta as it does to watch Zizkov, and the gap is widening all the time. Once inside the ground the experience is entirely different. Sausages have given way to Pepsi, popcorn and burgers, and the beer is conspicuously absent. Executive boxes now flank the stadium's central feature, two cars built into the main stand on behalf of the club sponsor, Opel. Tickets are obtained through a computerised booking system, and seats on all four sides then offer impressive views unless, that is, you end up in the Sparta home end, where, Umbro-clad, acned youths masquerading as England fans, mix with older skinheads.

Security is tighter – a perfect opportunity for former Communist Party officials to find a new vocation as matchday stewards – and consequently there is no free movement at half time. The Badge Van is relegated to the car park, and distraction is instead supplied by fifteen minutes of deafening techno, Queen and a long time favourite, *Daddy Cool* by Darts.

When the match kicks off again, spectators' lug holes are further battered with the arrival of every goal, which is greeted not by the roar of the crowd, but by an ear-piercing 30 seconds of the can-can, followed by an equally deafening silence, the thrill of the goal washed away amid misplaced marketing: wrap it up; sell it; forget what it meant in the first place.

Sparta are the current champions, but the nature of last season's triumph is currently a matter of some controversy. In July, former QPR keeper Jan Stejskal, now with Slavia, resigned from the Czech national side in protest at alleged corruption, saying: "I can hardly shut my eyes to what we could see on the league's pitches this spring... it is impossible for this to be ignored any more." He went on to describe the Czech league as "a comedy", and accused league officials and referees of favouring Sparta.

Stejskal's outburst was accompanied by admissions from two top referees that they had received a number of bribes, and that members of the Czech FA were amongst the perpetrators. The picture has been clouded with a series of further claims and counter claims, but the matter is currently in the hands of the Czech police and remains unresolved. Some sort of exchange visit to the Hampshire Police headquarters does, however, seem more than likely.

For the new entrepreneurs at Sparta and elsewhere, bribery may well be an option in the short term, but other, more market-oriented imperatives dominate the longer view. Given the admission prices, a familiar picture is emerging of a new type of spectator more suited to the role of the commercially aware football club chasing a place in the Champions League. In fact, in contrast to most grounds, Sparta already appear to operate some sort of moustache ban for home matches, with the crusty miner favoured by older Czech males almost entirely absent from the stadium.

With more clubs falling into the clutches of ambitious businessmen, the threat to footballing traditions in the Czech Republic is very real.

Whilst the younger generation is understandably anxious to shed the trappings of the old regime, the questions remains: how to modernize, but not to sterilize? Even at Zizkov, the half time competitions and the beer have disappeared. As one Zizkov fan lamented in a national daily, "How can you eat a grilled sausage with Coca-Cola?" O

Opportunity Knocks?

It is not just in Britain that black footballers have a hard time in the game after they retire. Osasu Obayiuwana looked at how reverse discrimination has been applied in African football.

WSC No 106, December 1995

EVERY YEAR MORE BLACK FOOTBALLERS RETIRE FROM PLAYING THE GAME. IF they were white, a significant proportion would move straight into coaching or management jobs. But, as we know, that just doesn't happen if you're black. And it's not just a problem in Britain. The story is the same even in countries where black players have been long-established, such as France and Portugal. Jean Tigana, now with Monaco, was the first ever black player to take charge of a first division side when he took over the reins at Lyon in 1993. In Portugal the exception to the rule is Eusebio, of World Cup '66 fame, who has spent several years working with Benfica's youth team. (The picture is brighter in South America, where Francisco Maturana is rated as Colombia's best-ever coach and several Brazilian club sides have been coached by blacks, though none has yet taken charge of the national side.)

If this disturbing state of affairs in England and mainland Europe can be logically ascribed to racism, what could be said for the preference of African football associations for European coaches, some of whom cannot get jobs as Third Division managers back home, at the expense of the indigenous ones?

Godwin Dudu-Orumen, presenter of *The Best of Football*, a popular sports programme on Nigerian television, argues that most African coaches are unable to manage a high profile national side, not only due to the old cliché that they are "technically incompetent" but also because of their inability to withstand intimidation and politicking by meddlesome

FA officials on sensitive issues, such as team selection.

He argues that only competent European managers, like the strong-willed Clemens Westerhof, who left his Nigerian managerial job after the 1994 World Cup finals, have the wherewithal to make the kind of contribution that has raised the profile of African football in the last decade, even if it meant treading on a few toes. "Westerhof was uncompromising in his attitude towards Nigerian FA members who tried to undermine his authority. Most local coaches wouldn't have the guts to call the FA's bluff if they're treated badly," Dudu-Orumen says.

But what incentives are given to the local coaches who work with the 'Super Eagles'? On arriving in Nigeria in 1989, after a stint as caretaker coach with Feyenoord, Westerhof was offered a US $60,000 annual salary, exclusive of match bonuses, a chauffeur-driven car and a plush suite at the Lagos Sheraton, later moving on to a duplex in one of the city's most exclusive districts.

It was a slap in the face for Christian Chukwu, officially designated chief coach during Westerhof's tenure. Chukwu, who rose to stardom as captain of the Nigerian side that won the African Nations Cup in 1980, was paid a paltry 30,000 naira yearly salary – the equivalent of US $400 per annum, less than a tenth of Westerhof's monthly salary. Hmm.

The 'technical incompetence' charge can be laid aside with just a cursory glance at the career of a coaching legend in Ghana. After an Englishman, George Ainsley, was recruited as their first national coach in 1957 and a Swede, Andreas Sjoberg, a few years afterwards, the Ghanaian FA sent ten ex-internationals to take coaching courses in Czechoslovakia and West Germany.

One of the lucky ten was Charles 'CK' Gyamfi. His depth of tactical knowledge led Ghana to three out of its four Nations Cup wins – the first in 1963 before a home crowd in Accra, the second in Tunisia, two years later, beating the home side 3-2 in the final match, and later the 1982 win in Libya. Only another local coach, Fred Osam Duodu, comes close to Gyamfi's record. He piloted the 'Black Stars', as they are popularly called, to their third African Nations win in 1978 and a near triumph at the 1993 World Youth Championships in Australia, where Ghana were beaten in the final by Brazil.

Since 'CK' retired to the post of Ghana's technical director, none of the foreign handlers contracted to manage the national team have been able to notch up a Nations Cup win. The German, Otto Pfister, came closest at the 1992 finals in Senegal, but was stopped at the final hurdle by another

African coach of note, Ivory Coast's Yeo Martial, who kept to his promise of giving the country's late President, Houphouet Boigny, his dying wish – Africa's most coveted soccer trophy, never won by the country in 26 years of participation at the tournament.

Martial was supposed to be a stop gap while the Ivorian Football Federation (FIF) searched for a new European coach. In spite of his achieving what no local or foreign coach had been able to do in the country's history, FIF relegated him to the background during the African zone preliminaries of the 1994 World Cup, employing instead a Frenchman, Philippe Troussier, who was sacked before the conclusion of the campaign. By the time Martial was recalled to work a miracle, it was too late.

You might expect that an FA would only recruit a national team coach who could speak at least one language understandable to the players. Yet the Russian, Valery Nepomniachi, supposedly in charge of Cameroon at Italia '90, spoke neither French, the working language of most players in the side, nor English, spoken by those from western part of the country. How he managed to overcome this difficulty remains a mystery to all but his assistant, Manga Onguene, a member of the Cameroon team at the 1982 World Cup, whom many believe to be the real brain behind the Lions' superlative showing at the tournament.

Despite the frustrations felt by black managers and retired players with managerial ambitions the world over, the tide could change quite rapidly in the near future. Never before have there been so many high profile black players with big European clubs. The likes of Ghana's Abedi Pelé, currently with Torino, and AC Milan's Liberian striker, George Weah (already a highly influential figure in his own country), are quite likely to move into team management when they hang up their boots, which would not only help to give African coaches the respectability they need and deserve but would surely boost the chances of black Europeans getting the opportunity to put their playing experience to practical use. ○

Rugby Special

Newcastle United were charging ahead with ambitious plans to become a multi-sports organization, but Ken Sproat would have preferred them just to stick to football.

WSC No 107, January 1996

THE THINGS IN FOOTBALL THAT CAUSE JIMMY HILL TO SPLUTTER WITH righteous moral fury include blatant obstruction, deliberate handball, on the field violence, niggly running battles and stop-start action. I can see his point. And rugby is the hideous manifestation of these evils. It has no place in my life. Tuning in to Radio 5 to listen to the football, there is nothing worse than having to endure reports from rugby matches. When the Five Nations championships are on, and the rugby replaces the football as the main commentary, I could weep. It is more boring than people telling you how many numbers they had on the lottery. I have never been interested and I never will be interested. This view is not typical of all football fans, but it is common enough. I am not the only one who wants to jail football fans who sing *Swing Low, Sweet Chariot*.

When football wasn't trendy and Newcastle United were a mediocre mediocrity, I was regarded as an eccentric for living and breathing football. These days, the people who used to be quite vicious to me for supporting Newcastle ("What! You pay how much? To watch them!") now worship at the shrine of St James'. Those merry folk who used to jest, "You'd watch black and white shirts drying on a washing line" (Ha ha, please stop, pick my ribtickled body out of the Gallowgate End urinals) now carefully wash their precious replica kits and do watch them dry on the washing line in case they get stolen.

Sir John Hall wants to develop 'The Sporting Club of Newcastle' in a similar vein to that of Barcelona. The aim is that every self-respecting Geordie will join up to the cause. Using the 'you'd watch a washing line' concept, Newcastle fans are now expected to watch fifteen men foul each other just because the team is associated with Newcastle United Football Club. Not only that. Ice hockey, basketball, athletics, motor racing, a health club and God knows what else are to be bought and brought under Sir John's huge umbrella.

The ink on rugby union's new professional Magna Carta wasn't dry before Sir John purchased Newcastle Gosforth Rugby Union Club. England star Rob Andrew (portrayed as a local lad – after all, he did go to a school in Barnard Castle, fifty miles south of Newcastle) has been brought in to 'do a Keegan'. The gravy train north has brought a bevy of star ovoid ball merchants to Tyneside. Rob Andrew was introduced as a special guest before a match. Most of those that were in their seats applauded. Not in some apoplectic fit of adoration, though, just in politeness.

Plans to develop the rugby team's Kingston Park ground into a "super stadium" will no doubt come to fruition. Star names will fill the team, and next season they will waltz the Courage National, er... Third Division. Impatience with opposition is a Sir John trademark. At present the rules state that a transferred player has to wait 120 days before he can play for his new team in a competitive match. As the stars kick their heels, the current rugby team gets a good hiding every week in the Second Division. Expect a court battle between Sir John and the RFU on this one.

I have a liberal attitude to other sports. If you want to watch them, go on, feel free to do so. Have a nice day, but keep off the back pages, get off my TV set and don't expect me to give them money. Here is the worry for most Newcastle fans. It has never been satisfactorily explained how Rob Andrew et al are being funded. Newcastle Gosforth play to crowds that would make the average Third Division football club chairman ill with worry. I remain to be convinced that professional rugby will be self sufficient on Tyneside. I may be selfish, but I don't care. I want every penny I pay to watch football to go into football.

Ice hockey is also undergoing something of a transition. Where a Premier League is mentioned you will find Sir John. Like the crocodile that chases Captain Hook in *Peter Pan*, he is omnipresent. Along with a clock ticking inside, there are catch phrases. "Big plans... tick tick tick... top ten in Europe... tick tick tick... there is a price for success." Sir John bought the long-established Durham Wasps and, until he builds an arena for them (plans already bedevilled with controversy), they will play in Sunderland under the name of Newcastle Wasps.

The other major ice hockey team in the area, the Whitley Warriors, have been bought by another consortium who have moved them the few miles from Whitley Bay to another new arena in Newcastle. On the face of it, the Warriors have stolen a huge lead to catch the hearts of the armchair/remote button all-sport-following public who might want to actively support a team. I predict, however, that Sir John will throw money at the problem and when his team of all stars finally skate into Newcastle they will wipe the ice with the Warriors, both financially and in sporting terms.

This is all well and good, but I don't care, and I don't wish my season ticket to subsidise it. My fears that you won't be entitled to a ticket for the football unless you are in The Sporting Club of Newcastle have yet to be allayed. The phone rang the other night and a semi-polite United sales-person wanted to know why I hadn't bought a £500 bond to guarantee my season ticket for the next ten years. The dissenters are being rooted out. My nightmare of being unable to travel around Northumberland without showing the 'Sir John Geordie Passport' to black-and-white-striped mind control operatives is a step nearer. How long before the stewards require you to know last week's rugby score before they let you in?

Helpfully, the match programme now carries two pages devoted to Newcastle's rugby and ice hockey fortunes. The programme for the Blackburn game carried the subtle message "Underwood Loves The Sporting Club Concept". It smacks of a slogan on a billboard in Tiananmen Square. The point is obvious – this is what the right thinking Geordie should be thinking.

When Sir John Hall said he had big plans for Newcastle, I used to think he just meant the football team, but he sees it as more than that. I have a feeling that he will not cease in his quest for Tyneside to be at the centre of the world until the North Pole is shifted from its axis and the earth revolves around Byker. He can have his dream, but don't expect anything more than a shrug of the shoulders from me. ○

Son of my Father

For Howard Byrom, the football nostalgia boom had a strange
consequence — it meant that his dad, former Blackburn and
Bolton striker John Byrom, was back in fashion.

WSC No 107, January 1996

IN RECENT TIMES, FOOTBALL HAS RECEIVED THE HIGHEST ACCOLADE BRITISH
culture can bestow – it has become hip. Fashion magazines feature
models in football shirts. Effete pop stars trill about the virtues of a kick-
about. Dining rooms now resound to newly authoritative chatter about
the mid-week game, and their favourite Seventies star. The past is
constantly being trawled for old heroes and relics.

Who could have predicted the sudden massive nostalgic interest for
those happy days? Orange footballs, toilet rolls on the terraces, sprawling
bungalows replete with shag pile carpets, gold plated bathroom fittings and
a Capri on the driveway. As the son of a Seventies soccer star, these things
were a major part of my childhood. Personally, I find it deeply ironic that
once again my father is back in vogue. As part of this so-called 'Generation
X', it's doubly ironic that my father is now more hip than I am.

At 15, Johnny Byrom (rummage through those bubble-gum cards!) was
signed up by Blackburn Rovers, recent runners-up in the FA Cup. In
1961 he played alongside the England captain, Ronnie Clayton, and a
host of other early Sixties mega-stars. He scored plenty and played up to
his cheeky nipper persona in front of forty thousand plus crowds.

In 1964, the team were invited to summer in the States. Imagine a
bunch of Herberts, from assorted northern and Scottish origins, on an
all-expenses-paid holiday to Babylon at the very zenith of its excesses.
They were greeted on the runway then taken to a Tiki Club for some hula-
hula hospitality. The swimming pool of their Hollywood hotel was awash
with women. The team received an invite to Stan Laurel's pad. Peter
Sellers was there when they arrived and together they swilled Stan's
private stash of Red Barrel. One player dated Miss Los Angeles and
everyone cruised on Sunset Boulevard.

When sideburns were still too hip for footballers, sometime before the
advent of the coarse nylon soccer shirt, I made my debut during
Christmas '67. The *Daily Mirror* was there for the photo. They ran a

caption alluding to my father's reputation for Boxing Day hat-tricks. For a while these kind of events seemed ordinary to me. Unfamiliar men would greet me in the street and girls would hang around the driveway wearing huge badges with my dad and his mates grinning from them. I hadn't yet sussed the novelty value – not everyone's father was a soccer icon.

Just before I was born, dad transferred to Bolton Wanderers, 15 minutes up the road, but another universe entirely to the supporters. It created a terrific buzz in Bolton, and murmurs of contempt from Blackburn, where we continued to live.

I vividly recall a ribald ditty chanted to me by some kids on the way home from school, "Oh, wanky, wanky, wanky, wanky, wanky, wanky, Wanderers!" Being inquisitive, I asked what "wanky" meant, smartly receiving a clout around the head. Nice one, dad. Anyhow, it was always a pleasure when the headmaster, Mr Painter, himself a Bolton boy, would enter the classroom on Mondays and compliment me on my father's performance the previous Saturday.

As the recipient either of a generous bonus for the season's contribution or some serious spivving on the Cup final tickets, JB took the family on exotic holidays abroad. Benidorm, Majorca, Marbella and, one summer in true jet-set style, the Bahamas. We would often chance upon some soccer peer or celebrity – we met Eric Morecambe in Albufeira. Dad would shoot the shit, my sister and I would stand around bored not knowing them from Adam. We enjoyed the good life. Already I was sold on the concept of minimum effort for maximum gain.

However, the expiry date on JB's Playboy Club Card was approaching. While carrying a hamstring injury, he became involved in an acrimonious dispute with Wanderers' new management and then returned to Blackburn Rovers on a free transfer. Everyone in town was made up. After one season he jacked it all in, turning down an offer to play in the States. It's amazing how quick the phone stops ringing. He was still stood a pint in the pub, but free trainers and sportswear soon became a thing of the past. For the next 20 years Johnny Byrom had to work for a living, though, mysteriously, around the end of May his grin was always broader than usual.

Being Johnny Byrom's lad, I had a strange knack of always being first to be picked. I was expected to sprinkle a little Byrom magic around the schoolyard each dinnertime with hat-tricks and thirty yard banana shots. It was a lot to live up to. Not yet out of short pants and already a disappointment. I approached the old feller for coaching. His main concerns seemed to feature on which girls fancied me and which lads I could gob. My inability to dribble and shoot with my left were definitely secondary. He did give me handy hints on butting an adversary in the face before punching them, and skilfully controlling the ball whilst slyly bruising an opponent's shin. It took practice but I eventually developed it to full effect. He came through with the goods, though; my Eusebio autograph on the back of a '66 World Cup ticket stub became a source of great envy.

I always enjoyed a kick-about but never progressed beyond Saturday afternoon amateur footy. On the whole my old man wasn't forthcoming with encouragement, deliberately guiding me away from football and towards a glamorous career as a telephone engineer. I had no plans, though, still don't in fact. I cruised through school, always copied my homework and allowed plenty of time for the important things in life; free time, music and fun. I scraped onto an apprenticeship, endured four years, then left to see the sights.

Dad set me a great example. He was no striver, always in bed when my sister and I left for school, usually around when we returned. He only worked Saturdays and the occasional week-night for 90 minutes. He was an extremely talented and charismatic player, though, through his own lack of drive, greatly underrated. But by the look of his grin as he skipped over the spreadeagled frame of Gordon Banks, he sort of enjoyed it.

He hit the headlines again a few years ago. Loafing with some friends in Santa Barbara, I received a news clipping through the post. John Byrom fined £700 for head-butting a guy in his local over allegations of squeezing his girlfriend's arse. Nice one, dad. ○

The President's Eleven

Neil Wills explained why Guatemala's chances of gaining a world ranking significantly higher than 163 were fairly slim (unlike their president).

WSC No 107, January 1996

Try to imagine this. You are an anally-retentive football fan (all right, it gets harder later on). After a failed self-coup by the latest incumbent, you suddenly find yourself president of a Central American country (there, I told you). You arrange a cup game between your national team and a group of odds and sods who you then claim represent the Rest of Central America. Full of confidence, you provide a trophy and blithely name it after yourself.

However, just to make certain of victory, you take the precaution of not letting your opponents see each other before the match, let alone train together. You invite four neighbouring presidents to watch the game with you. You lose 2-1. The other presidents try not to laugh at you. They fail in the attempt, quite badly.

If you were, or indeed are, Guatemalan president Ramiro De León Carpio, you would not have to imagine this scenario, you would be in the enviable position of being able to remember it. It is said that every night the spectre of that match returns to haunt him because, unlike some fairweather footie-fan politicians, this man's a Fan. Attend a match of current champions Communicaciones (they started life as the post office team) and the bloke behind you with the moustache is likely to be none other than *el presidente*.

Furthermore, he doesn't just watch the game – he's also a real footballer. Earlier this year he and his authentic striker's paunch took the field for a game between the National Palace side and a Media XI. The climax of the encounter was the goal notched by *el máximo líder*. Not, as you might imagine, a dodgy rebound off the left clavicle or anything so uncouth as a penalty, but a blistering drive from outside the area. Just how many other presidents can you name who have notched from outside the area? How many people do you actually know who have scored from outside the area? Exactly.

Given these credentials, one's heart goes out to a man who must be filled with deep, unbridled shame every time a representative eleven takes the field (Ipswich fans will no doubt be able to empathize). Guatemalan club sides are routinely dumped out of the UNCAF and CONCACAF tournaments (the equivalent of the European trophies) in the first or second round, and the national side has never qualified for a World Cup, nor looks like doing so for a good couple of centuries to come. In fact *Los Chapines* (to give them their cuddly nickname) currently hold sway over that coveted 163rd slot in the FIFA world rankings. This locates them between Tajikistan and Laos and a hefty 94 behind Honduras, the current top dogs of the isthmus.

Since Guatemala has a healthy 43,516 registered players, compared with just 2,000 in Laos, one is forced to ask just how the the country's team came to be so unremittingly dire. The answer has little to do with football. There are no less than three bodies that purport to represent the nation's footballing interest: the league, the football federation and the government's own Autonomous Sporting Confederation of Guatemala (CDAG). Naturally, each of these spends every waking minute fighting the other two.

The federation are apparently in charge of the national team; CDAG charge the federation with incompetence (reasonably enough) and say they ought to hold the reins; whereas league club presidents habitually refuse to release players for national duty, preferring them to turn out for the league's Guatemalan League XI (though why they bother is beyond me, because it has proved even less successful than the official national team).

However, one cannot just point the finger at the administrators. The players themselves are also at fault. What follows is a common scenario: Major League club brings in foreign coach (usually from a mountainous but IMF-friendly South American country). Foreign coach attempts to instil discipline and proper training programme. Players complain that this interferes with their busy schedule. Foreign coach perseveres. Two weeks pass. Foreign coach stops persevering, throws hands in air, and returns home, where they make tortillas better anyway.

What is frightening about this is that the players are telling the truth – they are too busy, for they not are just professional footballers but *chamusqueros* to boot. The *chamusqueros* (a slang term meaning 'those who sell themselves cheaply') are professionals who turn out on days off for spectacularly-amateur amateur teams on the wastelands of 7-Up cans, avocado stones and animal bones (at least I hope they're animal bones) that pass for football pitches in the capital. Some managers of professional sides therefore have no idea whether their star forward will be fit for Sunday's game against the league champions or whether said boy wonder will have turned his ankle on a piece of dead cow whilst helping Los Ineptos de San Brezo to victory over their rivals from the other side of the tracks.

To earth the scenario, imagine that you play for Rusholme Asbestos Works First XI (which you probably do anyway) in the Third Division of the Banned Carcinogens Midweek Torchlit League. For an extra couple of quid on the weekly subs you could hire Ryan, Eric or Lee to slot in to your well-oiled footballing machine. Guatemalans laugh hysterically and not a little unkindly when I try to explain the concept of Fantasy Football. For a small outlay, they argue, why settle for fantasy?

Yet if the authorities and the players are at fault, sadly the fans themselves cannot be held blameless. In a recent Olympics qualifier at home to El Salvador (who seemed visibly disappointed only to have won 1-0), objects were thrown at the opponents and linesmen, causing FIFA to hand out a 20,000 Swiss Franc fine, which won't help any. Friendly old USA actually wanted Guatemala banned from international competition for two years, which might have turned out to have been something of a blessing (Guatemala in two-year unbeaten run shock etc), but sadly nothing came of it.

About the only group to which no blame can be attached is the UNRG, Guatemala's very own left-wing insurgents. The armed conflict has rumbled on since 1960 and currently holds the record for the longest-running civil war in Latin America. However, any aspiring know-it-all down the pub caught seeking to use the war as an explanation for the nation's cosmic footballing incompetence needs only to be pointed as far as neighbouring El Salvador who, with the minimum of fuss, qualified for the 1982 World Cup whilst the FMLN guerrillas were busy launching their 'final offensive'.

That said, there are pinpoints of light at the end of the tunnel which, friends tell me, can clearly be discerned with the aid of infa-red night-sights. Uncle João has invited Guatemala to send five coaches to Brazilian club sides to gain experience. Pele is to visit the country and make a critique of the way the game is run, which should prove pretty scary night-time reading. And last but not least, De León Carpio himself has doshed out about £33,000 to ensure (hem hem) qualification for the Panamerican Games.

And if that fails, at least the president has something else to keep him warm at night: constituionally prevented from seeking a second term, he will be out of office in January, leaving him available to be selected for the national side in the forthcoming *Copa de Naciones*, a competition for which, thankfully, there is no qualifying tournament. ○

United we Lounged

Sheffield United 2 Leeds United 3, April 26th, 1992, First Division. Tim Bradford was there. Sort of.

WSC No 108, February 1996 – More Than A Match

ON APRIL 27TH 1992, I WAS LYING BY A POOL IN VENEZUELA, SIPPING A VODKA and taking in the sun, when my copy of the *Daily Journal* arrived. This was a classic ex-pats rag – a mixture of syndicated articles by high-profile right-wing American journalists, a few cartoons, Auntie Doreen's problem page, think pieces by out-of-work Venezuelan politicians and three pages of sport.

On a normal day my eyes would scan the pages feverishly like a wonky searchlight, over the baseball and boxing news stories to a few brief lines about the English League.

Being a Leeds United fan wasn't too difficult in South America. After all, in the previous few years I had only been to see them on a handful of occasions (and one of Django Reinhardt's hands at that), so a whole season away wasn't troubling me unduly. Except that I had made a bet with fortune on an unlikely double-header; the Labour Party winning the general election and Leeds winning the championship.

I had figured, after two or three minutes of research, that the second couldn't happen without the first. Leeds' first-ever title in 1969 was about a year before Ted Heath ousted Harold Wilson's Labour Government on the strength of the slogan, "We're posh and rich and hate hippies". Then in spring 1974, with the Labour Party just back in power, Leeds did it again. (It's no coincidence that in 1982, with the Falklands War raging and the country in the grip of Thatcherite patriotism, Leeds did the decent thing and got quietly relegated.)

However, a week before my poolside reverie with the expertly-mixed cocktail, the dream of a two pronged victory by teams beginning with 'L' had been shattered. My brother and I had gone out on a gigantic all-day celebratory bender, before getting home to watch the the election results on CNN surrounded by bottles of vodka.

As soon as the TV was on and John Major's grinning face appeared outside 10 Downing Street, I realized that Howard Wilkinson was going to have to come up with something special to save the day.

I took some consolation from the *Daily Journal*'s coverage of both competitions. Even on the day of the British election they had run stories about Labour being absolute certainties, and their sports department had also been studying the form rigorously for the previous month, deciding that Manchester United, too, could not be beaten.

I sensed that the season would go to the final weekend – I was expecting draws for both Leeds and Man Utd – but knew that with a bit of luck it could also be over after the 26th, when Leeds travelled to Bramall Lane and Man Utd were at Anfield.

So, having seen no football throughout the whole of the 1991-92 season, I prepared myself for the biggest sporting weekend of the decade so far. I was about to experience Sheffield Utd v Leeds. In black ink on newsprint paper, with perhaps a photograph or two.

You have to be totally ready and relaxed to cope with instant gratification of this sort, where the match is over in the second it takes you to find the score at the top of the page. Pre-match rituals (the triple wink, the clutching of the left ear lobe) done and dusted, shorts on, body smeared with factor eight suncream, ice-box crammed with, well, ice, and drink by my side, I turned the paper over to look at the back page.

Own Goal Secures Leeds As English Champions read the rather snappy headline (and to think I couldn't get a job on this publication as a junior sub editor). Without bothering to read the rest of the report I screamed my delight, downed the drink and jumped into the pool.

It wasn't the best game I had ever witnessed, but for sheer value for money – about 30p for the paper and £275 for a one-way ticket from Heathrow to Caracas – it was hard to beat.

So what if the Tories were in until virtually the end of the century, I thought, as my face hit the cool water. I mean, it wasn't as if they were going to destroy the health service and inflict damage to public transport and the education system that might take decades to put right. Leeds were champs. And I had a great tan. Caramba! ○

Fit for Nothing

Mark Perryman thought the growing trend for players to get injured during pre-match warm-ups was a sympton of clubs' disregard for some basic principles of physical training.

WSC No 108, February 1996

"THE GAME IS ABOUT GLORY. IT'S ABOUT DOING THINGS IN STYLE, WITH A flourish, about going out and beating the other lot, not waiting for them to die of boredom." And with these words from Danny Blanchflower the Spurs Way was born.

It's a fine philosophy and can be used to justify the misdemeanours of many a flair player. It is certainly a lot more attractive than anything likely to be provided by the dull followers of work-rate and route one. But at its heart this philosophy has also too often been used to explain away football's bewildering ignorance of the importance of physical fitness.

Gerry Francis has worked many a miracle at White Hart Lane, the first of which was introducing his famous sprint sessions on a Tuesday morning. But this is hardly revolutionary stuff. A basic part of athletics training is known as interval running, timed sprints with a timed recovery time, with distances gradually increased and recovery time progressively reduced. For any professional football club not to have this as a basic part of their training programme is a disgrace, for their use to be complained about – however jovially – by the players is an insult to the fans who pay their wages.

It has been estimated that in a competitive football match a player will run between six and nine miles. If half that distance consists of fairly lengthy sprints up and down the length of the pitch, the player will run some three miles at full pace, the rest at a jog.

This means the basis of a player's physical training would be remarkably similar to a bog standard club athlete training to run 10km road races off about 50 miles a week. A regime of early morning runs of six to eight miles, a long run of 10-12 miles, hill sessions to strengthen the thighs plus interval training sessions of 10 x 400m, and 4 x 1 mile should be the staple of a footballer's life.

Such a programme might sound quite heavy to the uninitiated; it's in fact precisely what is followed by tens of thousands of amateur athletes all year round. It amounts to some 50 miles a week, fitted in before work. You might have to be a bit mad to do it, but it's a hobby for many runners. But for a lucky few professional footballers, such a programme could make the difference between winning and losing, not to mention the attraction of continuing to collect a hefty pay cheque. Unfortunately, physical fitness is too often portrayed as something to be played off against skill and flair, something the likes of Wimbledon might pride themselves on as they go for the pre-season photo shoot on an army assault course, but not quite the done thing for the effete skill merchants. Nothing could be further from the truth.

The physique of a typical club runner is not dissimilar to what one might consider a footballer should look like. But how many times have we resorted to chanting 'you fat bastard' to one of our erstwhile heroes after they return for the new season? In a sense, though, it would be unfair to blame the players for abusing their bodies when so few clubs employ nutritionists to instruct their playing staff – employed, after all, exclusively because of their physical attributes – on what they can or can't eat or drink.

The next time some clown trumpets at a post-match interview that he'll be sinking a few pints with the lads tonight, or a manager coyly explains away his charge's drink-driving charge as boyish mischief, I'll scream. No other sport would put up with such behaviour, and a professional, very well-paid sport that does so betrays the trust of its fans.

The trouble is, football doesn't take the science of sport seriously. Complete with magic sponge and endless playing drills, the game seems blissfully unaware of the incredible advances made in almost every other sport that takes fitness, and, crucially, injury prevention, seriously. And yet football, far and away the best-resourced sport in Britain has scarcely made a single contribution to this work. This is testimony to the amateurish approach to a game where winning is worth millions.

Take the joke of a pre-game warm-up. Players rush around on a freezing cold day in T-shirt and shorts, a brilliant combination if you're looking for a pulled muscle or hamstring. Through a huge investment in research, and the use of materials such as Gore-Tex, which reduce perspiration but maximise body warmth, running kits are now designed to aid performance rather than simply to look good.

It's years since runners woke up to the fact that the only result of running a cross country race in shorts and vests will be a freezing cold body, boosted macho ratings in the changing room and quite possibly an injury. So why do footballers largely decry gloves, long sleeves and, yes, thermal tights? They're not proving anything other than some ill-conceived notion of being 'ard.

The players' stretching exercises are rarely supervised, are often cursory at best, and then the manager complains about his injury list! The game begins and again it's all bare flesh to prove our manliness instead of protecting million-pound muscles from a strain or pull that could sideline a player for weeks.

There's not much that can be done about contact injuries, but muscle pulls and the like are overwhelmingly caused by sloppy preparation and the wrong clothing for winter games. The number of hamstring pulls and groin strains easily outstrips the number of similar injuries a runner would expect to suffer from. This goes on season after season, with coaches and managers blissfully unaware of what could be done to prevent injuries which can easily cost a club a championship or cup run.

I'll never forget the sight of Teddy Sheringham hobbling off the pitch, unaided, then walking the entire touchline in order to get to the changing room after being felled by Bryan Robson. He promptly reappeared to watch the rest of the game in the cold from the bench. Sheringham took some six months to recover from that injury. I've seen too many such instances like this – except where the injury is very obviously severe, treatment is ill-advised and the player is virtually left to his own devices. Support, ice-packs, getting the player into the warm, all basic measures that are hardly attended to.

Fitness and injury prevention will aid the flair of a team, not diminish it. It's also quite possible that fitness could broaden the tactical options available to the players. Why do so few clubs have full-backs who can carry out a long throw-in? No-one can be turned into a Steve Backley lookalike, but a few sessions on a weight machine instead of the proverbial afternoon rounds of golf would significantly lengthen a player's throwing capacity.

Similarly, how come so many goalkeepers can neither throw nor kick a ball with any length or accuracy? A combination of weight-training and practices drawn perhaps from javelin-throwing and rugby penalty-taking would work wonders. The trouble is, football remains insulated from the world of sport. It's become so infatuated with its own capacity as a business that it won't listen to what it could learn from others who take their sport a lot more seriously.

This is a record football should be ashamed of. It remains light years behind sports with far scarcer resources, and yet the rewards for getting it right are manifold. When will we read of a club that is pioneering new techniques for injury prevention, rather than a manager whinging on about the length of his injury list?

And will clubs ever consider themselves part of a wider sporting community at both an élite and general level, helping to fund sports scientists, nutritionists and health education workers? It is about time the academy of football meant a bit more than a misty old memory of West Ham stringing the odd pass together. O

A Striking Example

Mention Iain Dowie's name in 1996 and nine out of ten people collapsed in gales of laughter. Davy Millar was the odd one out.

WSC No 109, March 1996

EACH GENERATION OF FOOTBALLERS PRODUCES ITS OWN CROP OF HEROES, THE men whose talents single them out for mass adulation. The rest can briefly rise to national prominence only by persistently psychotic tackling or by becoming a national joke.

Iain Dowie is a select member of this group. Ridiculed by lazy comedians and desperate fanzine editors, he is doubly cursed as his physical appearance is considered as amusing as his performance on the pitch. Everybody now knows that he is an anti-Adonis with the footballing ability of a carthorse in labour.

Well, not everyone. Iain can rest assured that there is one part of the world that considers him a star. In his (almost) native Northern Ireland, Dowie is the King of the Penalty Box, the Sultan of the Niggling Feud and the Lord of All He Surveys. In short, he's popular.

Of course, Northern Ireland fans have a head start when it comes to recognizing previously underrated players, especially centre-forwards. Their role isn't to score goals but to create as much confusion as possible among the opposition, thereby relieving the pressure on a leaky defence where the Third Division full-back is running amok and the part-timer in the nets is throwing in anything more dangerous than a back-pass.

Historically, we've been well served by our strikers. Back in the

Seventies the blessed Sammy Morgan, all bony elbows and knees, did a fine job of holding up play, usually by accidentally rendering a skilful opponent unconscious. Morgan was frequently paired with Derek Spence, as fine a dribbler with his knees as I've seen, who charged down more attempted clearances than you've had hot dinners. Between them, they were able to irritate even the most composed of defences.

By the time Billy Hamilton and Gerry Armstrong appeared, Northern Ireland possessed a stronger team than usual, which allowed this pair to spend time in the traditional striker's role of scoring goals. Not that they neglected their other duties; Hamilton could frequently be seen physically dragging two or three opponents into the area to get on the end of a cross, just in case Armstrong's barging runs provided such an item instead of the throw-ins they were intended to achieve.

Iain Dowie came into the side when his immediate predecessor, Colin Clarke, became too fat to move. He first demonstrated his potential in a match against Norway by playing a part in the last-minute winner. Jumping to meet a corner, he crashed into the keeper and another defender, allowing somebody else to score from a free header. True, this was in our penalty area and meant that we lost 3-2 but it was obvious that, at the right end of the pitch, he could prove very useful.

It took some time, but Iain eventually won over the crowd. The turning point was the 1995 game against the Republic in Dublin. Up front on his own, he kept the whole Republic defence occupied and prevented them from joining in the siege around our goal. He chased every lost cause, won every high ball and, of course, scored our first-ever goal in Dublin. He was so good that even the home fans laughed when Steve Staunton was named man of the match.

Since then he has thrived, scoring four goals in six games. One of those admittedly went down as an own-goal, but the defender would never have got the final touch if Dowie hadn't been pushing him. Iain's style is not appreciated by the purists who would prefer everybody to play the Ajax way. Sadly for them, football matches are not won on artistic merit but on which side scores more goals. Iain scores those goals. He's also playing a vital role in the team's increasingly successful attempts to play attractive football: Gillespie, Magilton and Hughes have more space to work with when Iain's pulling defenders all over the place.

You can laugh if you want, but we wouldn't swap Dowie for Ginola. OK, so Iain isn't likely to dance down the wing, beat three players and put in a dangerous cross, but the Frenchman could never wrestle two defenders to the ground whilst sticking out a foot to divert that cross into the net.

Keep ignoring the critics Iain, just as you've done throughout your life. They are jealous, you're the star. ○

Wishful Thinking

WSC celebrated its tenth birthday by writing the longest sentence ever seen outside Colin Murphy's programme notes.

WSC No 110, April 1996 – Editorial

SO WE'RE TEN. AND THEREFORE ENTITLED TO GRANT OURSELVES A FEW birthday wishes. In no particular order, they are as follows:

– the police to be persuaded that the law does actually permit them to eject people from a ground for systematic racist abuse, but that, equally, there's no need to confiscate someone's sandwiches, or comb, or glasses case on the basis that they might be offensive weapon;

– no stands to be named after a team's sponsors, or fast food franchise holders;

– no footballers to confess to political allegiances until after a general election, unless it's Vinnie Jones or Barry Fry, both surefire vote losers for the Conservatives;

– politicians to be forced to choose between rival teams with substantial support in their constituencies – and none of this "I want football to be the winner" nonsense, either they're fans or they're not;

– David Mellor to be brought back into the cabinet – that way, with luck, he'll be too busy to appear on Radio 5;

– no half-time interviews with celebrities keen to show they're on first name terms with the team's manager;

– 'personality'-led FA Cup draws to be made pay-per-view, so the FA will quickly come to realize how teeth-grittingly bad they are;

– Bob Wilson to go on a crash course in basic communication techniques so he'll grasp that if you ask someone a question you have to give them longer than five seconds to answer before interrupting;

– the BBC to impose a moratorium on 'themed' commentary of the "It may have been raining cats and dogs on Merseyside but it was the visitors who went home with their tails between their legs" variety for the Premiership highlights;

– Ian St John to have his chuckle surgically removed;

– stiff custodial sentences to be imposed on any person held to be responsible for inviting Denis Law to be a pundit for a televised match;

– use of the words, "To paraphrase Oscar Wilde" to be banned in broadsheet sports pages;

– the phrase "What Pelé once called 'The Beautiful Game'..." to be locked in a black box and buried at a secret location;

– all journalists to pay to see at least one Premiership game per season, and no claiming it back on expenses;

– the football authorities henceforth to refuse to take any action whatsoever against players named in four-in-a-bed/love cheat/reefer madness stories in the tabloids unless the events described took place on the pitch during a match;

– strict rationing to be introduced on use of football metaphors in articles about politics/the arts/genetic engineering/everything else, with an outright ban on their 'ironic' use on *Newsnight* ("Just when they should have been penning the government in their own half, the opposition were busy scoring an own goal");

– an end to moving Saturday matches to Monday night;

the FA Cup contract to be conditional on screening a live match from every round (with no enforced kick-offs between 9 pm and 12 noon);

– Graham Kelly to take assertiveness classes ("Bugger off to your European league, then, see how far you get");

– João Havelange to explain once and for all just exactly who he is and what he is up to;

– Sepp Blatter to be gradually weaned away from hair-oil, allowing his dark locks to go their own way naturally;

– one place in the World Cup finals to be decided by a lottery for all those teams who fail to qualify, to make all that effort seem worthwhile for the likes of Dominica, Macau and England;

– the old myth that 'the crowd wouldn't stand for it' to be dispensed with as a reason why English teams couldn't adapt to a more 'continental' style of play;

– managers to be prohibited from offering a player's nationality as an explanation for his actions;

– Brian Clough to be sent backwards in time to 1991, where he'd resign after the Cup final and not 'write' an autobiography;

– anyone who already wears a uniform in their day job or who lists 'amateur dramatics' among their interests to be prevented from becoming a League referee;

– and just for once, a new club owner to admit that he's aiming for a mid-table position in the First Division rather than the World Club Championship within five years.

That'll do for now. Should we add that this seems to have the makings of a board game for two-to-four players, seven years old and upwards, and that interested manufacturers should drop a line to the usual address? Hell, yes. ○

Family Planning

The death of Cissie Charlton drew attention to the mysteries that still surround England's most famous footballing dynasty.
Harry Pearson looked back on an extraordinary life.

WSC No 111, May 1996

THE NAMES OF FOOTBALL'S GREAT AND GOOD ARE ROUTINELY PREFIXED WITH the word 'legendary', as if it is the most natural thing in the world for the media to suggest that, say, Sir Stanley Matthews is a partly fictional creation. The press coverage of Cissie Charlton's death on March 26th followed this familiar pattern. In some ways this was fitting since the most well-known aspect of Cissie's life, the hours spent patiently teaching her second son Bobby the skills of the game, was entirely the product of overheated journalistic imaginations.

That a story concocted, according to Bobby Charlton, "because it made good copy" should come to be the most famous facet of Cissie Charlton's extraordinary life is one sad by-product of the media's capacity for mythologising.

Cissie Charlton was born Elizabeth Milburn on November 11th, 1912. Her grandfather, Jack 'Warhorse' Milburn, was a renowned player in the local leagues and sported the receding forehead that would later become a familial trademark; her father Jack 'Tanner' Milburn kept goal for Ashington during the club's brief spell in the Football League. 'Tanner' was also bald – Cissie would later thump a Scotsman who called Bobby a

"Baldy ****" during an international match because, "[while] I know it is irrational I have always been sensitive about my four sons' lack of hair ... I have never been able to shake off the feeling that somehow the failure was mine; that I was responsible." Thankfully Billy Bremner's father intervened before the situation could get out of hand.

Her four brothers all played professionally, Jack, George and Jim for Leeds, Stan for Leicester; her cousin was 'Wor Jackie' Milburn (another set of cousins, the Cobbledicks, kept away from football, doubtless put off by the barracking they knew the announcement of their name would provoke); her two elder sons were Jack and Bobby.

Between them the Charlton-Milburn clan, in which Cissie played the role of sturdy pivot, amassed 154 international caps and fourteen winners' medals in major competitions. Other footballing families might have produced more players, none can match the quality.

Cissie Charlton's place at the centre of such a family alone would have marked her out, but there was more to her than just that. She was born into the kind of north-eastern hardship that would have daunted even the hardiest of Catherine Cookson heroines; endured a miserable time as a maid in Watford; survived a mastectomy and the shock of the Munich aircrash a few months later; nursed a husband with pneumoconiosis; and at 73 she still had the energy left to coach a local infant football team.

Cissie married Bob Charlton in 1934 after he had won the money to buy her wedding ring in a fairground boxing booth. Bob – often perceived as a shadowy Denis Thatcher-like figure – seems to have been an amiable and at times comical man. Once, when Manchester United had put the couple up in a ritzy hotel, Bob overcame his embarrassment at the unfamiliarity of the surroundings by drinking too much and Cissie stayed up all night for fear he would wake and use the wastepaper bin as a chamber pot.

The Charlton's first child, Jack, was born the following year. Whatever footballing talent Jack had was clearly of a particularly subtle variety: when Cissie was approached by a scout 15 years later and asked if her son would consider going for a trial with Leeds, she thought he must have got the wrong woman. Bobby, born two years later, was a different matter.

There has been a lot of speculation in the press about a rift in the family, most of it centring on Bobby's relationship, or lack of one, with his mother and brothers. In truth, Bobby always seems to have been separate – introspective and self-contained where his parents and siblings were outspoken and gregarious. Jack seems to have inherited his taste for plain speaking from his mother. In the Fifties, unhappy that Bobby was not being selected for Manchester United as often as she thought he should be, Cissie bearded Matt Busby and asked if her son was being cold-shouldered because he wasn't a Catholic. After he'd picked his jaw off the floor, Busby put her straight.

How Bobby came to be this way is as unfathomable as why it should be that it was he, rather than Jack, Tommy or Gordon, who turned out to be the brilliant footballer. In the final analysis, Jack and Bobby are such obviously and completely different characters that were it not for the fact that they are brothers no-one would expect them to get on at all.

In the nurture versus nature debate, those who are on the side of the latter can happily point to Cissie's antecedents as proof of her formative influence on her two eldest sons. Husband Bob had no such footballing pedigree. Indeed, he showed so little interest in the game that he had gone to his shift down a pit shaft just before the kick-off of the 1966 World Cup semi-final (the BBC intervened on his behalf and brought him up to watch the game on the mine manager's TV set).

The nurturers have a more difficult time of it, and it is here the legend comes in. One of the most famous photos of Cissie shows her kicking a ball to a baggy-panted Bobby. They are flanked by sooty brick, she is wearing a pinafore dress; the pair are watched by her two younger sons, Gordon and Tommy, both in knee-length shorts. It is an arresting image, one which seems to sum up the popular view of the Charltons' story: football mad mum coaches talented son to fame and glory in the back streets of Ashington.

Sadly this inspirational tale is completely made up. Though not by either of the two main protagonists. Cissie never claimed to have taught her sons to play football and Bobby went out of his way to deny the myth. In his 1968 autobiography, *This Game of Soccer*, he expends only three paragraphs before telling the reader: "The story has evolved... that it was my mother who taught me all I know. Apparently, being a Milburn, she knew more about football than most men and spent all her time teaching me the tricks of the trade! That's how the story goes but there is no truth in it whatsoever."

Yet despite Bobby's protests, the story has now been repeated so often it has come to be taken as fact. It has cropped up in book after book and featured in practically all the obituaries. Does it matter? After all, it's harmless enough and does discredit to nobody. Well, in a way it does.

A while ago a friend and I were talking about Arie Haan's goal against

Italy in the 1978 World Cup. He said: "The thing with that goal is, every time anyone talks about it Haan shoots from further out. First it's 30 yards, then 35, then 38, then, well, I mean, it was practically 40 give or take a few inches. And it goes on like that until when you do finally see the goal again it's an anti-climax. Compared to what you've heard about it, it's practically a tap-in."

And that is the trouble with myths. Stood next to them the truth looks small. Luckily Cissie Charlton lived a big enough life not to be too seriously over-shadowed. ○

Patriot Games

Dave Hill, author of the newly-published book England's Glory: 1966 And All That, addressed some of the misconceptions about England's finest two hours.

WSC No 112, June 1996

ANYONE WITH A HEALTHY SUSPICION OF NOSTALGIA AND A WHOLESOME DISLIKE for chest-beating patriots can be forgiven for feeling cynical about England's triumph in the 1966 World Cup. After all, if you delve beneath the standard memories of the final against West Germany, of Kenneth Wolstenholme saying what Kenneth Wolstenholme said as Geoff Hurst completed his hat-trick, of Bobby Moore wiping his hands on his shorts before shaking hands with a laughing Liz Windsor, and of Nobby Stiles' woodentops war dance during the lap of honour, what are the unvarnished facts?

Not, as older readers may recall, wholly glorious. The final, of course, was the complete football drama, but it wasn't until they eclipsed Portugal (and the marvellous Eusebio) in the semi-final that England summoned a performance of dash and glamour. Before that they had been hugely ordinary against mostly unexceptional opposition. They had an excuse for their impotence against Uruguay in the tournament's opening game: the tension was tremendous and Uruguay (though weakened by the absence of several key players contracted to uncooperative Argentinian clubs) were an accomplished defensive side. In such circumstances a goalless draw, though disappointing, could be forgiven.

But recalling the grace and power of Bobby Charlton's opening goal in the ensuing fixture against Mexico, as people often do, helps obscure the fact that England had looked clueless in attack until that moment and the home crowd had signalled it's impatience with a chant of "We want goals!" They got one more and England won 2-0. Yet in beating France by the same scoreline three days later Alf Ramsey's side were again incoherent, Substitutes were not allowed in (to give it its full title) the Final Series of the Eighth World Cup Competition, so France were effectively reduced to ten men. Yet still England floundered for long periods.

Thus the host side advanced to the quarter-final against Argentina with trepidation, not simply because the South Americans, captained by the imperious Antonio Rattín, were infamous spitters and off-the-ball ankle-tappers, but also because they had looked a better team. Apart from Rattín, who ran the midfield at a lofty canter, they had a daring artiste in Ermindo Onega and a dandy striker called Luis Artime, known in Buenos Aires as The Handsome One. Artime had scored three times in the group games and Onega was sufficiently feared as his chief supplier to be made the special responsibility of Stiles, England's totemic midfield harasser.

Adulatory accounts of England's triumph rarely acknowledge that Stiles might easily not have played against Argentina at all. Towards the end of the match against France he committed what many regarded as a terrible foul on the artful Jacques Simon . Yet it went unpunished by the Peruvian referee Arturo Yamasaki, and it was while Simon lay clutching his leg that England penetrated a distracted French defence for a second time to make victory safe.

However, a watching FIFA official made use of his curious power to 'book' a player from the stand, and in the post-match furore pressure was put on Ramsey not to select Stiles to play against Argentina who had already had a player sent off in a blood-curdling goalless showdown with West Germany.

Ramsey, who had little time for officials, would have none of it. But, of course, the Argentina match eventually entered the national folklore not because of anything Stiles did but because Rattin was sent off after 36 minutes by the prickly West German referee Rudolf Kreitlein, a dismissal which acquired an epic quality thanks to the towering Argentinian's contemptuous stalk back towards the Wembley tunnel pursued by vindictive cries of "Dago!" by fair-minded Englishmen in the crowd. Rattín's removal was undoubtedly deserved, yet the ensuing chorus of chauvinistic glee all but drowned out the observation made (surprisingly) by a member of the House of Lords that England had committed more fouls in the match than the South Americans and so had nothing to be pious about. Little has changed since.

In mitigation, though, the team could point to the goal by Geoff Hurst which finally separated the two sides, the sublime near-post header from a wide-angled Martin Peters cross which the pair had practised to perfection on the West Ham training pitch at Chadwell Heath. It marked the start of Hurst's marvellous contribution to the England campaign, a contribution which, despite his three goals in the final, has not been appreciated as fully as it should.

And maybe that's the problem with the more sceptical perspectives on the most celebrated sporting achievement in England's post-war sporting history. Yes, the romantic view is too rose-tinted to be true. And yet dissident readings of the events of July 1966 tend not to give Alf Ramsey and his players the praise they deserve. Indeed there are those – pundits and fans alike – who go so far as to argue that the day the Jules Rimet trophy was hoisted at Wembley marked the onset of a dark age in English football.

Such contentions usually spring from an aesthetic complaint about the way Ramsey's team played. Yet this is based on the dubious assumption that the stone-faced England manager was in abject thrall to defensive instincts. Sure (or, as the posh public Alf would have put it, "most certainly"), there's no doubting his dedication to eliminating risk. Yet although the winning team is famously recalled as the 'wingless wonders', Ramsey's record shows that he consistently picked specialist wide players (even though he sometimes asked them to play deep, as he had done to such brilliant effect with Jimmy Leadbetter when winning the championship with Ipswich). He only dispensed with them completely when the exceptional challenge of the Argentina contest caused him to recall the combative, short-passing Alan Ball rather than give another chance to John Connelly, Terry Paine or Ian Callaghan, who each had a turn on the flanks in the group matches.

After that grim quarter-final victory Ramsey was unlikely to change a winning team as the tournament approached its climax. And this brings us to the eternal controversy over Jimmy Greaves. The great goalscorer's omission from the final line-up despite recovering from a gashed shin sustained against France was undoubtedly a personal tragedy, and today erstwhile squad colleagues murmur their agreement with the widely-held theory that his sad descent into alcoholism was hastened, even triggered, by this desperate disappointment.

But was the absence of Greaves a tragedy for English football? Is it further proof that Ramsey profoundly mistrusted flair and had a thoroughly negative approach to the game, an approach which contaminated the national team for years, if not decades, after?

Again, the evidence does not really sustain the accusation. For a start (as Greaves himself has acknowledged), it's hard to argue with Geoff Hurst's presence on the score-sheet. Furthermore, Ramsey's record shows that, far from looking for excuses to dump Greaves, he had always wanted the Tottenham man in his England attack. Absences through injury and, notably, through a bad bout of jaundice during the first part of the 1965-66 season partly conceal the fact that Greaves was the only forward who Ramsey consistently regarded as his first choice for his position up to and including the group matches in 1966.

It is also sometimes implied that the reserved, mannered Ramsey thought that the incorrigibly chirpy Greaves a flawed character. The two men's very different attitudes to their roots in working-class Dagenham make this a tempting conclusion. But it is less easy to argue that any such personal opinion affected Ramsey's assessment of Greaves as a player. In any case he seems to have had at least as many off-the-field run-ins with Greaves' friend and drinking partner Bobby Moore and Ramsey's dedication to his young captain is beyond dispute.

You often hear claims that Ramsey knew what his England team would be long before the tournament started. This is a myth. Agreed, he'd found his ideal defence in April 1965 when the established Banks, Cohen, Wilson, and Moore were joined by debutants Jack Charlton and Stiles, who generally augmented the back four as (as Ramsey once put it) an advanced sweeper. But his forward preferences were unclear right up until he was obliged to name his World Cup squad of 22 in June 1966. Strikers Barry Bridges, Frank Wignall, Alan Peacock, Mick Jones, Fred Pickering, Joe Baker and Johnny 'Budgie' Byrne (like wingers Gordon Harris, Alan Hinton, Peter Thompson, Derek Temple and Bobby Tambling) were all contenders at various points in the 18-month run-up, but none of them made the squad. In comparison Greaves was an ever-present.

Geoff Hurst actually came into the picture very late, winning his first cap at Wembley only in February 1966 against, of all opponents, West Germany. The match proved a dismal rehearsal for the incredible final to come with Stiles – wearing nine for the night – scoring the only goal. But Hurst retained his place and was allotted the number ten shirt in the squad suggesting that he had secured a place in Ramsey's provisional first choice side as Greaves' striking partner.

Yet for the curtain-raiser against Uruguay Hurst was displaced by Roger Hunt. 'Sir Roger', darling of the Kop, is often demeaned as a typical Ramsey player, a reliable artisan rather than an artiste. Surely, it is often implied, if hindsight justifies Ramsey's retention of Hurst for the final it cannot do the same for Hunt. But again the record books render this judgement arguable. Few would dispute that Greaves was the more gifted player, and although Hunt was an established member of Ramsey's squads he was essentially Greaves's understudy. Yet Hunt had a better ratio of goals per game under Ramsey – prior to the World Cup Greaves had scored 21 times in 26 matches and Hunt 11 times in 12. And in the group matches Hunt scored three of England's four. True, none had been classics. But the Liverpool man could hardly be punished for doing what he had been picked for.

Greaves meanwhile looked below par and would very likely have been dropped by Ramsey for the Argentina match even if he had been fit. Faced with the prospect of penetrating a packed and knowing defence the options offered to Ramsey by the tall, athletic Hurst – so good in the air and at receiving the ball selflessly with his back to goal – were persuasive. And after the Hurst-Hunt pairing functioned well in the thrilling defeat of Portugal, dropping either would not only be painful but would have risked damaging the chemistry of the whole team.

So the wingerless, Greaves-less, 4-4-2-shaped England that walked out to face the indestructible Uwe Seeler, the lithe young Franz Beckenbauer, the imposing Willi Schulz and company was not straight-forwardly the reflection of a soulless, suspicious, over-cautious man as Ramsey was often accused of being.

Nor was it mechanically produced from some soccer-science master plan. Although the defensive personnel remained unchanged, the rest of the side owed its make-up to a combination of team selections which were perfectly logical in their context (and which all paid off) and an appreciation that a team that prevails against top-class opposition gathers cohesion from experience.

And how they needed that cohesion – that strength – in the final, a match whose ebbs and flows, errors, moments of brilliance and sheer dramatic intensity still make compulsive viewing thirty years and many re-runs later. Furthermore, it was a team whose members (and reserves who watched in agony from the stands) retain a wholly admirable loyalty to each other to this day.

It may not have been total football but it was, for the most part, honourable, brave, and true. That's worth applauding. It may even justify millions of English folk continuing to kid themselves that the late Tofik Bakhramov of Azerbaijan was definitely right to tell Gottfried Dienst of Switzerland that, yes, it crossed the line. ○

Conduct Unbecoming

Brian Homewood described the Brazilian football authorities' matchless talent for bizarre decision making.

WSC No 113, July 1996

DURING THE FIFA INTERNATIONAL BOARD'S JAUNT DOWN TO RIO DE JANEIRO for their annual meeting (it had originally been scheduled for Belfast but was moved to Rio "as a tribute to Dr João Havelange"), general secretary Sepp Blatter launched into a spiel in which he described his determination to stamp out violence on the field. He could not have chosen a more inappropriate venue for his speech.

Brazil does more to encourage violence on the pitch than possibly any other of FIFA's members, thanks to a chaotic disciplinary system which appears to be geared exclusively to letting thugs get off the hook. The tribunal that recently imposed yet another minimum ban on Corinthians forward Edmundo is the latest example of the farcical depths to which the system can plummet.

Edmundo – readers may remember his goal at Wembley in the Umbro Cup – was sent off for the first time in a Corinthians shirt (but the umpteenth time during his career) in a São Paulo championship match against Santos. Along he went to the São Paulo federation tribunal (each Brazilian state has its own federation with its own tribunal) with a representative from his club, who took a video of the incident which he believed would prove that Edmundo had not really meant to whack Santos defender Sandro in the face.

When the video was put on, however, the tribunal was treated to an excerpt from *Scooby Doo* as the Corinthians rep had brought one of his son's tapes by mistake. Brazilian newspapers were left to speculate on which video the tribunal would watch at its next meeting – *Tom and Jerry* and *Wacky Races* (which still gets shown on TV in Brazil) were early favourites. Meanwhile, by a spectacular coincidence, Edmundo was freed to play in the following Sunday's derby game against Palmeiras. His absence would, of course, have detracted from the game and many felt this was why he had treated with kid gloves once again.

When a bad foul is committed, it is quite normal for the referee to hesitate before reaching for his pocket and the television commentator to say: "He's looking to see if the player has been booked already." If the player has been booked already, the yellow card remains where it was. If the player is actually dismissed, there is a more than reasonable chance that someone from the other team will go shortly to 'compensate'.

The result of all this is bloodshed. A total of 50 to 60 fouls in a game is common in Brazil and the ball is rarely in play for more than 45 minutes. Edmundo has been one of the chief beneficiaries. He was sent off five times in 1993 (when he was playing for Palmeiras) and showed his displeasure at one red card by shoving his hand into the referee's face. Of his five punishments, only one – a four-month ban – was significant, but it was quickly overturned.

In 1994, he sparked a brawl in a São Paulo v Palmeiras derby which ended with six players sent off and a 15-minute delay as police were forced to intervene. He was initially suspended for 40 days, but Palmeiras responded by bringing in their first 'suspensive effect', a masterpiece of Brazilian footballing legislation which allows any player who is banned for two games or more to appeal against his punishment and carry on playing until the appeal is heard. If the appeal hearing re-imposes the ban, he can re-appeal and continue playing until the re-appeal hearing takes place.

The hearing took place after a six-week delay, but actually increased the penalty. This was a pretty pointless exercise as Palmeiras merely had to bring in the second suspensive effect. While he was waiting for his second hearing, Edmundo was able to play in the final of the Brazilian championship and played a decisive role as Palmeiras won the title.

Last year, Edmundo was finally given an exemplary 40-day suspension by the CBF (this was for an obscene gesture with his genitals at Vasco da Gama supporters during a game), but it was largely irrelevant as he had broken his toe only a few days earlier. The obvious conclusion: the CBF wanted to be seen to be tough without having to do anything. The one saving grace is that Edmundo is a player of talent who is usually sent off for retaliation. More worrying is that many of the beneficiaries are hatchet men who threaten the integrity of the real players.

Gremio could not possibly have won last year's Copa Libertadores if FIFA had managed to enforce the new laws about which they like to brag. Gremio, from southern Brazil, are a throw back to the darkest days of Argentinian and Uruguayan football and their midfielder Dinho, who earned four red cards last year, is one of the most unsavoury characters in the game. Eric Cantona's karate kick was nothing compared to the one Dinho aimed at an opponent Wagner during Gremio's quarter-final at home to Palmeiras. The incident instigated a brawl which held up play for ten minutes and in which Palmeiras manager Carlos Alberto Silva accused Gremio players of encouraging local police to hit his players.

There has long been a suspicion that Gremio deliberately try to cause fights in home games to get local police involved. Two years ago, there was a free-for-all in a home match with Peñarol of Uruguay. At the first sight of trouble, the Gremio fans started chanting "bring on the riot police". The riot police came on, and although the Peñarol players put up a good rearguard action, they had to make a serious dash for the dressing-room to avoid a good beating.

Gremio have been accused of employing the 'kicking rota' system. This involves defenders taking it in turns to foul the opposition's best player instead of employing a man-to-man marker to do it. This way they can reduce the risk of a player being sent off for repeatedly fouling the opposition's top men.

Ferroviaria defenders deployed the tactic so effectively last year that their victim – Guarani's Amoroso – was stretchered off after 20 minutes. Amoroso was one of Brazil's top players at the time, but the battering caused a recurrence of a knee injury which needed an operation. Amoroso, 21, only returned to first team football this year, on loan to Flamengo, but has yet to recover his form.

At least São Paulo can boast minimum bans. Until last year, the Rio de Janeiro federation did not impose automatic suspension on red card offenders. Players sent off on Sunday matches were usually judged by a tribunal held on Thursday nights and routinely let off to play the following Sunday. The Rio federation has the odd opening hours of 2pm to 10pm. Jorge Luis Rodrigues, a reporter from *O Globo* newspaper, explains that this was to allow its most stupid decisions to be made "in the middle of the night".

Automatic bans were imposed, however, for accumulating three yellow cards. This led to several cases of players deliberately getting themselves sent off. Fluminense midfielder Claudio was given his third yellow late in a game against Flamengo: within two minutes he committed a blatant foul and a deliberate handball before finally earning the red for not retreating ten yards at a free kick. That meant a visit to the Thursday night tribunal which duly let him play in the next game.

Red cards get an automatic suspension in the Rio championship this year, but when a player accumulates three yellows, clubs can buy their way out of the suspension by paying the measly sum of $500 to the federation. "This will just encourage violence and it will be the clubs who start whinging when one of the star players gets hurt," said Gerson, the 1970 World Cup midfielder, now a television commentator.

Referees are more likely to be punished than rewarded for upholding the law. Clubs are able to veto officials they do not like through skilful backroom manoeuvring and if a referee correctly sends a player off for, say, timewasting, he can quickly find himself out of favour. The punishment will be undeclared: instead of being told that he is banned, the ref will be, to use the local term, 'put in the fridge' – he will not get any more big games. ◯

Guilty as Charged

Rich Zahradnik came over from America for Euro '96 and, much to his surprise, found himself in a Catholic country.

WSC No 114, August 1996

I ARRIVED ON THE MORNING OF THE FIRST MATCH OF EURO '96 TO FIND A nation still recovering from "THE SHAME!" Members of the England team had had some drinks in a dentist's chair then, played rough with the interior of an airplane. Shame was everywhere, the same shame felt by the entire British nation when one of its politicians, vicars, talk show hosts, policemen, soldiers, dogs, cats or royals does something the rest of us probably do all the time anyway.

There is no individual sin in British journalism, only group sin, sin that reflects on a whole nation of polite people in their sitting rooms. How else to explain this sense of collective guilt? I hadn't encountered it since I spent the fourth grade incarcerated in a Catholic school. I'd always associated the English with a quiet, prim sort of Anglicanism. This shame, it came from my Catholic upbringing, maybe mixed with a little of the Jewish guilt from my mom's side of the family.

Shame began the tournament, but once things got going, journalists called up a vast range of operatic emotions – in ways that would have got them laughed out of most any newsroom in America. Check out this from Paul Hayward, profiling Tony Adams in the *Daily Telegraph* on June 8th: "Adams talks with such unrelenting fervour about pulling on an England shirt that you half expect the three lions on his chest to leap off their badge and give the opposition a good mauling..." I'll interrupt it there. Now imagine an American writing something similar, something like, "Cobi Jones talks with such unrelenting fervour about pulling on the US shirt, you half expect the three stars on his chest to fly off their badge like kung fu throwing weapons and embed themselves in the opposition." Sound ridiculous to you? Does to me.

Hayward wasn't finished: "He is a product of the kind of English yeoman stock upon which military commanders once drew." Ahhh... the class thing! Translated, this meant, "He is the kind of working class dude some upper class twit ordered over the top in the Great War so he could be turned into Essex tar."

You can see now why I couldn't wait to get to the papers every morning. In two weeks travelling around, watching everything from Turkey v Croatia to England v Spain, I read some wacky stuff.

– Time travel: The City Comment section of the *Daily Telegraph*, writing about Sky's £184 million-a-year purchase of Premiership TV rights, informed readers: "Following the game has turned from a Saturday afternoon diversion for yobs into a fashionable, classless entertainment." At least some folks remain quaintly wed to their misconceptions of the sport's history.

– Historical and cultural references to English opponents I hardly knew existed: David Lacey of the *Guardian*, whose work I like, managed to get the date of the Armada into the second paragraph of his report on England v Holland. Do English sports writers have a special desk reference that gives them the dates of all the battles England has fought with potential football opponents? And what happens to these same writers, in the ever-expanding football world, when England meets some nation against which it does not have some historical grievance? Is there such a nation?

– Reverse! Reverse! Reverse! (but without SHAME!): After the victory over Holland and before the quarter-final with Spain, the *Mirror*, in a photo splash, put most of its sports staff in the stocks and showed chief writer Harry Harris and a guy in matador gear being threatened by a Beefeater with an axe. The broadsheets over the next couple of days gleefully reported Harris had refused to participate in the exercise – so his picture had been superimposed – and was taking legal advice. I wondered if that helped sell any more copies of the *Mirror*.

– A rotter's manifesto: John Jackson, calling himself ex-Chief Rotter, took the front page of *Media Guardian* to justify the behaviour of the Rotters, that group of reporters that works for the tabloids' news desks during a tournament trying to find out nasty things about "our brave lads," and bait – sorry, aggressively report on – hooligans. According to Jackson, the rotters' work is critical to the stability of society and a vibrant sports culture. My thinking is, if they're the crack journalists Jackson claims they are, send them where they're needed: Liberia, Bosnia or maybe a Hillary Clinton seance.

– The Football Consumers' Protection Commission: In the middle of the first week, before that great redemptive victory over Scotland, the *Mirror* sent one of its own rotters, Peter Allen, to Gascoigne's house. Allen's job, seemingly as self-appointed chairman of the FCPC, was to tell Gazza "that ordinary fans deserved more from massively paid stars". Gazza yelled obscenities, booted a football into the river. This was, I assumed, the *Mirror*'s contribution to helping the team's key midfielder prepare for his next match.

Ordinary fans probably do deserve more from their newspapers. But then I'd have nothing to read on vacation. And that would be a real... SHAME!!!! O

Trial of Nerves

Premiership superstars swap clubs for millions but down in the lower divisions the picture is rather different. Tom Findlay reported from the twilight world of the pre-season trialist.

WSC No 116, October 1996

IN THE SUMMER MONTHS, WHEN FOOTBALL IS SUPPOSED TO TAKE A BREAK, thousands of 'free agents' trawl around the smaller playing fields of England desperate to find a club. Loanees, refugees and YTS trainees trying to fulfil their dream. It's not a pretty business. Cambridge United, who have spent the last two seasons bobbing round the nether regions of the Third Division, played some 20 games through August featuring a small army of trialists. The first game of the shopping season featured 22 players the club had never seen before – none survived.

Quite simply, with almost no money available for players' wages and none for fees, Cambridge will give anyone a game. As a local journalist, Trevor Lord, explained: "Trying everyone and anyone becomes a pain, but you're frightened to death that you might miss someone." Who knows, he might be the next Ian Wright – a famous late-starter in football. In fact Cambridge really aren't that choosy – the next Iain Dowie would do.

Down in Billericay, the Essex commuter town, Cambridge have come to play the latest in their warm-up games – their sixth this week. Tommy Taylor will expect to beat the local ICIS League side with their mix of local lads and seasoned former pros.

On a brilliant August day the club fielded an extraordinary line up of footballing wannabes: Billy Hudson, once of Tottenham, Crewe and Crawley and nephew of Alan; a Czech, 'Sasha' Spirov; Brixton's Franklyn Dixon; and a man who'd played against England just three months before, Otis Roberts, once of the Hong Kong Select XI and for 20 gruesome minutes a Cambridge United player: aged pros, cocky youths and exotic internationals all chasing Cambridge's £200 per week. Sasha Spirov turns up half an hour before kick off. He claims to be a former Czech under-21 keeper, who played with Peter Kouba ("he was my understudy"). After military service, Spirov is now importing pink sparkling wines into the UK, living in Croydon and using his "friends and business partners" to get him a club in England. He warms up in his Pavel gear – dark tracksuit tucked neatly into his socks – bouncing and rolling, Grobbelaar-fashion.

He's given the first half – though no-one realizes who he is or what he can do – least of all Tommy Taylor. Still, there is a buzz on the sidelines: it's a good time to be a footballing Czech. A couple of skidding kicks, one fine save and a floodlight threatening throw later, his half and his Cambridge career is over. Tommy Taylor is not impressed, and it is clear that Sasha has some pretty radical work to do on his distribution.

Others starting their careers have found out a bit about marketing and self-promotion. Franklyn Dixon, a 20-year-old striker, has adopted Chris Bailey as his 'advisor'. Bailey, who is currently performing a similar role for Dalian Atkinson, is also a writer and producer of Manchester United's FA Cup songs and retains an infectious confidence: "I've got a bit of a name, I've got a network of managers," he confides, adding: "This lad's the first person to score six goals for Crystal Palace in one game since 1933." He then blows it all by confessing the opponents were Croydon in the FA Youth Cup.

Apart from those trying to make their first mark, these desperate exhibitions are full of names you nearly remember. Every year, every League club releases an average of ten players – very few others choose to leave. The result is thousands of former pros trying to get reconnected at the end of every season. The axed player has to fill in a 'disengaged player's card' (a pink form full of statistics), which is circulated round the country and to a number of lesser clubs abroad.

The PFA are also able to offer professional advice, some personal counselling and, in many cases, a great deal of practical help. Currently their education department has just under 1,000 former pros and over 1,500 former YTS players taking on a wide range of courses – NVQs in Leisure Management, working HGV licences, or just learning a bit of basic financial awareness.

Alex Dyer, once of Watford, Blackpool, Crystal Palace and Charlton, is one of football's definitive journeymen. Three years ago, he turned down a new contract with Barnet, hoping to return to a higher level. He is a free agent, who, with just two weeks until the new season, is getting more than a little anxious. The expected offers from the Nationwide League's bigger clubs never came, and with his pink form doing the rounds he's been "waiting all summer, just waiting for the phone to ring". For a man who moved to Palace for £250,000, it's hard to step back into such an atavistic arena: "It's tough when you've played over 400 games and someone takes you on a trial down here like you've just come out of school – that's the most heartbreaking thing about it." Dyer has no security, no contract – a highly-talented player now reliant on the opinion of an unproven Third Division manager. If asked, he will probably sign for a basic wage of some £250 a week.

Football is different from any other part of the entertainment industry. Everybody would love to do it, but so few can, and the majority of those struggle on for very little reward. Tommy Taylor has less than £1,000 a week in total to spend on wages for his two or three signings.

Paul de Luca, a local trialist with a degree in hospitality management that strikes awe into his colleagues, spent three months at Lincoln with

John Beck: "He was really complimentary... over complimentary really, in fact he told me that I had the best left foot that he had ever seen." But after a brief, if hardly headline-grabbing, tug-of-war between Lincoln and Cambridge, neither manager wanted him: "You get to the stage when you think, for God's sake just speak the truth." Keith Oliver, a 20-year-old axed from Hartlepool, looks better than all his short-term team-mates, but he's a midfielder and United have loads of them. He's left without a club, and worse still the prospect of pursuing a career in Sweden – "where everyone forgets you".

The PFA can only do their best, but there is no formalized system in place that would support players as they look for work. Against this background Shearer's £15 million, or even Mike Newell's £750,000, looks more than a bit obscene. Lacking professional representation the vast majority of trialists rely on tenuous connections, the 'good men' of football, and a huge dose of luck. And if it all fails? In the words of Billy Hudson: "If nothing's happening, I don't know what's gonna happen." ○

Osasuna the Better?

Phil Ball examined why the city of Pamplona in northern Spain has long been a haven for expatriate British footballers.

WSC No 117, November 1996

SINCE THE CONSTRUCTION OF THE NEW MOTORWAY, SAN SEBASTIAN TO Pamplona only takes 50 minutes by car now, over the rainy mountains and down into the *meseta* that opens out into southern Navarre. To the east of the city, on the old road up to the French Pyrenees, Club Atlético Osasuna are training in a downpour. You can tell they're in the Second Division now – First Division sides regularly attract hundreds, sometimes thousands to training sessions. Here there are at most a dozen assorted kids and pensioners moping on the cold stone steps of the training ground.

The players are going through a space-finding routine, each side trying to keep possession as long as possible, but they're only allowed two touches. Jamie Pollock, recently of Middlesbrough, is instantly recognizable by his relative lack of ball control and tired trot. The Osasuna coach immediately confirms my guess, bollocking Pollock for giving the ball away; "*Vamos* Jamie!" he screams, adding a startling "Move your ass!" which booms across the length of the pitch and echoes in the stand. Must have been on an American coaching course. Pollock laughs and continues to trot around aimlessly.

Rob Ullathorne, the other new recent English recruit, is harder to spot. The little boy sitting next to me points him out. "He was a substitute on Wednesday in the cup match," he tells me, "but when he came on he played really well." And straight away, you can see which player is adapting more quickly, which one is more likely to succeed. Ullathorne looks fit – he controls the ball like the Spanish players and is already bantering with them, shouting out the necessary basic vocabulary for getting the ball. He even looks vaguely Spanish.

There's still an hour to go, so I seek out the local journalists in the coffee bar behind the changing rooms. I want to know why Osasuna have often been in the habit of signing British players, especially before anybody else thought of it. I mention Michael Robinson, Sammy Lee and Ashley Grimes, the terrible triumvirate of the Eighties. The journalist wafts away my question into the air; "We've always signed foreigners here. Not just the English." I persist, pointing out that Pamplona, though only recently descended into the Second Division, is not exactly the place you'd expect this phenomenon to have occurred with regularity, pre-Bosman. "The foreigners have always been useless, that's why," he explains. "They think it's all fiestas and bulls and drinking. But this is a shitty place in the winter. Someone should tell them."

Pamplona is indeed a strange place, with a football team called 'Health', which is the meaning of 'Osasuna' in Basque, and a culturally schizophrenic air about it, neither truly Basque nor truly Spanish, hated in the north for its collaboration with the Franco regime. Again, my journalist friend dismisses me. "It doesn't mean health. It means strength, balls, like the bulls – big *cojones*. Urban [from Poland, signed in 1991] was the only one who had any," he rants. In calmer afterthought he adds, "And Robinson. He had some. Now he's got lots of money. Where did they find that Grimes?" he laughs. "In an orphanage?"

Later on the rain's turned to drizzle and Pollock has remembered that I've come all the way from San Sebastian to talk to him. He emerges from the changing rooms still in his kit and sits on the stone wall that surrounds the pitch. "The trouble with me is that I'm a fat bastard," he begins, sounding like Harry Enfield in north eastern mode. He seems so used to giving interviews that he just babbles on, anticipating in his own amicable way what he thinks I'm interested in. "I've come here to get fit. I need discipline," he adds revealingly. "Nothing against the lads back home, but fucking hell (he mimes slaking a pint). Here we can't be seen in the bars, like. We'll get fined. And if I want to leave Pamplona I have to get permission. That's what I've come for – some discipline." I decide not to ask him about Bryan Robson's policy vis-à-vis alcohol. "The *People* tried to get me to shop some dirt on the club the other day – but I wouldn't do it. They've been good to me. Smashin' hotel."

As he banters on, I try to imagine what it must be like for a young bloke like Pollock to come and try his luck. He seems sadly convinced that the club is destined for promotion, although of course he may be right. Without any clear idea of whether he should learn Spanish or not, with a couple of his cousins in town to help him out over the first few days, he jumps at my suggestion that he should ring me if he comes over to San Sebastian for a day at the seaside. Indeed, after a while, it's obvious that he's more interested in what I'm doing and if I like Spain I tell him about the fiestas and he immediately looks brighter, as if there's something to look forward to. He only goes to get changed when Ullathorne comes along, as if his English colleague will already have heard what he's had to say to me.

Ullathorne is a different fish altogether, and ostensibly, one much less out of water. His wife and child are here, he already has a house – to which a Spanish teacher comes every day – and he has signed a three year deal. Whilst he concurs on the discipline bit, he doesn't seem so concerned about it. He's here to learn a new language, a new culture. Immediately you can sense that while he will be matey to Pollock, there'll be only so much socializing they'll be able to do – and that Pollock will have to find his own way.

Ullathorne is less impressed too by the standard of play. "Most of the sides I've seen so far wouldn't stand a chance in the English First." He adds that they only lost to Toledo the week before because their striker had insisted on trying to win penalties by diving instead of just going for goal. I tell him that Sammy Lee had almost left after the first training session, when the theme had been how best to dupe the ref. He's scathing about the referees, too – "Make the Brits look brilliant. One minute they're friendly, the next they're playing the headmaster with you."

How about the training? "It's all about control and space," he explains. "They have great ball skills, but they're not that great, really. They've no idea about tackling. They think I'm hard." He looks up and down at himself ironically, a tiny sparrow of a man. "I like it here though. So what you doing here then?" he asks, and goes down the same path as Pollock, asking about the health care (his wife's about to give birth again), Spanish, if I speak Basque etc. He doesn't seem to fit the dismissive journalist's profile at all and seems exactly the sort of person who'll do all right.

Maybe Osasuna will walk away with it, and Pollock and Ullathorne will become feted heroes, rather like Aldridge was at Real Sociedad. Or rather that talking to them, no notes, no dictaphone, revealed what it must be like for your average player, post Bosman, when it's no longer such a big thing to be a foreigner at the club, you've played in the Premiership but you can't even be guaranteed a first-team place at Atlético Health and you're stuck in a hotel with a couple of your cousins hiding under the bed.

The questions is – when the club pays the final accumulated hotel bill, does the chit specify how much was spent on room service? No problem, Jamie. We believe you. ○

Kind of Blue

When Chelsea's vice-chairman Matthew Harding was killed in a helicopter crash, he was feted as a hero. Mike Ticher felt the tributes struck the wrong tone.

WSC No 118, December 1996

READING THE NEWSPAPER TRIBUTES TO MATTHEW HARDING IN THE DAYS AFTER his death, it was hard not to be struck by how easily the bare facts of his life could have been presented to paint an entirely different picture of the man.

He had recently left his wife and four children for a woman 17 years younger. He claimed to one journalist he had "more love children than you've had hot dinners". His most celebrated gesture while on the board at Chelsea was to charter a plane at a cost of £27,000 to fly him back from Morocco in time to watch a Cup tie at Newcastle.

If circumstances had been different, it's not hard to see how the newspapers could have turned his domestic affairs and occasional extravagance against him. If, say, his millions had turned out to have the same credibility as Robert Maxwell's. Or if the tabloids had decided to back Ken Bates during their battle last year.

Needless to say, that would have been a very unfair portrayal. But it wouldn't necessarily have been much more inaccurate than the almost unreserved adulation which was heaped on Harding after his death. He was, wrote the ubiquitous David Baddiel, "the friendliest man in the world". His three-year financial involvement in the club apparently entitled him to be called "Mr Chelsea", a tag which Bates would be justified in privately resenting. He was "the people's tycoon" and the "saviour" of Chelsea.

Such fulsome tributes did less than justice to Harding. He was no saint, and certainly not a starry-eyed benefactor. The money he put into Chelsea was an investment, for which he was already getting a handsome return. That's not a criticism. First, it was his right to do so. Second, it benefited the club enormously, perhaps more so than if the money had been a gift.

Yet this point, among many others, was lost in the flood of fawning articles which elevated Harding to such untouchable status. Why? The one key recurring phrase, surely, was that he was at heart "one of the lads". He loved (in no particular order) drinking, football, women and making money. But for his devotion to Bob Dylan, he would have been the perfect role model for readers of *Loaded*. "I don't believe in women going to games," he once said half-jokingly (but isn't it always?).

Harding's life virtually defined the boundaries of acceptable laddishness at a time when nothing could be more fashionable. As the *Guardian*'s Matthew Engel pointed out in one of the few level-headed profiles: "This is Britain in the 1990s. A Labour-supporting multi-millionaire who liked a beer with the lads and put his wealth into football seems like an authentic hero."

Despite a fondness for startling public gestures with his money, all the accounts of Harding's friendly and generous attitude towards ordinary fans ring true. He clearly did not do what he did at Chelsea out of a craving for the limelight. Rather, as Ken Bates himself pointed out in his programme notes for the Tottenham game, Harding "wanted to be loved by everyone, had many acquaintances but had few close friends".

Which is why Harding was not a hero, for heroes can't afford to be loved by everyone. They have to upset people's expectations of them and stand by unpopular positions. They have to change engrained mindsets, not reinforce them. One of the strangest cameos in the days after his death was the laying of flowers in his memory at Stamford Bridge by members of the Chelsea Headhunters. Somehow, being mourned by

Power, Corruption and Pies

self-proclaimed hooligans was interpreted in the media as another plus point for Harding.

Indeed, much was made of Harding's ability to mix easily with Chelsea fans, having spent years standing in the Shed as well as the period of enforced exile in the North Stand during his row with Bates. That was justifiably read as a testament to his lack of pretension, despite the fabulous wealth. But it also means he could have been under no illusions as to the fans' faults as well as their virtue of following Chelsea as fanatically as he did.

Thanks to the status he held among them, Harding was in a unique position to influence behaviour at Stamford Bridge, and there were more difficult challenges at Chelsea than investing vast amounts of money and spreading general bonhomie. As chance would have it, the first game after Harding's death was the one date remaining in Chelsea's fixture list when mass racist chanting is still the norm.

What a fantastic tribute it would have been to him if the club had taken advantage of the emotion of the day to finally suffocate the tirades against the 'yids' from fans (many wearing black armbands in Harding's memory) which poisoned the occasion as they have every Chelsea-Tottenham game for three decades.

But Harding left no unambiguous legacy which Chelsea could invoke to make Stamford Bridge a genuinely friendlier place for people who don't already share the values or the skin colour or the gender of the bulk of their fans. Perhaps he wanted to be one of the lads too much for that. ○

Moving the Goalposts

Travelling Cliftonville fans were dragged into Northern Ireland's sectarian politics. Conrad Thomas came to their defence.

WSC No 118, December 1996

IN SEPTEMBER, CLIFTONVILLE WERE DUE TO PLAY THEIR NORTH BELFAST RIVALS Crusaders in a cup semi-final. This was to be played at a neutral venue, The Oval, in predominantly Protestant East Belfast. The majority of Cliftonville fans are Catholic but we have happily travelled to The Oval on many occasions to watch our team play Glentoran. The route that we take to the ground is strictly decided upon by the police.

That night police stopped the Cliftonville supporters buses en route to the ground. We were told that a local residents group were staging an allegedly spontaneous demonstration in protest against our presence in their area. They claimed that we were guilty of vandalism and sectarian abuse. Rather than remove the protesters the RUC decided not to allow our fans to go any further. There was an angry stand off. Devoid of any support, we lost 4-0.

Whilst the incident was condemned in most quarters, some local politicians suggested that if issues were not resolved, Cliftonville may have to withdraw from the league. One Unionist politician, Jim Rodgers even had the audacity to say that there were Sinn Fein activists among the Cliftonville support. David Chick, the Glentoran chairman, said that he sympathised with the residents' views. He had never complained about our many previous visits.

Prohibitive restrictions on tickets and numbers were placed on Cliftonville's next visit to The Oval, despite our club having a very large away support by Irish League standards. In between these two games, Glentoran visited Cliftonville's ground, Solitude, to play a league match. Their supporters were encouraged and welcomed.

In Portadown, a mob waving placards baring the slogan 'No Republican Scum in Mid Ulster' prevented Cliftonville supporters getting to the ground. Buses were attacked and the windows were smashed, as the RUC confirmed. Only evasive action from the bus driver saved the loss of life. Our players, fearing for the safety of their families, refused to reappear after half-time and the match was abandoned. Again, the media begged the question as to whether Cliftonville would have to leave the League, despite our supporters doing nothing wrong.

Cliftonville supporters are being used as innocent pawns in a much wider game. The actions taken by some members of the Loyalist community are a blatant attempt to link the rights of travelling football supporters to political issues. Each summer Northern Ireland politics is dominated by the 'marching issue', whereby residents of some Catholic areas have sought to be consulted on the size and scale of what they perceive to be sectarian marches proceeding through their areas. The protesters are trying to directly link this issue, the polemics of which have nothing to do with football, to the rights of Cliftonville fans.

This is a complete red herring. Firstly, none of the three main Cliftonville supporters' clubs have ever been approached by residents of areas near to away grounds to express their concerns. Secondly, the protests are not spontaneous. As the placards from last Saturday show, this is a highly-organized action to try to forcibly remove Cliftonville from the league.

However, the most worrying thing is that it is being seen as our problem when surely it is up to individual clubs to guarantee the safety of away supporters. There is a precedent: after an incident in the early Seventies when our ground was being used as a neutral venue for a cup match and a Linfield supporter was injured close by, a police decision was taken that Cliftonville would have to play future home games against Linfield at their Windsor Park ground. The reason given for this decision was to guarantee the safety of Linfield fans. Will we be given the same opportunity?

In the past Cliftonville matches have been at the centre of some misbehaviour which our board (the majority of whom are Protestant) and supporters' clubs have publicly and consistently condemned. This time, though, we are being made to pay the price for the actions of others.

The fans of other clubs agree that this should not be allowed to happen. A survey in the *Belfast Telegraph* showed that 79 per cent of supporters wanted Cliftonville to remain in the League. Peter Shirlow, a lifelong fan of Linfield, told me of the "genuine anger in the stands at Windsor" when news of the Portadown incident filtered through. Paul Donnelly, a Glentoran fan said that it was "organized sectarianism, being exploited by some Unionist politicians. Cliftonville and their fans have a positive role to play in the Irish League. They should be respected and encouraged".

Politicians have a lot to answer for, we do not. Branding us as 'activists' only adds to the demonising of Cliftonville fans that will eventually lead to one of us being killed. Instead of our being forced out of the league, we should be encouraged and supported by the Irish Football Association, other clubs and the Irish League (who have maintained a disappointing silence). As Dr Alan Bairner, an expert on sport and society at the University of Ulster points out, "People involved in Northern Ireland sport have complained about the adverse impact of the political situation on their activities but the time has come for them to recognize their own responsibilities and take a positive approach to sectarianism." Cliftonville have tried their best, others must now follow suit. ○

Male Order

Sarah Gilmore and John Williams argued that Glenn Hoddle ducked the issue when newspapers carried pictures of Paul Gascoigne's wife after she had sustained a beating.

WSC No 119, January 1997

WHO COULD DOUBT THE AWFULNESS OF THE DAILY EXISTENCE OF PAUL Gascoigne, given the culture of the 'tabloid celebrity' shaped for us by the popular press over the past decade? A goldfish bowl nightmare if ever there was one. But the precarious PR profile being created of Gazza as 'new-ish' man fell apart at Gleneagles. The subsequent press mêlée which focused on his inclusion or exclusion from the England squad revealed some extremely unpleasant and morally suspect views so prevalent in the game and in the liberal media.

The argument used to justify his place in the England squad varied from the shamelessly pragmatic: he's a midfield genius who had a wonderful Euro 96; to the indignant assertion that football should not be the scapegoat for social and individual problems as advocated by Johnny Giles. "Wife beating is a despicable activity," he wrote in the *Express*, "but I do not see how Glenn Hoddle could have excluded Paul Gascoigne from the England team on this. Hoddle is a manager not a judge of morals." Oh really? The 13th apostle said that we had to forgive. He had obviously forgiven Gascoigne (he did pick him after all), and he urged us to follow his Christian example of tolerance. Not a moral judge? Bah, humbug.

Finally, Gascoigne himself said that he could understand the views of women's rights groups who were condemning his actions and he got a nice little ovation from the press corps assembled for his unscheduled announcement of penance at Bisham Abbey. Even broadsheet reporters present at the press conference claimed that it was one of the press pack's most inglorious days.

Paul Gascoigne should not be playing for England. He should not be playing because he should be punished for unacceptable behaviour. It is as simple as that and it has nothing to do with Hoddle's arrogant assertions that he has spoken to "the lad" – he's a bloody man for God's sake – and feels that it is better for him and his family for him to play for England than to leave him out (did Glenn speak to Sheryl about this, then, or are we missing something?).

There seem to be some very fluid moral arguments being asserted here. What do you have to do these days to get excluded, even temporarily, from the national team? Does there come a point when the player actually needs to be left out because his conduct is unacceptable, and if 'yes', then where exactly should that line be drawn?

The truth is harsh, but it is this: notwithstanding the outrage expressed over Gascoigne's offence, the culture of the game still feels more at ease with a man who likes a drink and a laff with the lads, belches and farts for TV and who, OK, publicly rows with and beats his wife every now and again, than with one who because of his quiet interest in the arts is viewed with suspicion, like Graeme Le Saux. Or with a quixotic Buddhist like the puzzling and madly-talented Roberto Baggio; or even a British Asian player, a prospect still so patently distant for all sorts of reasons (blimey, he might even go to the mosque rather than the pub). There is some exaggeration here, of course, but the old fears still reside among many English footballers: fears of thinking and theorizing, of talking, of not being a 'lad' and the association of all of these with 'the feminine'.

No wonder top players from abroad, including the new unsettled Brazilians, are beginning to question the qualities of British coaching, man management and the leadership currently available in some dressing rooms. Ask yourself this: if you really knew, would you come half way round the world to be coached in the narrow English tradition of 'playing from the heart' and sometimes crass, schoolmasterly discipline?

You don't have to admire the muscular sterility of the current Norwegian national side to know that there is much to what their coach, Egil Olsen, said recently about the "shocking" lack of feedback or analyses of player performance from managers and coaches in the British game, and his view that Scandinavian players in England are less developed now in terms of skill, and an understanding of the sport and of themselves, than if they had stayed at home in part-time football. They would also be more likely to get a sensible dressing room conversation about politics, relationships, the family, or virtually anything else nominally off limits to most British footballers until, as David Platt and others found, you get a move abroad.

Football clubs prefer the arrested state of development, the Peter Pan state of existence where you never have to grow up and thereby take responsibility for your actions because there is always the forgiving womb of the club to protect, nurture and forgive you whilst they lie on your behalf, explaining away any transgression.

All of which is so damaging because the culture that footballers become a part of in their mid-teens is far more pervasive than the normal workplace environment. A crucial part of that culture depends on women – women as carers, mothers and wives. It is usually a woman who picks up the pieces or feels the brunt of any difficulties as many players are encouraged to marry young and to marry family-minded, 'ordinary' women who will take up where mummy left off.

It was left to women's rights groups, of course, to make the obvious points about players as role models; that playing for the national team was not actually a 'job' and that sidelining Gascoigne may have carried an important message for boys and girls. Interestingly, the 'radical' supporters' organization was thunderously silent, as usual, on the matter of gender politics; what if Gascoigne had been involved in a racist assault? We might have seen some action then. Who speaks for supporters on sexism in football? Or do 'women' here translate into 'middle class', and are therefore anathema?

Incidentally, don't go looking for a discussion about football, gender and 'politics' – or any kind of politics – in the new football glossies, even with their proud female editorial boards. Walter Hale in *FourFourTwo* – presumably with editorial consent – recently warned that as soon as the sex of the editor or writer affected the content they would be out on their ear, and quite right too. It is obviously only men, like Walter himself, who are able to write in a gender-neutral mode. Anyway, who wants female football writers if they write the same kind of tired rubbish that most of the men do?

The message which came over to women from those at the highest level of the game, the liberal media, supporters' organizations *et al* is that domestic violence is not very nice, but sometimes men shouldn't be punished for their brutal treatment of women. Wrong. Domestic violence is much more wrong than snorting coke, being an alcoholic or having a ruck on the plane with your mates. It is about fundamental abuse of power, of hurting someone weaker than you. It is behaviour which is at the logical, extreme end of bullying and is a physical way of reminding women of their inequalities.

What people like Glenn Hoddle are doing is using their Christian principles of forgiveness to reinforce discrimination which women are less tolerant of than ever before. Women want men to be themselves but women also want men to behave. For most men that is not an issue. Some, however, do not need an excuse to behave badly: give them one and they'll probably behave even worse. When that happens, when it goes too far, you need to say so, you need – sometimes – to punish.

Hoddle might be staking all on Gascoigne undergoing a Saul-like conversion, but, deep down, we all know the harder, and the right, thing to do was to leave him out. Not cast him aside, or reject him, or jettison him or anything else. Just get him some counsel and leave him out; even if only for one match. A sign that some events – that do actually say important things about sport itself – are just more important than having your preferred football side. Even, or perhaps especially, if you manage England. ○

Share and Share Alike

Patrick Harverson of the Financial Times explained why football clubs suddenly became eager to be listed on the stock market.

WSC No 120, February 1997

SIX YEARS AGO, NEWCASTLE UNITED TRIED TO SELL SHARES, BUT THE CLUB couldn't give them away such was the lack of interest among fans and financial investors. In the next few months Newcastle will try it again. Only this time things will be a little bit different. The queue to buy shares in NUFC plc will stretch from St James' Park, across the Tyne Bridge and down the M1 to London where pension funds, insurance companies and other blue-chip City institutions will be lining up around the block for a piece of the Toon pie.

Newcastle's decision to join the stampede to list on the stock market – in 1996 nine clubs floated or unveiled plans for a flotation – is powerful evidence of how much football has changed in the past six years. Football boasts many new, modern stadia. Newcastle, not content with one big, smart ground, plan to build a second. Football is awash with glamorous foreign stars. Newcastle have Ginola and Asprilla. Football has a huge wage bill to meet. Newcastle pay Alan Shearer £25,000 a week. And now they are following the latest fashion and floating on the stock market.

But why? Why have Newcastle and so many others decided to go public, and why is the City – which only a few years ago would not have touched most clubs with a bargepole – suddenly so excited about investing in football? The answer, inevitably, is money. The clubs need it to pay for new stadia and new players and to exploit the commercial opportunities newly available to football, and the City sees a chance to profit from the sport's remarkable growth. Professional investors used to shy away from putting money in football because they did not trust the people who ran the clubs – but then who did? Also, they were unimpressed by the modest revenues the game generated and the poor, or non-existent, profits record of most clubs. And they did not like the idea that their investment could be damaged by an ill-timed injury, a run of bad form and the subsequent death rattle of relegation.

Now, however, investors are comfortable about the idea of handing their money over to football. Although there is still room for improvement, the financial management of top clubs is better. Revenues from television rights, ticket sales, merchandising and sponsorship have exploded since the creation of the Premier League. And the growing disparity between rich and poor, and the increased depth of squads at the top clubs, has guaranteed what appears to be lifelong protection from relegation to a sizable number in the Premiership.

If investors had shared any lingering doubts about the wisdom of investing in football, the performance of club shares on the London stock market last year provided all the reassurance that was needed. Last year, the stock market as a whole rose by 11 per cent. In contrast, the top five football shares – Celtic, Leeds, Manchester United, Tottenham Hotspur and Chelsea – rose by an average of more than 200 per cent. The price of shares in Celtic increased almost fivefold, while shares in the company that owns Leeds almost tripled in value.

The astonishing performance of football shares (even the sector's only dud, Millwall, did better than the market average last year) has left investors goggle-eyed and eager for more. It has also left the game's heavy-hitters – the owners and directors of the big clubs – a hell of a lot richer than they were at the beginning of the year.

At Manchester United, chairman Martin Edwards took the opportunity several times last year to cash in on his new-found riches by selling some of his shares. At Chelsea, the late Matthew Harding, and more recently the executors of his estate, bought options to buy stock in the club's parent company at prices well below the market share price, netting huge paper profits in the process. At Leeds, three directors redesigned the share structure of the club in 1995 to give themselves 98 per cent of the shares, and a year later made millions of pounds each when they sold Leeds to the Caspian media group.

Of course, the people who own and run the clubs will argue – in some cases justifiably – that they deserve their rewards because they have risked their money for many years to keep their clubs in business and continue to do so. Yet it remains an inescapable fact that one reason why many clubs have gone public is that it has enabled owners and directors to realize a market price – and a very substantial price at that – for their shares.

Not surprisingly, club chairmen put this somewhat differently, arguing that flotations offer fans an opportunity to own a stake in their club. Peter Maclean, head of public relations at Celtic, says that for many years before the flotation in 1995, supporters had clamoured to own a part of their club. "They were unhappy with the direction the former board was taking the club," he says. "Now we have over 10,000 owners of Celtic and they have the opportunity to voice opinions as shareholders as well as supporters. That's a welcome change."

Maclean, however, is being disingenuous. Sure, owning a share means a fan can turn up at the club's annual general meeting, but whether he or she has a real say in the running of the club is another matter. Sid and Doris Bonkers may own 500 shares in British Gas or British Telecom, but they cannot tell the board what to do. The boards of public companies only listen to powerful City institutions and rich investors who own millions of shares, not hundreds. Why should it be any different in football?

Just ask Spurs fans, who are unhappy that their club doesn't spend more of its money on new players. Chairman Alan Sugar appears more determined to keep his shareholders sweet than to win the hearts of the club's supporters by forking out £20 million on a couple of big overseas names. Yet Sugar's parsimonious policy has gone down well in the City.

Paul Wedge is an analyst at stockbrokers Collins Stewart and a financial advisor to Tottenham, and he says the club's institutional shareholders are quite happy with Sugar. "Investor sentiment about Tottenham is good – they feel he is running the club on a proper basis. You can't have a club that consistently loses money. The supporters won't be happy unless they win everything. But there are only three trophies to be won in England and 20 clubs chasing them in the Premier League, which means the majority of clubs are going to be unsuccessful. So while spending lots of money appeases supporters on a short-term basis, it does not guarantee success."

This is how the new money men in football think. They would rather a club makes a profit playing competent if unexciting football than it loses lots of money by hiring expensive stars to play thrilling football in front of appreciative fans. But Spurs supporters, of whom only a few are also shareholders, don't give a fig about the share price or the state of the balance sheet at the end of the financial year. They care about the team and the type of football it plays, and whether it is capable of competing for top honours every season.

Yet it would be wrong to characterize football's City investors as obsessively profit-oriented. Some of them are also fans, which is why they became interested in buying football club shares in the first place. Michael Goldman is a Chelsea supporter who also happens to invest millions of pounds in football as manager of the City's only specialist sports investment fund. He worries that in their search for off-the-field commercial success some clubs may be alienating themselves from their supporters. "I ask myself whether Newcastle moving to a new ground is a good thing. You can tamper with the roots too much."

He fears the trend towards putting the interests of shareholders and owners before those of supporters is irreversible. "By and large fans are being looked after, but slowly and surely they will be less catered for. The time to worry is when it becomes self-evident that clubs don't care about the fans any more." But how will we know when football has finally sold its soul to the corporate devil? "When Man Utd run on the field with Mickey Mouse on their shirts because they've been bought by Disney," he says.

Don't laugh. It could happen. In America, Disney owns a professional ice hockey team. Why not an English football team? Profits are profits, whatever the language, whatever the culture, whatever the sport. ○

Ultra Cautious

Simon Evans recounted how the bad old days of English football came to be re-enacted in stadia throughout the old Soviet bloc.

WSC No 122, April 1997

ATTENDING A GAME IN EASTERN EUROPE FOR AN ENGLISH FAN IS A STRANGELY familiar experience: you could be at an English Third Division match circa 1981 – the crumbling, half-empty terraces, stinking toilets, the alcohol, the drunks and the 'boys' staring each other out through fences topped with barbed wire.

Travelling to a big derby on public transport, you find yourself watching your back, there are skirmishes in the underground and inside the ground, coins and bottles fly. The police who once had licence to crush anything remotely resembling an unruly crowd, are uncertain of their role today and lack the resources, manpower or technical capability to deal with a problem which is sprouting up all over the former Soviet bloc.

In the Czech Republic, the 'Rowdies', particularly those in Brno, have grown in strength in recent years. In one incident Sparta Prague fans assaulted and hospitalized an opposition goalkeeper. Clashes between skinhead groups and police are regular occurrences at Polish games. Ferencvaros of Budapest have been fined by UEFA several times because of crowd disturbances and this season were given a final warning after incidents surrounding their UEFA Cup tie with Olympiakos. Croatia Zagreb received the ultimate punishment by UEFA, banned from Europe because of the behaviour of their hooligans – the 'Bad Blue Boys'.

The youths chasing down metro stations in Budapest, Bucharest, Prague and Warsaw take their influences from various countries. One prominent inspiration are the ultras – the Italian, Spanish and Portuguese groups, with their group names proclaimed proudly from huge banners, scarves wrapped over their faces like the *keffiyah* of the Palestinian *intifada*. In recent years the ultra movement has taken off in Hungary and Romania, although it had been part of the Yugoslav scene for over a decade. It is not always violent, as the Hungarian documentary film *Ultra Renaissance* showed, with its tale of Kispest-Honved's Ultra Red Boys with their satchels full of sandwiches taking a bus ride to Debrecen and doing little more than yelling abuse out of the window at peasants.

But that film also has a scene which reveals the stranger side of east European hooliganism. One Debrecen fan being interviewed in the pub before the game is explaining the modern fans' mentality – "Read *Fever Pitch* and you'll understand," he tells the reporter. Forget the ultras with their smoke bombs and banners – the serious hooligans look to England for inspiration. Never mind that Nick Hornby doesn't write a word in praise of hooliganism, that he's probably never even shouted "You're going home in an Arsenal ambulance". He's an English fan so he must be a hooligan. The prejudice that plagues the few decent fans who travel abroad with England, the belief that we are all psychopaths ready to stick the boot in, is actually seen as a positive by young east European fans.

The skinhead in the pub, where Slovan Bratislava hardcore fans meet for a few Budweisers before the game, found out I was English. "I'm a Chelsea fan," he tells me proudly, "but I like Millwall too." The large bonehead to his left is wearing an England shirt, behind him on the wall is a Combat 18 poster. He starts telling me tales of battles past at Stamford Bridge. He speaks limited English but while he was over for Euro 96 supporting, interestingly for a Slovak skinhead, the Czech Republic, he picked up some interesting technical vocabulary. He talks of "firms", "running", "kick-offs".

Kids like this are not hard to find around the grounds of western Europe. Across the region the clothing, the language and the lifestyle of the cartoon early Eighties English thug is *à la mode*. If it weren't for the stiff-arm salutes and booing of black players inside the stadium later it would be almost laughable. I ask the Slovan skin how Ruud Gullit fits in with his idea of Chelsea or if he knew that Millwall won awards for football in the community and that no one sings "We are evil" or dresses up in surgeons' outfits any more. I tell him no one is really into "running" and "firms". He looked sad, went quiet for a moment, before coming back to life: "Yeah, but what about England at Lansdowne Road?"

In Budapest, there is a 16-year-old who actually bought a video of that foreshortened game. His bedroom in his parent's shoebox flat is crammed with ultra and hooligan memorabilia. With the dedication of a trainspotter or stamp collector he has on file hundreds of photos of German "kick-offs" he got by mail order along with videos of infamous incidents in Italy and Hungary.

Indeed there is a blossoming cottage industry in hooligan paraphernalia –some of it can be got via magazines, some at ultra shops and some for free as several groups have gone to the trouble of uploading action shots to the Internet. There is an even bigger trade in bringing in the tools of the trade – smoke bombs and Greek flares.

But the business is not entirely import-led. There is a local market supplied by amateur photographers and film-makers. One of these in Budapest, whose nickname is 'Chelsea', spends his Saturdays with his sidekick 'Tottenham', filming the terraces with a Camcorder. Many of the major ultra groups have their own photographers, whose lenses are firmly fixed on the terraces. In bars frequented by ultras, lads gather at tables and ogle over pictures of Italian away ends covered in coloured smoke.

But while it all may seem to be rather silly, there is a sad sense of history repeating itself. Just as in Britain in the Seventies and Eighties, hooliganism is becoming accepted as part of football culture by a generation of young fans. Modern British hooliganism emerged in an era of economic dislocation, high unemployment and alienation among working-class youth – just what the former Socialist countries are going through now. It was allowed to get out of control due to poor policing, badly-organized stadia and a lack of action by football's authorities, all equally common to eastern Europe. It has been widely documented how the far right infiltrated hooligan gangs in Britain, and there is growing evidence to suggest the same is happening in several east European countries. On top of it all, eastern Europe now has a tabloid press ready to give all the media exposure the hooligans need.

UEFA regularly slaps the wrists of clubs like Croatia Zagreb and Ferencvaros, whose fans consistently cause trouble. But it does little to help ease the huge disparities between western and eastern European football which could themselves cause more problems. UEFA is ordering all clubs in Europe to follow the English example and remove perimeter fencing from grounds. That might work in Germany or Denmark but I dread to think what could be on the horizon if some of the east European derbies are played without fencing: the former communist countries are just heading into the stage Britain was at when fences were put up.

It took British police decades to develop a modern method for dealing with trouble in and around football stadia. But that experience could be shared now with their colleagues in the east. Cash could be offered from the millions being reaped across the continent to help eastern Europe tackle the problem before it gets out of hand. So far there has been no Heysel in eastern Europe, no tragedies to focus attention on the problem. Organized football violence in the east is just in its infancy. Will it be allowed to grow into the beast we once knew? ○

Dutch Uncle

Simon Kuper paid a 50th birthday tribute to Johan Cruyff.

WSC No 123, May 1997

THIS MONTH THE DUTCH CELEBRATE TWO BIRTHDAYS. APRIL 30TH, THE DAY that Juliana, the Queen Mother, lights her candles is traditionally the main national holiday, with market stalls, beer and orange flags. But the big day this year is April 25th, when the most remarkable living Dutchman turns 50. Almost every newspaper and magazine in the country is publishing a special Johan Cruyff supplement, and The Maestro himself has been invited to hundreds of parties.

The celebrations will cover up a few feelings of guilt. For the past 35 years Cruyff has been known to his compatriots chiefly as The Money Wolf, The Little One, and Nose. Now, as he moves into semi-retirement after 35 years as a workaholic, it is dawning on the Dutch that he was not merely a great footballer but a pretty interesting character too.

They recall, for instance, his penalty on St Nicholas Day 1982 against Helmond Sport. You might think that there is only one way of taking a penalty: you run up to the ball and try to kick it past the goalkeeper. Not so. Cruyff ran up as usual but then, instead of shooting, passed the ball forward and to his left, where it was picked up by Jesper Olsen, running into the box. As the Helmond team and keeper watched transfixed, Olsen passed the ball back into the middle for Cruyff to tap it into the empty net.

Cruyff never stopped thinking. He could do everything, but he also did everything in a new way. As manager of Ajax, he hired an opera singer named Lo Bello to teach his players how to breathe. On the coach to away games, Cruyff would lecture them on the right way to play cards. He explained to them that the traffic lights in Amsterdam were in the wrong places, and that he, Cruyff, therefore had the right to drive through them. He invented total football. Interviews with him were fascinating. When you hear Ruud Gullit talking about football on the BBC, he is mostly reciting things he learned from Cruyff years ago.

All this turned Cruyff into the classic prophet without honour. "The worst thing," he said, "is that you always knew everything better. It meant you were always talking, always correcting." (Unlike most great footballers, who talk about themselves in the third person, Cruyff uses the second person.)

Willem van Hanegem, another great Dutch player of the 1970s, describes Cruyff teaching him how to insert coins into a soft drink machine. Van Hanegem, who had spent minutes wrestling with the machine, was told to use "a short, dry throw" – and of course, the method worked. This, said Van Hanegem, was incredibly irritating.

Many of the rows Cruyff got into were his own fault. He believes that conflicts motivate people because they give everyone something to prove, and he can never admit that he is wrong. He still denies that he ruined Marco van Basten's career and doomed him to a lifelong limp by making him play with a severe ankle injury. Cruyff has complex theories on medicine, and the surgeon who gave him a triple bypass had to debate the operation with his patient beforehand.

"You must die with your own ideas," said Cruyff, and as a manager he sometimes suffered for his dogmatism. At Barcelona, he fielded a goalkeeper named Busquets who was manifestly not up to the job. When the press wrote that playing Busquets had been a mistake, Cruyff's pride was fired and he insisted on keeping the poor man in the team. He played his son Jordi too much, too, but that was because Cruyff is only human and a family man. Still shaken by his father's death when he was only 12, he obeys his wife Danny in every regard. And Danny, who is terrified he will die young, now wants him to retire. Cruyff appears to agree.

It was clear in his last couple of years at Barcelona that he was losing his touch. "The tooth of time has done its work," he admitted. Throughout his career he appeared quite nerveless, sometimes forgetting whether his team was winning or not. But the years of chain-smoking and forcing his body through pain barriers have ruined his health. He ran out of ideas and when Barcelona sacked him he discovered for the first time that not working can be fun, particularly if you are a multimillionaire with three lovely children.

This is a shame for English clubs, because Cruyff regrets never having managed a club here. An Anglophile, he comes from the generation of Dutchmen to whom England meant the BBC radio under the blankets during the war, Tommies with cigarettes, and the best football team in the world. Cruyff has spoken perfect English since his early teens, when the Ajax managers Keith Spurgeon and Vic Buckingham used to fatten him up with warm English lunches. On his first ever holiday, when he was 18, he and Michael van Praag, the present Ajax chairman, drove around England and stayed in Norwich with a boy Cruyff had met during a youth tournament.

Cruyff was tempted by last summer's offer to manage Arsenal, and left to his own devices he would even consider Everton. But Danny wants them to stay in Barcelona, and Cruyff himself loves the city. He races around it on his motorbike, and entertains himself by fighting a vendetta against the Barca chairman, Josep Lluís Núñez. With Bobby Robson having got little further in Spanish than "mucho", "muy" and "no", and revealing little insight about soccer even when speaking English, the fans and the local press are pining for Cruyff.

It is hard to see him coming back, though. For the first time in his life he is looking rosy-cheeked and healthy, and with nothing left to prove, he has become charming. He commentates on television, using words that he often makes up himself, and spinning theories even when the microphone has been turned off – Cruyff has never quite grasped how television works.

"Cruyff sometimes talks nonsense," wrote the author of his fantastic biography, Nico Scheepmaker, "but it is always interesting nonsense." Cruyff was a Shakespearean character, the Einstein of football, and a man who could hit 50-yard passes with the outside of his left foot. He could place a team-mate in front of goal so unexpectedly that the TV cameras sometimes failed to keep up. The Dutch are already starting to miss him. Without Cruyff, Holland would have had no footballing tradition, and without a footballing tradition, not all that many people in the world would have heard of Holland. ○

Tyne Tease

God knows there have been some fearsomely bad programmes about football on television, but David Hayes thought viewers in the north east were being subjected to the worst yet.

WSC No 123, May 1997

ANYONE COMING TO LIVE IN THE NORTH EAST SOON ENCOUNTERS THE DISTINCT football culture of the area. Intense local rivalries divide, but there is also a wider ethic – the product of tradition, geography and social experience – that bonds clubs and fans. An innovation in local media coverage last year was *The Football Show* (Tyne Tees) on Thursday nights. In many ways a familiar format – interviews with local heroes, filmed reports, past glories and disasters – it was saved from banality by the element of fan participation, the natural warmth of presenters Roger Tames and Dawn Thewlis, and the quality of the features.

Most of the attention naturally went to the 'big three', but every (hour-long) programme focused on the travails of Hartlepool or the giant-killing of York City as well. A favourite item showed Whitby Town's visit to Wembley for the FA Vase final, with fascinating film of their reception in the town and an interview with their groundsman of 60 years.

Far from the iconoclasm of *Fantasy Football*, and hardly a fanzine on the box, yet the makers had obviously thought carefully about representing the full range of the north-east game. The programme closed with a contact address; I received a friendly response to the suggestion of a feature on Berwick Rangers to coincide with the 30th anniversary of their Scottish Cup defeat of Rangers (Berwick's unusual position leaves them in a media limbo). *The Football Show* left you no room to breathe amidst the deluge of football fluff.

The second series began in March. First shock: new studio with resident band, a 'panel' format instead of the hosts being among the fans, and a huge Highbury-style mural behind the audience giving the impression of a cast of thousands. This illusion was an apt symbol of what followed. Second shock: Nick Owen as presenter, introducing the panel: Shelley Webb, Sid Waddell (darts man), Terry Christian, Andy Darling (comedy writer) and John Burridge (clown). And they're off.

In the first half, I learned that Newcastle (remembering Princess Grace) have to watch for dangerous corners in Monaco; Middlesbrough's only problem is to find a Teesside coach driver who knows the way to Wembley; David Mellor has stuck it in more times than Sunderland. Shaka Hislop is called 'The Cat' because he's always having kittens; it's rumoured Newcastle's defence is sponsored by a string vest company; and (after film of Malcolm Macdonald in his prime) it was nice to see Supermac when he had a different kind of bottle. Derek Whyte came on. Webb: "You've got a little girl called Chelsea. How did that come about?" Owen: "So why do you do so well in the cups and not in the League?"

Time for Budgie's 60 seconds with Les Ferdinand: "Who is your favourite Spice Girl? What is your most unappealing personal habit?" Now it's quiz time: the Italian club which upset the Pope is called Punto Rosso Sexy Shop – true or false? Time for music from house band Paul Smith's Flat Back Four.

Owen's smile: "There's talk of bringing back the terraces. Yep, they want to re-introduce two-up, two-down" (an actual drum-roll). Waddell: "Vinnie Jones was asked to fill in a questionnaire and he knocked seven bells out of the doorman." Quiz time: Who would run out to *Tears of a Clown?* Grobbelaar. Picture round: winners win tickets for Arsenal's next home game, losers for two games. Owen: "I think foreigners have a different attitude to drink, so while talking about foreigners what do you think of Newcastle's chances in Europe?"

Enough. You get the picture. To say that this putrid pap, this mind-numbing garbage, is a gross insult to every fan is blindingly obvious. In the wider scheme of things the fact that a modest show with a genuine feeling for the area has been replaced by a marketing junket designed only to sell products that appear during the commercial breaks – far worse things happen every day. In the context of what went before and what TV could offer, its another piece of larceny of the true spirit of the game.

It's a cast iron certainty that the word *Loaded* made ears burn in planning this series. Programming by numbers; a panel selected by admen's categories (Webb for the likely lads, Waddell for the pub bores, Christian for the zany kids); a soundbite formula in which any spontaneity or real feeling is totally extinguished.

The region has shrunk to the big three. A revealing moment came when Owen said, "Let's remember that the last north east club to reach Wembley was Darlington in the play-offs... so, er, let's remember that." An insert from an eager researcher? A producer with a conscience? The link went nowhere. This was the only mention of any other club in the first two programmes.

Another tiny incident with the patently decent Frank Clark. (Owen: "You played 450-odd games, some of them very odd... What did you win? And what was Cloughie like to work for?") Quiz time: who would run out to *Farewell My Summer Love?* Clark quietly offered: "Well, a farewell to Bournemouth would be sad..." Wrong answer.

I tuned in for the second and last time. Owen announced – I kid you not – a feature on "sex, lies and tabloids with Dean Holdsworth's stunning wife, Sam". And it came to pass ("You must have been distraught at the papers? Did you really say that your rottweiler is better looking than that girl?") Then "at the start of her singing career", Sam closed the show with *You're So Vain*. Breakfast TV meets *Opportunity Knocks*.

There are ways to register the fate of football in the 1990s, but *The Football Show* with the wife of Dean Holdsworth singing (execrably, as if it mattered) a song about Warren Beatty, in front of a panel including Terry Christian and a darts commentator, takes some beating.

A last-minute goal by Paul Pitman won the FA Vase semi-final in front of 2,000 ecstatic fans. Whitby Town are going to Wembley. A million stories untold. ○

The Right Result

Having survived a decade of vitriolic WSC editorials, the Tory government finally came out with its hands up. Not a bright, new dawn for football perhaps, but at least a chance to take stock.

WSC No 124, June 1997 – Editorial

A WEEK THAT BEGAN WITH THE DEATH OF LORD JUSTICE TAYLOR ENDED WITH the demise of the Conservatives, whose assault on football was stopped in its tracks by the Taylor Report.

The Thatcher government's proposed ID card scheme would have required anyone wishing to see a game to have such a card, without which it would have been an offence to enter a ground. No more casual fans; no more birthday trips for kids without filling in forms in triplicate. This didn't matter; football fans were a menace to society and had to be controlled. This from a government containing such familiar faces in the crowd these days as John Major, David Mellor and Kenneth Clarke.

The bill that could have killed football had already had a first reading in the House of Commons when Taylor's verdict on the Hillsborough disaster appeared and recommended that the scheme be shelved, on the grounds that the ID cards would just have made the crush outside the ground worse, and its repetition more likely. While the report's views on terracing remain controversial, Taylor expressed a view guaranteed to be unpopular with those who gave him the job.

Eight years on, with football now indelibly stamped with the core characteristics of Conservatism (stock market listings, an emphasis on individual greed, the widening gulf between rich and poor) it seems hard to imagine that the Tories once actively presented themselves as the anti-football party, secure in the knowledge that such a stance would pick up considerable support from the public.

The mood in Whitehall was echoed by a press, both tabloid and broad-sheet, which rarely missed an opportunity to push the message that football stadia had become little more than a battleground for anti-social elements. Today no politician, or newspaper, would dream of denigrating football for fear of losing votes, or readers. In at least one politician's case, fear of damaging a post-election media career ensured a pro-football stance. After losing his seat in Putney, David Mellor's diatribe against the barracking he received from the Referendum Party included the comment that James Goldsmith "had behaved like a rugby fan". A few years ago he would have said "soccer fan" on the assumption that his audience would have absorbed the message without complaint.

No doubt a fair proportion of the wavering voters in middle England courted by all the parties in the election are among those who have discovered football in post Taylor Report times – and in some cases bought into it. Businessmen such as Alan Sugar, only too eager in the build up to the election to declare his support for New Labour now that it has shifted far enough to be acceptable to Rupert Murdoch, would not have cared a jot had football been ground into the dust in the 1980s by the Thatcher administration of which he was so fond.

Graham Kelly was effusive in his praise of Taylor – "the magnificent stadia which are springing up all the time will be his epitaph" – but didn't dare mention one of the principal reasons why the FA had cause to be so grateful: if it doesn't sound unseemly to use such a word in association with Hillsborough, the FA were enormously lucky, both to have wriggled out of any significant degree of culpability for the tragedy and to have since benefited hugely from the restructuring of football that followed on from the massive loss of life.

For years before Hillsborough the football authorities paid scant attention to supporters' organisations' warnings about the woeful safety standards at football stadia, and had not learned any lessons from a narrowly averted disaster at a previous Cup semi-final at Hillsborough. When Spurs played Wolves in 1981, fans arriving just before kick off after travelling up from London spilled on to the pitch to avoid the crush building up in the overcrowded pens at the Leppings Lane end.

That event was commemorated by the Hillsborough Justice Campaign day of action on May 3rd. This joint initiative between the FSA and fanzines culminated in the crowd and players at the Liverpool v Spurs match at Anfield holding up cards and banners demanding a fresh inquest, in the light of the new evidence which prompted last year's drama documentary. (Sky's coverage of the match gave it scant attention, of course – much better to keep the audience's mind firmly fixed on important stuff like percentage of possession and shots on target.)

Tony Blair has missed no opportunity to play the football card and unlike those who have occupied the government benches for the last 18 years, he didn't play a part in the assault on the game. If the new administration wishes to send out a positive signal to those who supported both Labour and football during their wilderness years, it could do a lot worse than take note of what that crowd at Anfield on May 3rd were calling for and re-open the Hillsborough inquest. ○

Appearances can be Deceptive

Al Needham made an unscheduled cameo on Star Soccer which got him banned from the City Ground, but ultimately saved him from a much worse fate.

WSC No 125, July 1997

THE YOUTH OF TODAY MAKE ME SICK. THEY'VE GOT MORE FREEDOM, ARE taken more seriously in the media, have better cars to break into and joyride, they have sex all the livelong day and, with the invention of Hooper's Hooch, they've got their own alcoholic beverage.

But the one thing that really grates is the fact that, if they stray within sight of a floodlight, they get their runty faces on the telly. Just look at the match previews on Sky – a good 50 minutes of pasty-faced raggamuffins 'larging it' while Richard Keys tries manfully to convince the nation that Leeds v Coventry is worth staying in for. Slap a bit of face paint on, and the bastards hog so much airtime they get their own VideoPlus number. How things have changed.

Ever since my sister's best friend was the talk of the estate after her appearance on *ATV Today*, I vowed to immortalize myself in a televisual context. And what better place to do it in 1977 than at a Forest game? After all, we were barnstorming up the league, and for most people a big match is one of the few times in their life when a TV camera is in the vicinity that isn't checking to see if they're pulling a shotgun on a garage attendant or stuffing pencil cases down their trousers.

Alas, I soon realized that in the late Seventies and early Eighties you had to put in some serious work in order to get your face on *Match of the Day*. There were three ways to attain this: sit next to a celebrity fan (Cilla, usually), kick the shit out of someone (or have the shit kicked out of you) or streak on to the pitch. These were not viable options for me, because: a) Nottingham had no celebrity fans (with the the exception of Paper Lace – no, scrub that, we had no celebrity fans), b) seeing as I was being laced at school on a daily basis, I deserved a break at the weekend, and c) I wasn't that desperate, mate. I crossed a bridge on my journey into Manhood, accepted the fact that I would be part of the anonymous herd, and packed in trying.

But Old Mrs Fate had plans for me, the cow. On my way to see Forest play West Ham, I found myself behind a cartel of ICF stormtroopers who couldn't have looked more Cockney and potentially violent if they'd been sporting white boiler suits with swastikas picked out in pearly buttons. As they approached a police van, I instinctively had a good listen for something that would electrify the playground and guarantee me a loan of someone's Rubik Snake.

"Cor blimey, guv'nor," said one of the Chirpies, "Ahhjer get to ver Trent End, Gawd bless ya?" (Yes, I know I'm exaggerating, but it's necessary to get the point across that these were West Ham supporters, asking the Nottingham Constabulary how to get to the Forest home end.) As soon as the coppers pointed the way, I feared the worst. And sure enough, 3.15, it all goes off. A space the size of a good-sized traffic island is cleared in the Trent End, and in the middle is the kicking and punching so redolent of that era. But this one is getting right out of hand, and people are surging towards the fence so frantically that, thinking about it now after what's happened since, it scares the shit out of me.

So I jump up, climb the fence, dodge a can of half-full cola whizzing past my head, lose my balance, awkwardly skitter down the other side like a budgie flying into flowered wallpaper, and stagger into the netting of a goal being tended by Peter Shilton. I'd smashed through the invisible wall separating player from payer, and he couldn't have shot me a look of more shocked bemusement if I'd have flung open the door of his lamppost-encrusted Jaguar while he was trying to pull his pants up.

Next day, the full horror of the event was played out within the confines of *Star Soccer* while I was at my Nana's. Well, she went berserk. She battered me, while Huw Johns aurally shook his head in despair at the Collapse of Society. When my Dad and Grandpa came back from the pub, they battered me too. My entire extended family made pilgrimages from all over the world to batter me. Seeing as I had become the General of a Firm (well, I was the first over the fence, so I'd obviously started a pitch invasion), I was banned from going to football and instead spent the remaining Saturdays of my youth pretending to be a mod, marching from the bus stations of one shopping centre to another.

But looking back on it now, that communal lynching I received was a blessing in disguise. Because if they hadn't have done it, I would have continued to go to Forest matches. And I know, I just know, that I would have run on to the pitch after the QPR League Cup tie. And Cloughie would have cracked me one. And then I would have had to kiss him. On TV. Thank you, Baby Jesus... ◯

Message Understood

Once football fans were told their obsession with the game was unhealthy. Now along came Sky with the idea that a state of dribbling devotion was the only way to be.

WSC No 128, October 1997 – Editorial

THERE WAS NO ESCAPING FOOTBALL THIS SUMMER. IF YOU LIVE ANYWHERE near a major town you will have seen the huge billboards featuring text taken from the new Sky advertisement for its coverage of the 1997-98 season. "Football is our life" says one, above a picture of two fans, one celebrating, the other with head in hands. "Football is our religion" says another, over a picture of fans sitting on a fence overlooking a ground. The TV commercial from which the posters are derived only lasts a minute or so but it's one of the most disturbing things ever seen on satellite television, weirder even than the 24-hour shopping channel or episodes of *Scooby Doo* dubbed into German.

Monochrome close-ups of Premier League stars staring moodily into the lens are intercut with Sean Bean, star of the worst football film yet made (you may know the title) striding about, declaiming lines intended to strike a great big booming chord in the heart of football fans. Football, you see, is "ecstasy, anguish, joy and despair. It should be predictable but never is. It's a feeling that can't be explained."

The clincher comes at the end. "We know how you feel... we feel the same way." If only they did – then Sky would have to close down its entire operation and publicly apologise for having been the driving force behind football's grotesque kowtowing to television over the past five years. Instead it was left to a grafitti artist to add a ring of truth to one of the posters by adding the words "...about money".

Where to begin to describe the awfulness of this ad? First, there's the patronizing message – Sky, involved with football for all of five years, would have us believe it understands the essence of football fan culture; something built up over a hundred years can be reduced down to stock images of men in replica shirts shouting and kids with painted faces.

Worse is the image of the fan as someone who has abandoned reason. This is a thread that has run consistently through the media depiction of football fans in the past few years. Innumerable advertising campaigns depict that new stock comedy character, the football nutter – sleeping in his scarf, painting his house in club colours, wearing his shirt 24 hours a day, naming a kid after a promotion-winning team. Every advertising agency now seems to want to catch on to football obsessiveness just as completely as they abandoned football altogether a decade ago in favour of the then fashionable American variety.

Obsessiveness has become a defining image of the fan, a badge of authenticity to be seized on by any celebrity or politician keen to show they've got the common touch, who will happily gabble on about how they would pack in their careers tomorrow for a chance to play centre forward for their favourite club. Of course, some fans are only too aware that football plays an unhealthily large role in their lives, but to have this ailment appropriated, glorified and advertised back to them with such blatant insincerity feels like manipulation of the highest order.

For years, of course, the media were happy to suggest that being a football fan made you abnormal. Now the opposite is true: the new stereotype suggests you're not a real fan unless you are incapable of conversing on any other subject. This has understandably produced a reaction among those who happen not to like the game, in some cases turning otherwise tolerant people against football fans, in the belief that all such people subscribe to the views in the Sky ad. In others it has reawakened an image of us as grunting knuckle-draggers which might have been understandable, however inaccurate, in the wake of Heysel.

As well as this reaction, the propagation of football as a commercial substitute for religion will create a hype monster that is sure to burst.

Already there are stories of ten-year-olds who support Man Utd or Liverpool in order to stay in playground conversations but don't actually bother to watch the matches on TV.

Meanwhile Sky subscriptions have gone up again, and they have started to charge for Sky Sports 2, previously 'free' to those who bought the other two channels. They make sure that their audience will pay for it, of course, by moving England's key World Cup games there from Sky Sports 1, the home of the Premiership. They will then, doubtless, spend the money on more degrading commercials, adding insult to extortion. While the game needs money, English football is now as unbalanced as the fans in the adverts, with all control in the hands of people who hadn't managed to stay awake for a whole match before Italia 90, and will turn their backs if there are no more profits to be made.

Sky seem to believe that the whole of British football history has been one glorious progression leading to their arrival, that their involvement represents the pinnacle of football's achievement. What luck that our little game, struggling along as the most popular sport in the world, should have attracted the attention of the benevolent Mr Murdoch. O

Fighting Between the Lines

John Williams looked at what the spate of books about Seventies and Eighties fan culture suggested about the state of the game.

WSC No 129, November 1997

At West Ham in late September, a few away travel truths struck home a little more sharply than I can remember before. The District Line train eastbound at 2.30 was thinly populated. A number of passengers were tourists, picking up a Premier League game between the Hammers and Liverpool while on holiday in London. Other Liverpool fans (and their kids) were openly wearing dispiritingly new team shirts.

I myself, a Kop season ticket-holder and regular away fan, was going with my LSE-attending step-daughter (who is 'interested', but not a mad Red; she goes to London games) and her (black) boyfriend who told me in the ground that, yes, he'd been to a game, once, he thought at Ipswich. He 'supports' Tottenham.

Entering the Lower Centenary we were searched (out of kilter, this) and found ourselves sharing the end with Hammers fans (they looked like the family club). Two years ago we'd paid £17 and had the whole end; now it was £24 and two-thirds of it. This is known as market forces. Liverpool's support was the by-now-usual mix of London Reds, people giving their kids a day out, and older Scouse accents. Plenty of female fans; some painted faces. No real singing (though the elephant-brained locals gave eight-years-away Ince the usual "Judas" shit). At half time a female dance troupe 'entertained' us; they were not abused (or enjoyed).

Afterwards a friendly older Hammer on the train couldn't quite believe how upset my mate was that we'd lost. A couple of Asian lads wearing new West Ham scarves looked busily for the next home fixture. We'd had a 'good day out', no messing, and no hassle, despite the defeat.

I wouldn't have dreamt of taking my daughter and her fella in the away end at West Ham in the late Eighties of course. For a start, he'd have got stick, and probably from Reds, too. She'd have been pissed off by not being able to see and by the intimidating trip to and from the tube and in the ground (I wasn't too keen on that myself). For these things I'm thankful; I wouldn't go back ten years. But at £24 a throw and with a theme park atmosphere in the away end, you can see the appeal of some current depictions of Eighties culture.

Of course, the celebration of Seventies and Eighties football has been in full swing for a while. Danny Baker has been doing the BBC TV version with some heavily sanitized commentaries on pitch invasions and 'offs' at home and abroad, presented as part and parcel of life on the terraces before the 'luvvies' and 'anoraks' took over. Club histories of the decade by fans also favour enticing and nostalgic depictions of real life adventures for (male) supporters. Eddie Cotton's *The Voice of Anfield* is full of this sort of stuff; bottle-throwing mobs, robbing, and the occasional away coach gang bang to keep 'the lads' breathlessly entertained, before everyone goes home to their mum. Particular versions of 'the truth' are highly sacrosanct here; one lifelong Red was recently assaulted at the match for suggesting on a TV history of the decade that Liverpool fans rightly shouldered some of the blame for Heysel.

This kind of material is meat and drink, of course, for professional Mancunian Richard Kurt's *United We Stood: the Unofficial History of the Ferguson Years* with its casual abuse of all things Scouse. Kurt is troubled, too, naturally, by the struggle over modern-day Old Trafford between the day trippers and the die-hards. But there is also a refreshing approach here to female fans who don't, er, live in Manchester. For Kurt, the 1990s promise world domination; why dwell overmuch on the alehouse Eighties, when the Mancs can now party in the Camp Nou? (Great diagrams here, as well, of Old Trafford's fan base in transition; anthropology awaits.)

Nationally, Colin Ward led the hoolie nostalgia trip for a while, firstly with the racy *Steaming In* ('I know this happened, but it wasn't me guv') and then the more transitional *All Quiet on the Hooligan Front*, a kind of European football travelogue in which a French-speaking, Guardian-reading 'face' (Colin) does much damage to press expense accounts on trips abroad as the 'mobs' slowly fade away. Some of this is funny, but the tiresome Metropolitan flavour of Ward's work – "John was as wide as the Thames" – has also been picked up in the recent highbrow (sic) fiction of John King in *The Football Factory* and *Headhunters*. Presumably, this is meant to be Martin Amis meets King's mate Irvine Welsh, but it reads much more like the editor of *Loaded* ghosting tales of football lads for Bret Easton Ellis. Unreadable and pointless.

But all these pretenders must give way to the undisputed kings of this genre, the redoubtable Brimson brothers, Eddy and Dougie. These guys have got three (count them, but don't try to distinguish between them) volumes currently out on the bad-old-good-old-days. These are big sellers, too. You can see why. The secret here is to print, largely with no editorial comment, fans' accounts of their adventures and views of 'good times' past. So, we get just one, lengthy account of Hillsborough; from a Forest fan who blames ticketless Liverpool supporters for the deaths.

We also get a BNP member's judgements on the plight of the sport, which seem to fit comfortably with some of the authors' own views: they talk about "coloured" fans, the exaggeration of football racism, and the "do-gooders", academics and social workers who defend minorities and oppose good old English culture (for more on which, see inside). We get endless and mind-numbingly repetitive tales of firms, fights, offs and scams. In 800 gruelling pages there is not one female or black voice. This is mob masturbation; testosterone time travel. I just can't imagine who their readership is meant to be.

But the beauty of this is that Doug and Eddy now want to stop all this hooligan stuff (which is going on, just as it always has, as we speak). Their 'insight' is that men fight at football because they like fighting. If only the hapless FA could listen and understand this then we could do something about it (but what exactly?).

Contradiction then is heaped on contradiction; the new families are great for football, but 'nuclear' families are spoiling the atmosphere and they should clear off; fans will always be violent but we can solve the problem; organisations like the FSA are bollocks, but we need more fans' say in the game; English fans are the toughest around, but hooliganism is (of course) much worse abroad. And so on.

For the Brimsons and their gleeful publishers, and despite the 'policy' gloss, a day down at Upton Park is really incomplete without all the old attractions. They're right of course; down in the netherworld the corpse of the hooligan Eighties still twitches and more. In some places, and for some games, it is still given the kiss of life by this sort of stuff. (England in Rome has potential. There are Jurassic Parks for football firms all over the Midlands, for example.) Otherwise, they just don't get it. For good or for ill (mostly the former), going down the Hammers just ain't what it used to be. The question now is not can we get back to the Land That Time Forgot; more, does the future have to be quite so depressingly manufactured and wholesome? And so expensive? ○

Focus Pocus

Saturday lunchtimes changed irrevocably and for the worse. Cameron Carter surveyed the wreckage of a proud institution.

WSC No 129, November 1997

I USED TO LOOK FORWARD TO FOOTBALL FOCUS. PROBABLY BECAUSE IT USED to be good. Ten years ago, during its golden Arthurian period, you got crumply old Bob Wilson with a pen in his jacket pocket (which sometimes crept into his hand during those traumatic live link-ups with experienced managers), lots of football clips and a special focus on Crewe Alexandra at the end. Now, you get last weekend's goals you've already seen on *Match of the Day* with a satiny Britpop underlay. It's not right, and deep down everyone knows it.

The rot set in when Bob left to work for ITV, presumably to provide a better standard of living for his family. A troop of people related to football, let us say, only by marriage – Ray Stubbs, Steve Rider and the like – duly attempted to fill the gap, but were clearly only filling in while the BBC looked for a replacement with Bob Wilson's classic combination of authority and inoffensiveness. Finally they gave up and decided that what the kids wanted was a football DJ playing only the very latest stuff and so Gary Lineker has appeared on our screens ever since, squeaking away like a rusty fieldmouse.

It was quickly apparent what *Grandstand* had let us all in for. After a feature on the Liverpool team making a charity record in his first season in charge, Lineker undid a button on his pox-doctor's clerk's jacket and quipped, "I don't think Blur and Oasis have got anything to worry about." He probably thought this got him in with the kids. Well it didn't; we young people don't respect that kind of blatant currying of favour from people with stinking great streaks of grey in their hair, as a matter of fact, much preferring our football authority figures to remain conservative, remote and, therefore, dignified.

And anyway, there were people over 30 watching who rather like Mantovani and who fail to appreciate such lightning forays into the borderlands of youth-oriented humour. Chief among Bob Wilson's most alluring qualities, and I'm sure his wife would agree with me, was his obvious and profound ignorance of young people, their music and their lifestyle. A phrase like the one the man-child Lineker used that Saturday would be about as likely to pass Bob's lips as "Come on, let's trash the place", because he was and is a simple man who, perhaps naively, believed that football talk is what the viewers specifically want to hear when they tune in to a football magazine.

Now that we have Lineker with his Italian waiter cruise-ship charm, the material is extremely thin, like cheap toilet-roll your finger goes through, making you vow to buy the second-cheapest next time. A large percentage of each programme over the last two seasons has been taken up by a strenuous, in-depth Lineker interview with a current player in their beautifully appointed house in the suburbs. The footballing action was as limited as the questions:

"Tell me, Jürgen/Bryan/Dennis, how does the English game differ from the one back home?"

"Was this a very difficult time for you?"

"Looking back, do you regret your involvement in organised crime?"

After this patience-exploring period, Gary might pipe a slight joke if he was feeling confident, and then on we went to last Saturday's goals with guitar. As if this was not enough to convince the viewer that everything was better in the old days, there would generally then take place a folding of the hands for a serious chat with Mark Bloody Lawrenson about a player in the headlines, during which Gary would say "that's the nature of the man" as if he had hit on something final.

One hankers for Bob and the old days. You didn't have to look at Bob's jackets like you do Lineker's. They weren't meant to be looked at. They just Were. There was no gloss, no service-industry hokum, everything was purely functional. If the producers of *Grandstand* had ever approached Bob with the idea of managers' heads appearing in the middle of revolving footballs you can be sure that he would have told them gently but firmly to go back to lunch and he'd see them tomorrow.

The footballing public in Bob's day were given what they wanted – lots of clips. The top games of the day were lovingly previewed with action from the corresponding fixture the previous season, or maybe a few seasons before. There was a bit of context for you, a thread of care and preparation ran through the show. "The last time these two clubs met..." When did you ever hear Lineker introduce a piece of football action with those words. I'll tell you. You never did. Bob was always doing it, and that is why we loved him in a no-touching, share-a-bottle-of-whiskey-with-him-when-we're-older kind of way.

Also, just as he came to the end of his enticing introduction to the clip, Bob would crinkle his eyes into some kind of smile and leave you with completely good karma until the excerpt was over. It is true that Lineker has begun to try this himself recently, but as this makes him resemble a wine bar Lothario coming on to the girls near closing-time one cannot take it as sincere.

Another extra you used to get was the Focus On The Unfashionable Northern Club. There'd be a dragging overhead shot of some disused dock or railyard accompanied by a Gubba figure droning an introduction written up in the library after a brief visit to the Geography section: "For nigh on four centuries the port of Hull has been famous for its shipbuilding, but today with the shipyards standing idle as they have done for the past 20 years, it is football that provides the main talking-point in the pubs and offices of this historic northern city..."

Then there would be a very old guy on a leather sofa remembering things extremely slowly, interspersed with a few grainy old football clips of the club's past glories. Solid infotainment for all the family, and they never seemed to run out of Unfashionable Northern Clubs, either. The new boys can't be bothered with all that. Oh, I know they can't use Nationwide League action nowadays, but they hardly ever use old material any more in any context, not even when they are covering the FA Cup. It's almost as if the production team sacked two archivists to pay for the salary of one new set designer. Glitz and polish, you see, the modern disease. Never mind the quality – feel the service. As for Lineker, he won't shake your hand until you've been in make-up.

One last thing. In a recent edition, Garth Crooks's earnest little report was dressed up as an episode of *Holiday* by the boys in Titles & Effects. I was watching with a chap who had been living abroad for five years and I caught him staring in disbelief at the gyrating television screen in rather the same way people used to stare in disbelief at a man with no abdomen in a Victorian travelling circus. What could I say to him? That this post-modern grotesque was what his fondly remembered *Football Focus* had become? With its execrable, irrelevant theme tune and dreary live interviews with managers where the studio guest gets to ask a question and make a joke? In the end I didn't say anything, silence seemed the most appropriate response. Until now.

The way it's going at the moment, *Football Focus* will be presented a couple of seasons from now by Darren Day from inside a mocked-up ref's whistle to a background of heavy drum 'n' bass, with maybe the odd clip from last Saturday's big game included somewhere for nostalgia lovers among the deconstructional topical debate. This is a sad state of affairs because missing *Football Focus* (or *Top of the Pops*, incidentally) used to mean the whole week was a failure. Those days are gone. One recent Saturday I missed *Football Focus* because I was out in the kitchen testing myself on the exact ingredients of Alpen. ○

Rising in the East

Karsten Blaas explained why clubs from the former GDR had made more of an impact off the pitch than on it since Germany's reunification.

WSC No 129, November 1997

AT THE END OF LAST SEASON, GERMAN FOOTBALL COMMENTATORS WERE ABLE to announce some rare good news from the east: all professional teams from the formerly communist part of the country had avoided relegation. Hansa Rostock successfully completed their Bundesliga campaign while Leipzig, Jena and Zwickau secured their places in the Second Division. Energie Cottbus added some icing to the cake by winning promotion to the Second and reaching the cup final (which they lost).

All in all, we were told, football was about to pave the way for a 'rise of the east', an upswing of the entire region. This optimism, however, seems grossly exaggerated. East Germany shared the fate of other former Soviet bloc countries in being thrown into a free market environment without any preparation. But in football, the GDR was affected far more severely than the rest and it will take East German clubs much longer to recover.

East German football is now almost entirely a lower division appendix of the Western league structure. And while Czech or Hungarian clubs only lost their star players, East Germany has seen an exodus of enormous proportions that started immediately after the Wall fell and hasn't come to an end yet. Not only are there more than 100 native professionals playing for western clubs in the top leagues, among them big shots like Matthias Sammer, Ulf Kirsten and Steffen Freund, there are also innumerable others who have joined amateur or youth outfits in the west.

In the unification euphoria of 1990, supporters from the east began to head westward every Saturday, leaving their local teams with what were, even by GDR standards, tiny gates. The eastern football authorities were afraid that a delayed introduction of the Bundesliga might make things even worse. The DFB, West Germany's football association, were restructuring their own league system at the time of unification and originally intended to wait for at least two more seasons before admitting the easterners. When they reluctantly gave in, the eastern officials learned their first lesson in the laws of supply and demand: if you offer something that no one wants, you won't get very much for it.

Two harsh conditions were imposed: first only two of the eastern Oberliga's 14 teams were allowed in the Bundesliga, while a further six were placed in the Second Division. Second, there would be no special legislation to protect the financially unstable and inexperienced clubs from behind the Wall. The East Germans were to discover that it is not easy to live in a democracy when you belong to a minority.

So, when the western world and unsubdued capitalism came to Dresden, Rostock and Leipzig, it caught them on the wrong foot. Most of those who had run the clubs under the communists were removed and replaced by well intentioned but overstretched new boards. Investors were extremely hard to find in an area with an unemployment rate of over 20 per cent, so the new club executives gratefully let in any-body who promised to help them.

As a result, they became easy prey for incompetent and often criminal speculators. Dynamo Dresden, one of East Germany's most successful sides over many decades, were the most spectacular case. Between 1991 and 1995, they were run by Rolf-Jürgen Otto, a building contractor from Frankfurt with a criminal record. After running the club into the ground, Otto is now in prison again for tax fraud, while Dynamo are flat broke. They were relegated to the Third Division for continuous breach of the DFB's licensing regulations, committed under Otto's leadership.

With similar turbulence happening all over the place, the DFB was forced, periodically, to change its harsh line – a Bundesliga without an eastern participant would have caused political embarrassment in a nation that was officially attempting to overcome the old divide. When Dresden's fi-nancial chaos became plain to see at the end of 1992-93, they were deduct-ed four points for the following season, a dubious and unprecedented de-cision, since normally clubs get penalised for forged accountancy in the same year it occurred. This, however, would have meant relegation for the GDR's then only First Division representative.

Another of the DFB's occasional concessions to eastern clubs was a prolonged period of time during which they were to get their grounds into shape. Nothing much has happened yet, which makes away trips to eastern stadia, with their unsegregated terraces, insufficient policing and indifferent stewarding, a tricky experience for Western visitors.

Hooliganism and fascist skinhead violence in the east aren't a result of the post-unification period, having been obvious problems since the mid-Eighties. Hansa Rostock supporters caused a nationwide outcry in 1995 when they threw tear gas grenades on to the pitch during a home match against St Pauli. Two of the latter's players were injured and had to be substituted. Again, the DFB's punishment was ridiculous: they merely ordered Rostock to hold one of their subsequent home match-es on neutral ground. St Pauli, who had been the target of the assault, didn't get a replay, let alone the three points, while Hansa drew the biggest crowd in the club's history when they nearly filled Berlin's Olympic stadium for the visit of Frankfurt. In fact, they voluntarily went to Berlin for a second time a few weeks afterwards when their home pitch was iced over.

On both occasions, more than 50,000 people from all parts of the east came to watch them. Hansa Rostock, a team that never had any success or reputation while the GDR existed, are now the only Bundesliga team that easterners can emotionally relate to (apart from Bayern Munich, whose merchandising machine has lured fans from all over the globe).

Today there is a new mood of self esteem in eastern football, with most of the region's clubs preferring to appoint homegrown managers and board members, rather than importing journeymen from the west. The other side of the coin, however, is a very aggressive form of terrace xenophobia, which includes unrelenting hostility towards black players as well as hatred of those who are seen as representing the unjust new capitalist system: western players, referees and fans.

Despite the fact that disturbances at international and European club matches in recent years have mostly been caused by eastern thugs, the German football association apparently think it's none of their business, an attitude that seems doubly strange in light of their application for the 2006 World Cup. Meanwhile, fans of Rostock, Cottbus and Jena are completely free to loudly invoke the former leaders of the GDR and Germany's Nazi past on matchdays. The east has indeed risen, though not in the way the predominantly western media would like to see. The people of the GDR took a long time to realize that the brave new world is a fake. Now, Nazi dimwits think that they have every right to act accordingly. ○

When in Rome

After England's World Cup qualifier against Italy produced violence on the terraces, Mike Ticher offered some reasons why the pervading image of England fans abroad is a negative one.

WSC No 130, December 1997

"MULTICULTURALISM IS A DIVISIVE FORCE... ONE CANNOT BE LOYAL TO TWO nations any more than a man can have two masters." So said Norman Tebbit in the week before England qualified for the World Cup with an accomplished performance on the field and a hideous mess off it.

Although I was born and brought up in England, my instinct is always to want the national team to lose. It's not so much the violence and racism of the hooligans. It's the image of England as a nation that emerges every time the team plays which is so alienating.

Tebbit's perfectly-timed intervention made the connection explicit this time around. Anyone who wasn't sure what his preferred monocultural society looked like didn't even need to travel to Rome to see the England fans in action. They could just stay at home and read the papers to wallow in the ugly combination of paranoia, self-pity and naked aggression that goes by the name of patriotism in this country.

Football's appeal depends on its 'us v them' character. When national teams are involved there is bound to be some blurring of the boundary between pride in your country and denigration of someone else's. But the ambiguous symbols of England's pride and the casual racism of the denigration are reminiscent more of a newly-established and still insecure state like Croatia than the oldest one on the continent.

The treatment of all things Italian before and after the game was wearily familiar from Euro 96, and not just from the tabloids. The ref was suspect because he liked pasta (*Daily Mail*); the Italian players were a dirty bunch of cheats ("how they get away with it I don't know," said Teddy Sheringham); their police "didn't understand the England fans' culture of drinking and mass singing" (Colin Ward) – which was surely the one thing to their credit.

And everywhere the creaking military metaphors were wheeled out to explain England's triumph. "Led by Captain Ince and Sergeant-Major Adams, with Lance-Bombardier David Batty producing another performance worthy of being mentioned in dispatches, England... blocked Italy's avenues of approach, sabotaged their lines of communication and silenced their guns," David Lacey crowed in the *Guardian*. We all know what happens to the Italians in a war.

So we knew what we were up against. But who are 'we' exactly? Norman Tebbit, at least, knows what he thinks. If you want to be English you have to renounce any other loyalties, something he believes is much harder for black or Asian people to do. And the iconography of English nationalism has even stronger overtones of racial purity.

In some countries – Germany is the obvious example – the far right has its own flags and emblems, which may rear their ugly head in football grounds, but would never appear in the pages of a national newspaper. But what *God Save The Queen*, the Union Jack, the St George cross and the bulldog represent at a football match is completely interchangeable as 'England' and 'fascist'.

After the match in Rome, Glenn Hoddle was asked to comment on the violence in the stands. "It's not a night to be talking about crowd trouble," he said, "it's a night to be talking about a proud nation that's qualified." But that's the problem with England. You can't invoke the "proud nation" without summoning up the same symbols and emotions that also stir the thugs and the rag-tag army of replica-shirted drunks that staggers after them wherever England play.

The result is an incongruous image like that of Graeme Le Saux posing in the *Sun* with one of their St George bowler hats. When England play football, everyone – perhaps especially if they are intelligent, articulate and ever so slightly exotic – has to accept those symbols if they want to belong. England's style of patriotism is defined by our man slumped in the Rome fountain with the tatty Union Jack ("Slough Town") and the "Do it for Princess Di" T-shirt.

In some other countries, football has played a key role in making the idea of what is 'us' a little more sophisticated. Take Ireland and Australia, for example, which I also theoretically 'belong' to through citizenship. Ireland under Jack Charlton were pilloried for exploiting the rules that allowed the incorporation of players who weren't 'really' Irish in the opinions of some. Yet the unprecedented success of that team helped spark a serious debate about what it means to be Irish. People found that, thanks to a history of emigration, there was a whole range of new definitions of Irishness.

You might be black, you might speak with an English accent, you might never have been to Ireland. Yet when they pulled on the green shirt, no one cared. The cosmopolitan nature of the team helped to blow away a lot of frankly racist myths about the centrality of blood, religion and language to Irish identity. It turned out that almost anyone could join, and in 1990 and 1994, lots of people wanted to.

While Ireland's team has been shaped by emigration, Australia's is almost entirely the result of immigration. If the Socceroos make it to France, their squad will be dominated by players who, though born in Australia, owe their upbringing in the game to their parents' origins in Greece, former Yugoslavia, Italy, Germany, Malta or almost anywhere else in Europe you care to name. The national team is as good an example of multiculturalism in action as you would ever wish to see. During the last World Cup campaign, at the height of the war in the Balkans, there were players in the team with origins in several of the former Yugoslav republics. Yet if anything, it was the team's cohesion and single-mindedness that overcame its technical limitations.

The widespread acceptance of dual or multiple identity, the dreaded beast which Tebbit would have us slay with the steadfast sword of St George, is one of the things that makes Australia a more relaxed place than England. It would be silly to pretend that no national chauvinism accompanies the country's sporting teams. But the kind of abuse heaped on any country that England play is never likely to find a home in the Australian press. The howls of rage from people who consider themselves both Australian and, say, Italian, would make sure of that.

There are good reasons to identify with the national team in both those countries which do not depend on antagonism towards other people – or raw emotion – namely that it is OK to be a mongrel rather than a bulldog. England is lumbered with a different and seemingly more intractable heritage and football is only one of the escape valves through which it expels its noxious gases. While England remains semi-detached from the idea of becoming part of Europe on a political level (something the Scots and Irish seem to find much less threatening), it's no surprise that the national team should be the focus for, at best, a sullen, stupid and exclusive form of patriotism. But knowing that doesn't make England's football campaigns any less of an ordeal.

I ended up watching the second half of the game in a pub while being harangued by an England fan who protested that Italians "weren't human". If England geared up for a football match is the pinnacle of humanity, count me in with the aliens. ○

The Trial of Roy

Almost all Roy Hodgson's coaching experience before arriving at Blackburn had been abroad. All, that is, save for a fraught few months at Ashton Gate in 1982. Matt Nation remembered it well.

WSC No 130, December 1997

ON TURNING TO YOUR SUNDAY TABLOID, YOU OFTEN FIND PAGES FIVE TO EIGHT plastered with a 'seedy past' exposé. The host of a sofa-based chat show, for example, is revealed to have once visited a topless bar, dropped a couple of tabs and then thrown a cloakroom attendant through a plate-glass window. The nation smirks behind its collective hand for a couple of days, then loses interest, comes over all moral and decides to let bygones be bygones.

While he has never shared settee and banalities with June Whitfield, Roy Hodgson is currently enjoying levels of attention which could, potentially, catapult him further towards the front of the paper. Already itinerant, tactically astute and a folk-hero in Switzerland, Roy could now also be credited with having pulled off a minor miracle in making Blackburn a great deal less unpopular than they were three or four years ago. In fact, it's difficult to imagine anybody less deserving of having muck and detritus from the past smeared all over them.

But it is precisely the nice guys, Roy, who get it in the neck, particularly when there are people out there who just cannot let bygones be bygones. Like my father, who, on seeing your craggy-dressed-up-as-cosmopolitan features staring out from newspaper and television alike, went all of a doodah until his son helped him to place his head between his knees and draped warm towels over the back of his neck. Like my sister's first boyfriend, whose father-in-law-in-waiting threw him out of the house the very first time he came round because his name was the same as yours, Roy.

I wonder whether you know just how much it hurt back then. When you and Bob Houghton managed to do what nobody else had ever managed to do, namely drag the City down into the Fourth Division at the beginning of the 1980s. I know the descent through the divisions had already started before you arrived, Roy; I know that the club was in a desperate financial position, that the backbone of the team was forced to tear up their contacts and accept voluntary redundancy; I know that you were only the assistant, Roy, and that it was Houghton who had the final word. Nevertheless, Roy, you were part of the big picture, that great big, farraginous Jackson Pollock of an eyesore which, at that time, passed for Bristol City.

And you even became the boss for three months in early 1982, Roy, those unedifying three months when your charges won three games in 20. What on earth did you say during the pre-match team talks that made them go out on to the pitch with the verve of a long-term inmate of Death Row? "Go out there and get it over with"? "One day we'll all look back at this and laugh our heads off"?

Can you remember the players you imposed on us, Roy? Terry Boyle, the man who ran like Stan Laurel going the wrong way on a Travelator; Alan Nicholls, spindle-shanks centre-half with the bifurcate clearances, who would have been dragged out of position much more often but for the fact that he was never where he was supposed to be to start with; and what about Errington Kelly, Roy, possibly the only free transfer that even Bristol Rovers didn't want? You might be multi-lingual, but you didn't know that Errington is a name fit only for a big band leader or a North Sea seaside resort; it's not a footballer's name, Roy, not in any language.

You may not have signed all these players yourself, Roy, you may have inherited some, blooded some, or simply had no others available. But they are all inextricably linked with your time at the City; you filled in the team sheets, you let them stay when you could have banned them from the training ground.

These names mean nothing to most people and they probably mean even less to you, Roy. You will have consigned them to the murky twilight zone which you inhabited before you went away and got reinvented. In fact, if we ever manage to catch a glimpse of your CV, we'll probably find the years 1980-82 accounted for by some euphemism such as "travelling" or "managerial research in England". They've probably got a word in the army for people like you.

What has become of the damage cases whom you left behind? My father is now retired and currently awaiting delivery of a defibrillator to counteract the effect of seeing you on *Football Focus*. My sister is happily married and appears to have suppressed the events surrounding the ignominious exit of her first love, save for the fact that she hasn't spoken since. Even Roy the Boyfriend, who was so shaken by the whole affair that he has never married, seems to have come to terms with bachelorhood and the resultant evenings spent playing with electric train sets. They're settled, they're making do.

Maybe you should get settled too, Roy. You seem to have forgotten where you came from, and other people are doing their best to forget it as well. And should wanderlust or a Bristol City chairman asking you to name your price ever cause you to remember, then fight the urge to do anything about it. Make sure you never return to Bristol, unless you want to be sent packing back up the M5 with the toe of my father's slipper wedged up your backside. Leave my family alone, Roy, they've suffered enough. ○

Pay and Display

Patrick Harverson looked at what will be in store for viewers
when football clubs launch their own TV channels.

WSC No 131, January 1998

HERE WE GO AGAIN. PREMIER LEAGUE CLUBS ARE FALLING OVER THEMSELVES
in their hurry to sign deals with broadcasters to establish their own television channels, just as they flattened everything in sight in their stampede to the stock market last year.

And, as in their rush to sell their shares to the City, the eagerness to
create new TV channels raises some doubts about the clubs' ability to
make good business decisions. There is a place on the stock market for
a few well-run clubs, but there are some who have floated in the past
year who don't belong there – a point painfully highlighted by the performance of some clubs' share prices recently.

Similarly, while the recent news that Manchester United will launch
its own channel in partnership with Sky Television and Granada next
season made business sense, some of the other clubs planning to take
the same route might want to think again.

United may be big enough to pull it off – the club reckons it need only
attract ten per cent of its three million UK fans to the channel to break

even on the project – but what about Newcastle United, Leeds United, Arsenal, Chelsea and Southampton, all of whom are considering setting up their own channels? It seems that any decent-sized member of the Premiership with ambitions to be a player in the brave new media world of digital and pay-per-view television is likely to be doing the same.

So what is all this about? Surely there is enough football on television at the moment to satisfy even the most fanatical supporter. And without the ability to broadcast live Premiership games (the exclusive rights to which remain firmly in Sky's grip), who is going to bother to tune in?

The clubs are clearly hoping to make money from their channels. Yet it is unlikely that any of them, even Manchester United, will be in a position to make a profit from their club channels within the first couple of years. Filling hours of air time is an expensive business, says Don Perretta, head of business development at Chrysalis Sport, the country's leading independent producer of sports programming, responsible for, among others, Channel 4's Italian football and ITV's Formula One.

It can be done quite cheaply in terms of the cost per hour, but the overall cost will be tens of millions of pounds. You have to have the technical staff, the satellite uplink, ten cameras at a match, the editorial staff, everything, he says. To make it pay, the clubs will have to attract a good number of subscribers. Yet they will not be able to charge high fees, given that fans are increasingly unhappy with the overpricing of tickets, merchandising and – not least – subscriptions to Sky Sports. And if the clubs fail to attract many subscribers, they will struggle to attract advertisers, who would provide the other main source of revenue.

Admittedly, clubs might be able to make some money from selling merchandise on their channels, but this is hardly likely to endear them to their viewers. Nor will lengthy ad breaks to sell replica kits and other club gear make for compelling television. The likely lack of quality is something that Chrysalis's Perretta believes could kill some club channels at birth. He believes they will be simply too boring to last very long. He may have a point, although few people have lost money overestimating the devotion of football fans to their clubs.

Essentially, the channels will be televisual versions of club call phone services. Instead of being told that Darren Anderton is still on the injured list, fans will be able to see him receiving treatment from the physio, accompanied no doubt by cheery comments from the player predicting his imminent return. Team and club news (or propaganda) will be the first order of the day.

There will also be archive material, live reserve and youth team games, coverage of pre-season friendlies or testimonials, and endless player profiles. Much of it will look like football's answer to afternoon television: At home with Becksy and Posh; Cooking the Calderwood way; Ferguson's Fashion Hour (Duncan, not Alex).

While this might be moderately entertaining for a while, the novelty factor could quickly wear off. Alan Sugar, who says Tottenham have no plans to start their own TV channel, dismisses the entire idea as a "non-starter". He adds: "You might just have enough material to last the first two days." And then what?

So why are the clubs so keen on starting their own channels? The answer is they are playing a very long game. The ultimate prize is not the chance to snag a few viewers, flog them some merchandise and maybe make a few quid, but the opportunity for clubs to broadcast live coverage of their own Premiership games on a pay-per-view basis.

Manchester United, Newcastle, Leeds and the rest are preparing for the day when football clubs will own the broadcast rights to all their home games. If, though more likely when, that happens, what better place to show them than the club's own channel? Instead of sharing the bounties of football's popularity with Sky, in selling subscriptions direct to their fans the clubs could keep most of the profits for themselves.

The clubs are quite confident this day will come. The law dictates that the rights to any televised event reside with the owner of the venue staging the event: in other words, the home club. Until now, the clubs have been happy to award these rights collectively to the Premier League to sell on to broadcasters, because they believe they can earn more money from pooling the rights than from selling them separately.

However, this arrangement is under investigation by the government, which believes the clubs may be operating as an illegal, anti-competitive cartel against the interests of the game and its supporters. The courts will decide some time in the next two years whether the government's concerns are justified, but if – as some lawyers predict – the current Premier League contract with Sky (which runs until 2001) turns out to be the last collective deal of its kind in league football, the biggest clubs want to be ready for a new era that allows them to sell their live games to anyone they want, including their own channels.

The clubs are not alone in manoeuvring themselves into position for a possible TV free-for-all. The national and regional broadcasters are also aware that clubs may eventually be able to sell the rights to their own games – after all, it happens already in Dutch and Spanish football, so why not here? As a result, they are keen to join forces with the clubs in readiness for the rights revolution.

So don't be surprised if Sky does a few more deals like its joint venture with Man United and Granada. That way, if Sky does lose Premiership football in 2001, at least it would still be closely involved in the sport as co-owners and co-producers of club channels. It is quite conceivable, in fact, that by 2001 Sky could have signed deals with almost every top club. There is no way Rupert Murdoch is going to give up the Premier League – which saved Sky from oblivion in 1992 – without having established a fall-back position. In the big-business world that is Premiership football today, club channels don't seem such a stupid idea after all. ◯

The Enemy Within

Ray Gilbert recounted the sorry saga which led Doncaster to record the worst season of any club in recent League history.

WSC No 132, February 1998

DONCASTER'S RESIDENTS FOUND 1997 MORE THAN A MATCH FOR HER Majesty's notorious *annus horribilis*. The district auditor blew his whistle on the gifts accepted by the nucleus of Labour members who have controlled local politics for years, and are now suspended. The new Doncaster prison, Doncatraz to locals, remained the privatisation flagship of the Wackenhut Corrections Corporation of Florida and has the worst record for inmates attacking each other of any prison in the UK.

Doncaster College sailed on as the UK flagship of all that is wrong with further education colleges with a principal widely accused of featherbedding himself. On top of all that we have Doncaster Rovers FC. The League's worst team is dying as the Anton Johnson-led consortium riding to its rescue is kept waiting for the signatures of major shareholders Ken Richardson and the Dinard Trading Company of the Isle of Man.

Richardson first hit the headlines in 1984 when convicted at York Crown Court of conspiracy to defraud. Racehorse Flockton Grey won a race for two-year-olds by 20 lengths at odds of 10-1. It looked like a good pay day until the jury decided Flockton Grey was really another horse, the three-year-old Good Hand. Richardson picked up a suspended prison sentence and heavy fines. Banned from the turf for five years by the Jockey Club he turned to football. His first club, Bridlington Town, reached Wembley in the FA Vase with a group of players on big wages, then swiftly disappeared after a short spell as tenants at Doncaster, after the Rovers board had sold up to Richardson and Dinard.

According to a recent filing Dinard is an "Import/Export" company. This year its three directors resigned to make way for Mr JT Donnelly of Sark, Channel Islands (where there is no company law), Mr BM Shimmin of the Isle of Man and Mr FH Perry, also of the IoM, who acts as company secretary. It may still be owned by Cameo Trust Corporation of 80 Broad Street, Monrovia, Liberia although one former director says Cameo has severed its link with Dinard. None has any real connection with Doncaster or football. You would need to be Sherlock Holmes, Maigret and Poirot rolled into one to fathom the affairs of this lot and find the link between Richardson and Dinard. Yet link there must be.

Richardson has never been registered as a director of the Rovers, but his mates have been installed as chairman from time to time. The current one is Ken Haran of Bradford who happened to give evidence at the racehorse trial in York. Richardson's daughter and niece are the other two directors, with his daughter taking over as company secretary. The club's old auditors, based in Doncaster, say they were asked to resign by Richardson who brought in a new outfit from North Yorkshire.

Until his recent decision to stop attending matches Richardson always fixed the transfers, picked the team, gave the team talks and made the substitutions. Good managers were hired, then fired or forced out. Ian Atkins, Steve Beaglehole, Sammy Chung and Kerry Dixon were all admired by the fans and ditched by Richardson. Chung, as manager, came to a home match at the start of last season only to find that Dixon was also there as player-manager.

An early storm signal went up on October 25th 1993, when the club advertised the ground for sale in the *Daily Telegraph* and sought a developer for retail and hotel use. This move conveniently overlooked the fact that the ground has always been owned by Doncaster Council, who let the club have it on a 99-year lease. Most other clubs have left the Rovers years behind in the upgrading of ground amenities. The council was willing to help relocation to a new stadium until it had to consider the merits of dealing with Richardson. There has been stalemate ever since.

Yet there was one attempt to break it. On a night in June 1995 there was a fire in the main stand. It caused plenty of damage but far from total destruction. Three people from the north east were quickly arrested. This story, hilarious in parts, will come out at a trial to take place at Sheffield Crown Court. It will be a good read, not least because Richardson will be there as well. He was arrested at a night match on March 25th 1996 and charged with conspiracy to burn down the stand.

Between times the playing standard went from decent to indifferent to appalling. We now hold the record for the worst start to a season. By November 29th it read 20 games without a win. The direction of the club became yet more bizarre. The fans knew that Richardson had favourites and non-favourites among the players. Last season Paul Birch joined the club and always played well. The day came when, to everybody's disgust, he was pulled off part way through the second half whereupon the match sponsors rightly declared him man of the match. He hardly played another game for the Rovers after that, went to Torquay and received an ovation from the Rovers supporters when he turned out at Doncaster in their opponents' colours.

Kerry Dixon kept the Rovers in the league last season by a whisker. He had the complete loyalty of the players, the crucial strength of Darren Moore at centre back and the quick feet of Colin Cramb as striker. At the season's end we were told that Richardson's skill had saved us from Dixon's ineptitude as a manager! In the summer Moore and Cramb declined to sign again and left for more ambitious pastures. Dixon left to safeguard his sanity soon after this season's start. Richardson was then seen on the bench directing his large collection of non-League signings on match days (the goalkeeper only saw his team mates on match days when he arrived from his week's work).

The protests grew and the attendances dwindled. Brighton's fans came with their well-honed loathing of football's asset strippers and helped mount a protest so rowdy the police advised Richardson and his 'general manager' sidekick, Mark Weaver, to leave at half time.

Since January 1997 a consortium including former Rovers directors has been ready to negotiate a takeover from Richardson and Dinard. The minor shareholders favoured this takeover but Richardson and Dinard blocked it until Richardson suddenly appeared to have a change of mind. The Brighton fans had been the catalyst. After a shocking display at Darlington in the middle of October, Richardson announced he was coming to no more matches. "I saved them from relegation last season

– even Kerry Dixon would admit that – but they are just not responding this year and I don't want to be associated with losers. Dinard can do what they like and Mark Weaver will act for them and probably appoint a manager. But I'm not wasting my time any more."

Weaver produced his neighbour as goalkeeper for one first team match. Dave Cowling was appointed manager and lasted nine days. Then came Danny Bergara, master of maladroit man management, who soon made his mark by sacking a real goalkeeper, Dean Williams. Three days after Darlington, the consortium and Richardson met, but negotiations don't seem to have moved on. At the year's end Richardson and Dinard were still in control, content to be 12 points adrift at the bottom and more than happy to charge League prices to watch a team that wouldn't win a match in a pub league.

On December 11th the funeral cortege of Billy Bremner, one of Doncaster's best managers, slowed to walking pace as it passed Belle Vue. What a tragedy that he should die with his once proud little club still in the clutches of the enemy within. ○

Postscript: In January 1999, Ken Richardson was found guilty of conspiracy to commit arson and sentenced to four years in prison.

What a Send-Off

Richard Darn wondered if he was the only Barnsley fan to retain his sanity during an explosive match with Liverpool at Oakwell.

WSC No 135, May 1998

IN JUST 40 TRAGIC MINUTES, MR GARY WILLARD, A "TOP" REFEREE FROM Worthing, was crossed off 16,500 Christmas card lists in Barnsley. His crime was to cack-handedly preside over a home defeat at the hands of Liverpool. For most of the crowd, a bit of foul-mouthed bellowing sufficed. Others were moved to throw coins and spit. A few carted their beer-inflated carcasses onto the pitch to exact instant revenge.

There have been some pretty odd games at Oakwell this season, but this entered the twilight zone. Three Barnsley players sent off (previously only a couple had been dismissed in the past two seasons), a referee who vanished up the tunnel for five minutes ("he's even sent himself off" chortled one wag) and an eight-man Barnsley team making Liverpool look like a set of frightened bunnies. Reason was suspended as home fans saw conspiracies everywhere. Surely Mr Willard shot JFK? My cousin, a mild-mannered systems analyst, was convulsed with rage. He couldn't say why apart from blathering something about being cheated and favouritism to top teams. It was that sort of game.

But this anarchy had very little to do with the "return of violence to the national game" as the editorials in the pathetic *Daily Mail* and the *Express,* intoned, seemingly free from the constraints of actually having been at Oakwell. The "pitch invasion" was in fact seven individuals coming onto the playing area at intervals. One did get near the referee, before he was bowled over by a Barnsley player. The others ran out of steam after a few escapist yards, one being subdued by a tiny policewoman. Not much hope of invading even Lilliput with that lot.

Meanwhile, I felt sorry for the referee. Obviously, I didn't say so at the time. Apart from making a complete balls-up of one sending-off, most other things were done by the book or open to interpretation. That didn't register with our local MP, who accused him of nearly starting a riot. True, Mr Willard's overall performance was poor, something which had much to do with his authoritarian streak. But he hardly deserved to be pilloried as a heretic, threatened with violence and smuggled out of town in an unmarked car.

In fact, the occasion said far more about the current state of English football and the Premiership in particular. Whether it's money, Sky-induced hype or too many violent videos, it's the crowd, players and managers who have lost the plot. A few years ago everyone was crying out for referees to be more consistent. Now they are, we want them to use more discretion. As more and more seems to hang on every decision on the pitch, so the pressures on a referee's fallible human senses increase.

Why is the standard of refereeing going down? It isn't. It's just that blanket TV coverage with up to five camera angles reveals what many have always suspected: the interpretation of an offence depends on where you are standing. Mr Willard honestly saw two offences which added up to red cards. He didn't see Paul Ince raise his arm, so he stayed on. The third Barnsley player walked on the say-so of the linesman. I'm risking life and limb saying this, because the prevailing mood in the town is to hire a coach, load the rocket launchers and get down to Sussex. But if mistakes were punished by capital punishment, every Barnsley defender this season would be in the cemetery. I felt sickened by the situation Willard found himself in. He was isolated and, in my opinion, frightened. Arguably the pressures of football, both financial and athletic, have overtaken the ability of one man to maintain effective control.

The time has come to to beef up the officials by having four linesmen – two in each half – and giving these individuals greater power to call for an offence. In the cauldron of Oakwell, having a video replay facility wouldn't have worked. But the referee could have benefited from having four other sets of eyes around the pitch to rely on. In that situation, referees would be obliged to consult assistants before reaching decisions where possible. It's only a theory and for a tiny, tiny minority of Barnsley's following, being confronted by four linesmen might simply mean taking more loose change to games. But anything has to be better than the shambles witnessed at Oakwell. ○

Favour of the Month

With refereeing controversies breaking out everywhere, Richard Mason reported on the scandal of the season in Serie A.

WSC No 136, June 1998

THERE IS A CRISIS IN ITALIAN FOOTBALL. AN UNPRECEDENTED SERIES OF refereeing errors (or "favours", as many prefer to believe), nearly all of which have benefited Juventus, has led to a degree of soul searching rare even in a country so frantically passionate about football as Italy.

The most recent occurred in the "match of the season", Juventus v Inter on April 26th, when Ronaldo was denied what seemed the clearest of penalties by referee Piero Ceccarini who then, within seconds, awarded a penalty at the other end. Admittedly, Del Piero missed it, but the damage had already been done. Inter's president Massimo Moratti left the stadium 20 minutes from the end, commenting that referees were conditioned to favour Juventus, and that he did not wish to be made a fool of any longer. Ronaldo called the decision "a disgrace". To add insult to injury, Inter's Ze Elias, sent off for a foul less heinous than one for which Juve's Edgar Davids was let off, was suspended for three matches and Ronaldo and Zamorano for two.

Had all of this been an isolated case of a referee having a bad game it would probably have blown over, even allowing for the importance of the occasion. But it wasn't. Throughout the season Juventus have benefited from a series of decisions which can be euphemistically described as "strange". Back in the autumn, Ciro Ferrara cleared a shot from Udinese's Oliver Bierhoff when it was clearly over the line. The score at the time was 1-1, and the game was in the second half. The final result was 4-1, but it is reasonable to think that had Udinese been awarded the goal, a draw was probably the maximum Juventus would have achieved.

In February, Roma were denied what seemed a clear penalty by international referee Messina for a foul by Didier Deschamps with the score at 2-1 late in a game Juventus won 3-1. Against Lazio in Rome, Italy's "top"' referee, Pierluigi Collina, first sent off Pavel Nedved for protesting, then judged as involuntary a case of hands by a Juventus defender as he jumped with a Lazio forward at a corner. It was the last minute and Juve won 1-0. On April 19th at Empoli, with 15 minutes to go and Juventus winning 1-0, Stefano Bianconi's header was clearly over the line before Angelo Peruzzi scooped it out, but referee Rodomonti said no. Comically, television showed him mouthing "I saw it all, I saw it all".

As I write, Juventus lead Inter by four points, but it could be argued that these five decisions gave them ten points they had not earned, and they are not counterbalanced by any points "lost" for mistakes against Juventus. Also, the events I have described are only the most glaring – there have been many others of a more minor nature. After 27 games Juventus have committed 625 fouls (only Atalanta have committed more) and had two players sent off, while Sampdoria, with 496 fouls one of the cleaner sides, have seen no fewer than 11 red cards.

The commonest theory, to which I subscribe, is that referees are "conditioned" to favour Juventus, and to a lesser extent other big city clubs. Juventus are an institution, and possibly a third to a half of Italy's fans, whatever team they watch on Sundays, are Juve supporters at heart. Juventus are also very strongly identified with the corridors of power because of their umbilical links with the Agnelli family, owners of Fiat. This can result, among other things, in staggering arrogance. After the Inter game, their president, Vittorio Chiusano, denied the evidence of his own eyes in claiming that there was no penalty and that the referee had not helped Juve. The general manager Luciano Moggi contented himself with lecturing Ronaldo for "having learnt Italian too quickly".

If we add the increasing commercialisation of the game, with the consequent "need" to be successful not occasionally but always, we can understand why a referee designated to control a Juventus match may not always be ecstatically happy. Especially if you consider that it has emerged that Rodomonti, the villain of the piece at Empoli, went more than three years without refereeing Juventus after he was "guilty" of awarding Genoa a goal that wasn't in December 1994. This fact suggested to many that even if they don't actually pay referees, Juventus can dictate who does or does not referee their games.

Now people are rushing to suggest all sorts of radical changes. They range from electronic equipment to determine whether the ball has crossed the line to the use of two referees and even slow motion replays during matches. The first might be acceptable, though eventually one of these machines would be bound to give a false reading and then we would be back where we started. As for the rest, forget it (I hope).

If the thesis that referees are conditioned by the importance of certain teams is correct, it doesn't matter what technology you introduce, ways will still be found to favour those teams, and the game in the meantime will have been irreparably impoverished as a spectacle for no advantage.

I think there are simpler solutions. First, an end to the system whereby referees for Sunday's matches are announced on Wednesday and the newspapers regale us with details of their previous games – how many home wins, draws, away wins, penalties, red cards etc. Let people find out as they arrive in the stadium, as they do in England. Second, a bit more honesty and humility – when your team has clearly been the recipient of a piece of good luck, say so. Just a word in that direction from the Juventus backroom staff and perhaps some sympathy for Inter and the average fan in the street would have been satisfied. Third, remind referees that the old dictum, the best referee is the one nobody notices, happens to be true. Lastly, and most important of all, referees who are patently unable to apply the laws in the same way for all teams should be suspended indefinitely.

Of course, it is now quite possible that the pendulum will swing back against Juventus for a time, as referees bend over backwards to be "impartial". In the meantime, Juve's last game is away to Atalanta. It is just possible that both teams will need the points for opposing reasons. If this is the case, any volunteers to referee? God himself, who is quite popular in this country, would have his work cut out to come out of that one unscathed. ○

French Lessons

England went out of the World Cup and great wails of anguish went up all over the nation. Not here though.

WSC No 138, August 1998 – Editorial

AT THE RISK OF PROMPTING A WAVE OF CANCELLED SUBSCRIPTIONS, YOUR OLD pals at *WSC* have to admit that in some respects we enjoy the World Cup more when England aren't in it. This has something to do with being able to remember a time when football wasn't ubiquitous, when it existed for the benefit of those who were interested in it, but didn't intrude into the lives of everyone else. Nothing could support the weight of expectation heaped upon France 98 months before it started, and if England had not been there we might at least have been spared some of the crowing boorishness that surrounded the tournament.

It was apparent even during the breaks. A nasty, xenophobic stench hung around the ads for one of the official sponsors, Vauxhall, in which foreign fans, players and managers were dubbed with voices and 'dialogue' that would have been rejected as too crude in *'Allo 'Allo*. Worse was the beer commercial in which a group of supporters walk into a pub intending to watch a World Cup game but discover Vinnie Jones sitting by himself in front of the TV. He snarls at the group who back off immediately. The message was stark: respect the hard man, otherwise he may lose control – and it will be your fault if he does.

Many fans took this attitude with them to France. Determined not to adapt in any way to wherever they happen to be, they welcome the "provocation" that gives them the chance to prove their toughness. And they keep receiving what could easily be construed as messages of support. Alongside the usual blather about the "shame" heaped on the nation by the fighting, the *Sun* produced a highly ambiguous front page on June 16th with the headline **Two–Nil** above pictures of Alan Shearer and one of the boneheads arrested in Marseille, two Englishmen making an impact at the World Cup given equal prominence.

In other papers, some of the fans who were subsequently arrested were shown wearing *Sun* bowler hats that had been distributed outside the bars in Marseille before the trouble started. Yet Des Lynam and sports minister Tony Banks were photographed wearing the same hats in the paper's build-up to subsequent England games. Banks will have had official approval for his stunt, given that the government is only too keen to cuddle up to Rupert Murdoch, but why should the BBC have allowed their main presenter to be aligned with a paper that was bound to take the most chauvinistic approach to reporting the World Cup?

Another reason for feeling ambivalent about England is the team itself, characterised under Glenn Hoddle by petulance, immaturity and a refusal to acknowledge any fault – much the same tendencies displayed by the hooligan followers. The instinct of many fans in Marseille to blame someone else for provoking an English reaction was to be mirrored by the David Beckham incident which undermined England on the pitch. Beckham's dismissal was the low point of a bad night for the quartet of England players, Ince, Batty and Shearer being the others, who most frequently cross the line between legitimate aggression and intimidation and are also among the most reluctant to accept criticism.

Shearer, above all, seems to have cultivated a narky persona which refuses to engage with reasonable criticism or even normal standards of social interaction, as demonstrated in his TV interviews. It fell to Shearer to explain the game where each player had to work a song title into his interview, which he did with obvious relish. True, the questions are almost invariably banal, but the open refusal to take them at all seriously showed a contempt for the viewer as well as the interviewer.

Shearer's sullen demeanour is matched by the man who made him captain. Glenn Hoddle plainly does not rate communication as one of the jobs of an international manager. His habit of giving out deliberately misleading information about injuries and his fatuous insistence that every selection he made was pre-planned left him open to attack from those who might otherwise have given him the benefit of the doubt. And his spiky, humourless manner left him with no reserves of affection when things went wrong on the pitch, dulled the enthusiasm generated by elements of the team's performance and did nothing to counter the poisonous legacy left by a faction of England fans wherever they went.

England's inability to admit defeat gracefully and depart with a semblance of dignity was familiar and wearisome enough. But the air of malice around the campaign seems set to continue into the domestic season in a new form – the ritual hounding of David Beckham. It is tempting to respond that those who live by the hype run the risk of dying by it, but not when some people seem to think that's what he literally deserves.

Neither football nor England should matter that much. O

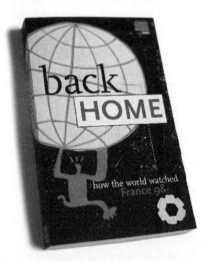